HISTORY AND LITERATURE
OF EARLY CHRISTIANITY

Hermeneia

FOUNDATIONS AND FACETS

Volume Two

INTRODUCTION TO
THE NEW TESTAMENT

HISTORY AND LITERATURE
OF EARLY CHRISTIANITY

HELMUT KOESTER

FORTRESS PRESS
PHILADELPHIA

WALTER DE GRUYTER
BERLIN AND NEW YORK

Translated from the German, *Einführung in das Neue Testament,* Chapters 7–
12, by Helmut Köster, copyright © 1980 by Walter de Gruyter & Co., Berlin,
Federal Republic of Germany, and New York, United States of America.

Library of Congress Cataloging in Publication Data

Koester, Helmut, 1926–
    Introduction to the New Testament.

    (Hermeneia—foundations and facets)
    Translation of: Einführung in das Neue Testament.
    Includes bibliographies and indexes.
    Contents: v. 1. History, culture, and religion of
the Hellenistic Age—v. 2. History and literature of
early Christianity.
    1. Bible. N.T.—History of contemporary events.
I. Title. II. Series.
BS2410.K613   1982   225.9'5   82-71828
ISBN 0-8006-2100-X (v. 1)
ISBN 0-8006-2101-8 (v. 2)

TYPESET ON AN IBYCUS SYSTEM AT POLEBRIDGE PRESS

9608G82   Printed in the United States of America   1-2101

To the Memory of my Teacher
Rudolf Bultmann

Contents

§7. The Sources for the History of Early Christianity

§12. Asia Minor, Greece, and Rome

Illustrations

MAPS

PHOTOGRAPHS

CHARTS

Acknowledgments

Grateful acknowledgment is made for permissions to use a number of photographs in these volumes: to the Agora Excavations, Athens, Greece, for the photograph of the Library of Pantaenus Inscription (vol. I, p. 92); to the Fogg Art Museum, courtesy of the Sardis Excavation Office of Harvard University, for the photograph of the Synagogue of Sardis (vol. I, p. 221); to the Freer Gallery of the Smithsonian Institute, Washington, D. C., for the photograph of a page from Washingtonianus (vol. II, p. 28); to the Houghton Library and Semitic Museum of Harvard University for the photograph of Oxyrhynchus Papyrus 655 (vol. II, p. 151); and to the Institute for Antiquity and Christianity of the Claremont Graduate School for photographs of a page from Codex II of the Nag Hammadi Library and of the site of the discovery of that Library (vol. II, pp. 210 and 227).

Additionally, the author wishes to express his thanks for permission granted him to take photographs, also used in these volumes, at the following institutions: the Archaeological Museum, Thessaloniki, Greece (vol. I, pp. 163, 204, 305); the Byzantine Archaeological Administration, Thessaloniki, Greece (vol. II, p. 85); the National Museum, Athens, Greece (vol. I, p. 175); the Archaeological Museum, Verria, Greece (vol I, p. 330); the Louvre, Paris, France (vol. I, p. 125); the Staatliche Museen Charlottenburg, Berlin, German Federal Republic (vol. I, p. 37; II, pp. 243, 289); the Pergamon Museum, Berlin, German Democratic Republic (vol. I, p. 83; II, pp. 115, 339); the Museum für Kunst and Gewerbe, Hamburg, German Federal Republic (vol. I, p. 185); the National Archaeological Museum, Copenhagen, Denmark (vol. I, p. 7); the National Museum Numismatic Collection, Athens, Greece (vol. II, p. 75); Museum Ancient Ethesus, Turkey (vol. II, p. 249); Corinth Excavations of the American School of Classical Studies (vol. II, p. 123).

A final work of thanks is due the research team for Religion and Culture of the Lands of the New Testament (ASOR) who supplied the remaining photographs used in this volume.

FOUNDATIONS AND FACETS

FOREWORD TO THE SERIES

The publishers of *Hermeneia: A Historical and Critical Commentary on the Bible* are pleased to present the first volumes in a companion series to be known as *Hermeneia: Foundations and Facets*. The new series will include works foundational to the commentary proper and works treating facets of the biblical text.

At present *Foundations and Facets* is confined to the New Testament division of *Hermeneia*.

Foundations and Facets is designed to serve two related functions.

Much of the more creative biblical scholarship on the contemporary scene is devoted to facets of biblical texts: to units smaller than canonical books, or to aspects of the New Testament that cut across or exceed canonical limits. An intensive treatment of the sermon on the mount, for example, need not require a full commentary on Matthew, any more than a generic study of the great narrative parables of Jesus demands a complete study of Luke. *Facets* in this sense refers to any textual unit or group of such units that does not coincide with canonical books. Such units may be as short as an aphorism or as extensive as source Q, as limited as the birth and childhood stories or as diffuse as hymns in the New Testament. Again, tracking the various strands of the gospel tradition from the time of Jesus down into the second century can better be pursued independently of specific biblical books. In this second sense, *Facets* refers to strands or trajectories of early Christian tradition.

Further, *Facets* indicates features of biblical books themselves, such as the literary method of Luke, the use of irony in the Fourth Gospel, or the formal structure of the gospel as literary genre. While such features might well be included in the commentary proper, there may be reason to isolate one or more for special and extended consideration.

As it turns out, these creative and innovative impulses in current scholarship are linked to emerging new methods in biblical criticism or to the reconception of old ones. Accordingly, a second function of *Foundations and Facets* is to accommodate the creation or revision of correlative foundational instruments and tools. Such foundational works, properly conceived, will form the basis for the next phase of biblical scholarship.

The pioneering work of Martin Dibelius and Rudolf Bultmann in form criticism more than a half century ago rested on comparative evidence then newly acquired. Recent efforts to interpret the same oral forms—parables, pronouncement stories, miracle tales, and the like—have led to revised and expanded collections of comparative data. *Foundations and Facets* will be open to these primary materials, so that every student of the New Testament will be able to examine the comparative evidence firsthand.

Similarly, new methods allied with literary criticism, the study of folklore, and linguistics bring with them newly conceived grammars and lexica. Grammars include a poetics of biblical narrative, a handbook of hellenistic rhetoric, and a systematic hermeneutics. Other alliances with the social and psychological sciences are producing correlative new methodologies, which will themselves eventually require precise formulation. To be sure, older methodologies are being revised and refurbished as well. The cultural and religious milieu of the New Testament, together with its sociological and economic substratum, remain ingredient to an understanding of early Christianity and the literature it produced. And New Testament "introduction" is as pertinent today as it was when New Testament science assumed its modern form a century earlier, although it should by now be apparent that this traditional discipline must reorient itself if it is to lead into the text. It is fitting that the series should begin with a work of just this order: a classical form of scholarship with provocative new content.

The new series is thus aimed at both the *Foundations and Facets* of the biblical canon, seeking to harness mature as well as creative and innovative impulses impinging upon it.

The complete scope of *Foundations and Facets* has yet to be determined. It is the plan of the series to adapt itself as nearly as possible to the unfolding requirements of sound biblical scholarship. The series may thus eventually embrace works the exact dimensions of which are at present unknown, and it may well omit projected works for which suitable authors do not appear.

The expansion of biblical instruction into secular contexts, such as the public university, presents biblical scholarship with a fresh and serious challenge: in addition to exposition for the reader trained in the fundamental disciplines of biblical science, exegetes must now make the text intelligible for persons generally rather than technically literate. It is the intention of the authors and editors of *Foundations and Facets* to meet this challenge: they aspire to a mode of biblical scholarship that will illumine the text for the general reader, while simultaneously serving the most stringent requirements of the advanced student. If the series succeeds in achieving this goal, it will have attained a new level of scholarly integrity.

Polebridge Press
Riverbend 1982

Robert W. Funk, editor

The concept of an "Introduction to the New Testament" in the form of a history of early Christianity in its contemporary setting, including a survey of the political, cultural, and religious history of the Hellenistic and Roman imperial period, stems from the predecessor of this book, the *Einführung in das Neue Testament* by Rudolf Knopf (revised edition by Hans Lietzmann and Heinrich Weinel) in the series "Sammlung Töpelmann" (now succeeded by "De Gruyter Lehrbücher"). Thus, the *Introduction* presented here in its English version does not aspire to be an "Introduction" in the technical sense nor a "History of Early Christian Literature" which treats the scholarship, date, integrity, and literary structure of each of the New Testament writings. To be sure, these questions are encompassed in the present work, but they are discussed within the context of a reconstruction of the historical development of early Christianity. My primary concern is to present the history of the early Christian churches, since it seems to me that the student of the New Testament must learn from the outset to understand the writings of the earliest period within their proper historical context.

It is obvious that this attempt to reconstruct the history of early Christianity requires one to relinquish some strictures of traditional introductions. I do not limit the discussion to the twenty-seven canonical books, but treat also sixty other early Christian writings from the first 150 years of Christian history, whether or not these writings are preserved fully or only in fragments. These non-canonical works are witnesses to early Christian history no less valuable than the New Testament. A historical presentation of these materials requires that clear decisions be made about authorship, date, and place of each writing; in other words, the results of historical-critical inquiry have to be consulted fully in each instance. I have also made an effort to discuss the problems in making such decisions. If these issues remain controversial with respect to some parts of the New Testament, they are even more difficult for non-canonical literature: traditionally scholarly debate has focused on the canonical literature, whereas the so-called "apocrypha" and other non-canonical writings have received only scant attention. Furthermore, quite a few of the latter have been discovered only recently, and their critical evaluation has just begun.

Nevertheless, it is much better to advance scholarship, and thus our understanding, through hypothetical reconstruction than to ignore new and apparently problematic materials.

In view of the present situation of New Testament scholarship, it would be misleading to suggest to the students of early Christian history that they can expect largely secure results. The New Testament itself furnishes evidence that the history of early Christian communities was a complex process, full of controversies and difficult decisions. Understanding this process requires critical judgment as well as the construction of trajectories through the history of early Christianity. The recent discovery of even more early writings not only demands a basic reorientation of our views, but will also enable the student to appreciate more fully the depths and riches of this formative period, especially as it is seen in the context of the general history of the culture in which Christianity began.

The scope of this book does not permit me to base my entire presentation upon the results of my own research. There are many topics in my survey of the Hellenistic and Roman world on which the specialist will have better insights and judgment. I am not only indebted to the published works of many scholars, but also owe much to my students at Harvard University, who have enriched this book in its various stages of writing and re-writing with their suggestions and criticisms, and equally to my colleagues, from whom I have learned a great deal during the last two decades in seminars and in discussions. I wish to express my special thanks to colleagues and friends: to Klaus Baltzer, of the University of Munich, and to Frank M. Cross, Dieter Georgi, George MacRae, Krister Stendahl, John Strugnell, and Zeph Stewart, all of Harvard University.

This book is the author's own translation of the German *Einführung in das Neue Testament,* published 1980 by Walter De Gruyter, Berlin and New York. Only in a few instances has the text been changed; one chapter was added (§6.3d). However, a number of minor errors and a few major mistakes were corrected. For this, I am particularly indebted to Eckhard Plümacher's review of this book (*Göttingische Gelehrte Anzeigen* 233 [1981] 1–22) and to the extensive notes which he kindly made available to me.

The bibliography has been redesigned so that editions and translations of texts are quoted first in order to encourage the student to read further in primary materials. English translations of texts are cited in the bibliographies wherever available. I am grateful to my colleague Albert Henrichs of Harvard University for suggestions regarding the revision of the bibliography. The bibliography is not meant to be exhaustive, but is designed to emphasize what is, in my opinion, the most valuable and more recent material, and what will best lead to further study. I have, however, included the most important "classics" which are still basic guides for scholarship today. For further reference, the reader should consult the standard reference works: *The Interpreter's Dictionary of the Bible* (especially its recently published supplement), *Reallexikon für Antike und Christentum, Der Kleine Pauly, Die Religion in Geschichte und Gegenwart,* and *The Oxford Classical Dictionary* (specific references to these works are normally not given in the bibliographies).

The English edition (as already the German work) would scarcely have been finished in such a brief time without the patience and interest of my wife and my children. Numerous persons have given their help in the various stages of translation and production of this work: Philip H. Sellew (editing, bibliography), Jonathan C. Guest (editing, copyediting, and proofreading), Gary A. Bisbee (maps), Pamela Chance (typing), Robert Stoops and Douglas Olson (bibliography). I am very grateful for their expert and untiring help. Rarely does an author enjoy such experienced and congenial production assistance as I had from my friends Charlene Matejovsky and Robert W. Funk of Polebridge Press at Missoula, Montana. Their dedication, care, competence, and advice accompanied every step of the book's production.

Inter Nationes, an agency of the government of the Federal Republic of Germany in Bonn, made a major grant to offset the cost of assistance for this translation. Thanks are due for this generous help.

This book is dedicated to the memory of my teacher Rudolf Bultmann. He encouraged me more than thirty years ago to deal more intensively with the extra-canonical writings from the early Christian period. His unwavering insistence upon the consistent application of the historical-critical method and his emphasis upon the investigation of early Christian literature in the context of the history of religions must remain basic commitments of New Testament scholarship.

Harvard University
Cambridge, Massachusetts
May 1982

Helmut Koester

Abbreviations

Serial and Journal Titles

AAWG.PH	Abhandlungen der Akademie der Wissenschaften zu Göttingen. Philologisch-historische Klasse
AB	Anchor Bible
ADAI.K	Abhandlungen des deutschen archäologischen Instituts, Kairo, Koptische Reihe
AHR	*American Historical Review*
AGSU	Arbeiten zur Geschichte des Spätjudentums und Urchristentums
AJP	*American Journal of Philology*
AKG	Arbeiten zur Kirchengeschichte
AnBib	Analecta biblica
ANRW	*Aufstieg und Niedergang der Römischen Welt*
ANTT	Arbeiten zur neutestamentlichen Textforschung
ASNU	Acta seminarii neotestamentici upsaliensis
AThANT	Abhandlungen zur Theologie des Alten und Neuen Testaments
AVTRW	Aufsätze und Vorträge zur Theologie und Religionswissenschaft
BAC	Biblioteca de autores cristianos
BEThL	Bibliotheca ephemeridum theologicarum Lovaniensium
BEvTh	Beiträge zur evangelischen Theologie
BFChTh	Beiträge zur Förderung christlicher Theologie
BHTh	Beiträge zur historischen Theologie
BibOr	Biblica et orientalia
BJRL	*Bulletin of the John Rylands Library*
BKP	Beiträge zur klassischen Philologie
BT.B	Bibliothèque de théologie, 3. Ser.: Théologie biblique
BWAT	Beiträge zur Wissenschaft vom Alten Testament
BZNW	Beihefte zur Zeitschrift für die neutestamentliche Wissenschaft
CBQ	*Catholic Biblical Quarterly*
CGTC	Cambridge Greek Testament Commentary
ConB	Coniectanea biblica
CRI	Compendia Rerum Judaicarum ad Novum Testamentum
EHS.T	Europäische Hochschulschriften. Reihe 23: Theologie
EKKNT	Evangelisch-katholischer Kommentar zum Neuen Testament
EPhM	Etudes de philosophie médiévale
EPRO	Etudes préliminaires aux religions orientales dans l'empire romain
ErJb	Eranos-Jahrbuch
EtBib	Etudes Bibliques

Et J	Etudes Juives
EvTh	*Evangelische Theologie*
FKDG	Forschungen zur Kirchen- und Dogmengeschichte
FRLANT	Forschungen zur Religion und Literatur des Alten und Neuen Testaments
GBSNTS	Guides to Biblical Scholarship, New Testament Series
GCS	Die griechischen christlichen Schriftsteller der ersten drei Jahrhunderte
GLB	De Gruyter Lehrbuch
GRBS	*Greek, Roman, and Byzantine Studies*
GTB	Van Gorcum's theologische bibliotheek
GWU	*Geschichte in Wissenschaft und Unterricht*
HAW	Handbuch der Altertumswissenschaft
HDR	Harvard Dissertations in Religion
Hesp.S	Hesperia. Supplements
HeyJ	*Heythrop Journal*
Hist	*Historia. Zeitschrift für alte Geschichte*
HNT	Handbuch zum Neuen Testament
HNT.E	Handbuch zum Neuen Testament. Ergänzungsband
HSM	Harvard Semitic Monographs
HSS	Harvard Semitic Series
HThK	Herders Theologischer Kommentar zum Neuen Testament
HTR	*Harvard Theological Review*
HTS	Harvard Theological Studies
Hyp.	Hypomnemata. Untersuchungen zur Antike und zu ihrem Nachleben
ICC	International Critical Commentary
IDBSup	*Interpreter's Dictionary of the Bible. Supplement*
Int	*Interpretation*
JAC	*Jahrbuch für Antike und Christentum*
JAC.E	Jahrbuch für Antike und Christentum. Ergänzungsband
JAL	Jewish Apocryphal Literature
JBL	*Journal of Biblical Literature*
JEA	*Journal of Egyptian Archaeology*
JHS	*Journal of Hellenic Studies*
JQR.MS	Jewish Quarterly Review. Monograph Series
JR	*Journal of Religion*
JRomS	*Journal of Roman Studies*
JSHRZ	Jüdische Schriften aus hellenistisch-römischer Zeit
JTC	*Journal for Theology and the Church*
JTS	*Journal of Theological Studies*
KlT	Kleine Texte für (theologische und philologische) Vorlesungen und Übungen
LBS	Library of Biblical Studies
LCL	Loeb Classical Library
LHR	Lectures on the History of Religions, Sponsored by the American Council of Learned Societies
MAPS	Memoirs of the American Philosophical Society
MBPF	Münchener Beiträge zur Papyrusforschung und antiken Rechtsgeschichte
MH	*Museum Helveticum*
Mn.Suppl.	Mnemosyne. Bibliotheca classica/philologica Batava. Supplements
MThSt	Marburger theologische Studien

MThZ	*Münchener theologische Zeitschrift*
NAWG.PH	Nachrichten der Akademie der Wissenschaft in Göttingen. Philologisch-historische Klasse
NHS	Nag Hammadi Studies
NovT	*Novum Testamentum*
NovTSup	Novum Testamentum. Supplements
NTDSup	Das Neue Testament Deutsch. Supplementband
NTS	*New Testament Studies*
NTTS	New Testament Tools and Studies
NumenSup	Numen. International Review for the History of Religions. Supplements
OBO	Orbis Biblicus et Orientalis
OTS	*Oudtestamentische Studien*
PBA	*Proceedings of the British Academy*
Ph.S	Philologus. Supplement
PTS	Patristische Texte und Studien
PVTG	Pseudepigrapha Veteris Testamentis graece
RAC	*Reallexikon für Antike und Christentum*
RB	*Revue biblique*
RechSR	*Recherches de science religieuse*
RGG	*Die Religion in Geschichte und Gegenwart*
RechBib	Recherches bibliques
RPS	Religious Perspectives (series)
RVV	Religionsgeschichtliche Versuche und Vorarbeiten
SBLDS	Society of Biblical Literature Dissertation Series
SBLMS	Society of Biblical Literature Monograph Series
SBLSBS	Society of Biblical Literature Sources for Biblical Study
SBLSCS	Society of Biblical Literature Septuagint and Cognate Studies
SBLSS	Society of Biblical Literature. Semeia Supplements
SBLTT	Society of Biblical Literature. Texts and Translations
SBS	Stuttgarter Bibelstudien
SBT	Studies in Biblical Theology
SC	Sources chrétiennes
SCHNT	Studia ad Corpus Hellenisticum Novi Testamenti
SEÅ	*Svensk Exegetisk Årsbok*
SG	Sammlung Göschen
SHCT	Studies in the History of Christian Thought
SJ	Studia Judaica
SJLA	Studies in Judaism in Late Antiquity
SNTSMS	Society of New Testament Studies Monograph Series
SÖAW.PH	Sitzungsberichte der Österreichischen Akademie der Wissenschaften. Philosophisch-historische Klasse
SPB	Studia Post-Biblica
SQAW	Schriften und Quellen der Alten Welt
SQS	Sammlung ausgewählter kirchen- und dogmengeschichtlicher Quellenschriften
StANT	Studien zum Alten und Neuen Testament
STL	Studia Theologica Lundensia
StNT	Studien zum Neuen Testament
STRT	Studia Theologica Rheno-Trajectina

SUNT	Studien zur Umwelt des Neuen Testamentes
SVTP	Studia in veteris testamenti pseudepigrapha
TEH	Theologische Existenz heute
TF	Texte zur Forschung
ThBü	Theologische Bücherei
ThF	Theologische Forschung
ThHK	Theologischer Hand-Kommentar
ThLZ	*Theologische Literaturzeitung*
ThR	*Theologische Rundschau*
ThZ	*Theologische Zeitschrift*
TSJTSA	Texts and Studies of the Jewish Theological Seminary of America
TU	Texte und Untersuchungen zur Geschichte der altchristlichen Literatur
UB	Urban-Bücher
VC	*Vigiliae Christianae*
VTSup	Vetus Testamentum. Supplements
WdF	Wege der Forschung
WMANT	Wissenschaftliche Monographien zum Alten und Neuen Testament
WUNT	Wissenschaftliche Untersuchungen zum Neuen Testament
WZ (J)	*Wissenschaftliche Zeitschrift der Friedrich-Schiller-Universität Jena*
YCS	Yale Classical Studies
YPR	Yale Publications in Religion
Zet.	Zetemata
ZNW	*Zeitschrift für die neutestamentliche Wissenschaft*
ZThK	*Zeitschrift für Theologie und Kirche*

Works often Cited

Barrett, *Background*
    C. K. Barrett (ed.), *The New Testament Background: Selected Documents* (London: SPCK, 1956; reprint: New York: Harper, 1961).
Bauer, *Orthodoxy and Heresy*
    Walter Bauer, *Orthodoxy and Heresy in Earliest Christianity* (Philadelphia: Fortress, 1971).
Betz, *Galatians*
    Hans Dieter Betz, *Galatians: A Commentary on Paul's Letter to the Churches in Galatia* (Hermeneia; Philadelphia: Fortress, 1979).
Bihlmeyer, *ApostVät*
    F. X. Funk and Karl Bihlmeyer, *Die Apostolischen Väter* (SQS 2,1,1; 2d ed.; Tübingen: Mohr/Siebeck, 1956).
Black and Rowley, *Peake's Commentary*
    Matthew Black and H. H. Rowley (eds.), *Peake's Commentary on the Bible* (London: Nelson, 1962).
Bornkamm, *Experience*
    Günther Bornkamm, *Early Christian Experience* (London: SCM, New York: Harper, 1969).
Braun, *Studien*
    Herbert Braun, *Studien zum Neuen Testament und seiner Umwelt* (3d ed.; Tübingen: Mohr/Siebeck, 1971).
Bultmann, *Exegetica*
    Rudolf Bultmann, *Exegetica: Aufsätze zur Erforschung des Neuen Testaments* (ed. Erich Dinkler; Tübingen: Mohr/Siebeck, 1967).
Bultmann, *Existence and Faith*
    Rudolf Bultmann, *Existence and Faith* (ed. Schubert M. Ogden; New York: Meridian, 1960).
Bultmann, *Theology*
    Rudolf Bultmann, *Theology of the New Testament* (2 vols.; New York: Scribner's, 1951).
Calder and Keil, *Anatolian Studies*
    W. M. Calder and Josef Keil, *Anatolian Studies Presented to William Hepburn Buckler* (Manchester: Manchester University, 1939).
CambAncHist 7–10
    S. A. Cook, F. E. Adcock, and M. P. Charlesworth, *The Cambridge Ancient History,* vol. 7: *The Hellenistic Monarchies and the Rise of Rome;* vol. 8: *Rome and the Mediterranean 218–133 B. C.;* vol. 9: *The Roman Republic 133–44 B. C.;* vol. 10: *The Augustan Empire 44 B. C.–A. D. 70* (New York: Macmillan, 1928–34).

Cambridge History of the Bible 1
  P. R. Ackroyd and C. F. Evans (eds.), *The Cambridge History of the Bible,* vol. 1: *From the Beginnings to Jerome* (Cambridge: Cambridge University, 1970).
Cameron (ed.), *The Other Gospels*
  Ronald D. Cameron (ed.), *The Other Gospels, Introductions and Translations* (Philadelphia: Westminster, 1982).
von Campenhausen, *Tradition*
  Hans von Campenhausen, *Tradition and Life in the Church: Essays and Lectures in Church History* (Philadelphia: Fortress, 1968).
Cartlidge and Dungan, *Documents*
  David R. Cartlidge and David L. Dungan (eds.), *Documents for the Study of the Gospels* (Cleveland: Collins, 1980).
Conzelmann, *Outline*
  Hans Conzelmann, *An Outline of the Theology of the New Testament* (New York: Harper, 1969).
Cullmann, *Vorträge 1925–1962*
  Oscar Cullmann, *Vorträge und Aufsätze 1925–1962* (Tübingen: Mohr/Siebeck, and Zürich: Zwingli, 1966).
Foakes Jackson and Lake, *Beginnings*
  F. J. Foakes Jackson and Kirsopp Lake (eds.), *The Beginnings of Christianity* (5 vols.; London: Macmillan, 1920–33, and reprints).
Foerster, *Gnosis*
  Werner Foerster, *Gnosis: A Selection of Gnostic Texts* (Eng. trans. ed. R. McL. Wilson; 2 vols.; Oxford: Clarendon, 1972–74).
Fraser, *Alexandria*
  P. M. Fraser, *Ptolemaic Alexandria* (2 vols.; Oxford: Clarendon, 1972).
Grant, *ApostFath*
  Robert M. Grant, *The Apostolic Fathers: A New Translation and Commentary* (6 vols.; New York: Nelson, 1964–68).
Grant, *Hellenistic Religions*
  Frederick C. Grant (ed.), *Hellenistic Religions: The Age of Syncretism* (The Library of Religion 2; New York: Liberal Arts, 1953).
Haenchen, *Acts*
  Ernst Haenchen, *The Acts of the Apostles: A Commentary* (Philadelphia: Westminster, 1971).
Haenchen, *Gott und Mensch*
  Ernst Haenchen, *Gott und Mensch: Gesammelte Aufsätze* (Tübingen: Mohr/Siebeck, 1965).
Käsemann, *New Testament Questions*
  Ernst Käsemann, *New Testament Questions of Today* (Philadelphia: Fortress, 1969)
Kee, *Origins*
  Howard Clark Kee, *The Origins of Christianity: Sources and Documents* (Englewood Cliffs, NJ: Prentice Hall, 1973).
Kirche: Festschrift Bornkamm
  Dieter Lührmann and Georg Strecker (eds.), *Kirche: Festschrift für Günther Bornkamm zum 75. Geburtstag* (Tübingen: Mohr/Siebeck, 1980).
Lake, *ApostFath*
  Kirsopp Lake, *The Apostolic Fathers* (LCL; 2 vols.; Cambridge, MA: Harvard University, 1912, and reprints).

Layton, *Rediscovery of Gnosticism*
  Bentley Layton (ed.), *The Rediscovery of Gnosticism* (Proceedings of the International
  Conference at Yale, New Haven, 1978; NumenSup 16; 2 vols.; Leiden: Brill, vol. 1,
  1980; vol. 2, forthcoming).
Lightfoot, *Apostolic Fathers*
  J. B. Lightfoot, *Apostolic Fathers: A Revised Text with Introductions, Notes,
  Dissertations, and Translations* (2 parts in 5 vols.; London: Macmillan, 1885–90).
Lipsius-Bonnet, *ActApostApoc*
  Richard Albert Lipsius and Maximilian Bonnet, *Acta Apostolorum Apocrypha* (2 vols;
  Leipzig: Mendelssohn, 1891–1903; reprint: Darmstadt: Wissenschaftliche
  Buchgesellschaft, 1959).
NagHamLibEngl
  James M. Robinson (ed.), *The Nag Hammadi Library in English* (Leiden: Brill, and
  New York: Harper, 1977).
Neusner, *Religions in Antiquity*
  Jacob Neusner (ed.), *Religions in Antiquity: Essays in Memory of Erwin Ramsdell
  Goodenough* (NumenSup 14; Leiden: Brill, 1968).
Nilsson, *Griechische Religion 2*
  Martin P. Nilsson, *Geschichte der griechischen Religion,* vol. 2: *Die hellenistische und
  römische Zeit* (HAW 5,2,2; 3d ed.; München: Beck, 1974).
Nock, *Essays*
  Arthur Darby Nock, *Essays on Religion and the Ancient World* (2 vols.; Cambridge,
  MA: Harvard University, 1972).
NTApo
  Edgar Hennecke, *New Testament Apocrypha* (ed. Wilhelm Schneemelcher; 2 vols.;
  Philadelphia: Westminster, 1963–65).
Robinson and Koester, *Trajectories*
  James M. Robinson and Helmut Koester, *Trajectories through Early Christianity*
  (Philadelphia: Fortress, 1971).
Schmithals, *Paul and the Gnostics*
  Walter Schmithals, *Paul and the Gnostics* (Nashville: Abingdon, 1972).
Morton Smith, *Clement*
  Morton Smith, *Clement of Alexandria and a Secret Gospel of Mark* (Cambridge, MA:
  Harvard University, 1973).
Vielhauer, *Geschichte*
  Philip Vielhauer, *Geschichte der urchristlichen Literatur* (GLB; Berlin: De Gruyter,
  1975).

HISTORY AND LITERATURE
OF EARLY CHRISTIANITY

The writings which are now included in the twenty-seven books of the New Testament are the product of the early history of the Christian churches in the eastern countries of the ancient Mediterranean world and, eventually, in Rome. In addition, numerous other writings from this early Christian period belong to the same historical developments. This book endeavors to introduce the student of the New Testament to all of these writings in the context of a reconstruction of the expansion and growth of the Christian communities from their beginnings to the middle of the second century CE.

The political, cultural, religious, and economic factors that constituted the setting for early Christian history have been discussed extensively in the first volume, including the history of Judaism of the Hellenistic and Roman imperial periods. What has been said in that volume is essential for the understanding of the development of early Christianity. The importance of this is indicated by the cross references in this volume, for it is difficult to understand Christian history without studying its environment.

The sources for early Christianity, which are almost exclusively Christian writings, present significant problems that have been the subject of the specialized works of many scholars. Some acquaintance with the scholarly approaches to these ancient writings and with the present status of their learned investigation is prerequisite to the study of this literature in its historical context. Therefore, the first chapter of this volume (§7) is devoted to the various problems of the investigation of the New Testament and other early Christian literature.

Although Christianity emerged from the ministry of Jesus and in the first communities in Palestine, soon spreading to other parts of Syria and to Egypt, its most significant literature, which was to determine the future of this religious movement, developed in the urban culture of the eastern Mediterranean, particularly the cities around the Aegean Sea. Thus, the history of the Christian churches will be treated not only in chronological sequence, but also with respect to the different regions in which the

establishment of the churches in the major economic centers of the
Hellenistic world (Antioch, Ephesus, Corinth, and even Rome) marks the
end of the formative period of early Christianity and thus concludes the
production of most of the New Testament writings.

THE SOURCES FOR THE HISTORY
OF EARLY CHRISTIANITY

1. SURVEY OF THE SOURCES AND THEIR TRADITIONS

(a) The Formation of the Earliest Christian Writings

The Bible of early Christianity was the Old Testament (OT), or more precisely, "the Law and the Prophets." This is what was meant when early Christians spoke generally of the "Scripture" or when they used the quotation formula "it is written." Side by side with the "Scripture" there was from the beginning an oral tradition which was transmitted under the authority of the "Lord." It comprised the sayings of Jesus as well as short narratives about him. The words of the "Lord" were not restricted to sayings of the earthly Jesus, but also contained words of the risen Lord (§7.4a–c). At an early date the medium of written communication and transmission also came into use. To be sure, the primary activities of the earliest Christian communities required oral communication because preaching, instruction, and common celebrations were of major importance. But it is certainly wrong to picture the early Christian missionaries and church leaders as uneducated people who could neither read nor write. The culture of the Hellenistic and Roman periods was to a large extent a literary culture. This is especially true for Judaism in that period, which became the matrix for the formation of early Christianity. Learning how to read was expected for all male members of the Jewish religious community. Accordingly, in early Christianity oral traditions also seem to have been written down for ecclesiastical use at an early time. Such written materials would have included catechetical collections of Jesus' sayings, church orders, or collections of parables and miracle narratives. Some of these were later incorporated into larger writings, such as the early collection of parables, first written down in Aramaic, that is preserved in Mark 4, and the early church orders that were used by the author of the *Didache* (§10.1c).

The oldest written documents of early Christianity that are preserved as such are the letters of the apostle Paul, which were written in the 50s of

I CE. These letters are not occasional writings, nor can they be classified as "literature." Rather, they are instruments of ecclesiastical policy, which functioned alongside the political and propagandistic medium of oral communication because this was required in an organization of churches distributed over a wide geographical area. The literary form of the letter which Paul used is certainly related to older Greek and Jewish prototypes, but was primarily fashioned through the demands of the Pauline missionary situation, which gave it its essential imprint. Beginning with the last decades of I CE, the use of the written medium for new communication and for transmitting the tradition became more prominent, but this

Bibliography to §7

Martin Dibelius, *A Fresh Approach to the New Testament and Early Christian Literature* (New York: Scribner's, 1936).

Philipp Vielhauer, *Geschichte der urchristlichen Literatur* (GLB; 2d ed.; Berlin: De Gruyter, 1978).

Werner Georg Kümmel, *Introduction to the New Testament* (translated from the 17th German edition of 1973; Nashville: Abingdon, 1975).

Alfred Wikenhauser and Josef Schmid, *Einleitung in das Neue Testament* (6th ed.; Freiburg: Herder, 1973).

Bibliography to §7.1

Hans von Campenhausen, *The Formation of the Christian Bible* (Philadelphia: Fortress, 1972).

Paul Wendland, *Die urchristlichen Literaturformen* (HNT 1,3; 2d and 3d ed.; Tübingen: Mohr/Siebeck 1912).

Helmut Koester, "Aprocryphal and Canonical Gospels," *HTR* 73 (1980) 105–30.

Idem, "Literature, Early Christian," *IDBSup* (1976) 551–56.

Bibliography to §7.1a

Kurt Aland, "The Problem of Anonymity and Pseudonymity in Christian Literature of the First Two Centuries," *JTS* n.s. 12 (1961) 39–49.

Horst R. Balz, "Anonymität und Pseudepigraphie im Urchristentum," *ZThK* 66 (1969) 403–36.

Norbert Brox, *Falsche Verfasserangaben: Zur Erklärung der frühchristlichen Pseudepigraphie* (Stuttgart: Katholisches Bibelwerk, 1975).

Wolfgang Speyer, *Die literarische Fälschung im heidnischen und christlichen Altertum* (HAW 1,2; München: Beck, 1971).

Pseudepigrapha I (Entretiens sur l'antiquité classique 18; Geneva: Vandoeuvres, 1972).

Adolf Deissmann, *Light from the Ancient East: The New Testament Illustrated by Recently Discovered Texts of the Graeco-Roman World* (New York: Doran, 1927).

Hans von Campenhausen, "Das Alte Testament als Bibel der Kirche," in: idem, *Aus der Frühzeit des Christentums* (Tübingen: Mohr/Siebeck, 1963) 152–96.

William G. Doty, *Letters in Primitive Christianity* (GBSNT; Philadelphia: Fortress, 1973).

Robert W. Funk, "The Apostolic Parousia: Form and Significance," in: W. R. Farmer, C. F. D. Moule, and R. R. Niebuhr (eds.), *Christian History and Interpretation: Studies Presented to John Knox* (Cambridge: Cambridge University, 1967) 249–68.

did not mean the end of the ongoing oral transmission. As late as about 130, Papias of Hierapolis still placed a higher value on the oral tradition from the apostles that was passed down by their successors than on written gospels. On the other hand, the instrument of church policy that Paul had created had a strong impact on the following period, so that the use of the literary instrument of the letter for the purpose of propaganda and church organization became quite popular. It also must have become evident rather soon that the written forms of the traditions about Jesus, used as foundations for church order and as a device for the propagation of the Christian message, were in many instances better suited than the orally transmitted materials—not, however, because of any beliefs in the greater reliability of written sources. Oral traditions, as is demonstrated by the rabbinic parallels, could achieve a high degree of reliability, while authors of books sometimes treated their materials with much more freedom. Rather, the primary reason for preferring the written medium was a cultural one: the use of writings and books was more natural in the culture of that time.

The model of the Pauline letter was first taken up and further developed in the circles of his students. The result is the creation of the so-called deutero-Pauline letters: 2 Thessalonians, Colossians, Ephesians, the Pastoral Epistles (1 and 2 Timothy, Titus), *Laodiceans,* and *3 Corinthians.* Not only do all of these use the model of the Pauline letters, they also continue the Pauline tradition under his authority. But soon other authors began to write under their own names, or under the names of other apostles, still using the model of the Pauline letter for their own purposes. *1 Clement,* written from Rome, is designed to achieve the same result which had earlier been produced in Corinth by Paul's letters, namely, to make the Corinthians patch up their quarrel. Bishop Ignatius of Antioch, while travelling to his martyrdom in Rome, wrote a series of letters to churches in Asia Minor in order to assist them in clarifying their problems. Letters are preserved even under the names of other apostles which use the Pauline model for their church-political designs. Among these are the two Epistles of Peter in the New Testament (NT), and probably also the three Johannine Epistles, which can be compared to the Pastoral Epistles of the Pauline corpus. The prophet John included in his Book of Revelation seven letters to churches in Asia Minor, through which he used his influence to counsel and advise those troubled communities. In the second half of II CE, bishop Dionysius of Corinth wrote to a number of churches in Asia Minor and on Crete in order to warn them about heretical forms of asceticism, though not without complaining that his letters had been tampered with. 2 Peter indeed warns that the Pauline letters could be misunderstood. Of the abundant letter-writing from the period which followed only very little is still preserved (such as those of Clement of Alexandria and Irenaeus). But the letters of bishop Cyprian from the middle of III CE have come down to us in more complete form. Seen as a whole, the letters from the period of early Christianity— whether they are "genuine" or "pseudepigraphic"—are an important source for early Christian history.

The next important corpus of literature includes those collections and compilations of various materials which focus on the person of Jesus and began to be called "gospels" by the middle of II CE. The early writings of this kind were simple, written versions of traditions about Jesus in various forms, which corresponded to the particular theological interests of the respective churches. Literary models from the Hellenistic world influenced the shape and content of these gospel writings from the beginning. Collections of miracle stories of Jesus are closely related to the genre of the aretalogy (§3.4d) and at the same time reveal a christology which presents Jesus as the prototype of the miracle healer and exorcist. Collections of Jesus' sayings are influenced by the genre of the Jewish wisdom literature and correspond to a christological orientation for which Jesus is the teacher of wisdom or the earthly appearance of heavenly Wisdom. One example of this literary genre is preserved: the *Gospel of Thomas,* which was found among the writings from Nag Hammadi. There is also a rather extensive literature in which Jesus appears as the heavenly revealer. The oldest writing of this genre is the Revelation of John. Under the influence of Jewish apocalyptic literature, a number of Christian apocalypses were produced, such as the *Apocalypse of Peter* and *Shepherd of Hermas,* and additions to Jewish apocalyptic books such as *5* and *6 Ezra.* The rich Christian gnostic revelation literature is closely related and is now fully visible through the discoveries of Nag Hammadi (§10.5b).

In those Christian communities that became the matrix for the later orthodox churches, the written and oral traditions of Jesus were composed in writings that took their point of departure from the kerygma of Jesus' cross and resurrection. At the same time, the literary model of the biography (§3.4d) strongly influenced the formation of this genre of Christian literature. The four gospels of the NT are representatives of this literary genre of the gospel, as well as several apocryphal gospels which are preserved only in fragments (the *Gospel of Peter* and the Jewish-Christian gospels). The effect of a very popular genre of Hellenistic literature can be clearly seen in these writings, and this is even more evident in the production of the various acts of the apostles. In the canonical Book of Acts, the intention to write history has played a role, in addition to aretalogical interests and several elements of the Hellenistic romance (travel narrative and story of the shipwreck). In the apocryphal acts of apostles the model of the romance is even more clearly evident (§3.4e).

Writings which sought to be primarily theological treatises had only gradual success. Paul's Letter to the Romans does not really belong in this category, because its role as an instrument of church policy remains the primary intent, despite a clearly visible influence from apologetic literature. A theological treatise appears for the first time in the Epistle to the Hebrews; with its allegorical interpretations of passages from the OT, it can be compared to the treatises of Philo of Alexandria (§5.3f). Among the noncanonical writings, the *Epistle of Barnabas* belongs in this category. The further production of theological treatises is closely related to the development of Christian apologetic literature, which is a continuation of Jewish apologetic writings (§5.3e), but also shows points of contact with the philosophical genre of protreptical literature. The Christian creed is a new element in this literature and provides its basic structure. These writings were composed in such a way that scriptural proof for the individual statements of the creed was given point by point. The treatment of an individual statement of the creed could also be expanded into a treatise on a particular topic. Though there are few examples from II CE, a large number of such treatises are preserved from III CE (e.g., Origen's *De principiis* and several treatises of Tertullian). The apologists of II CE used the schema of apologetic writings, which was also based on the Christian creed, in polemical literature directed against the heretics and against the Jews (Justin Martyr's *Dialogue with Trypho the Jew* and Irenaeus' *Adversus haereses*).

Only very few writings document the life of the Christian churches and their worship services. Several writings may be sermons in published form. *2 Clement* could be such a writing, and perhaps also the co-called *Gospel of Truth* from the Nag Hammadi writings. The *Passover Homily* of bishop Melito of Sardis was composed toward the end of II CE. The accounts of martyrdoms which were written as circular letters were also designated to be read in worship services. Several of these come from II CE: the *Martyrdom of Polycarp*, of *Justin and His Companions*, the *Acts of the Martyrs of Lyon and Vienne*, and the *Acts of the Scillitan Martyrs*. Finally, the church orders should be mentioned here. Of these only the *Teaching of the Twelve Apostles (Didache)* can be dated with certainty into the early period of Christianity, while the (Syriac) *Didascalia*, the *Church Order of Hippolytus*, and the *Apostolic Church Order* were all written after the year 200.

(b) The Canon of the New Testament

1) *The Lord and the Letters of Paul.* During the first decades of the expansion of Christianity, the Lord was the only authority which assured the validity of the Christian message and the reliability of the Christian tradition. In controversial questions, one would rely primarily on "what

the Lord had said," or one would ask a Christian prophet what the "Lord" had revealed to him. In addition, other authorities could be called upon, such as "the Law and the Prophets," the possession of the Holy Spirit, "Nature," general morality, or rational judgment. Not until the end of the period of the first apostles did Christians begin to appeal to the authority of specific apostles. The first evidence for this is the witness of the Pauline communities, which soon began to collect and distribute the letters of Paul, and which also started to produce new letters in his name, incorporating them into the collection of Paul's letters. It has been conjectured that the Epistle to the Ephesians was connected with the first collection of the Pauline letters and was written as a covering letter for it. However that may be, we nonetheless possess clear evidence that the authority of a particular apostle was used for writings that originated from his former realm of activity.

2) *Peter, Thomas, and John*. Unfortunately, the sources are otherwise missing that could provide us with direct insights, similar to Paul's, into the ministry and sphere of activity of any other apostle. It is striking, however, that in several limited geographical areas later traditions and writings are grouped around the name of a specific apostle, whose authority they claim. A number of writings are preserved from western Syria that claim to be written by Peter: the *Gospel of Peter,* the *Apocalypse of Peter,* the *Kerygma of Peter* (and if not identical with the last writing, the *Doctrina Petri*), furthermore a source of the *Pseudo-Clementines* which is known as the *Kerygmata Petrou*. After all, Paul's Letter to the Galatians reports that Peter stayed for some time in the Syrian city of Antioch (Gal

Bibliography to §7.1b: Text

Eberhard Nestle, Erwin Nestle, Kurt Aland, and others (eds.), *Novum Testamentum Graece* (26th ed.; Stuttgart: Deutsche Bibelstiftung, 1981).

Bibliography to §7.1b: Studies

Wilhelm Schneemelcher, "History of the New Testament Canon," *NTApo* 1. 28–60.

Werner Georg Kümmel, *Introduction to the New Testament* (Nashville: Abingdon, 1975) 475–510.

Robert M. Grant, *The Formation of the New Testament* (New York: Harper, 1965).

Idem, "The New Testament Canon," in *Cambridge History of the Bible*, 1. 284–308.

Floyd V. Filson, *Which Books Belong in the Bible? A Study of the Canon* (Philadelphia: Westminster, 1957).

Ernst Käsemann (ed.), *Das Neue Testament als Kanon* (Göttingen: Vandenhoeck & Ruprecht, 1970).

David L. Dungan, "The New Testament Canon in Recent Study," *Int* 29 (1975) 339–51.

Albert C. Sundberg, "The Bible Canon and the Christian Doctrine of Inspiration," *Int* 29 (1975) 352–71.

2:11ff). It is therefore quite possible that the later writings under the authority of Peter derive from a Petrine tradition which is related to the actual missionary activity of that apostle in this particular area. This seems to be confirmed by the Gospel of Matthew, certainly a writing from Syria, which contains the famous word of Jesus to Peter designating him as the rock on which Jesus will build his church (Matt 16:17ff).

The tradition of Thomas from eastern Syria might result from a similar pattern, although it is impossible to prove that the legend of Thomas' missionary journey to the east, including even India, rests on historical foundation. All that is certain is the eastern Syrian provenance of the *Acts of Thomas,* which were written in early III CE. Most likely two other writings belong here which appear under the authoriy of this apostle in the Nag Hammadi library: the *Gospel of Thomas* and the *Book of Thomas.* The first of these writings was composed not later than the beginning of II CE while the second cannot be dated with any certainty. If all these writings indeed come from eastern Syria (Edessa?), they might rest on a tradition under the name of Thomas which had its origin in his mission in this realm.

Finally, the tradition which is preserved under the name of John must be mentioned. The place of origin of these writings cannot be determined with certainty. Many scholars have good reasons to believe that they stem from one of the border areas of southern Syria, or from Palestine (not from Antioch or Edessa). Others, however, maintain that this tradition originates from Asia Minor—to be sure, at a later time it was believed that the tomb of John was in Ephesus. In addition to the Fourth Gospel of the NT, three letters (1–3 John) and several apocryphal writings are preserved under his name (*Acts of John, Apocryphon of John*). The gospel and letters are closely related with each other. The gospel itself is complex and rests on several stages of development in its traditions or sources. It is possible that the name of John was connected already with the oldest stage, but we have no proof for this assumption.

3) *The Twelve Apostles.* In addition to the assertion of authority under the name of a specific apostle, a new authority emerged under the designation of the Twelve Apostles. Paul knew only of the "Twelve," which he distinguished from "all the apostles" (1 Cor 15:5 and 7). General appeals to the "Apostles" without giving a specific number appear in the Epistle to the Ephesians, in Ignatius of Antioch, in *1 Clement,* in Polycarp of Smyrna, and in 2 Peter. This is a widely used appeal which cannot be identified with a specific tradition. The "Twelve Apostles" as a more narrowly defined authority are called upon for the first time in the *Teaching of the Twelve Apostles* (*Didache*), where they function as the authority for the ordering of the church. Many later church orders also used the au-

thority of the (Twelve) Apostles (*Apostolic Constitutions, Apostolic Church Order,* etc.). In the canonical Acts, the Twelve Apostles are the guarantors of the tradition and the prototype of an ecumenical presbytery.

Gnostic sects and schools used the names of individual apostles abundantly as the authorities for their teachings. A number of gnostic writings or revelations claim the names of apostles, who are in each case the recipients of the heavenly revelation which is written down in that book (e.g., *Apocryphon of John*); writings of theological instruction also appear under apostolic names (e.g., the so-called *Gospel of Philip*). Since the formation of the concept of apostolicity, which became basic for the canon of the NT, took place in the ongoing controversy with the gnostic sects, it must be assumed that it was exactly the gnostic appeal to apostolic authority which prompted the fathers of the church to emphasize on their part the apostolicity of the orthodox writings. However, as will be shown, the actual theological basis of the formation of the NT canon did not quite agree with such an emphasis.

4) *Marcion.* The impetus for the formation of the canon, that is, for the singling out of a limited number of traditional writings of Christian authors as authoritative Holy Scripture, came from a radical theologian of the tradition of the Pauline churches: Marcion (on Marcion's life and teaching, see §12.3c). Shortly after 140 he was excommunicated from the Roman church, whereupon he founded his own church, which quickly spread. The most striking feature of his teaching was the rejection of the OT on theological grounds. Until then, the OT had been the generally accepted Holy Scripture in all churches. This is also true for the Christian gnostics, who were able to overcome their difficulties in understanding the OT with the aid of the allegorical method; Marcion, however, rejected that method of treating the Hebrew Bible. He considered the OT as a historical document which testified to the activities of the just God who ruled this world; but salvation through Jesus came from a very different, "foreign" God. Since the authority of the OT had thus been annulled, the question arose whether there was some other scriptural authority for the Christian church, which had now been redeemed by the foreign God. Conscious of the significant role which the Law and the Prophets had played as Holy Scripture in the churches of his time, Marcion created a new Holy Scripture which became binding for his communities. It consisted of the Gospel of Luke and those letters attributed to Paul in the later canon of the NT except the Pastoral Epistles.

Marcion, however, came to the conviction that these writings were not preserved in their original form. He therefore made a critical edition to purify the books of his canon from all later additions. Before censuring Marcion because of his critical purification of the Pauline letters, one should remember that Marcion's opponents also tried to correct the image of Paul transmitted in the genuine letters, not least by the addition of the Pastoral Epistles to the Pauline corpus (Marcion apparently did not know of these epistles). Marcion's new edition of Luke conforms with a widespread custom of his time: Luke itself (as also Matthew) was already a new edition of the older Gospel of Mark. Thus Marcion's treatment of the Christian writings which he used for his canon was quite in agreement with the general attitude of his time. The novel element in Marcion's work was the elevation of these newly edited Christian writings to the status of Holy Scripture and the simultaneous rejection of the OT. Marcion himself was convinced that he was simply continuing a development which had been started by the great apostle Paul.

5) *The Reaction to Marcion.* How did those circles of the Christian church react which had insisted upon Marcion's excommunication, and which at the same time had tried to demarcate the borderline between the Christian church and Gnosticism? Only a part of this reaction is known, and what we learn is surprising. Justin Martyr is the principal witness. He was active in Rome at that time and wrote the first known (but not preserved) book against Marcion. Justin used the gospels of Matthew and Luke (perhaps also Mark), but he does not seem to think that his own new, harmonizing edition of these gospels might be just as questionable as Marcion's new edition of Luke. The letters of Paul, the most significant section of Marcion's new canon, were never quoted by Justin. Did he avoid them consciously? There are a few parallels to the Gospel of John in Justin's writings, but they derive from an older tradition related to John, not from the gospel itself. It is not impossible that Justin rejected that gospel because it was particularly popular among his gnostic opponents. The position and authority of the gospels in Justin's writings is striking. They are the authoritative "Memoirs of the Apostles," which are occasionally quoted with the formula "it is written," otherwise the customary citation formula for the OT. The fact that Justin thus moves the gospels as written authorities into close proximity to his standard of Holy Scripture, the OT, may be evidence of Marcion's influence.

Justin reveals that although it was apparent that the time for the creation of a Christian canon—a step which Marcion took—had come, the church still was at a loss as to how to go about it. This is shown by Justin's ignoring the Pauline epistles and by his imprudent continuation of the deliberate redaction of written gospels. A constructive alternative to the Marcionite solution did not appear. Justin's emphasis upon the authority of the OT and use of new recensions of the LXX (§5.3b) merely attempted to fortify what was current before Marcion. A generation after Justin, Irenaeus started on the path which would lead out of the perplexity caused by Marcion. Irenaeus was bishop of Lyon in Gaul, but as a theologian he belonged to the tradition of the Pauline churches in Asia Minor, where he had grown up. From there he also knew the tradition of the Johannine writings, which had been combined with the memory of the prophet John in Ephesus, who wrote the Book of Revelation. He boasts that he had sat at the feet of the famous bishop Polycarp of Smyrna, even if he was still a child at the time. Though a bishop of a western church, he was in his (Greek) writings a representative much more than Rome of an ecclesiastical tradition in which the Pauline letters, in spite of their great esteem in Marcionite and gnostic circles, were still a highly valued and obvious apostolic inheritance. The Pauline letters were still read in Asia Minor despite the warnings of 2 Peter (2 Pet 3:15f). At the same time, Irenaeus could appeal to the Johannine writings, which had meanwhile found their home in Asia Minor.

The NT canon of Holy Scripture, which was thus essentially created by Irenaeus, and which he placed side by side with the OT, included all the Pauline letters as well as some of the "Catholic" epistles (i.e., those which were directed to all churches). Thus its basis was broader than the Marcionite selection, which was based exclusively on the writings of Paul. Although traditionally the "Apostle" had been Paul alone, Irenaeus stretched this term to approximate the term "Twelve Apostles." As for the gospels, Irenaeus also did not try to create one exclusive authority; rather he accepted the four "separate" gospels (i.e., not in a harmonized form) of Matthew, Mark, Luke, and John. The idea that the gospels were four rather than one he tried to defend with a cosmological speculation that they corresponded to the four ends of the earth. It is clear that Ireneaus had to defend himself here against the widespread concept that, properly speaking, there could only be one gospel.

The inclusiveness of Ireneaus' conception of the Christian Scripture which is evident here has extraordinary significance. Everything that had been in use in the Christian communities from the beginning was included, if the tradition of the churches would confirm its use. Therefore, writings from the early period of Christianity were included, even if one knew very well that they had not been written by an "Apostle" (e.g., the Gospel of Mark and the writings of Luke). And after all, the strict definition of an apostle as a disciple of Jesus would not fit Paul anyway. On the other hand, recognized writings used by the churches were excluded if it was known that they had been recently composed. The question of inspiration did not play any role whatsoever in this process of canonization, because the claim to possess the Holy Spirit was so common that this criterion would have only caused confusion. The concept of apostolicity appears in a modified form: the authors of the writings collected in the canon were, to be sure, either apostles or disciples of apostles—with Paul counting as an apostle; but actually they only expressed what was the real criterion of the canon, namely, the teachings of the churches in the earliest period, meaning whichever of these writings had actually remained in use since that time. The fact that the usage in the churches of Asia Minor and Greece conformed to Irenaeus' collection, and that Antioch, Carthage, and later also Rome confirmed this usage, was the actual church-political basis of the canon, which was thus created at the end of II CE.

6) *The Muratorian Canon.* The oldest list of NT canonical writings which is preserved is probably the *Muratorian Canon,* written about 200, although some scholars would date it at least a century later. This list enumerates the four gospels and the Book of Acts, thirteen letters of Paul (without the Epistle to the Hebrews), the Revelation of John and the *Revelation of Peter,* the Epistle of Jude, two Epistles of John, one of Peter, and the Wisdom of Solomon. Explicitly rejected are the letters of Paul to the *Laodiceans* and to the *Alexandrians,* and the writings of the heretics (Valentinus, Marcion, and others). If this canon list can be dated early, it would be evidence for the early acceptance of all the major writings of the NT and for the relative openness of the canon to catholic epistles and revelations.

But this situation did not change much in the two following centuries (thus a later date would also be possible for the *Canon Muratori*). Individual manuscripts of the whole NT included some writings of the Apostolic Fathers (*Barnabas, Shepherd of Hermas, 1* and *2 Clement*) as late as IV and V CE. The canon list of the codex Claromontanus includes among the writings of the NT (where only Hebrews seems to be missing) the *Epistle of Barnabas,* the *Shepherd of Hermas,* the *Acts of Paul,* and the *Revelation of Peter.* Uncertainty with respect to the Fourth Gospel prevailed in the west for some time, while in the east the Revelation of John remained under suspicion for centuries. Origen was the first to defend the Epistle to the Hebrews as a canonical writing, although he knew that Pauline authorship was quite uncertain. Eusebius of Caesarea, at the beginning of IV CE, raised doubts about the canonicity of the Revelation of John and accepted James, Jude, 2 Peter, and 2 and 3 John only with considerable hesitation. A definitive decision about the exact content of the Bible, Old and New Testaments together, has never been made by the Christian church as a whole. But a consensus about the twenty-seven writings of the NT eventually emerged, particularly by the distribution and general usage of a Byzantine recension (the Imperial text, see §7.2a–d), which was widely disseminated in order to replace the texts which had been destroyed during the Great Persecution at the beginning of IV CE. After V CE the Latin edition of Jerome, known as the Vulgate, which contained the same twenty-seven NT writings, eventually became the generally accepted Latin Bible.

(c) Noncanonical Writings of Early Christianity

1) *The Apostolic Fathers.* In addition to the writings of the canon of the NT, there are several other ancient and modern collections of early Christian writings. They include books which were recognized and used by the fathers of the church as well as those which were rejected as heretical. The most significant collection is that of the Apostolic Fathers, which was made in XVII CE. The title "Apostolic Fathers" (*Patres Apostolici*) was chosen at that time because it was believed that all those writings were composed in the apostolic period by followers of the apostles. If, however, the "apostolic period" is more strictly understood as the time up to the Jewish War, namely, from 30 to 70, the claim of origin in the apostolic period cannot be maintained for any of these writings. In fact, even in the NT itself only the genuine Pauline letters were actually composed in this period. Nevertheless, the Apostolic Fathers comprise a number of books which can be dated with certainty in the last decade of I CE and the first decades of II CE. Among these are *1 Clement,* the *Didache* (added to this collection when it was discovered in 1883), the letters of Ignatius of Antioch, the fragments of Papias, and perhaps also the *Epistle of Barnabas,* while *2 Clement,* the major part of the *Epistle of Polycarp,* and the *Martyrdom of Polycarp* were written in the middle of II CE. The *Epistle to Diognetus,* which is usually included in editions of the Apostolic Fathers, is an apologetic writing from a later period (ca. 200). The *Shepherd of Hermas* has its rightful place in this collection, though it is difficult to determine its exact date. In contrast to the NT, whose writings are preserved in an immense number of manuscripts and translations, very few copies of the Apostolic Fathers have survived, in some cases only a single manuscript (the only known manuscript of the *Epistle to Diognetus* was burned in the municipal library of Strasbourg in a bombardment of the city during the war of 1870).

Bibliography to §7.1c: Texts

F. X. Funk and Karl Bihlmeyer, *Die apostolischen Väter* (SQS 2,1,1; 2d ed.; Tübingen: Mohr/Siebeck, 1956).

Kirsopp Lake, *The Apostolic Fathers* (LCL; 2 vols.; Cambridge, MA: Harvard University, 1912 and reprints).

Edgar Hennecke, *New Testament Apocrypha* (ed. by Wilhelm Schneemelcher; 2 vols.; Philadelphia: Westminster, 1963–65).

Eduard Schwartz (ed.), *Eusebius: Kirchengeschichte* (Ed. min.; 5th ed.; Berlin: Akademie-Verlag, 1952).

Kirsopp Lake, *Eusebius: The Ecclesiastical History* (LCL; 2 vols.; Cambridge, MA: Harvard University, 1926 and reprints).

2) *Manichean and Gnostic Collections.* Ancient Christian sects, of course, also collected their own literature. The Manicheans are best known in this respect. They developed a high literary culture and produced a number of major collections of religious literature, in which they also included canonical and apocryphal books from the first two Christian centuries. Numerous fragments of such Manichean collections have been discovered in Central Asia, in the Turkish, Iranian, and Chinese languages. Upper Egypt has yielded a Manichean library in Coptic. Of these Manichean collections, only the edition of the apocryphal acts of the apostles became at all influential; in the west it circulated in Latin translation, but only partial copies and translations are preserved. A gnostic collection, almost complete, was discovered in 1945 near Nag Hammadi in Upper Egypt. Its writings, comprising a library of thirteen volumes, all written in Coptic, are translations of Greek originals, of which some were composed in II CE (or earlier).

3) *The Apocrypha.* The corpus known as the New Testament Apocrypha is a modern collection of early Christian writings which have come down to us in many different ways and are often preserved merely in fragments. Some of these books were still read in the Middle Ages and were first published during the Renaissance; others became known through quotations and excerpts made by the church fathers. But most of this material originates from discoveries of manuscripts during the last hundred years. In many instances the Greek original is not preserved, and all that is available are translations or secondary translations into Latin, Coptic, Syriac, Armenian, Georgian, or Arabic. Frequently the original form of such a writing can be reconstructed only through painstaking comparison of various source materials. It goes without saying that this poor state of preservation of most of the apocryphal writings makes it much more difficult than in the case of the canonical books to decide the questions of authorship, date, and the original form of the text.

It seems quite unlikely that any of the apocryphal texts was written during the apostolic period, but some of these writings may have been composed as early as the end of I CE and a very large number are products of II CE. The NT Apocrypha are therefore sources for the history of early Christianity which are just as important as the NT writings. They contain many traditions which can be traced back to the time of the very origins of Christianity. They provide us with a spectrum that is much more colorful than that of the canonical writings and permit insights into the manifold diversity of early Christian piety and theology, in short, a perspective which the polemical orientation of the canon of the NT often obstructs or seeks to limit.

(d) Extra-Christian Testimonies

Non-Christian testimonies for the beginnings of Christianity are unfortunately not very informative. There is a report about Jesus in the *Antiquities* (18.63) of the Jewish historian Josephus, but it is not preserved in its original form, since it was thoroughly redacted by a Christian scribe. Reconstructions of the original text of Josephus' report have been attempted, yet they remain uncertain. Josephus also tells of the death of James, the brother of Jesus (*Ant.* 20.9). The earliest Roman testimonies appear in Suetonius and Tacitus. Suetonius (*Vita Claudii* 25.4) gives a short notice about the expulsion of the Jews from Rome during the reign of Claudius, because they constantly caused disturbances "incited by Chrestus" (*impulsore Chresto*). Whether or not this refers to the Christians must remain an open question. In the *Vita Neronis* (16.2) Suetonius reports that the Christians, who were following a new and evil (*maleficus*) wrong belief (*superstitio*), were expelled from Rome by Nero. Tacitus reports in greater detail that the Christians, who derived their name from Christ, crucified under Pontius Pilate, were executed in a most cruel fashion by Nero. He adds that they were not so much punished because of a suspicion of arson, but because of their hatred for humanity (*Ann.* 15.44.2–8). Dio Cassius, finally, reports the execution of the consul Flavius Clemens and the banishment of his wife because they were accused of atheism; he says that they perished together with others who were executed for inclining toward Jewish beliefs (*Epitome* 67.14). It is possible that this information refers to the persecution of Christians by Domitian.

The first extensive report about the Christians by a pagan writer comes from the younger Pliny. In 112 CE he was governor of Bithynia in Asia Minor, and in this capacity he wrote a letter to the emperor Trajan asking for advice as to how he should treat the Christians, and what steps he should take against them. From this letter (*Epist.* 10.96) we learn that the Christians met early in the morning, took oaths not to commit any crimes, and that they would gather together later for a common meal. Pliny's correspondence with Trajan, as well as Hadrian's rescript to the proconsul of Asia, Minucius Fundanus, will be discussed later in more detail (§12.3d).

Information from non-Christian writers about the Christians begins to flow more abundantly in the middle of II CE. Lucian of Samosata reports

Bibliography to §7.1d

W. den Boer, *Scriptorum paganorum I–IV saec. de Christianis testimonia* (2d ed.; Leiden: Brill, 1965).

fully about the death of the Cynic philosopher Peregrinus Proteus, who had once been a Christian. In his book about the pseudo-prophet Alexander he places Christians, atheists, and Epicureans into the same category. The emperor Marcus Aurelius makes some negative remarks about the Christians in his *Meditations*. The Roman orator Fronto published a speech against the Christians which is now lost. The most detailed reports about the Christians are preserved in a writing of the Platonist Celsus, quoted in part by Origen in his refutation of Celsus' writing. This material, however interesting, contributes little to the history of Christian beginnings. It has more significance for the controversy between paganism and Christianity, which began in II CE.

2. THE TEXT OF THE NEW TESTAMENT

(a) Problems of the Tradition of New Testament Texts.

Not a single autograph of any book of the NT has been preserved. The oldest copies which have survived were made ca. 200 CE, except for a tiny fragment from the Gospel of John from a manuscript written in the first half of II CE. All early copies were written on papyrus, which was probably also the writing material for the originals. Most of these are fragmentary, and all were found in Egypt, where the dry desert sand retards the decomposition of the writing materials, a process which moves much fas-

Bibliography to §7.2

Bruce M. Metzger, *The Text of the New Testament: Its Transmission, Corruption, and Restoration* (2d ed.; Oxford and New York: Oxford University, 1968).

J. N. Birdsall, "The New Testament Text," in *Cambridge History of the Bible* 1. 308–77.

K. W. Clark, "The Textual Criticism of the New Testament," in: Black and Rowley, *Peake's Commentary*, 663–70.

Frederick G. Kenyon, *The Text of the Greek Bible* (3d ed.; rev. A. W. Adams; London: Duckworth, 1975).

Bruce M. Metzger, *Chapters in the History of New Testament Textual Criticism* (NTTS 4; Leiden: Brill, 1963).

Eldon J. Epp, "The Twentieth Century Interlude in New Testament Textual Criticism," *JBL* 93 (1974) 386–414.

Idem, "A Continuing Interlude in New Testament Textual Criticism?" *HTR* 73 (1980) 131–51.

J. K. Elliot (ed.), *Studies in New Testament Language and Text: Essays in Honor of G. D. Kilpatrick* (Leiden: Brill, 1976).

Kurt Aland, *Studien zur Überlieferung des Neuen Testaments und seines Textes* (ANTT 2; Berlin: De Gruyter, 1967).

Idem (ed.), *Materialien zur neutestamentlichen Handschriftenkunde*, vol. 1 (Berlin: De Gruyter, 1969).

Hans Lietzmann, "Textgeschichte und Textkritik," in: idem, *Kleine Schriften* (3 vols.; TU 67, 68, 74; Berlin: Akademie-Verlag, 1958–62) 2. 15–250.

ter in a humid climate. It is not likely that any of the most ancient surviving copies were made from the autograph itself, especially since none of the NT writings was actually composed in Egypt. The oldest surviving copies of the NT as a whole were written in IV CE (Codex Sinaiticus and Codex Vaticanus). Like all other ancient "uncials" they are parchment codices. The codex, rather than the scroll, became the predominant form of the book among the Christians as early as II CE and all surviving papyrus manuscripts of the NT are codices or fragments of codices. Uncials, also called majuscules, are manuscripts written in capital letters and in continuous script without separation of words, and usually without accents. They are the most important foundation of the NT textual tradition. Later manuscripts are called "minuscules"; they are written in small cursive letters, connecting several letters to groups and syllables (for the writing materials, see §2.6d).

In some respects the problems of NT textual transmission are the same as those found in the transmission of other ancient authors. The same mistakes are made in the copying of manuscripts in both instances: inversion of letters; omission of single letters, resulting in a different word; haplography (omission of identical letters or groups of letters; dittography (copying a letter or group of letters twice); confusing similar letters; and finally "homoeoteleuton," that is, omission of a group of letters or words because it ends with the same letters as a preceding group—a very frequent mistake; sometimes whole lines are omitted in this way. We also find deliberate corrections of NT texts. After these writings obtained canonical recognition, such corrections were often made on the basis of a comparison with other manuscripts. Biblical quotations in NT writings were also corrected by comparing them with manuscripts of the OT. Parallel texts of the gospels were often assimilated to each other. Other corrections are due to the influence of a more literary Greek style (Atticisms). Dogmatic motifs also caused corrections, for example, in Mark 6:5 with the statement that Jesus was not able to do miracles in Nazareth. Finally, there are a number of additions to the original text: even after II CE material from other traditions was still added to the gospels, such as the pericope of the laborer on the Sabbath in Luke 6:5 (Codex D) and the pericope about Jesus and the adulteress, which can be found in many manuscripts after John 7:52. One example of dogmatic addition is the mentioning of the trinity in Latin manuscripts in the text of 1 John 5:7f (the so-called *Comma Johanneum*).

But in other ways the problems of NT textual criticism are quite different from those of its classical sister discipline. Classical authors are often represented by but one surviving manuscript; if there are half a dozen or more, one can speak of a rather advantageous situation for reconstructing the text. But there are nearly five thousand manuscripts of the NT in Greek, numerous translations that derive from an early stage of the textual development, and finally, beginning in II CE, an uncounted number of quotations in the writings of the church fathers. The only surviving manuscripts of classical authors often come from the Middle Ages, but the manuscript tradition of the NT begins as early as the end of II CE; it is therefore separated by only a century or so from the time at which the autographs were written. Thus it seems that NT textual criticism possesses a base which is far more advantageous than that for the textual criticism of classical authors.

Nevertheless, the advantages which this rich textual tradition seems to offer should not be overestimated. Special difficulties arise from the very richness of the manuscript tradition, while, on the other hand, the problems in the reconstruction of the original text are to a certain degree independent of the number of the surviving manuscripts. The primary difficulty arising from the wealth of the manuscript tradition is the complexity of the interrelationship of the manuscripts, which makes the construction of a stemma (a family tree of manuscripts) impossible. But in classical textual criticism the construction of a stemma is the basis of the method. As soon as the relationships and dependencies of the various manuscripts are clear, it is easy to eliminate all secondary variants. For NT manuscripts, however, dependencies can be established only occasionally, and for a limited number of manuscripts, and often only for individual variants or groups of variant readings. On the whole, the various branches of the manuscript transmission crossed and became mixed at such an early date and to such a degree that a stemma would become absurdly complex. This is also the case for those translations which are preserved in large numbers of manuscripts, such as the Vulgate. Instead of reconstructing a stemma, NT textual criticism tries to classify manuscript families.

Such classifications have had a certain success and can help bring some order into a seemingly overwhelming diversity of transmission. After some earlier attempts to establish families, the system of B. F. Westcott and F. H. Hort, the most influential British scholars of textual criticism (§7.2f), classified all manuscripts as either representatives or mixtures of four major families. The designations which Westcott and Hort applied to these families are still used today as a helpful device for preliminary characterization of any manuscript or group of manuscripts. Further research, however, has questioned the validity of the "Neutral Text" and has added the "Caesarean Text" as a possible additional family.

1. *The Western Text.* This type is extant in Codex D of the Gospels and Acts, the Codex D of the epistles, the Old Latin and Old Syriac

translations, and in quotations from second and third century authors (Marcion, Justin, Irenaeus, Tertullian, Hippolytus, and Cyprian). Thus, the witnesses of this text derive from a type that was in wide use as early as the middle of II CE, though it is often considered to have been a "wild," unrevised text with many unreliable readings.

2. *The Alexandrian Text*. The primary criterion for this family is the occurrence of its peculiar readings in the quotations of church fathers of Alexandria, from Clement and Origen to Cyril. Westcott and Hort assigned only a few uncials to this family (such as C and L) and the minuscule 33, as well as the Coptic translations; today we might also include in this type the codices ℵ and B as well as A, other uncials, and several papyri which were not known to Westcott and Hort. Whereas the Alexandrian text of the later period was clearly an edited text, showing considerable philological skill, it was preceded by an earlier text, closely related to it, which is in evidence in early papyri and quotations in Clement and Origen (perhaps also ℵ and B).

3. *The Neutral Text*. According to Westcott and Hort, the uncial manuscripts ℵ and B (especially the latter) were the witnesses of a text free of contamination. However, today most scholars classify these two manuscripts with the Alexandrian family.

4. *The Caesarean Text*. This type was not yet recognized by Westcott and Hort and appears to be least well attested. It is assumed that this type relies upon the text Origen brought from Egypt when he moved to Caesarea, but was later contaminated, especially by Western readings. Its extant witnesses are the uncial Θ, several minuscules, and the older Armenian and Georgian translations.

5. *The Koine or Byzantine Text*. There is no question that this family is, on the whole, a mixture of all older text families (a fact which does not exclude the possible survival of older readings in this family). It seems to derive from a revision prepared by Lucian of Antioch at the end of III CE. Although this family includes the vast majority of all extant manuscripts and translations, it is generally considered to be the latest and least trustworthy textual family. Indeed, the Textus Receptus, the "received text" of the Reformation and post-Reformation period, is more or less identical with this family.

One could try to make text-critical decisions simply on the basis of the family relationship of variant readings, but even this procedure is not entirely satisfactory, because many manuscripts contain "mixed" texts, that is, their readings sometimes belong to one family, at other times to another. Furthermore, the families become so large and contain so many different texts that it is necessary to construct subfamilies, which then adds more complexity. A further problem of the wealth of the transmission is quantity. One has to work through an immense amount of material in order to find witnesses for an important ancient reading in a late manuscript full of scribal errors and worthless variants. The evaluation of the quotations of the church fathers is also unusually difficult; such evidence is particularly significant for the geographical localization of manuscripts and their textual traditions. These witnesses have been only partially used, and their use is further complicated by the fact that many of these church fathers' writings are preserved only in medieval manuscripts in which scribes sometimes corrected the biblical quotations according to their own text. Moreover, reliable critical editions often do not exist. As for the numerous translations which frequently derive from the oldest stage of the transmission of the Greek text, and which are also important witnesses for the geographical localization of the transmission of the Greek texts, critical editions of all the extant evidence are not always available. Thus, seen as a whole, the very richness of the transmission confronts the scholar with comprehensive tasks and with many obstacles in trying to accomplish them.

But even if it were possible to use fruitfully all the valuable information for this text-critical work, the decisive problems of NT textual criticism cannot be solved, or are only partially solved, in this way. Though the largest part of the text by far can be considered secure on the basis of the text-critical work already accomplished, nevertheless a significant number of textual problems remains. These result from the fact that the manuscript tradition for the NT writings is uneven, and, for the first century of the manuscript transmission, even completely lacking. There are only about four dozen manuscripts which contain the entire NT anyway, and only the smaller portion of these are uncials from v to x ce, the others medieval minuscules. All other manuscripts contain but a part of the NT, and among these the majority are manuscripts of the gospels, while the Pauline epistles are represented less frequently, and manuscripts of the Catholic Epistles—not to mention the Revelation of John—are comparatively rare. For all that, it is possible to reconstruct with a great degree of certainty the most important text types which were current in early iv ce and which were the prototypes, on the whole, for most later manuscripts.

The beginning of iv ce was also an important divide, because the Great Persecution of 303–311 meant the destruction of uncounted biblical manuscripts. Information about earlier text types comes primarily from the older papyri and the older translations into Latin (the *Itala* or *Vetus Latina*), Syriac, and Coptic. Translations, however, are notoriously difficult evidence, because they provide only a relative certainty with respect to the text of their Greek original. As far as the older Greek papyri are concerned, one has to remember that all of these are fragmentary. Still, it is possible to determine the existence of some of the text types that correspond to the manuscripts of the full Bible in IV CE. But the primary problem still remains: even the papyri do not give us any information for the period before the end of II CE, i.e., they say nothing about the time which precedes the canonization of the NT writings (§7.1b). There can be no question that special care was given to the text of these writings only after their canonization. This intensifies the problem which also exists with respect to the textual criticism of classical authors. Decisive textual corruptions, changes, and revisions of ancient texts usually occur during the first hundred years of their transmission, that is, during the period in which the lasting significance of a text or its author is either not yet recognized or is still debated.

There are numerous examples of alterations and corruptions of the autographs of NT writings during the earliest period of transmission. These problems cannot be solved with conventional text-critical methods, but require the aid of literary criticism (§7.3a–d). The edition of the Gospel of Mark which was used by Matthew and Luke, for example, was substantially different from the Gospel of Mark we know as transmitted in all texts and manuscripts. In the Gospel of John, a redactor made several additions to an earlier work (the most significant is John 6:52–59). In the compilation of the writings which the manuscripts transmit as 2 Corinthians, the editor had combined a number of smaller letters of Paul to produce this major epistle; the same seems to be the case with Philippians. How severely such new editions and redactions could alter the original text is demonstrated in Marcion's edition of the Pauline letters— and Marcion had no intention but to restore the original text of Paul's writings. Also instructive is the example of 2 Peter, which, written in II CE, incorporated the entire letter of Jude in a new edition (2 Peter 2).

More directly related to textual criticism proper are the cases in which the text of a passage had become so corrupt that the scribe had no choice but to reconstruct hypothetically whatever he thought might have been the original, or cases of deliberate corrections in order to adjust a text to a new theological perspective. Marginal notes were also brought into the text accidentally in a number of instances. A particular difficulty is the text of the Book of Acts, which is preserved in Codex D in a textual form which so radically departs from the texts of the other manusripts that it has been surmised that at its base was a second revised edition made by the book's original author. In all these instances, the textual critic must turn to a hypothetical reconstruction (conjecture), for which there may be at least some justification in the uncertainty of the manuscript tradition, but never support from an actual manuscript reading. These then are the most important tasks of textual criticism, which can be solved only in the context of the entire interpretation of the writing in question.

(b) The Papyri

The papyri occupy an important place among the manuscripts of the NT. They are the only direct witnesses for the text of II and III CE. The first papyri of the NT were discovered in the last decades of the nineteenth and in the beginning of the twentieth century. These were all small fragments, often only measuring a few square centimeters. An exception was the Papyrus Oxyrhynchos IV, 657 (𝔓13) from III or IV CE, containing major portions of Hebrews 2–5 and 10–12. A large number of more extensive papyri began to come to light with the discovery (in 1930) and publication (1933–34) of the Chester Beatty Papyri (𝔓45 and 46) from III CE. These include a number of papyri which, according to paleographical judgment, that is, analysis of the form of the letters, were written in III and perhaps even in late II CE. The papyri have thus assumed an increasingly important role in NT textual criticism during the last decades. In text-critical editions of the NT the papyri are designated by a number preceded by a Gothic P. In what follows I briefly describe those papyri which are the most important for textual criticism (for full information about the present depositories of these papyri and their publications, see the bibliography).

𝔓13 (Oxyrhynchus Papyrus IV, 657) contains Heb 2:14–5:5; 10:8–22; 10:29–11:13; 11:28–12:17. It was written no later than the beginning of IV CE and contains a text which is closely related to Codex B (see below). Since the latter's text ends with Heb 9:14, 𝔓13 is an important witness for the text of Hebrews 10–12.

𝔓32 (Rylands Papyrus 5) contains only a few verses of the Letter to Titus (Tit 1:11–15; 2:3–8), but belongs to the oldest of all NT papyri (ca. 200 CE) and presents a text type which agrees with the famous Codex Sinaiticus (א, see below) from IV CE. It is thus a testimony to the early existence of this text type.

𝔓45 (Chester Beatty Papyrus I) contains thirty of originally 220 leaves of a papyrus book containing the four gospels and Acts, written in III CE. The leaves which are preserved include major portions from Matthew 20; 21; 25; 26; Mark 4–9; 11–12; Luke 6–7; 9–14; John 10–11; and Acts 4–17. Only the fragments from Mark, Luke, and Acts are well preserved.

Bibliography to §7.2b

Frederic Kenyon, *Our Bible and the Ancient Manuscripts* (rev. A. W. Adams; New York: Harper, 1958).

Joseph van Haelst, *Catalogue des papyrus litteraires juifs et chrétiens* (Série Papyrologie 1; Paris: Publications de la Sorbonne, 1976).

This text is of special interest because it does not agree with the otherwise prevailing "Alexandrian" text type of Egypt; in part, it contains readings of the "Caesarean" text and, to a smaller extent, "Western" readings. Thus it is an early witness for a "mixed" text.

𝔓46 (Chester Beatty Papyrus II) is a nearly complete papyrus codex of the Pauline letters from the beginning of III CE. Eighty-six of originally 104 leaves are preserved, in only slightly damaged condition. Parts of the Epistle to the Romans are missing at the beginning; parts of 1 Thessalonians and all of 2 Thessalonians are missing at the end. The text is related to the "Alexandrian" type, but is a century older than the oldest witness of this type previously known. 𝔓46 contains a number of peculiarities which are extremely significant for the early history of the Pauline corpus: Hebrews appears immediately after Romans, meaning that is was uncontested as a Pauline letter and put in its position after Romans because of its length; the Pastoral Epistles are missing completely (they could not have once occupied the pages at the end which are now lost from the codex), which means that the scribe of this codex did not know them as part of the Pauline corpus of letters; finally, 𝔓46 places the concluding doxology of Romans not after Chapter 16, but after 15; this seems to confirm that Romans 16 was originally an independent letter which Paul directed to another church (to Ephesus?).

𝔓47 (Chester Beatty Papyrus III) is the middle part (ten leaves) of a papyrus book of the Revelation of John (which originally contained thirty-two leaves). The text of Rev 9:10–17:2 is preserved with only a few lacunas. The readings agree frequently, but not always, with Codex Sinaiticus, thus testifying to the existence of its text in the middle of III CE, the date of this papyrus' writing.

𝔓48 contains Acts 23:11–17, 23–29. Its significance lies in the fact that it proves the existence of the Western text in Egypt in III CE.

𝔓52 (Rylands Papyrus 457) is a tiny piece with a few fragmentary verses from the Gospel of John (John 18:31–33, 37f) which attracted much attention, although its text-critical significance is minimal. But the type of its letters has been dated with some certainty to the first half of II CE. This would make it the oldest preserved fragment of any NT writing, removed from its autograph by half a century or less.

𝔓53 (Michigan Papyrus 6652) from III CE contains a "mixed" text of Matt 26:29–40 and Acts 9:33–10:1.

𝔓64 and 𝔓67, written ca. 200, are parts of the same papyrus codex with the text of Matt 3:9–15; 5:20–22, 25–28 and verses from Matthew 26. 𝔓70 (Matt 2:13–16, 22–3:1; 11:26f; 12:4–5; 24:3–6, 12–15) is also a witness for the early use of the Gospel of Matthew in Egypt; see also 𝔓45. A few verses of Luke appear in 𝔓69 from the same period (Luke 22:41, 45–

48, 58–61). 𝔓69 and 70 are the Oxyrhynchus Papyri XXIV, 2383 and 2384.

𝔓65, from III CE, contains 1 Thess 1:2–2:1 and 2:6–13 in the Alexandrian form of the text.

𝔓66 (Bodmer Papyrus II) is the first of a series of NT papyri from the collection of the Genevan bibliophile Martin Bodmer; these are the most significant biblical papyri to be found since the Chester Beatty Papyri. 𝔓66 was written ca. 200 CE, consists of 104 pages, and contains the text of John 1:1–6:11 and 6:35–14:26, as well as fragments from the remaining chapters of John. This papyrus is the most important early witness for the Fourth Gospel. Its readings belong partly to the "Alexandrian" and partly to the "Western" text types. It is remarkable that the scribe repeatedly corrected his "Western" readings in the margin and between the lines so that they agreed more fully with the "Alexandrian" text. This proves that both a "mixed" text and the "Alexandrian" text were known in Alexandria at that time. In one instance, 𝔓66 contains a reading which is not attested in any other manuscript, but which many scholars had already conjectured as the original text: in John 7:52 it reads the definite article before the word "prophet."

𝔓72 (Bodmer Papyrus VII and VIII) is a codex from III CE containing a number of different writings, including the apocryphal correspondence of Paul with the Corinthians, the *Passover Homily* of bishop Melito of Sardis, and the letters of Jude, 1 and 2 Peter from the NT. It is the earliest witness for these texts.

𝔓75 (Bodmer Papyrus XIV–XV) has been dated by its editors to the time between 175 and 225 CE. Of the originally 144 pages of the book, 102 are preserved (some only in fragments) containing the text of Luke 3–24 and John 1–15 with lacunas. It is so far the oldest witness for the text of Luke and one of the oldest for the Gospel of John, and is thus one of the most important NT manuscripts. Its text is closely related to that of Codex Vaticanus (B, see below).

(c) The Uncials

Almost all the papyri cited above were written before the middle of IV CE. Papyrus was still used for NT manuscripts in the later period, especially in Egypt; but with the official recognition of Christianity parchment became the more highly valued writing material for biblical manuscripts. We know today that parchment possesses many advantages over papyrus,

Bibliography to §7.2c

E. G. Turner, *The Typology of the Early Codex* (Philadelphia: University of Pennsylvania, 1977).

especially its greater durability. But it is likely that the parchment codex quickly found general acceptance from ɪᴠ ᴄᴇ on because of an order which the emperor Constantine gave. As Eusebius reports, Constantine ordered fifty manuscripts of the Bible "on parchment" to be produced for use in the new churches of Constantinople (331 ᴄᴇ), which made this writing material, so to speak, the official material for biblical manuscripts. The oldest complete manuscripts of the NT, several of which are also manuscripts of the whole Bible, are such parchment codices from ɪᴠ ᴄᴇ and later centuries. In addition, there are a number of parchment codices which contain only a portion of the NT, usually the gospels. Because of the use of only capital letters in their writing, the name "uncial" or "majuscule" has become the common designation for these manuscripts. Their sigla are capital Latin letters, and when these had all been assigned, Greek capital letters were used in addition; the Codex Sinaiticus is designated with the first letter of the Hebrew alphabet (‭א‬, sometimes also "S"). The American-born German text-critical scholar Caspar René Gregory had proposed a system which would have brought an end to this rather arbitrary way in which letters were used as sigla: all uncials would receive a number preceded by a "0," while the minuscules would be designated by a number without a "0." But despite its obvious advantages Gregory's new system has not found general acceptance. Only in cases where the capital letters of the Latin and Greek alphabet are used up for older manuscripts are Gregory's numbers used. There are now more than 250 uncial manuscripts recorded and known. The following list describes only those which occur more frequently in the text-critical apparatus of NT editions.

Codex Sinaiticus (‭א‬ = S = 01), discovered by C. Tischendorf in the years 1844 and 1853, is the most famous of all NT manuscripts (it also contains most of the text of the OT). It was found in the monastery of St. Catherine's on Mt. Sinai and the story of its discovery, frequently published, need not be repeated here. The codex was first presented to the Russian Czar; after World War I it was bought from Russia and came from Leningrad to the British Museum in London. Out of 346 leaves, 147 contain the text of the NT, which is almost completely preserved. In addition to the NT and the major part of the OT, the codex also preserves the text of the *Epistle of Barnabas* and the *Shepherd of Hermas*. Codex Sinaiticus and Codex Vaticanus (B, see below) are the two oldest complete manuscripts of the NT. Sometimes together with Vaticanus, sometimes alone, Codex Sinaiticus has greatly influenced the decisions of scholars in textual criticism, sometimes because it was seen as a "neutral" manuscript (i.e., not belonging to a particular textual recension), or because it was highly valued as a text related to the "Alexandrian" family or even as a "mixed" text. Although there is no question that this codex was indeed written in IV CE most scholars today would agree that Tischendorf and some of his successors overestimated its significance. Nevertheless, it remains one of our most significant textual witnesses, containing an "Alexandrian" text with strong "Western" influences. The corrections which were made at a later date show the influence of the text type which was then current in Caesarea.

Codex Alexandrinus (A = 02) also comes from Egypt. It was brought to the British Museum in the year 1628 via Constantinople. This codex was written in V CE and contains the entire Bible (with major lacunas) as well as *1* and *2 Clement.* In its gospel text it is one of the most important witnesses for the "Alexandrian" text type and often agrees with Sinaiticus and Vaticanus.

Codex Vaticanus (B = 03) rivals Sinaiticus for the title of the most valuable uncial manuscript of the Bible. Like Sinaiticus, it was written in the middle of IV CE. For many centuries it was kept in the Vatican library, where it was first catalogued in the year 1475. But Codex Sinaiticus, though only discovered in the last century, became known earlier than Vaticanus, because the officials of the Vatican who were responsible hesitated to surrender their codex to the scholarly world. Thus the first facsimile edition was not published until the end of the nineteenth century. In its NT part, Vaticanus lacks Heb 9:14 to the end of the letter, the Pastoral Epistles, Philemon, and Revelation. This is particularly regrettable, because this codex has been viewed as the most significant representative of a "neutral" text, that is, a text which has not been influenced by the various text types representing revisions or editions. However, Vaticanus is more appropriately valued as a comparatively pure representative of the "Alexandrian" edition, written with very few mistakes and with an excellent older textual basis.

Codex Ephraemi rescriptus (C = 04) is a "palimpsest." In V CE its pages were inscribed with the text of the Greek Bible, but in XIII CE that text was imperfectly erased and the pages were filled with a copy of the ascetic writings and sermons of the Syrian church father Ephrem (IV CE). Approximately five-eighths of the pages which contained the text of the NT are preserved and include parts of all its writings except 2 Thessalonians and 2 John. With the use of chemical devices Tischendorf painstakingly succeeded in deciphering the erased NT text. The codex seems to have been written in Egypt, but it contains readings of various text types including the "Byzantine" text.

Codex Bezae (or *Cantabrigiensis,* D = 05) is one of the most interesting manuscripts of the NT. Written in V or VI CE, it finally ended up, nobody knows how, in the possession of Calvin's successor Beza, who donated it in 1581 to the University of Cambridge. Since that time it has been published several times. Codex D contains the text of the Gospels and Acts, as well as one leaf of the text of 3 John 11–15 (how this leaf got into this codex has never been explained). The unusual feature of this manuscript is its presentation of both the Greek and Latin texts written on facing pages. The texts themselves are remarkable. The Latin text is that of the Old Latin translation, which was made before the Vulgate (§7.2e), while the Greek text is the primary witness for the so-called "Western" text type. This type is characterized by numerous additions (and also some striking omissions) in the text of the Gospels and by readings in Acts which diverge so frequently from the other manuscripts that it has been assumed that it derives from a second edition made by the author himself. It is debated whether the "Western" text is a secondary degeneration of the original text or a source for many valuable ancient readings. It is true, however, that the ancient Syriac translation of the Gospels and church father quotations from the first centuries often agree with peculiar "Western" readings as they are preserved in Codex Bezae.

Codex Claromontanus (D = 06; this codex must be distinguished from the Gospel/Acts Codex D described above) contains the text of the Pauline Epistles. Like Codex Bezae it is a bilingual Greek-Latin manuscript written in v ce. Codex Claromontanus is also a representative of the "Western" text type, which, however, in the letters of the NT has readings which are not as strikingly different as in the Gospels and Acts.

Codex Laudianus (E = 08) is again a bilingual Greek-Latin manuscript from vi ce with the text of Acts, containing many "Western" readings but also numerous "Byzantine" variants. The siglum "E" is also used for the eighth-century Codex Basiliensis with the text of the Gospels and for the ninth-century Codex Sangermanensis; the latter is a copy of Codex Claromontanus and therefore has no independent value for reconstructing any earlier stages in the text.

Codex Augiensis (F = 010), a bilingual Greek-Latin text of the Pauline Epistles, was probably written in ix ce in an Alemannic monastery. This manuscript was kept for a long time on the island Reichenau in the Lake of Constance (= Augia Dives); today it is in Trinity College in Cambridge. Another codex with the siglum "F" (= 09) contains fragments of the text of the Gospels.

Codex Boernerianus (G = 012) is also a bilingual text of the Pauline Epistles from ix ce. It is closely related to the Codex Augiensis. Many errors appear in both manuscripts and both belong to the "Western" text type. Either G is copied from F, or both are copied from the same manuscript. It is very peculiar that Codex Boernerianus on its last page introduces "Paul's" *Letter to the Laodiceans* without actually presenting its text. Codex G = 011 is a very fragmentary gospel manuscript.

Codex Coislinianus (H = 015; the siglum "H" is also used for two less significant codices with the text of the Gospels and Acts). This is a very important manuscript of the Pauline Epistles, unfortunately preserved only in fragments. It was written in VI CE and brought to Mt. Athos at some later time, where its pages were used to strengthen the bindings of other books. A total of forty-three pages are preserved, but are scattered through several of the world's libraries. Codex Coislinianus is a witness for the "Alexandrian" text type. At the end of the letter to Titus one finds the note that the text of this manuscript had been compared with a manuscript from the library of Pamphilus in Caesarea.

Codex Regius (L = 019), an almost completely preserved codex of the Gospels from VIII CE, shows close connections with the gospel quotations of Origen and agrees frequently with the text of Codex Vaticanus. Before the "Longer Ending of Mark," which appears in many later manuscripts (Mark 16:9–20), Codex Regius has copied a shorter ending that otherwise occurs only in a few witnesses in the margin.

Codex Purpureus Petropolitanus (N = 022), a deluxe manuscript of the Gospels, was probably written in Constantinople in VI CE. It was inscribed with silver ink on purple parchment, with the names of God and Jesus in gold ink. Almost half of the originally 462 leaves are preserved and now in the possession of several libraries. This codex was apparently divided into several batches and brought to Europe by the crusaders. Closely related to the text of this codex are the two purple manuscripts O and Σ. The texts of these magnificent manuscripts are less valuable, because they belong to the "Byzantine" text type.

Codex Porphyrianus (P = 025) is one of the very few uncials which contain the text of the Revelation of John in addition to the Pauline and Catholic epistles. P is a palimpsest (like C): the text of the NT, written in IX CE, was replaced by a commentary of Euthalius in the year 1301. The text of Revelation in this manuscript offers a number of important ancient readings.

Codex Borgianus (T = 029) is a bilingual Greek-Coptic manuscript and the oldest representative of this genre. Unfortunately only twenty leaves with the text of Luke 22–23 and John 6–8 are preserved. Written in V or VI CE with the Sahidic text in the left column and the Greek text in the right, Codex Borgianus attests readings which agree with Codex Vaticanus.

Codex Freerianus (W = 032), also called *Washingtonianus*, comes from the monastery of Shenute in Atripe near Achmim in Upper Egypt and is one of the important discoveries of the twentieth century. Presenting the text of the Gospels, it was written in IV CE or at the beginning of V CE. Its readings are such a "mixture" of the various text types ("Alex-

Page from *Codex Washingtonianus*

This page shows the text of Mark 16 with the unique interpolation of the "Freer-Logion" into the ending of the Gospel of Mark.

andrian," "Western," and "Byzantine") that it seems to call into doubt all the theories about ancient textual families. Within the (secondary) "Longer Ending of Mark," Codex Freerianus contains a very interesting expansion after Mark 16:14 (the so-called Freer Logion). This is the most interesting NT manuscript now in the United States, in the Smithsonian Institution in Washington, D. C.

Codex Koridethi (Θ = 038) was written in a monastery of the Caucasus, apparently by a scribe who did not know Greek, probably in IX CE or earlier. The codex attests the existence of different text types in the East (Armenia). Many corrections appear in the text side by side with the corrigenda. The Caesarean text prevails in this gospel codex in the texts of Matthew, Luke, and John, while the "Western" text appears in Mark.

Codex Zacynthius (Ξ = 040), another palimpsest with the text of Luke from VIII CE is the oldest known manuscript which also presents a commentary. The text is closely related to Codex Vaticanus. The commentary is a catena of quotations from the church fathers and surrounds the single-column text of Luke on three sides.

(d) The Minuscules

There are several thousand minuscules of the NT, that is, manuscripts written in a cursive hand. Most of them were produced in the late Middle Ages, and the text of the Gospels is best represented. Parchment was still in use as a writing material, but it was increasingly replaced by paper, which had been invented in China and became known in Europe as early as X CE. It began to be produced in Europe in XII CE and was commonly used for writing a century later. For biblical manuscripts, however, the more durable parchment was abandoned less quickly. Some minuscules used parchment and paper side by side in the same codex. Arabic numbers are used as the sigla for minuscules. All known minuscules have been catalogued today, but most have not been critically evaluated. The vast majority presents the less valuable "Byzantine" text type, but a careful scrutiny of these manuscripts has demonstrated that even later manuscripts of this kind may contain valuable ancient readings. Their testimony is, therefore, by no means without value, and it is an unsound method to neglect the minuscules in favor of the older uncials. Only a few of the better-known minuscules and their families will be listed here.

1 is a twelfth-century minuscule which contains the text of the whole NT with the exception of Revelation. It was already used by Erasmus for the first printed edition of the Greek NT. For Revelation, Erasmus relied upon a paper manuscript (once lost, but now rediscovered) which is also designated by the siglum *1*, containing all of Revelation except for 22:16–

21; since Erasmus did not have access to any Greek manuscript with the complete text of Revelation, he retranslated the missing verses from the Latin Vulgate, so that his first printing of the Greek NT would not be delayed. According to the studies of Kirsopp Lake, Minuscule *1* forms a family together with *118, 131,* and *209,* while a number of other minuscules show close affinities. The text of this family contains elements which are otherwise only found in the Old Syriac and Old Latin translations.

13, a minuscule written in xii ce in southern Italy, is the leading witness of a family known as the Ferrar Group. Other members of this group are *69, 124, 346,* and half a dozen other manuscripts. The text represented by this family is perhaps best preserved in the fifteenth-century minuscule *69,* and the archetype was certainly written before the year 1000. Characteristic for this family is the position of the pericope of Jesus and the adulteress after Luke 21:39 instead of after John 7:52. The text type shows remarkable connections with the Old Syriac translation and Tatian's *Diatessaron.*

33 is one of the oldest minuscule manuscripts, written in ix ce. It has been called the "Queen of the Minuscules," contains the whole Bible (except for Revelation), and has a text closely related to that of Codex B.

81, written in the year 1044, contains only the Acts of the Apostles and is one of the most important witnesses for that book.

157 is a gospel codex written in xii ce. Its readings often agree with Codex D, but also show affinities to Tatian's *Diatessaron* and to Marcion's text of Luke. At the end of each Gospel there is a colophon which is also found in about a dozen other manuscripts: "(copied) from the ancient manuscripts of Jerusalem."

565 comes from the Black Sea and was written in ix or x ce. It also contains the above-mentioned "Jerusalem colophon." The text of this gospel codex is closely related to the "Western" type, a type of the NT text which was known both in the east and west in the ancient period.

700 is a very peculiar gospel manuscript from xii ce. It departs 2,724 times from the "Textus Receptus" and contains 270 readings which are not found in any other manuscript. It seems that these peculiar readings derive from a very old text, since in the form of the second petition of the Lord's Prayer in Luke 11:2, this manuscript reads: "Your Holy Spirit come upon us and cleanse us." This form of the second petition is taken from Marcion's gospel text and is also attested in the church father Gregory of Nyssa, but does not appear in any other manuscript.

1424 is the main witness of a family identified by B. H. Streeter that includes another two dozen manuscripts. The codex contains the whole NT, and every book (except Revelation) is provided with a commentary written in the margin.

2053 contains only the text of Revelation along with a commentary of Oecumenius (VI CE) on it. Although this minuscule was written as late as XIII CE in Messina, it is one of the best textual witnesses for Revelation, sometimes even superior to the Chester Beatty Papyrus (𝔓47) from III CE and the Codex Sinaiticus.

(e) The Ancient Translations

A few remarks about the translations (or "versions") have already been made above (§7.2a). It is not easy to assess their value. The three most important older translations, the Syriac, the Latin, and the Coptic, have each had a complex history, including several recensions which show the influence of a Greek text that meanwhile had undergone its own further developments and editions. The oldest stages of these translations belong to II CE (or at least as early as early III CE in the case of the Coptic translation) and they presuppose a Greek text which is not always accessible through extant Greek manuscripts. Secondary translations are not without value, especially in those cases where the primary translation which they used is no longer fully extant. Of course, in this case, the reconstruction of the original Greek text is even more difficult than in the case of primary translations. To give a general orientation, the most important translations will be briefly listed and described, but the scope of this book does not permit a discussion of the problems which are involved in their text-critical evaluation.

1) *The Syriac Translations.* In the second half of II CE, Tatian composed a harmony of the Gospels which was called the *Diatessaron* (a name which seems to imply the use of four sources and is best translated as "harmony"). The basis for this harmony was the four Gospels of the NT canon. It is not certain whether he used the recently discovered *Gospel of Thomas.* It is also unclear whether the original of this harmony was written in Syriac or in Greek. In any case, it was in the Syriac language that this harmony was used in the east for many centuries as the generally accepted, authoritative version of the Gospels. A single page of the Greek *Diatessaron* has been found in the ruins of the Roman fortress Dura Europus on the Euphrates, which was destroyed by the Persians in 256/57 CE. No manuscript of the Syriac version is preserved. The best

Bibliography to §7.2e

Bruce M. Metzger, *The Early Versions of the New Testament: Their Origin, Transmission, and Limitations* (Oxford: Clarendon, 1977).

Idem, "The Early Versions of the New Testament," in: Black and Rowley, *Peake's Commentary,* 671–75.

Kurt Aland (ed.), *Die alten Übersetzungen des Neuen Testaments, die Kirchenväterzitate und Lektionare* (ANTT 5; Berlin: De Gruyter, 1972).

source was until recently the commentary, preserved in an Armenian translation, which the Syrian father Ephrem wrote on the *Diatessaron* in IV CE. Only recently about two-thirds of this commentary was discovered and published in the original Syriac. Gospel harmonies in other languages (Arabic, Persian, Latin, Middle Dutch, Old Italian) show a more or less strong influence from Tatian's work. Should it ever be possible to reconstruct the original Syriac (or Greek) text of the *Diatessaron*, an extremely important witness for the text of the Gospels in II CE would become available. As things stand at this time, the *Diatessaron* is at least noteworthy insofar as it has exercised a considerable influence upon the texts of the separate Gospels in both eastern and western Christianity.

Approximately at the same time as the *Diatessaron* was composed, a Syriac translation of the four separate Gospels was made, and perhaps also of the rest of the NT: the Old Syriac translation. Only the text of the Gospels is preserved of this version, in two fragmentary manuscripts, Codex Syrus Curetonianus (sy^c) and Codex Syrus Sinaiticus (sy^s) from V and IV CE respectively. It is debated whether its basis was a Syriac translation from II CE which was increasingly contaminated by readings from Tatian's *Diatessaron,* or whether "*Diatessaron*-readings" were present from the beginning and were later partially eliminated. Apart from this relationship to readings from Tatian, both manuscripts give evidence for a very close affinity to "Western" readings in a number of Old Latin manuscripts (see below) and in the minuscules of the Ferrar group (§7.2d). Such a coincidence of witnesses which come from the geographical periphery of the textual tradition demonstrates that their joint ancestor was a Greek text which was widely used in II CE and which therefore must be as seriously considered for the reconstruction of the original text as the Greek papyri and the uncial manuscripts from IV and V CE.

Another Syriac version which is known through several hundred manuscripts, some of these from V and VI CE, is called the Peshitta (sy^P). It is a later version which was developed gradually from the older Syriac translation in successive recensions, using Greek texts for comparison in each case. The oldest tangible stage in its formation is the edition of bishop Rabbula of Edessa, who died in 435. In the year 508, bishop Philoxenus of Mabbug on the Euphrates requested his suffragan bishop Polycarpus to make a "translation" (or edition) of the NT into Syriac. This recension is preserved in a later revision made by Thomas of Heraclea in 616, the so-called "Heraclensis" (sy^h). The older Peshitta, which does not include 2 Peter, 2 and 3 John, Jude, and Revelation, contains readings which are related to the Codex Vaticanus as well as to the "Byzantine" text type. The missing Catholic Epistles and the Book of Revelation were probably added in the "Philoxenia" of bishop Philoxenus. The "Heraclensis" is actually a text-critical edition, and has preserved a number of valuable ancient variants in its marginal notes (sy^hm), especially for the Acts of the Apostles. It is, therefore, the most important witness for the text of the "Western" text of this book in addition to Codex Bezae.

Independent of this Syriac translation is the translation into the Western Aramaic dialect of Palestine (sy^pal) which can be partially reconstructed from medieval lectionaries. Although this dialect is more closely related to the language of Jesus than the "Syriac" translations, this version from v CE has only minor text-critical significance.

2) *The Latin Translations.* The *Acts of the Scillitan Martyrs* and the works of Tertullian demonstrate that a Latin translation was known in North Africa as early as the end of II CE. This translation was made in Africa, was later used in a revised form in other western countries and in Italy, and is known as the *Vetus Latina* (Old Latin, also called *Itala*; its siglum is "it"). About thirty-two manuscripts are preserved, none of them a complete manuscript of the whole NT; small Latin letters are used for these in the text-critical editions. The dates of these manuscripts vary from v to XIII CE which shows that this translation was used into the medieval period and was completely replaced by Jerome's Vulgate only in the late Middle Ages. An old witness for the African text of the *Vetus Latina* is Codex Palatinus (e) from v CE, a gospel codex with readings closly related to the quotations of Cyprian and Augustine. Even older, but very fragmentary is Codex Bobbiensis (k), written ca. 400 and containing parts of the first two Gospels.

The European manuscripts of the *Vetus Latina* provide us with more complete evidence, but the text type as well as the manuscripts are of a later date. Codex Vercellensis (a) from v or VI CE is the oldest European manuscript of the Gospels. Codex Veronensis (b) represents a text which was used by Jerome for his revision, which became the Vulgate. The Latin column of Codex Bezae (D), designated with the small letter "d," also belongs here, because it represents an independent old Latin tradition and is not simply a translation of this codex's Greek text. The Old Latin text of Acts and Revelation is attested in Codex Gigas (gig), a manuscript containing the text of the whole Bible which is one of the largest manuscripts ever written: its pages are almost half a meter (over eighteen inches) wide and almost a meter (three feet) long. Although the Old Latin manuscripts are not uniform, there is no question that their readings belong to the "Western" text and thus are an important testimony for that peculiar ancient text type. A comprehensive edition of the *Vetus Latina* by the monastery of Beuron in Germany is in progress.

The lack of uniformity among the Latin versions used in various parts of the west was the primary reason that prompted bishop Damasus of

Rome to entrust Jerome with a new revision of the Latin Bible in the year 382. Jerome began with a new edition of the Gospels, where the lack of uniformity was most obvious. In a letter to Damasus, written in 384, Jerome gave an account of his work. This new edition, which was made very carefully for the Gospels but only superficially for the remainder of the NT, was not a new translation, but a revision on the basis of a comparison with those Greek texts which were in circulation at the time. Jerome's work became the basis for the so-called Vulgate (the "common" translation), which, however, was not immediately accepted everywhere and was further revised several times ("vg" is the siglum for the Vulgate, "vg^s" designates the recension of the Sixtina of the year 1590, "vg^{cl}" the Clementina of 1592; textual variants which occur in manuscripts of both the Vulgate and Vetus Latina are designated by the siglum "lat," variants attested in all Latin manuscripts by "latt"). Today there are more than eight thousand known manuscripts of the Vulgate which demonstrate that the lack of uniformity existing at the time of Jerome was by no means overcome by his edition.

3) *The Coptic Translations.* During the early Christian period a number of Coptic dialects were spoken in Egypt which had developed from the ancient Egyptian language. The two most important dialects into which the NT was translated were Bohairic in Lower Egypt and Sahidic in Upper Egypt. Very little is preserved of the translations into any of the dialects of Middle Egypt (Memphitic, Fayyumic, Achmimic, and Subachmimic), but these dialects have gained new significance through the recent discoveries of early Christian writings. The Sahidic translation (sa) is the oldest Coptic translation, probably made in early III CE. A number of manuscripts are preserved, some of them quite old. It is possible that several translations existed which were independent of each other. The text of the Sahidic translation is closely related to the "Alexandrian" type, but also contains many "Western" readings. The Bohairic translation (bo) was made later than the Sahidic and is attested in a large number of manuscripts, mostly of later date, because Bohairic became the official language of the Coptic church. The oldest known manuscript, discovered only recently, dates from IV CE and contains most of the Gospel of John. Again the "Alexandrian" text type prevails. Of the Fayyumic translation only a few fragments have survived. It is more closely related to the Sahidic than to the Bohairic translation.

4) The oldest translation of the NT into a Germanic language is at the same time the oldest surviving document in a Germanic language, the *Gothic translation* (got). It was made in the middle of IV CE as part of the translation of the whole Bible by the Cappadocian Wulfila (or: Ulfilas), who had been deported with his family by the Goths. He composed this

translation for Gothic Christians who were then settled in Moesia on the lower Danube. An incomplete text of the Gospels is preserved in the famous Codex Argenteus, which was written in v or vi CE in Northern Italy on purple parchment with silver and gold ink, and is now kept in Uppsala. Almost all other Gothic Bible manuscripts are palimpsests, but altogether parts of nearly every book of the NT are thus preserved. The Greek basis of the Gothic translation is the "Byzantine" text. It is uncertain whether the many "Western" readings were parts of the original translation or introduced later into copies made during the stay of the Goths in northern Italy; the latter is probably the case.

5) The *Armenian translation* (arm) was made ca. 400 CE. More than a thousand manuscripts have been catalogued, the oldest from the year 887, but a good critical edition does not yet exist. It is an open question whether the Armenian version rests on a Greek text or was made on the basis of the Syriac translation, which was later compared with Greek texts and revised during viii CE. The text type of the Armenian translation seems to be more closely related to the "Caesarean" than to the "Byzantine" texts. Less well known is the Georgian translation (geo). Christianity was introduced to the Georgians living at the foot of the Caucasus in v CE. The oldest manuscripts of this translation date to ix CE. It is probably a secondary translation, and its text type belongs to the "Caesarean" group.

6) The origin of the *Ethiopic translation* (aeth) is an enigma. Perhaps it was made in vi or vii CE, perhaps as early as iv CE, but the oldest surviving manuscript dates from xiii CE. It is possible that it does not rest on Greek texts but on a Syriac translation. On the whole its text is "Byzantine," but in the Pauline epistles its readings often agree with 𝔓47 and Codex Vaticanus, especially in instances where the readings of these two manuscripts are not supported by any other witnesses.

Other ancient translations have only little significance for textual criticism, or their use is burdened with too many difficulties. These include the Anglo-Saxon, the Nubian, and the Sogdian translations, as well as the translations into Persian and Arabic. Except for a small portion of the Arabic version, they were all made from other translations and not from Greek originals.

(f) The Printed Editions of the Greek New Testament

The first complete book printed after the invention of the printing press was the Bible in the Latin text of the Vulgate (the Gutenberg Bible of 1456 CE). But it would take more than half a century before the first Greek Bible appeared in print. In the year 1502 the Spanish cardinal Ximenes began with his preparations for a grand edition of the Bible in Hebrew, Aramaic, Greek, and Latin. The fifth volume of this polyglot with the text of the NT was printed in 1514, the other volumes within the subsequent three years. But the approval of the Pope was not given until 1520, and the final publication was delayed until 1522 for reasons that are unknown. Thus the "Complutensian Polyglot," as it is called from the Latin name of its place of publication, Alcala, was denied the honor of being the first printing of the Greek text of the NT.

This honor belongs to the famous humanist Erasmus of Rotterdam. In 1515 the Basel printer Froben suggested to Erasmus that he prepare an edition of the Greek NT. In July of that year Erasmus began with his preparations, type-setting was started on 2 October, and on 1 March 1516 the entire Greek text of the NT was published together with Erasmus' Latin translation. Though the publication was at first received with somewhat mixed feelings, undeniably it was a success. In the first two editions, 3,300 copies were printed and sold. With only minor alterations, this text persisted as the standard form of the Greek NT until the end of the nineteenth century. It was the basis of Luther's German translation, of the authoritative English translation known as the "King James Version," and of all other western translations which rest on the Greek text. Since Erasmus prepared this edition in great haste, it is no wonder that the text turned out to be quite inferior. Erasmus used only very few, late minuscules; the only superior minuscule manuscript available to him, Codex 1 from XII CE, he dared not use at all, because the text was so different from all the other manuscripts he knew! For the Revelation of John he had only one single manuscript with a text that was unreadable in many passages and which lacked its last page. Erasmus repaired these defects by translating the respective passages into Greek from the Latin Vulgate, creating in this process a number of Greek words which had never before existed. Later editions, to be sure, corrected hundreds of misprints of the over-hasty first edition. But Erasmus also introduced the *Comma Johanneum* (the mention of the Trinity in 1 John 5:7f) into his later editions, although it was missing in all Greek manuscripts: a Greek manuscript with the *Comma Johanneum* (translated from Latin) was forged in order to deceive Erasmus—and it succeeded!

During the sixteenth century several scholars began to add a text-critical apparatus to their printed editions, thus listing variant readings, first taken from other Greek manuscripts, but soon also from quotations of the church fathers and from translations of the NT. The Parisian publisher Robert Estienne (= Stephanus) printed several editions of this kind, and after him Beza, Calvin's successor, who had two ancient uncial manuscripts in his possession (Codex Bezae and Codex Claromontanus; see §7.2c), though he used them very little for his edition. Both editors printed a text which mixed readings of Erasmus' edition and the Complutensian

Polyglot. In the year 1624 the Dutch printing firm of Elzevir issued a handy and convenient edition of the Greek NT which again reproduced Erasmus' text as compared with the Complutensian Polyglot. They advertised this edition as "the text that is now received by all." The designation "Textus Receptus" is derived from this advertisement. Critique and confutation of this Textus Receptus has been the primary task of textual criticim ever since, into the twentieth century.

Until the eighteenth century many scholars were engaged in enriching the material for text-critical work by collating known and newly discovered manuscripts. Remarkable is the edition of John Mill (1707), the first major critical edition, listing thirty thousand variants from a hundred manuscripts, ancient versions, and quotations from the church fathers. It is characteristic, however, that Mill did not alter the Textus Receptus but reprinted it without change. Shortly thereafter Edward Wells published an edition which departed in 210 cases from the Textus Receptus (1709/ 19). The edition of Daniel Mace followed in 1729. But the former was ignored, the latter fiercely attacked and soon forgotten—the belief in the Textus Receptus as the inspired, original Greek text of the NT was too strong. A major step forward in method came through the edition of Johann Albrecht Bengel, which was published in the year 1734. To be sure, Bengel's printed text departed from the Textus Receptus only in those instances where such readings had already occurred in previous printed editions. But he had gained new insights from his elaboration of families of manuscripts and he indicated explicitly in his text-critical apparatus all readings which he judged superior to the Textus Receptus. Neither was Bengel spared from hostile attacks by ecclesiastical authorities and scholars of theology. In his monumental edition of the NT of 1751/52, Johann Jakob Wettstein again reproduced the Textus Receptus and banished all readings which he deemed superior to the apparatus. Wettstein was the first to designate the uncial manuscripts by capital letters and the minuscules by Roman numbers.

A new period in the printed editions, now primarily concerned with the publication of better Greek texts, began with Johann Jakob Griesbach, a student of Johann Salomo Semler. On the basis of Bengel's and Semler's insights (classification of the manuscripts into families, elaboration and rational application of the known principles of textual criticism), Griesbach produced a pioneering edition of a new Greek text which was published in the years 1774/75 and repeatedly reprinted in Germany and elsewhere (the primary editions were in 1796 and 1806 in Halle and London). A number of new editions followed until the middle of the nineteenth century, based upon the constantly increasing supply of new materials. Roman Catholic scholars also participated in this work. A new and independent point of departure is visible only in the edition of the Greek NT by the philologian Carl Lachmann in 1831 and 1842/50. With the objective methods which he had developed in his editions of classical and Middle High German texts, Lachmann sought to break once and for all the authority of the Textus Receptus, still commonly used as the basis for text-critical work. Lachmann replaced the Textus Receptus with the text which in his opinion was the most ancient text used in the east. But the arbitrarily chosen manuscript base for the reconstruction of this text was too small, and the methodological schema too rigid. Thus a major breakthrough was denied him.

The necessary broadening of the manuscript base for text-critical work is owed to Constantin von Tischendorf, who continued Lachmann's work. Beginning in 1841, Tischendorf published a whole series of editions of the NT, repeatedly attempting to improve the text in numerous passages. The manuscripts which Tischendorf had himself discovered and collated, especially the famous Codex Sinaiticus (ℵ), had a decisive influence on the Greek text of these editions. Tischendorf's chief merit was his indefatigable effort to collect and collate manuscripts. His *Editio octava critica maior* of 1869–72 and subsequent editions is unsurpassed even today in its abundance of information and still-indispensable critical apparatus. In rank and scholarly substance equal to Tischendorf's editions is the edition of the Greek NT by B. F. Westcott and F. J. Hort, which was published in 1881 as the fruit of many years of collaboration. In distinction to Tischendorf, Westcott and Hort were not collectors, but had their main interest in the production of a text on the basis of careful and well-balanced reconstruction of its history. Their extensive labors in the scholarly determination of the family trees of the individual manuscripts and translations led to the assumption of four manuscript families, which they called "Syrian" (= "Byzantine"), "Western," "Alexandrian," and "Neutral." The variants of these families were carefully weighed in each single instance, but in the final judgment, Westcott and Hort almost always preferred the readings of the "Neutral" text with its main representatives, Codex Vaticanus and Codex Sinaiticus.

A certain significance must also be ascribed to two further editions which appeared shortly before and after the turn of the last century. The first was published by Bernhard Weiss (1894–1900). In his text-critical decisions Weiss did not give primary attention to the history of texts and manuscripts, but based his judgment in each textual problem upon considerations of subject-matter and exegetical perspectives. This procedure led Weiss to conclude that the Codex Vaticanus (B) is the nearest representative of the original text, although he started from principles which were very different from those of Westcott and Hort. After Weiss, Hermann von Soden once more embarked on a large-scale text-critical experiment. In 1902 he began with the publication of his preliminary studies, and in 1913 the publication of the text with critical apparatus followed. It is still the major text-critical edition of this century, with elaborate collections of witnesses and a new reconstruction of the family histories of manuscripts. However, this willful and not always reliable work did not have its intended success. It was further burdened by an entirely new system of sigla for the textual witnesses, which is systematic and consistent but so complex that it is nearly inaccessible.

The greatest success and broadest influence fell to the pocket edition of Eberhard Nestle, which was published for the first time in the year 1898 and has been published since that time in twenty-five editions. Better and more useful than the competing editions of a more recent date (Merk, Bover, Souter) and equipped with a rich text-critical apparatus printed in the smallest possible space, it is nevertheless not an independent critical work of scholarship, but a school edition which was originally produced according to a purely mechanical procedure. Its text was produced following the principle (abandoned in part only in later editions) that the majority judgment of the three editions of Tischendorf, Westcott and Hort, and Weiss should decide the text to be printed. But since all three editions prefer the text of Codex Vaticanus (B) or the closely related Codex Sinaiticus (ℵ), the text printed in Nestle's edition primarily reflects the preferences and prejudices of the text-critical scholars from the second half of the nineteenth century. Thus it became the extension of the achievements of the great text critics of the last century, a new "Textus Receptus" of the twentieth century. Still, there is no question that this text was vastly superior to the old Textus Receptus and its defenders, who have not yet become a completely extinct species.

Further progress in more recent text-critical scholarship is visible in the new edition led by Kurt Aland, which builds on the edition of Nestle and has indeed been published as its twenty-sixth edition. Earlier editions had already increasingly discarded the mechanical majority-judgment of the nineteenth-century editors. The new edition of Aland presents a text which, according to the present judgment of scholars, reflects as closely as possible the archetype of the various manuscripts and families which must have existed shortly before the end of II CE. For the time being, this is a decisive new step in text-critical scholarship. The same efforts have also determined the text edition which has been published and distributed by the United Bible Societies. However, this edition presents so few variants, though with a full listing of all the manuscripts which are relevant in each instance, that is has limited usefulness for the serious student who is interested in the history and the problems of the NT text.

(g) Principles of New Testament Textual Criticism

In its historical development the method of NT textual criticism has been in each instance a combination of changing factors, such as the availability of manuscript materials, scholars' dogmatic judgments, step-by-step development of basic canons of criticism (here biblical and classical textual criticism influenced each other), statistical and mechanical procedures, reconstruction of families of manuscripts, and criticism of the subject matter, which occasionally led to conjectural emendation. At the present state of scholarship there is an attempt to consider all these factors in the most comprehensive way. But there is also no unanimity about how a decisive breakthrough with respect to the existing problems might be achieved.

Of course, a number of technical criteria are universally accepted. Mistakes which have been introduced in the process of the copying of manuscripts can be easily recognized (§7.2a). The ancient versions contain a number of mistakes which are detected without difficulty, such as misreading Greek words, mistaking one Greek word for another, or mistranslations. Conscious corrections by scribes have have also been frequently observed. In all these instances the principle has found common acceptance that the more difficult reading is to be preferred (*lectio difficilior placet*). Such decisions are, by all means, not always purely mechanical, but involve matters relating to the topics concerned. This is especially the case with respect to such scribal corrections as additions of complementary expressions, historical and geographical rectifications, and dogmatic alterations.

Judgments on the basis of insights into the history of the text are necessary, of course, and in the practice of textual criticism they play a considerable role. But the value of such judgments is limited, both because of the large number of NT manuscripts and because of the complexity of their transmission. The establishment of families has not led to a consist-

Bibliography to §7.2g

Kurt Aland, "Glosse, Interpolation, Redaktion und Komposition in der Sicht der neutestamentlichen Textkritik," in: W. Eltester and F. H. Kettler (eds.), *Apophoreta: Festschrift Ernst Haenchen* (BZNW 30; Berlin: Töpelmann, 1964) 7–31.

Ernest C. Colwell, *Studies in Methodology in Textual Criticism of the New Testament* (NTTS 9; Leiden: Brill, 1969).

Eldon J. Epp, "The Eclectic Method in New Testament Textual Criticism: Solution or Symptom?" *HTR* 69 (1976) 211–57.

Günther Zuntz, *The Text of the Epistles: A Disquisition of the Corpus Paulinum* (London: Oxford University, 1953).

John Strugnell, "A Plea for Conjectural Emendation in the New Testament," *CBQ* 36 (1974) 543–58.

ent stemma for the manuscripts, since the tracks of their transmission cross each other too frequently. Westcott and Hort had still been convinced that clearly distinguishable text types could be isolated as the oldest representatives of the various forms of the NT text. But the discovery of the papyri showed that even older witnesses appear to be "mixed" texts when measured against the standards of the reconstructed families. It is indeed by no means unlikely that the attainable archetypes of all known manuscripts and translations—should it ever be possible to reconstruct such archetypes with some degree of certainty—will be "mixed" texts in which several earlier strands of the transmission have been combined in various ways.

The limitations of purely text-historical procedure in working with classical Greek and Latin texts should not be ignored in NT textual criticism. The reconstruction of a stemma leads back to archetypes of first editions, but not necessarily to the original text. Even the most successful reconstruction of archetypes in NT textual criticism gives no more than information about the forms of the texts which were in existence at the end of II CE. Like the classical philologian, the NT textual scholar also has to remember that textual corruptions are most frequent during the first decades of the transmission, that is, in the period between the autograph and first edition. Such corruptions can be more severe in the very first years than in subsequent centuries, no matter whether our oldest manuscript witness comes from the Middle Ages or from III CE. It does not make much difference how many manuscripts written since the end of II CE have been preserved, since not a single manuscript provides us with a direct insight into the history of the text during the first fifty to one hundred years after the writing of the autograph.

Two other factors aggravate text-critical judgment in attempting to recover the original texts of the NT writings. The first of these is the Great Persecution at the beginning of IV CE. During this time, manuscripts of the NT were systematically confiscated and burned, with the result that the textual base for new editions greatly in demand later in IV CE, must have been comparatively small. Important ancient texts might have been preserved in the border areas of the Roman empire, which were not as badly affected by the persecution as the central districts, but textual evidence from those areas is scarce. All NT manuscripts from the time before IV CE have been found in Egypt; thus they may represent the textual tradition of only a geographically limited area, in which, besides, the tradition of the orthodox church did not become established until the end of II CE.

The insights gained from the necessary and indispensable reconstruction of the oldest families of manuscripts should therefore be modified by the following principles:

1) Even the best, though not always completely possible, reconstruction of the archetype of all available manuscripts and translations leads us back only to the second half of II CE, but does not give us any direct information about the textual history of the first fifty or one hundred years after the composition of the autographs.

2) The best-attained reading may in some instances be nothing but reconstruction of corrupt texts, because it can be expected that corruptions appeared in the period before the fixing of the archetype of the known textual tradition.

3) The oldest archetypes of the most important textual families belong to a geographically limited area, while the reconstruction of geographically more distant witnesses, such as the ancient translations, is burdened with numerous factors of uncertainty.

4) One must be prepared for the discovery of valuable ancient readings in manuscripts and translations which come from the marginal areas of the textual transmission.

5) A comparatively late manuscript may have preserved valuable ancient readings, while even the best ancient manuscripts contain readings which have no value in reconstructing the original text. The judgment about the general character of a manuscript is not always identical with a judgment about each one of its readings.

6) The agreement of witnesses which come from geographically distant areas, such as from the Syriac as well as from the Latin or Sahidic translations, should always receive a serious hearing, even if it contradicts the weight of all other witnesses.

7) Quotations are reliable guides to the texts which were actually in existence and used during the early centuries, and to their geographical location. They are valuable even in cases where only very few Greek manuscripts support their readings, all the more so since only Egypt has yielded manuscripts which can give us direct evidence for the texts which were used in the early period of Christianity.

8) If there are major uncertainties and a wide spread in the alternatives for a specific reading in the known witnesses, this can point to a very ancient corruption which came into existence before the period in which the oldest manuscripts were written. It is quite possible in such instances that not a single manuscript or translation has preserved the original text.

9) If it is impossible to reconstruct a sensible text with the help of all available textual evidence, hypothetical reconstruction of the original text (conjecture) cannot be excluded. Such a reconstruction, however, requires not only a skillful handling of all text-critical methods, but also an exact knowledge of the language, terminology, and theology of the author in

question. Textual criticism and criticism of subject matter are an insepa-
rable unit.

10) No single method, whether it takes its orientation from mechanical
or subject-related criteria, is capable of solving all of the many problems of
NT textual criticism. As one has to reckon with a multiplicity of causes for
the mistakes and corruptions in the transmission of NT texts, it is also
necessary to employ several methodologies for the solution of textual
problems.

If all that has been said suggests that the textual questions of the NT
can by no means be easily solved, it must be added at the same time that
only a very small proportion of the NT text is indeed subject to much
doubt. However controversial the solution of text-critical questions in a
number of passages may be, there is, on the whole, a high degree of
certainty with respect to the original text of the NT as a whole. As an
important discipline of biblical scholarship, however, textual criticism has
to be reapplied constantly, even in those instances where a solution seems
to have been reached, because the history of the NT text is at the same
time a history of its interpretation and thus of the problems inherent in the
content of the early Christian message. Variant readings demonstrate in
many instances how certain passages have been interpreted in the early
period, or which statements were seen as difficult or problematic by the
ancient transmitters of the text. This makes textual criticism one of the
disciplines which contributes to the interpretation of the subject matter of
the NT itself.

3. LITERARY CRITICISM

(a) General Remarks

Only a small portion of the writings of the NT and other early Christian literature can be viewed as the single product of an individual author.
All these writings had literary prototypes which influenced their shape;
most of them used sources which determined their contents and forms to a
large degree; many are not even preserved in their original form, but only
in later redactions, editions, and compilations. This presents the student
of the NT with many problems of literary criticism which, though they
frequently overlap, must be posed differently for each writing or group of
writings. The scope of this book does not permit us to present the earliest

Bibliography to §7.3

William A. Beardslee, *Literary Criticism of the New Testament* (GBSNTS; Phila-
    delphia: Fortress, 1970).

Christian writings within the framework of a comprehensive treatment of early Christian literature. The following discussion will instead sketch several central and characteristic problems, using in each case their main representative as a paradigm. Fuller treatments will be found in the histories of early Christian literature in the bibliography for §7.

(b) The Synoptic Problem and the Sources of the Gospels

"Synoptic Gospels" is the designation for the first three Gospels of the NT canon, Matthew, Mark, and Luke. It has long been noticed that these Gospels in large part present parallel materials in a similar framework and often in the same sequence of individual pericopes. Moreover, the wording of the respective parallel pericopes in any two or all three of these Gospels is often very close. If one compares the Synoptics with the Gospel of John, there are, to be sure, certain similarities in the external framework, but with the exception of the passion narrative only very occasional similarities occur in the content and wording of individual pericopes. In addition, a large portion of the material presented in the Fourth Gospel, especially Jesus' long revelation discourses, has no true parallels in the Synoptics. It is rather easy to print the Synoptic Gospels side by side to illustrate their sequences of parallel pericopes, while there are great diffi-

Bibliography to §7.3b: Texts

Albert Huck (ed.), *Synopsis of the First Three Gospels* (13th ed. rev. Heinrich Greeven; Tübingen: Mohr/Siebeck, 1981).

Kurt Aland (ed.), *Synopsis Quattuor Evangeliorum* (10th ed.; Stuttgart: Württembergische Bibelanstalt, 1978).

Idem, *Synopsis of the Four Gospels: Greek-English Edition of the Synopsis Quattuor Evangeliorum with the Text of the Revised Standard Version* (United Bible Societies, 1972).

B. H. Throckmorton (ed.), *Gospel Parallels: A Synopsis of the First Three Gospels* (4th ed.; Nashville and New York: Nelson, 1979).

Bibliography to §7.3b: Studies

Heinrich-Julius Holtzmann, *Die synoptischen Evangelien: Ihr Ursprung und ihr geschichtlicher Charakter* (Leipzig: Engelmann, 1863). The classic presentation of the two-source hypothesis.

Julius Wellhausen, *Einleitung in die drei ersten Evangelien* (2d ed.; Berlin: Reimer, 1911).

B. H. Streeter, *The Four Gospels: A Study of Origins* (first published, 1924; London: Macmillan; and reprints). The most detailed reconstruction of sources for the Synoptic Gospels.

Martin Lehmann, *Synoptische Quellenanalyse und die Frage nach dem historischen Jesus* (BZNW 38; Berlin: De Gruyter, 1970).

William R. Farmer, *The Synoptic Problem* (Dillsboro, NC: Western North Carolina, 1976). Farmer and Stoldt question the two-source hypothesis.

Hans Herbert Stoldt, *History and Criticism of the Marcan Hypothesis* (Macon, GA: Mercer University, 1980).

culties in trying to incorporate the Gospel of John into such a "Synopsis" or edition of gospel parallels.

This close relationship of the Synoptic Gospels has engendered a series of hypotheses about the literary relationship of these three Gospels to each other. In the history of NT scholarship the oldest hypothesis, which was at the same time a widely accepted ecclesiastical tradition, argued for the assumption of the priority of Matthew. In this case, Mark is seen as a condensation of the Gospel of Matthew, and Luke as a later composition on the basis of both Matthew and Mark. A second hypothesis, known as the "Fragments Hypothesis," was first proposed by Friedrich Schleiermacher. This suggests that there were originally individual compilations of older materials ("fragments") which were later composed in different, but not entirely dissimilar ways into larger gospels as they are now preserved in the NT. Another proposal to explain the Synoptic problem is the "Primitive Gospel Hypothesis" according to which the similarities and differences of the three (or all four) Gospels can be explained by assuming that each of the gospel writers made different selections for the composition of his Gospel from a more complete "Primitive Gospel," which was available to all of them but is now lost. Each of these hypotheses is burdened with considerable difficulties (for a more detailed discussion, see the appropriate secondary literature).

The studies of Lachmann, Wilke, and Weisse, published independently of each other in 1835 and 1838, argued persuasively that the Gospel of Mark is the oldest, and that Matthew and Luke are secondary elaborations of Mark. Weizsäcker and H. J. Holtzmann further developed this hypothesis by demonstrating that Matthew and Luke used a second common source, the so-called *Synoptic Sayings Source* (its abbreviation is the siglum "Q" from the German word *Quelle*). While the two later Gospels drew their general framework from the Gospel of Mark, as well as most of the material about the course of Jesus' life and his activities, the *Sayings Source* provided them with Jesus' sayings and speeches. This hypothesis, known as the "Two Source Hypothesis," has become the most widely accepted solution of the Synoptic Problem in the twentieth century, though strong objections continue to be raised against it.

The arguments for the Two Source Hypothesis have shifted somewhat during the history of scholarship. One of the strongest arguments was already propounded by Lachmann: Matthew and Luke agree in their sequence of pericopes only in those instances in which Mark also has that same sequence. But during the nineteenth century this argument was often connected with the assumption that that sequence reflected the actual course of events during the ministry of Jesus, and since it was thought to be more accurately presented in Mark, this Gospel was seen as the source for the other two. Shortly after the beginning of this century, William Wrede pointed out new directions for the investigation because he was able to show that the order of the material in Mark has little if any relationship to the actual course of Jesus' life, but results from the deliberate composition of these materials by the gospel's author. Wrede's work also forced scholars to recognize that the theological composition and interpretation of traditional materials which is clearly present in Mark also appears in a refracted and modified form in Matthew and Luke. The literary-critical argument for the priority of Mark must, therefore, be based upon a comparative analysis of the work of redaction and composition of the three gospel authors. This, however, demonstrates convincingly that Matthew and Luke presuppose both as a whole as well as in many details the literary composition of the "author" of the Gospel of Mark, and that each continues this work in his own way.

More difficult than the demonstration of Markan priority is the reconstruction of the second source of Matthew and Luke, the sayings source "Q." In a portion of the sayings common to Matthew and Luke the sayings not only occur in similar sequences and compositions (e.g., in the parallel portions of the Sermon on the Mount in Matthew 5–7 and the Sermon on the Plain in Luke 6), they also show close detailed resemblances with each other even in their formulation and wording. Another portion of the sayings, however, exhibits striking differences between its Matthean and Lukan forms. One has to assume, therefore, that "Q" was indeed a written source, but that Matthew and Luke used it at different stages of its development and redaction. Since the material transmitted through this *Sayings Source* in many instances exhibits features caused by translation from Aramaic, it is possible that it represents a very early collection of Jesus' sayings which was originally composed in Aramaic, and that was translated into Greek either as a whole or in the process of the compilation of smaller collections.

The hypothesis of the use of two written sources by Matthew and Luke, namely Mark and "Q," does not in itself solve all the problems of the sources of the Synoptic Gospels. Apart from the material drawn from Mark and "Q," the first and third Gospels contain much material peculiar to each book. Among these are the two infancy narratives in Matthew 1–2 and Luke 1–2, a number of parables in Matthew 13, a part of the Synoptic Apocalypse in Matthew 24–25, and for Luke, especially much of the material contained in the travel narrative of Luke 9:51–18:15. Such observations have prompted the suggestion of a further source "M" for the special materials in Matthew and a source "L" for the special materials in Luke. As far as Luke is concerned, it seems difficult to forego the assumption of such a special source, although determining its extent is problematic (did it contain only Luke's special materials, or also pericopes parallel to Markan passages?). In any case, refining source theories in more and more complex detail also leads the construction and usefulness of literary theories to their limits. Neither in the formative stage of the gospel nor in their later development is it possible to explain all the data exclusively with the assumption of the use of written sources. Rather, from the beginning there was also the oral tradition, which continued to be important even into II CE and into later periods (§7.4a).

The decisive question in the determination of literary sources is not whether some material was available in written form or not. Even material that is not "literature" in the true sense can occasionally be transmitted in written form. If one wants to posit the existence of a literary source, it is also necessary to determine that source's literary character and genre. With respect to the *Synoptic Sayings Source* used by Matthew and Luke, this is indeed possible. Its genre seems to correspond to that of the sayings books of the Jewish wisdom literature. Thus the *Sayings Source* represents a type of literature which has been called *Logoi Sophon*, "Words of the Wise" (James M. Robinson). Some of Luke's special materials may have been derived from a source of this type, because it consists largely of sayings and parables. Another representative of the same genre is the recently discovered *Gospel of Thomas*. With its wisdom sayings and parables it provides a good example for the kind of book that the *Synoptic Sayings Source* might have been in an early stage of its development.

The literary character of another early written form of the gospel tradition can also be recognized: the collection of miracle stories of Jesus which was used by the Gospels of Mark and John. This is a type of literature which enumerates the great deeds of a famous person. The Hellenistic world presents its analogy in the accounts of the deeds of gods and of divine men, namely, in the aretalogy. The content and sequence of several miracle stories in Mark and John share enough in common for us to conclude that their sources were different versions of the same literary collection. This source, which in the Gospel of John is called the *Semeia* or *Signs Source,* presents Jesus as a healer endowed with miraculous powers, who can control even the forces of nature (see the narratives about Jesus walking on the sea and feeding of the multitude).

The canonical Gospels thus essentially rely on two types of literary sources, which can be clearly defined, and which have provided most of the materials for them: sayings books and collections of miracle stories (aretalogies). The former present Jesus as a teacher of wisdom or as the divine Wisdom, the latter picture Jesus as the "Divine Man." But apart from these two types of literary sources, one finds materials of rather

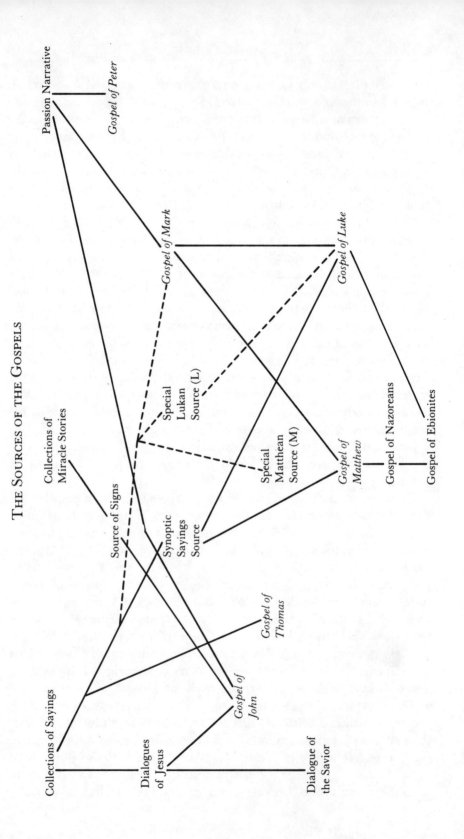

THE SOURCES OF THE GOSPELS

Passion Narrative

Gospel of Peter

Gospel of Mark

Gospel of Luke

Collections of
Miracle Stories

Special Lukan
Source (L)

Source of Signs

Special Matthean
Source (M)

Gospel of Nazoreans

Gospel of Ebionites

Gospel of
Matthew

Synoptic
Sayings
Source

Collections of Sayings

Gospel of
Thomas

Gospel of
John

Dialogues
of Jesus

Dialogue of
the Savior

different sorts, which also seem to derive from written sources. One of these is the collection of apocalyptic sayings which appears as a prophetic discourse about the future in the so-called Synoptic Apocalypse (Mark 13 and parallels). Such compositions must have circulated widely in early Christianity; a small apocalypse of this kind was used in the *Teaching of the Twelve Apostles* (*Didache* 16). The literary genre of such writings is related to the Jewish apocalypses of that period (such as the Book of Daniel; see §5.3c), which were also used as prototypes for Christian apocalyptic literature like the Revelation of John and others. Jesus does not necessarily have to appear as the speaker in such literature (in *Didache* 16, material closely related to Mark 13 is presented as written by the Apostles), but in ancient Christian prophetic words (e.g., 1 Thess 4:15ff) as well as in later gnostic revelations the risen Christ is frequently the author of revelation discourses.

Finally, there was certainly a written form of the Passion Narrative at an early date. It was used independently by Mark and John, and it is possible that the apocryphal *Gospel of Peter* employed a very similar source. If this were in fact the case, it would best explain the agreements of these three Gospels in their presentation of the sequence of the events in Jesus' passion, in their use of OT quotations, and in many other details. It is unnecessary to resort to the very unlikely assumption of a literary dependence of these three Gospels (Mark, John, and *Peter*) upon each other, although Matthew and Luke indeed did draw their passion narratives from the Gospel of Mark.

(c) The Acts of the Apostles

"Luke," the author of the Acts of the Apostles and also of the third Gospel of the NT, could scarcely have been a travel companion and fellow

Bibliography to §7.3c

Henry J. Cadbury, *The Making of Luke-Acts* (2d ed.; London: SPCK, 1958).

Henry J. Cadbury et al., "The Composition and Purpose of Acts," in: Foakes Jackson and Lake, *Beginnings*, 2. 3–204.

Rudolf Bultmann, "Zur Frage nach den Quellen der Apostelgeschichte," in: idem, *Exegetica* (Tübingen: Mohr/Siebeck, 1967) 412–23.

Haenchen, *Acts*, 81–90.

Idem, "Das 'Wir' in der Apostelgeschichte und das Itinerar," in: idem, *Gott und Mensch*, 227–64.

Idem, "Tradition und Komposition in der Apostelgeschichte," in: idem, *Gott und Mensch*, 202–26.

Idem, "The Book of Acts as Source Material for the History of Early Christianity," in: Leander Keck and J. Louis Martyn (eds.), *Studies in Luke-Acts: Essays Presented in Honor of Paul Schubert* (Nashville: Abingdon, 1966) 258–78.

Gerhard Schneider, *Die Apostelgeschichte* (HThK 1; Freiburg: Herder, 1980) 82–103.

worker of Paul, but belongs to a later generation (§12.3a). The more this view has found acceptance, the more scholars have tried to determine the sources from which this first historical work of Christianity obtained its information. Even though this book contains many invented speeches and the author more than once confuses literary conjectures with reliable information, it is still not possible to explain its composition without assuming that it used earlier sources. In the history of scholarship two suggestions have found the most widespread acceptance: the hypothesis of an "Antiochian Source" for most of the historically valuable material in Acts 6–12 and 15, and the hypothesis of a "We Source" for a portion of the travel narratives in Acts 16–28. Both theories, however, are burdened with considerable difficulties.

No one denies that Acts has preserved historically valuable information about the Hellenists in Jerusalem and the martyrdom of Stephen, about the beginnings of the Hellenistic communities, and particularly about Antioch. But the precise delimitation of such source materials is difficult. Did the author of Acts use a continuous and coherent report about the beginnings of the Hellenists' mission and about the church at Antioch? Or was it the author of Acts who combined partly legendary traditions and partly authentic documents to create a narrative of successive events? Moreover, the assumption of the use of a source by no means guarantees that material drawn from it contains trustworthy historical information— on the contrary! It is difficult to argue that whatever historically valuable material does appear in the first part of Acts was derived from a particular written document. At the same time, the written sources which were used in Acts seem to have contained thoroughly legendary materials; furthermore, the literary style of the author of Acts is so clearly visible in all its parts that a source analysis on stylistic grounds is impossible. The hypothesis of an "Antiochian Source" is therefore very precarious, although it cannot be denied that specific sections of Acts must have drawn on materials from sources and traditions. The situation is somewhat different with the "We Source." The first-person plural ("we"), often appearing unexpectedly in the reports of Paul's travels, leads to the conclusion that the author of Acts indeed used an itinerary or a travel report which a travel companion of Paul may have written. Valuable older materials appear in these sections. However, the occurrence of the first-person plural cannot be used to determine and define such a source, since the author of Acts also uses the "we" as a stylistic device in sections where he certainly did not use any sources whatsoever; this is most evident in his narrative of the shipwreck (Acts 27–28).

Acts presents still another literary problem since it is transmitted in two different versions which frequently vary. The text that is usually printed in the critical editions of the NT is that of the Egyptian uncials from IV CE (B, ℵ, etc.), whose readings are largely identical with those of the Alexandrian church fathers. The other version is found among the representatives of the so-called "Western" text (Codex D, Old Latin, Old Syriac) whose readings are often supported by the Latin fathers. It is a version that contains numerous special readings and additions; among these is the famous expanded version of the Apostolic Decree in Acts 15:29. Discoveries of older papyri and quotations in the church fathers prove that the "Western" text must have circulated as early as II CE. Thus, both versions of Acts are very ancient. An interesting suggestion would see in the version of the "Western" text the original edition of Acts beause this text contains some valuable information which is missing in the version of the Alexandrian texts (e.g., the information about places in Acts 12:10; 20:15, and times in 19:9; 27:5). But other variants of the "Western" text seem to be secondary (adjustments of contradictions and an anti-Judaic tendency). It is therefore more likely that this version is the result of a revision made in II CE, i.e., a second edition, not a degeneration of the original edition.

The problem of sources also raises the question of the literary genre of the Book of Acts. The author no doubt intended to write a historical work. This is visible in the conception of the whole book, a historical development which begins in Jerusalem and extends as far as Rome, and in the dovetailing of sources and traditions within this framework. Also typical for a historical work are the speeches, which the author composed in order to highlight significant moments. It cannot be assumed that these speeches are based upon any sources; rather, the composition of such speeches by the author fits the custom of Greek history writing. What contradicts the author's intention to write history are some of the sources and materials that are available. Only such information as that about the founding of the Antiochian church (Acts 11:19ff) is instrinsically suitable to the intention of historiography.

The incorporation of numerous miracle stories and legendary materials demonstrates that the author was just as uncritical as many other historians of his time, but it has a serious consequence: large parts of the book read like an apostolic romance, not a historical book. This impression is reinforced by the lengthy narrative of the shipwreck (Acts 27–28) which is so typical of the Hellenistic romance. The use of the itinerary, however rich in valuable historical information, resulted in a presentation of Paul's mission in which the travel motif (again a characteristic element of the romance) predominates, while the description of the actual missionary activity and the organization of the newly founded congregations recedes into the background. Therefore, with regard to its literary genre, Luke's

Acts of the Apostles belongs in the immediate neighborhood of the apocryphal acts, of which the older examples were written not long after Luke's own work (e.g., *Acts of John, Acts of Peter, Acts of Paul*). These apocryphal works also emphasize the travel motif, make uncritical use of a rich tradition of stories of miraculous deeds and events, insert frequent speeches by the apostles (which are witnesses for the missionary preaching of the time), but are not completely devoid of valuable historical information. Source criticism and the determination of the original version is equally as difficult in the apocryphal acts as in Luke's. Additional problems, of course, arise from the fact that the textual transmission of the apocryphal acts is very poor; there is, for example, not a single manuscript of the *Acts of John* that contains the whole work. But the fact that the apocryphal acts also went through several editions and recensions only shows how comparable they are with the canonical Book of Acts in yet one more respect.

(d) Literary Problems of the Letters of Paul

Only the certainly genuine letters of Paul will be discussed here (on the individual deutero-Pauline letters, see §12.1a; 12.2a, b, g). The following letters are generally accepted as genuine without doubt: Romans, 1 and 2 Corinthians, Galatians, Philippians, 1 Thessalonians, and Philemon. Their literary unity, however, has repeatedly been questioned with more or less adequate justification. In the cases of 1 Corinthians and 1 Thessalonians the arguments against unity are weighty, although perhaps not persuasive enough; but it can be assumed with a high degree of certainty that Romans, 2 Corinthians, and Philippians are each composed of several originally separate letters of Paul.

In the Letter to the Romans, chapter 16 is problematical. Rom 15:33

Bibliography to §7.3d

Walther Schmithals, "Die Korintherbriefe als Briefsammlung," *ZNW* 64 (1973) 263–88.

Dieter Georgi, *Die Gegner des Paulus im 2. Korintherbrief* (WMANT 11; Neukirchen-Vluyn: Neukirchener Verlag, 1964; English translation forthcoming) 25–29.

Joseph A. Fitzmyer, "Qumran and the Interpolated Paragraph in 2 Cor 6:14–7:1," *CBQ* 23 (1961) 271–80.

Hans Dieter Betz, "2 Cor 6:14–7:1: An Anti-Pauline Fragment?" JBL 92 (1973) 88–108.

B. D. Rahtjen, "The Three Letters of Paul to the Philippians," *NTS* 6 (1959/60) 167–73.

Günther Bornkamm, "Der Philipperbrief als paulinische Briefsammlung," in: idem, *Geschichte und Glaube 2* (München: Kaiser, 1971) 195–205.

J. Müller-Bardorff, "Zur Frage der literarischen Einheit des Philipperbriefes," *WZ (J)* 7 (1957/58) GS 4, 591ff.

ends with a concluding offer of peace. Quite unexpectedly Rom 16:1ff continues with a recommendation for Phoebe and goes on with a long list of personal greetings. It is unlikely that Paul personally knew such a large number of Christians in Rome, and the list moreover contains several names that really belong to Asia Minor (Prisca and Aquila, Epainetus, Andronicus). Furthermore, the vacillation of the manuscripts is interesting: a number of manuscripts put the doxology that occurs in most manuscripts at the end of Romans 16 (i.e., 16:25–26, which is certainly not Pauline) after Rom 14:23, while ℘46 and others place this doxology after Rom 15:33. The best solution of these problems is the recognition that chapter 16 was not originally directed to Rome, but was a letter of recommendation and greeting originally sent to Ephesus which was attached to the Letter to the Romans at a later date. Whether this allows the conclusion that the letter to Rome was also sent by Paul to other churches with appropriate greetings attached is unclear.

2 Corinthians is most heterogeneous. Although its individual parts are thematically related, several breaks in continuity cannot be explained as simply leaps in Paul's thought. The report about the situation in which Paul found himself is suddenly interrupted in 2 Cor 2:13 and not continued until 7:5. Chapters 8 and 9 each have a new beginning, and although they treat a similar topic they are addressed to different communities. Altogether surprising is the last part, 2 Corinthians 10–13, with its biting polemics: after all, in chapter 7 Paul had already said that he was reconciled! Among several possible solutions, some of which at least partly agree with each other, the following is the most persuasive. What is now transmitted as the Second Letter to the Corinthians is a composition of five different letters of Paul that was published in this form later than the first edition of a collection of other Pauline epistles (quotations from 2 Corinthians are missing in *1 Clement* and in the letters of Ignatius of Antioch). Of most of these original five letters, only the body of the letters is preserved, while the prescripts and final greetings have been dropped, except for those which now form the framework of the preserved composite letter. The first of these five letters is found in 2 Cor 2:14–6:13 and 7:2–4. It is Paul's first written reaction to the information from Corinth, received in Ephesus, that foreign apostles had come into the Corinthian church. The second of these letters, 2 Corinthians 10–13, presupposes that Paul meanwhile had made a personal, but fruitless, visit in Corinth. Only when Paul's fellow-worker Titus intervened in Corinth on his behalf did it later become possible to reestablish good terms with the Corinthian church. Paul, already on his way to the church, wrote 2 Cor 1:1–2:13 and 7:5–16 as soon as Titus had brought him the good news about that reconciliation. Together with this third letter, he sent two additional letters,

both concerning the collection for Jerusalem. One of these was addressed to the Corinthians and is now preserved in chapter 8; the second, directed to the churches of Achaea, appears in chapter 9.

Philippians must also be understood as a collection of several letters, even if the exact historical situation for the writing of each of these letters is not quite as evident as in the case of 2 Corinthians. The first of the letters now preserved in Philippians, Phil 4:10–20, is a letter of acknowledgment that Paul sent to Philippi after receiving a gift from that church, delivered to him through Epaphroditus. The second letter was written somewhat later: Phil 1:1–3:1. The situation had changed; Paul was now in prison in Ephesus, Epaphroditus had been severely ill, but had recovered and was the messenger of the second letter. The third letter, Phil 3:2–4:1 is part of Paul's controversies with rivalling Jewish-Christian missionaries. Of this letter, only a fragment is preserved in the present letter to the Philippians. How to assign the pieces in Phil 4:2–3, 4–7, and 8–9 to these three letters remains uncertain. All three letters were probably written to Philippi from Ephesus (on the Ephesian imprisonment, see §9.3e).

If the letters of Paul are thus not preserved as direct copies of the original autographs, but as later editions, it is not surprising that they also contain a number of editorial additions, which characteristically occur near the seams of the composite letters. Such an addition is clearly recognizable both by its topic and terminology in 2 Cor 6:14–7:1. Another appears in Rom 16:25–27: it reveals a vocabulary closely related to that of the Pastoral Epistles and was added by the editor to provide a proper conclusion for Paul's "Epistle to the Romans." Also related to the Pastoral Epistles is the interpolation of 1 Cor 14:33b–35 that forbids women to speak in church (cf. 1 Corinthians 11 with respect to 1 Tim 2:9ff). Smaller interpolations cannot always be determined with certainty, but cannot be excluded a priori. It seems likely, for example, that Rom 2:16, which shares the phrase "according to my Gospel" with Rom 16:25 and 2 Tim 2:8, was added by a later editor. Beyond that, some major sections of the Pauline letters have also been considered as spurious, such as the verses on obedience to the authorities in Rom 13:1–7, which reflects the spirit of the political parenesis of Hellenistic Judaism, and—much more likely to be inauthentic—the anti-Judaic polemic 1 Thess 2:14–16.

When we review all the preserved Pauline letters, what has been said demonstrates that a larger number of letters was transmitted than the current editions would suggest; in fact, at least fourteen letters. Only two among these writings are at all extensive: Romans (chapters 1–15) and 1 Corinthians. This observation is important for our judgments about the form and genre of the Pauline letter. The large majority of these letters does not belong to the category of the more voluminous didactic letter; they are instead occasional writings which were composed for a specific situation. Numerous letters of this kind have been preserved from antiquity, such as those in the Oxyrhynchus Papyri or in the published correspondence of the younger Pliny. The church-political interest is the primary concern of these Pauline letters: they are written in the interests of the organization of Christian congregations and their preservation, and are designed to solve problems that threaten the existence of these communities. These interests are clear in the letters of recommendation (Romans 16; Philemon), letters of credence (2 Corinthians 8 and 9), notes of acknowledgment (Phil 4:10–20), but also in the polemical letters (Galatians; Philippians 3; 2 Cor 2:14–6:13). Because the person of the apostle plays a significant role in questions of church policy and in polemical situations, two elements have primary significance in the letters: the personal apology (see especially Galatians 1–2; 2 Corinthians 10–13; Philippians 3) and the travel plans (see 1 Corinthians 16; 2 Cor 1:1–2:13 and 7:5–16). But all these factors also determine the more extensive letters of Paul. The foremost motive for the writing of Romans is Paul's intention to travel to the west, and Paul was therefore obliged to direct an explanation, or apology, of his message to the church in Rome: this apology grew into a major presentation of his theology. In 1 Corinthians, the main motif is the organization of the community and the regulation of Christian life: thus the letter became a church order, in which the various questions which had been addressed to Paul were treated point by point.

The formal schema of the Pauline letters corresponds to the Jewish letter formula, but also contains elements of the Greek letter. The prescript carries the name of the sender, the addressee, and the greeting in two sentences, according to the Jewish form. The wish of peace also reflects the Jewish form; thus the greeting is always "grace and peace" rather than the Greek "greetings." The proem follows directly upon this prescript and usually contains an extensive thanksgiving, speaking about the status of the church, its relationship to the apostle, but also about the personal experiences of the apostle and his travel plans. Such a proem may occupy the major portion of the letter, as in the case of 1 Thessalonians (1 Thess 1:2–3:13), but it can also take the form of a polemical eruption of angry surprise (Gal 1:6ff). The body proper of the Pauline letter form is the parenesis (1 Thess 4:1–12; Romans 12–15; 1 Corinthians 5–14) which is often followed by an eschatological section (1 Thess 4:12–5:11; 1 Corinthians 15). The conclusion is formed by the greetings, in which individual persons are specially named. The frequent striking peculiarities in the form of the Pauline letter can be explained as modifications of this basic schema. In Romans, the theological reflections that precede the parenesis (Rom 1:18–11:36) are elaborations of the thesis that

Paul has proposed at the end of the proem. The discussion of the travel plans can be resumed in the context of the final greetings (Rom 15:14–33; 1 Corinthians 16). Only a portion of some of these letters is preserved, of course; of the letter of recommendation in Romans 16 we have only the body proper, the actual recommendation (Rom 16:1–2) and the final greetings (Rom 16:3–23); of the letter of acknowledgment in Phil 4:10–20, only the body proper has survived. This is also the case with the two letters of credence concerning the Jerusalem collection in 2 Corinthians 8 and 9.

The same basic schema was usually employed in the composition of the deutero-Pauline letters. In Colossians the prescript (Col 1:1–2) is followed by an extensive proem (Col 1:3–2:5) which makes elaborate statements about the mission and fate of the apostle. The next section is a polemic interspersed with parenesis (2:6–4:6), and greetings form the letter's conclusion (4:7–18). In Colossians as well as in Ephesians, material is employed in the parenesis that has the character of a church order (Col 3:18–4:1; Eph 5:22–6:9). In the later Pastoral Epistles, church order material has become the primary content of the writing.

(e) The Second Letter of Peter and the Letter of Jude

The most striking case of literary dependence within the letters of the NT appears in the relation of 2 Peter to Jude. In its second chapter, 2 Peter reproduces almost the whole letter of Jude, although with many alterations. Jude was probably written toward the end of I CE and it is strongly and even explicitly dependent upon Jewish apocalyptic materials (see Jude 14). From this apocalyptic perspective, Jude argues against (gnostic?) heretics who claim to be the truly spiritual people (Jude 19) and are thus seen as a danger to the churches to which they belong, and in which they participate in the common *agape* meals (Jude 12).

For the perspective of 2 Peter, probably written about half a century later, the situation has changed fundamentally. The heretics have been excluded from the churches and there are relationships to them only on the private level (cf. 2 Pet 2:13 with Jude 12). The citation of apocryphal Jewish materials is apparently questionable to the author of 2 Peter. Thus all such passages are deleted or altered in 2 Peter's reproduction of Jude. But otherwise the whole design of Jude as well as many details are clearly reproduced in 2 Pet 2:1–3:2. There are also some borrowings from Jude in other passages of 2 Peter (cf., e.g., 2 Pet 1:5 to Jude 3; see §12.1b, 2f).

Bibliography to §7.3e

Walter Grundmann, *Der Brief des Judas und der zweite Brief des Petrus* (ThHK 15; Berlin: Evangelische Verlagsanstalt, 1971) 102–7.

(f) The Letters of Ignatius of Antioch

The letters of Ignatius were written in the beginning of II CE. They were read in the churches in the subsequent period, but are not nearly as richly attested as the writings of the NT. With respect to their transmission these letters present an interesting problem of literary criticism, which demonstrates that the train of transmission preserving a writing's original form and wording can be extraordinarily narrow under certain circumstances.

Eusebius of Caesarea mentions in his *Church History* (3.36.2–11) that the Antiochian bishop Ignatius, while he was being taken to Rome as a prisoner, had written several letters, namely to the Ephesians, Magnesians, Trallians, Romans, Philadelphians, Smyrneans, and to Polycarp, bishop of Smyrna. But the edition of the Ignatian epistles which circulated in the Middle Ages contained thirteen letters in its Greek version, and twelve letters in its Latin version. In addition to the seven letters mentioned by Eusebius, a letter of Maria of Cassobola to Ignatius, a letter of Ignatius to this Maria, letters to the churches in Tarsus, Philippi, and Antioch, and a letter to the deacon Hero of Antioch were included (the letter of Maria is missing in the Latin version). The authenticity of this collection of Ignatian letters, which is known today as the "Longer Recension," was questioned as early as the Renaissance. But in addition to this Longer Recension, there is a second version preserved in one Greek manuscript (the Codex Mediceo Laurentianus of Florence; see below) which was also known in the Middle Ages, when it was translated into English, Latin, and Armenian. This second version, though containing letters to the same addressees as the Longer Recension, differs from it in that those letters mentioned by Eusebius appear in a form that is much shorter than the corresponding letters of the Longer Recension. This second version is called the "Middle Recension." It was rediscovered in the seventeenth century, reprinted several times, and in the course of time it generally came to be thought that the seven letters of this recension which are mentioned by Eusebius were Ignatius' original letters. But in the year 1845, the English scholar Cureton published still another recension preserved in a Syriac translation and containing only three letters of Ignatius, i.e., to the Ephesians, Romans, and to Polycarp. Moreover, the text in this "Short Recension" turned out to be even shorter than the text of the cor-

Bibliography to §7.3f

Milton Perry Brown, *The Authentic Letters of Ignatius: A Study of Linguistic Criteria* (Durham: Duke University, 1963).
Theodor Zahn, *Ignatius von Antiochien* (Gotha: Perthes, 1873).

STEMMA OF THE TRANSMISSION OF IGNATIUS' LETTERS

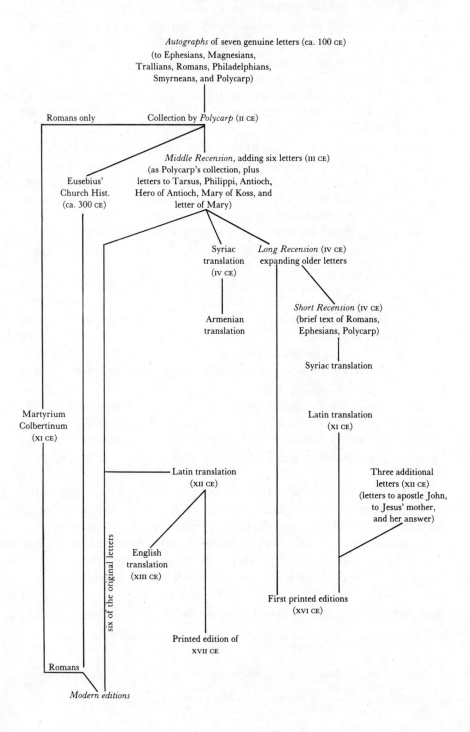

Autographs of seven genuine letters (ca. 100 CE)
(to Ephesians, Magnesians,
Trallians, Romans, Philadelphians,
Smyrneans, and Polycarp)

Romans only   Collection by *Polycarp* (II CE)

Middle Recension, adding six letters (III CE)
(as Polycarp's collection, plus
letters to Tarsus, Philippi, Antioch,
Hero of Antioch, Mary of Koss, and
letter of Mary)

Eusebius'
Church Hist.
(ca. 300 CE)

Syriac   *Long Recension* (IV CE)
translation   expanding older letters
(IV CE)

Armenian   *Short Recension* (IV CE)
translation   (brief text of Romans,
                            Ephesians, Polycarp)

                            Syriac translation

Martyrium   Latin translation
Colbertinum   (XI CE)
(XI CE)

                                        Three additional
        Latin translation   letters (XII CE)
        (XII CE)   (letters to apostle John,
                                        to Jesus' mother,
                                        and her answer)

six of the original letters

        English
        translation
        (XIII CE)

                    First printed editions
                    (XVI CE)

Romans

Modern editions

        Printed edition of
        XVII CE

responding letters in the Middle Recension. Some scholars subsequently accepted only these three letters in their short form as original Ignatian letters. Finally, another collection of Ignatian letters exists which is transmitted only in Latin and contains three letters not appearing in any of the other recensions: letters of Ignatius to the apostle John and to Mary the mother of Jesus, and a letter of Mary to Ignatius.

Thus the various collections and recensions contain a total of fourteen letters of Ignatius and two letters of others to Ignatius. Of the seven letters to the addressees named by Eusebius, four are transmitted in both a longer and a shorter version, and three in a longer, a shorter, and a very short version. The study *Ignatius von Antiochien* by the NT scholar Theodor Zahn, published in 1873, finally was able to prove conclusively that the seven letters of the Middle Recension to the addressees mentioned by Eusebius were the original letters, and that the longer version as well as the very short version of three of these letters are secondary—in fact the short version of three letters preserved in Syriac must be seen as an abbreviation of letters from the Longer Recension. All the other letters are pseudepigraphical, some of them not produced until the Middle Ages. The time of the production of the Middle Recension and the Long Recension is debated. The former may have been produced as early as III CE, the latter certainly not until IV CE. It is remarkable that the original Greek text of the genuine letters is preserved only in collections which at the same time contain spurious letters, most of which are in only one Greek manuscript, the Codex Mediceo Laurentianus from XI CE. The *Letter to the Romans,* which is missing in this codex, is found in several early medieval manuscripts that also contain the *Martyrdom of Ignatius.* Apart from these very few textual witnesses, textual criticism of the Ignatian letters must rely upon recensions and translations. There is also a recently discovered Greek papyrus for a portion of the *Letter to the Smyrneans.* The history of the transmission of the letters of Ignatius clearly demonstrates the possible fate of collections of early Christian writings that were not protected by becoming part of the NT canon. But even those writings which are now part of the NT must have been subject to such vicissitudes of transmission before the canon was created.

4. PROBLEMS OF FORM AND TRADITION CRITICISM

(a) The Synoptic Tradition

The true father of form criticism (*Formgeschichte*) was Johann Gottfried Herder, who also provided important stimuli for other areas of modern intellectual history. Herder was the first to recognize that the song, poem, and fairy tale have their true origin and setting in the life of the people. But it was not until a century later that this insight took effect in the work of biblical scholarship through the studies of Hermann Gunkel. Gunkel applied the new method primarily to the book of Genesis and to the Psalms. Following Gunkel, Rudolf Bultmann and Martin Dibelius investigated the Synoptic Gospels with the help of the form-critical method in studies published almost simultaneously shortly after World War I. These works provided a completely new base for all scholarship dealing with the gospels of the NT and other early Christian literature.

The fundamental thesis of the form-critical method is that the sayings and speeches of Jesus as well as the stories about him were first transmitted orally, not in written form; this is indisputable. Such oral transmission was not due to any lack of ability by the early Christians to produce written records—Paul's letters show that this was not the case— nor by a dogmatic preference for the oral medium of transmission (as in

Bibliography to §7.4

Gerhard Lohfink, *The Bible: Now I Get It! A Form-Criticism Handbook* (Garden City: Doubleday, 1979). An excellent introduction to form criticism.

André Jolles, *Einfache Formen* (2d ed.; Darmstadt: Wissenschaftliche Buchgesellschaft, 1958).

Eduard Norden, *Agnostos Theos: Untersuchungen zur Formengeschichte religiöser Rede* (2d ed.; Leipzig: Teubner, 1923; reprint: Darmstadt: Wissenschaftliche Buchgesellschaft, 1956).

E. Dinkler, "Form Criticism of the New Testament," in: Black and Rowley, *Peake's Commentary*, 683–85.

Vielhauer, *Geschichte,* 9–57.

Alfred Seeberg, *Die Didache des Judentums und der Urchristenheit* (Leipzig: Deichert, 1908).

Idem, *Der Katechismus der Urchristenheit* (Leipzig: Deichert, 1903; reprint: ThBü 26; München: Kaiser, 1966).

Bibliography to §7.4a

Rudolf Bultmann, *The History of the Synoptic Tradition* (2d ed.; New York: Harper, 1968). The classic and standard handbook for form criticism of the Synoptic Gospels.

Karl Ludwig Schmidt, *Der Rahmen der Geschichte Jesu* (Berlin: Trowitzsch, 1919; reprint: Darmstadt: Wissenschaftliche Buchgesellschaft, 1964).

Martin Dibelius, *From Tradition to Gospel* (New York: Scribner's, 1934). The works of Dibelius, Bultmann, and Schmidt are the foundations of the form-critical method.

Rudolf Bultmann and Karl Kundsin, *Form Criticism* (New York: Willet, Clark, 1934; reprint: New York: Harper, 1962).

Edgar V. McKnight, *What is Form Criticism?* (GBSNTS; Philadelphia: Fortress, 1969).

Norman Perrin, *What is Redaction Criticism?* (GBSNTS; Philadelphia: Fortress, 1969).

Vincent Taylor, *The Formation of the Gospel Tradition* (New York: St. Martin's, 1953) rabbinic Judaism); the interests and needs of the life of the early Christian communities were responsible. The tradition from and about Jesus was alive in the missionary propaganda and preaching, praxis and liturgy, and teaching and polemic of the Christian communities. In these contexts the sayings of Jesus were quoted and taught, and the stories about him told and retold.

The form and content of the tradition was thus shaped by the sociological and theological contexts which determined the life of the early Christians. This is also true, of course, for Jesus himself. The sayings, parables, and example stories of Jesus are dependent in their form upon the total theological setting of Jesus' preaching, and upon the cultural situation of Judaism in his time. It is possible to demonstrate in many instances how the different theological situations of the early Christian community after the death of Jesus and the new cultural horizons of the early church, which soon went beyond the limits of Judaism, provided new molds for the reshaping of the tradition.

The specific theological and sociological situation to which the various forms of the tradition belong in each case is called the "life situation" (*Sitz im Leben*). For example, the life situation for the tradition and formation of the Lord's Prayer is the religious practice of prayer in the early church. Example stories and parables have their life situation in the functions of the Christian sermon in edification and community building. In such a new life situation parables underwent many changes (e.g., allegorical elaborations), although they ultimately derived from Jesus. Collections of sayings have their life situation in parenesis and in baptismal instruction, miracle stories in the missionary propaganda of the early church. In each case, the term "life situation" refers first of all to the Christian community. To be sure, the tradition may not originate here, but in this context it has been formed and augmented. If one wants to speak of the "situation in the life of Jesus" for such pieces of the tradition that probably derive from Jesus, it is necessary to understand this "life situation" as the entire context of his message, mission, and deeds, but not as some specific time and place at which Jesus may have said or done some particular thing. The actual circumstances of the origin of such traditions in the life and ministry of Jesus can in no way be known, because the biographical framework by which the individual traditions are connected with each other in our written Gospels is an entirely literary creation, and therefore secondary as compared to the traditions used within this framework.

In order to define in more detail the individual forms of the tradition, it is necessary to distinguish between the sayings and the narrative materials. The authors of the gospels, of course, derived both types of materials from traditions which were formed in the life of the church. But many materials were preserved in the sayings tradition which ultimately goes back to Jesus himself, while the forms of the tradition of the narrative materials were one and all created by the Christian community. Among the sayings materials, prophetic sayings and wisdom sayings predominate. Their forms have analogies in the prophetic and wisdom books of the OT. Parallelism of phrasing is frequent in their formation; many of these sayings are similes, metaphors, and hyperboles. Some of the prophetic and wisdom sayings may well derive from Jesus himself, but the forms in which they are transmitted are normally determined by the usage of the church, such as their employment for catechisms. The preaching of Jesus about the rule of God is otherwise most clearly preserved in the parables. To this category belong actual parables, parabolic narratives, and example stories. It is striking that the closest analogies to these parables are found in the parables of the prophets of the OT, while in Judaism of that period the allegorizing parable is much more frequent. In the tradition of the church, the parables of Jesus were sometimes provided with allegorical interpretations, according to the method of interpretation which was typical of the time. Rules of the community and legal sayings which are concerned with ordering the Christian life are creations of the church in their entirety, with the exception of those sayings that contain a prophetic criticism of the Law. A portion of the legal sayings as well as some of the wisdom sayings were probably derived directly from the Jewish environment of the early church. The Synoptic tradition also contains sayings which were formed in analogy to traditional words of Jesus or to Jewish sayings.

A characteristic form of the Synoptic tradition is the apophthegm (Bultmann; Dibelius speaks of the "paradigm"). Apophthegms are short scenes in which a question is asked or a problem posed, to which a saying of Jesus provides the answer. Questions are asked by the disciples, by the opponents of Jesus, by Jesus himself, or by any other individual. In several instances questions of either the disciples or the opponents are provoked by some action of Jesus, such as the exorcism of a demon. The majority of the apophthegms are controversy dialogues, while others can be classified as scholastic and instructional dialogues. The occasion for the formation of both types of apophthegms was the interests of the communities which needed materials for polemical purposes and for the instruction of their members. The gospels also contain biographical apophthegms which owe their origin to the interest in the life and ministry of Jesus, which is thus presented in short paradigmatic scenes. It is necessary to distinguish between those apophthegms that provide a framework for an older traditional saying of Jesus, and those in which the scene and the word of Jesus were composed as a unified piece. Only in the first case is it possible that a genuine word of Jesus has been preserved. Characteristic for the tradition of the apophthegms is the attachment of further related sayings or secondary analogous formulations, so that it is not rare to have in one single apophthegm several competing answers to the question that was raised.

Most of the traditional narratives are miracle stories. A type of the miracle story which is characteristic for the Synoptic tradition is the exorcism. Exorcisms are told according to a fixed schema: encounter of the possessed person with Jesus; recognition of the power of the exorcist; Jesus threatens and drives out the demon, often with a demonstration; presentation of the success, and acknowledgment by the witnesses. In the healing miracles the encounter of the sick person with Jesus is usually followed by a remark about the severity of the disease; the healing is accomplished either through a word of Jesus (magical terms from Aramaic are occasionally preserved here), through some manipulation, or a combination of both; the conclusion tells of the success of the healing and the applause of the bystanders. Nature miracles are comparatively rare in the Synoptic tradition (e.g., the Stilling of the Storm and the Walking on the Sea). As in the exorcisms and healing miracles, the brevity of the narrative is a striking feature of these stories' style. There are numerous parallels to each type of Synoptic miracle story in Jewish and pagan traditions and in the Christian acts of the apostles; they all exhibit the same basic schemata and narrative forms. However, secondary embellishment and expansions, novelistic features, and elaborate descriptions of the healing process (occasionally including complex manipulations) are the rule in these stories, whereas such features are almost completely absent from the Synoptic miracle stories.

A number of legends also belong to the Synoptic tradition. A "legend" is a story which relates a particular event by using wondrous or amazing details. The only cult legend in the Synoptic tradition is the story of the institution of the Lord's Supper. All the other legends are biographical in nature (the birth and infancy narratives, the story of the Baptist, the temptation of Jesus, his entry into Jerusalem). The passion narrative also belongs here; although the underlying structure may be a report shaped by the Christian kerygma, it contains numerous legendary elaborations. It is typical for the legends of the Synoptic tradition that they highlight only one single event and use descriptive embellishments very sparingly. Novelistic features are rare (but see the Emmaus story in Luke 24).

Epiphany stories include the story of Jesus' baptism, the transfiguration, and the appearances of the risen Jesus (the latter have a close parallel in the story of the calling of Paul; see Acts 9:1ff). These epiphany stories share many features with stories of the same genre in the OT and in Jewish apocalyptic literature: a special place (desert, mountain), description of the situation, extraordinary appearances (a dove, bright light, the risen Lord), a voice from heaven or the self-revelation of the figure who appears, description of the impression made upon the persons present, and finally a command or a commission. Remarkably, there is no mention of a commission in the stories of Jesus' baptism and transfiguration. These stories did not become stories of the calling of Jesus; rather the emphasis is always placed upon the word that is directed to the disciples.

The quest for the historical kernel of the stories of the Synoptic narrative materials is very difficult. In fact such a quest is doomed to miss the point of such narratives, because these stories were all told in the interests of mission, edification, cult, or theology (especially christology), and they have no relationship to the question of historically reliable information. Precisely those elements and features of such narratives which vividly lead to the climax of the story are derived not from actual historical events, but belong to the form and style of the genres of the several narrative types. Exact statements of names and places are almost always secondary and were often introduced for the first time in the literary stage of the tradition. Unexpected features may sometimes reflect some historical information, such as that Jesus was baptized by John, the leader of another sect which was competing with the Christians (§8.1). It is possible, however, to draw some conclusions about reliable data from an evaluation of the totality of the narratives of a particular genre. The prominence of the exorcisms allows the conclusion that Jesus' ministry was indeed characterized by his activity as an exorcist. The several stories of the resurrection, which are throughout stories of the appearance of the risen Christ (with the exception of the story of the empty tomb), are derived from the fact that such appearances were by all means experienced and then told by those who had "seen the Lord," and repeated in the style appropriate for such narratives. The differences between the original reports and the later epiphany stories can be observed by comparing Gal 1:12–17 (Paul's personal report) with Acts 9:1ff (the report received by Luke and further elaborated by him). It must be noted here that both reports are given in the proper style of such forms as established in the OT: Paul echoes the report of the call of Jeremiah, while Luke follows the form of the calling of Ezekiel. In the context of such narratives the proper names are in fact also historical: Peter, the women (or at least Mary of Magdala), James (cf. 1 Cor 14:7; the story itself is told in an apocryphal gospel).

(b) Early Traditions in the Letters of the New Testament

Materials which were not created by the authors of the NT letters but were derived from the traditions of the church are preserved in great richness and variety. Only rarely is such material explicitly quoted or identified as traditional, and whether or not this is the case, the question of the exact wording of such traditions, and of their delimitation from the context in which they appear, remains a notorious problem. Since external indications for the employment of traditions are usually absent, the identification of traditional material in a given passage has to rely upon other criteria, such as terminology that differs from the normal vocabulary of the author, metrical or poetic language within a section of normal letter prose style, stereotyped formulaic sentences and phrases, and finally the occurrence of parallels in other writings where there is no literary dependence. Sometimes it is also possible to discover contradictions or differences between quoted materials and the statements of the author.

Kerygmatic formulas about the suffering, death or cross, and raising or resurrection of Jesus are frequently used (e.g., 1 Cor 15:3ff). This basic schema was further expanded at an early date by such characteristic items as the idea of Jesus' death as expiation (see Rom 4:25 and the typical and frequent formula "for us"), which is expressed in a number of kerygmatic formulations (Rom 3.25f; Gal 1:4f; 1 Pet 2:21–25). The expectation of the parousia was also combined with this confession (1 Thess 1:10). A different theological perspective appears in the traditional formulas speaking of Jesus' suffering and death and his exaltations or enthronement (Heb 1:2b–3; 1 Pet 3:18–19 and 4:1). Later Christian confessions combine the statement about the resurrection with that of the exaltation.

Christological hymns are quoted repeatedly. They have an easily recognizable form with strings of relative and participial clauses for which Christ is always the subject. For the content of these hymns, the mythic story about the descent of the redeemer, his work among human beings, and his enthronement is typical. The oldest of these hymns, Phil 2:6–11, already takes up the statements of the myth of heavenly Wisdom from Judaism. In particular, the presentation of Christ as the mediator of

Bibliography to §7.4b

Martin Dibelius, "Zur Formgeschichte des Neuen Testaments (außerhalb der Evangelien)," *ThR* NF 3 (1931) 207–42.

Amos N. Wilder, *Early Christian Rhetoric: The Language of the Gospel* (Cambridge, MA: Harvard University, 1971).

Walter Bauer, "Der Wortgottesdienst der ältesten Christen," in: idem, *Aufsätze und kleine Schriften* (Tübingen: Mohr/Siebeck, 1967) 155–209.

Erich Dinkler, "Form Criticism," in: Black and Rowley, *Peake's Commentary*, 683–85.

James M. Robinson, "Die Hodajot-Formel in Gebet und Hymnus des Frühchristentums," in: W. Eltester and F. H. Kettler (eds.), *Apophoreta: Festschrift für Ernst Haenchen* (BZHW 30; Berlin: Töpelmann, 1964) 194–235.

Ernst Käsemann, "Sentences of Holy Law in the New Testament," in: idem, *New Testament Questions*, 66–81.

creation, which introduces many of these hymns, is derived from the wisdom myth (Col 1:15–20; John 1:1–5, 9–12, 14, 16). In most instances only fragments of such hymns are quoted (Eph 2:14ff; 1 Tim 3:16; 2 Cor 9:9; cf. 2 Cor 5:19).

Like the hymns, the doxologies are also derived from the liturgical tradition. They sometimes appear in the conclusions of the letters (Rom 16:27), but are also found in the body (Rom 11:36; 1 Cor 8:6). The blessings at the end of letters may also preserve liturgical materials (see especially 2 Cor 13:13). From the liturgy of the eucharistic celebration Paul quotes the words of institution (1 Cor 11:23–27) and the call "Our Lord, come!" (1 Cor 16:22; cf. Rev 22:20). It is quite possible that various passages have preserved liturgical material from the rite of baptism, but it has been difficult to identify such passages with any certainty. The short confession "Jesus is Lord" (1 Cor 12:3) and the call "Awake, o sleeper!" (Eph 5:14) could be parts of baptismal liturgies.

Even parenetical sections have been assigned to the liturgy of baptism. But traditional parenetical material did not have its exclusive life situation in the instruction of catechumens. There are two basic forms in which parenetic materials were transmitted, namely, as catalogues of virtues and vices, and as compositions of groups of sayings. A third form appears later as parenesis in the schema of household duties (*Haustafeln*). Parenesis in the form of sayings was typical for the Jewish tradition of the Hellenistic period. One letter of the NT is nothing but this sort of parenetical sayings collection: the Epistle of James. Traditional parenesis in the form of sayings frequently appears in the concluding parts of the letters (Rom 12:9–21; Gal 6:2–10; 1 Thess 5:14–22; Heb 13:2ff). Catalogues of virtues and vices had already been taken over by Judaism from Hellenistic philosophy, and are frequently used in early Christian writings. They occur in a parenetic context as simple lists (1 Cor 6:9–10; Gal 4:19–21; Col 3:5–8; cf. Gal 6:22–23; Col 3:12) or as the underlying structure of more elaborate admonitions (1 Thess 4:3–7; Eph 4:17–5:6; and frequently in the Pastoral Epistles). The table of household duties derives from the Stoic diatribe. It speaks of the obligations of the individual members of a house (man and wife, parents and children, masters and slaves), and about one's duty toward friends, foreigners, governments, and so on. They are used in Christian literature for the first time in the deutero-Pauline epistles (Col 3:18–4:1; Eph 5:22–6:9; cf. 1 Pet 2:13–3:7; *Didache* 4). The Pastoral Epistles used this traditional schema for the development of church order; thus not only are the duties of old and young people mentioned, but also the obligations and qualifications of various church officers, namely bishops, presbyters, deacons, widows (1 Tim 2:1–3:13; 5:1–21; 6:1–2; Tit 1:7–9; 2:1–10).

Sayings of Jesus are also used in parenesis (1 Cor 7:10–11; cf. 1 Tim 1:15). Apocalyptic materials are occasionally quoted as words of the Lord. These are probably pronouncements of early Christian prophets, who made predictions about the future in the name of the Lord who had revealed it to them. Paul cites such a "word of the Lord" in 1 Thess 4:15–17, but at another time as a "mystery" (1 Cor 15:51). References to such mystery traditions, that is, revelations about the future which are accessible only to the initiated, are not rare. They include such traditions as those referred to by Paul in Rom 11:25ff and 1 Cor 2:6ff (also 2:1?). In these instances, as also in 1 Cor 13:2 and 14:2, these "mysteries" are traditional sayings that are derived from inspired pronouncements of Christian prophets (see also 2 Thess 2:7; Rev 1:20ff; etc.). Later, the kerygma of Christ is called a "mystery," so that *euangelion* and *mysterion* become synonymous terms (Eph 3:1ff; Col 1:26ff; Rom 16:25ff; 1 Tim 3:16). There was still another activity of the prophets in the Christian communities which manifested itself in sentences that became traditional: the formulation of sentences of sacred law; these are pronouncements which state the *ius talionis* (the law of equal retribution), formulated for the sacral and religious realm of community life. Paul quotes such sentences several times (1 Cor 3:17; 14:38; 16:22; Rom 10:11, 13). Such pronouncements by prophets also influenced the formulation of sayings of Jesus (cf. Mark 8:30 with 2 Tim 2:11–13).

The use of traditional materials is visible last but not least in the quotations and interpretations of passages from the Old Testament. A number of OT quotations were drawn from traditional collections of testimonia for specific topics (e.g., Rom 10:18–21; Heb 1:5–13). But entire interpretations of OT passages were also employed (1 Cor 10:1–10; Hebrews uses such materials to a large extent), or interpretations created by one's opponents were quoted with critical comments (which is certainly the case in 2 Cor 3:7–18).

(c) Traditional Materials Preserved in the Apostolic Fathers, the Apocrypha, and the Apologists

It is evident that early materials are frequently quoted and used in these writings. The noncanonical writings, however, have all received much less attention than the NT itself, and therefore much less certainty prevails in their interpretation. Numerous older traditions used in these writings have not been clearly recognized. In the following I refer to only a few examples and limit my comments to those traditions which are significant for the history of early Christianity.

Words of Jesus and traditions about Jesus which are comparable to the Synoptic tradition are found in special writings belonging to the genre of the gospels and in quotations in other literature. There is no literary dependence upon the canonical Gospels in many instances. Rather, the source of such traditions is either oral transmission or independent written tradition. *1 Clement* quotes two small collections of sayings (*1 Clem.* 13.2; 46.8). A similar collection has been inserted into the first chapter of the *Didache,* and *2 Clement* apparently used a collection of Jesus' sayings. In the latter case, however, this collection depended upon the canonical Gospels. An independent tradition of Jesus' sayings has recently come to light in the newly discovered (Coptic) *Gospel of Thomas* that contains mostly prophetic sayings, wisdom sayings, and parables of Jesus. The fragment of an *Unknown Gospel* (Pap. Oxy. 840) and the gospel fragment *Papyrus Egerton 2* present sayings that have been set into scenes resembling the Synoptic apophthegms, but are somewhat more elaborate. Bishop Papias of Hierapolis collected sayings of Jesus in the first half of II CE from the oral tradition, including legends and apocalyptic revelations. Finally, in later centuries one still finds so-called *Agrapha* quoted by church fathers, that is, sayings of Jesus which do not derive from the canonical Gospels. Even if most of these *Agrapha* cannot be claimed as genuine words of Jesus, they are still important witnesses for the development of the early Christian churches and their traditions about Jesus. Miracle stories of Jesus seem to recede somewhat in the noncanonical tradition (though miracle stories of the apostles are told in great numbers). But legends that deal with the birth and childhood of Jesus were very popular. Collections and editions of such stories led to the publication of the *Protevangelium of James* and the *Infancy Gospel of Thomas.* Epiphany stories are not rare in the extracanonical tradition, especially those featuring the appearance of the risen Lord. The fragment preserved from the *Gospel of Peter* tells the story of the empty tomb in the form of an epiphany story that may in fact be an ancient tradition of which fragments are preserved in Mark 9:2–9 and Matt 27:51–53, 62–66; 28:2–4. Ignatius of Antioch (*Smyrn.* 3.2–3) has preserved a story of the appearance of Jesus to his disciples which is related to Luke 24:36–43 but can be shown to derive from an older tradition. The so-called *Gospel According to the Hebrews* contained a report of an appearance of Jesus to his brother James; there is no reason to doubt that this is an old traditional story. It is highly questionable, however, whether the numerous epiphany stories that introduce instructions of Jesus after the resurrection in gnostic revelation writings rest on ancient tradition, though in some individual instances this might have been the case.

Kerygmatic and confessional or creedal formulas are frequently quoted. The variety of citations demonstrates that even the second century did not know any generally valid formulation of the Christian creed, and that traditional formulations could be freely modified. But the preliminary stages of the development of the later ecclesiastical creeds can be clearly recognized. Rich material is presented by Ignatius. His anti-docetic tendencies led to the inclusion in the creed of a statement about the birth of Jesus by Mary—in order to emphasize the humanity of Jesus! (*Eph.* 18.2 and often elsewhere). He also quotes formulations that juxtapose Jesus' divinity and humanity in antithetical sentences, and that assume almost hymnic character through their frequent repetitions (*Eph.* 7.2); other creeds enumerate in chronological fashion the events of salvation from the birth of Jesus to the resurrection (*Smyrn.* 1.1–2). Similar creedal formulas are quoted by Justin Martyr (*Apol.* 1.31.7; *Dial.* 85.2; 132.1). In Justin's citations, the ascension of Jesus and his second coming for judgment may have become firm parts of the confession. One can also observe the beginnings of a division into three parts, the confession of God the Father and Creator, of Jesus Christ the Savior, and of the Holy Spirit. That such confessions had their life situation in the liturgy of Christian baptism is shown by Justin *Apol.* 1.61; as soon as the older baptismal formula "in the name of Jesus" was replaced by the trinitarian formula (Matt 28:19; *Did.* 7.1), the creedal formulations were also expanded accordingly.

Hymns were especially transmitted in writings from gnostic circles. The *Acts of John* (94–96) preserves a very long hymn of the Christian community as a "song of Christ," together with its responses. The *Acts of Thomas* quotes a "wedding hymn" (6–7) that speaks allegorically of the sacred marriage of the church with her celestial bridegroom. The same book also recites the famous "Song of the Pearl" (*Act. Thom.* 108–113), a gnostic proclamation in the form of a mythological poem. Both "hymns" are certainly older than the *Acts of Thomas*, a third-century writing. An originally pagan hymn about God and the soul which was used in a superficial Christian revision among the gnostic Naassenes is quoted by Hippolytus. In the *Odes of Solomon* a whole Christian hymn book has been preserved, in which gnostic tendencies are also clearly recognizable. Some scholars date these hymns—a total of forty-two—as early as I CE.

Liturgical materials are quoted abundantly. The *Didache* preserves an instruction for the baptismal liturgy with the quotation of the trinitarian formula (perhaps the oldest use of this formula), cites the Lord's Prayer in a form closely related to Matthew 6, as well as eucharistic prayers and parts of the liturgy for the eucharist (*Didache* 7–10). In his report about the baptismal praxis of the Christians, Justin Martyr quotes an expanded baptismal formula (*Apol.* 1.61.3), and in his description of the eucharist one finds a formulation of the words of institution which is shorter than the versions preserved in the NT (*Apol* 1.66). Numerous doxologies and invocations appear in the aprocryphal acts of the apostles, especially in the *Acts of Thomas* (see sections 27 and 50).

Quotations of parenetic traditions are so frequent that a full account is impossible here. Tables of household duties and catalogues of vices also form an important part of the noncanonical literature (cf. *Did.* 4.9–11; 5.1–2; *1 Clem* 1.3; *Barnabas* 20). The predominance of materials from the Jewish teaching of the two ways is striking. The description of the way of death is usually nothing but a long catalogue of vices. Traditional Christian and Jewish sayings material is otherwise customarily connected with admonitions and prohibitions related to the Decalogue or to various catalogues of virtues and vices (see *Didache* 1–4; *Barnabas* 19; and especially the *Mandates* of the *Shepherd of Hermas*).

FROM JOHN THE BAPTIST TO THE EARLY CHURCH

1. JOHN THE BAPTIST

(a) Life and Message

Our primary sources for the life and ministry of John the Baptist are the canonical Gospels. But the birth narratives preserved there are legends that the Christians inherited from the sect of John the Baptist. Their information may be trustworthy that John, who must have been slightly older than Jesus, came from a priestly family. The presentation of John's ministry (Mark 1:2–8; Matt 3:1–12; Luke 3:1–18; John 1:19ff) contains a number of Christian features, such as the description of John as Elijah, his activity in the desert, and his "social teaching" (Luke 3:10–14). The information that John was active as an eschatological prophet, not only in Judea, but also in other parts of Palestine, is historically reliable. Herod Antipas, who imprisoned and executed John, was the ruler of Galilee and Perea. John's message announced the coming of God's final judgment (the "stronger one" to come after him was originally God; the Christians later interpreted this saying as one referring to Jesus) and offered a unique opportunity for repentance and conversion. Baptism with water was the eschatological seal for those who were converted, while the coming "baptism with fire and spirit" (Matt 3:11) designated the divine judgment from which no one would escape (Matt 3:12). The baptism of John was thus an instrument which reconstituted the elect people of God, who would be spared in God's judgment. John the Baptist was imprisoned by Herod Antipas and was executed during the time of Jesus' ministry; according to Mark 6:17–29, this happened because John had criticized Antipas' marriage with Herodias. The report of Josephus (*Ant.* 18.116–19) confirms this picture of John. Josephus suppresses the eschatological component of John's preaching, however, and says that the reason for his execution was Antipas' fear of a popular insurrection.

(b) The History-of-Religions Background

Unfortunately, it is scarcely possible to add much to the general statement that John the Baptist was an exponent of the movement known as

Jewish apocalypticism, from which a number of messianic preachers and eschatological prophets emerged at his time. Josephus mentions several such prophets: Judas the Galilean (*Ant.* 18.23ff), Theudas (*Ant.* 20.97f), the Egyptian prophet (*Ant.* 20.169f), and others. Josephus also counted John the Baptist and Jesus among these persons, as did "Gamaliel" in Acts 5:36ff. But beyond this statement, a more precise definition of the background in the terms of comparative religion is difficult, not only for John, but also for Jesus. Most of the suggested parallels do not stand the test. John's preaching of baptism is not related to Jewish proselyte baptism, because in that practice (which is attested only much later) there is no eschatological component. The ritual washings of the Essenes at Qumran are rites of a very different sort; these were priestly ceremonies which could be repeated and sought to guarantee cultic purity, although from an eschatological perspective.

It is striking that in John's preaching, insofar as our sources tell us anything, there is no expectation of a messianic figure who will appear on earth, nor any allusion to a political role for the people or the elect. It is, therefore, not possible to understand John—or Jesus!—as a representative of the political messianism which finally led to the Jewish War. John speaks solely about the coming judgment of God—as Jesus speaks solely of the coming rule of God (§8.2c). There is probably only one clear derivation: this kind of religious message made recourse to the pre-exilic prophecy of Israel, which knew no messianic figures nor any messianic role for the people of Israel. If the theme of the renewal of Israel in the wilderness also played a role in this prophecy, the baptism of John can be understood on the basis of the Exodus typology (passage through the sea). Whether John was at all connected with other baptist movements of his time is unknown due to the incomplete nature of our knowledge.

Bibliography to §8.1

C. H. Kraeling, *John the Baptist* (New York: Scribner's, 1951).

Charles H. H. Scobie, *John the Baptist* (Philadelphia: Fortress, 1964).

Roland Schütz, *Johannes der Täufer* (AThANT 50; Zürich: Zwingli, 1967). Comprehensive listing of literature.

Walter Wink, *John the Baptist in the Gospel Tradition* (SNTSMS 7; Cambridge: Cambridge University, 1968).

John A. T. Robinson, "The Baptism of John and the Qumran Community," and "Elijah, John and Jesus," in: idem, *Twelve New Testament Studies* (SBT 34; London: SCM, 1962) 11–27 and 28–52.

Bibliography to §8.1b

W. H. Brownlee, "John the Baptist in the Light of the Ancient Scrolls," in: Krister Stendahl (ed.), *The Scrolls and the New Testament* (New York: Harper, 1956) 33–53.

(c) The Effects of John's Ministry

John the Baptist no doubt created a religious movement that lasted beyond his death. Mark 2:18–19 is proof of this, since it juxtaposes the disciples of John with the disciples of the Pharisees and those of Jesus. The episode reported in Acts 18:1–7 does not itself prove the continuing existence of the baptist sect, however, because it is constructed entirely on the basis of Luke's theory of the mediation of the holy spirit (but cf. John 1:35–37). Nothing more is known about the fate of John's sect, though it is not impossible that the Mandeans, a religious group still in existence today in Mesopotamia (Iraq) which must have had its origin in the country of the Jordan, derives from the sect of John the Baptist; however, this is debated. But most momentous was the influence that John exercised upon Jesus and his disciples. That Jesus was baptized by John—this report should not be doubted—proves that Jesus was a disciple of John. We do not know why Jesus parted from John and his movement; it is not necessary to assume that there was any opposition or hostility involved. If the information in John 3:22–23 is correct (cf. John 4:1), Jesus and John would have been active at the same time (John 4:2 seeks to correct that somewhat). Indeed, Jesus' message as a call for repentance and the proclamation of the coming of God and his rule was analogous to John's message. An important testimony of Jesus about John is preserved in Matt 11:7–11. According to this text, Jesus called John the Baptist "greater than a prophet" and "the greatest among all born by a woman" (i.e., "among all human beings": Matt 11:10 and 11b are later, restrictive additions of the Christian church).

2. JESUS OF NAZARETH

(a) The External Data of his Life

Jesus came from the Galilean town of Nazareth, that is, from the north of Palestine, which also boasted a fair number of Hellenistic cities (his birth in Bethlehem is a later theological interpretive fiction). His family was Jewish, which is clear from the names of his parents (Joseph and Mary) and his brothers (James, Joses, Judas, and Simon). Jesus' father was a building artisan or a carpenter (Matt 13:55), as was perhaps Jesus himself (Mark 6:3; according to Justin *Dial.* 88 he made yokes and ploughs). Jesus' mother tongue was Galilean Aramaic, or perhaps even a Hebrew dialect that had survived in Galilee. Presumably Jesus could also speak Greek, yet many of his sayings that are preserved in Greek derive from an Aramaic original. Aramaic must therefore have been the language of his proclamation. No reliable information about Jesus' education has been preserved. But it must be assumed that Jesus was by no means uneducated; he was certainly able to read and write.

At some point after he had joined the sect of John the Baptist, Jesus parted from them and began his own ministry. The places where he was active are not known with any certainty because most of the specific place names in the gospels were added to the tradition at a later date. But it is striking how strongly Galilee stands out as the place of his activity, and how completely the most important Hellenistic cities (Caesarea, Sepphoris, Tiberias) are missing in the tradition. But the essentially non-Jewish areas in the north (Caesarea Philippi) and east of Galilee (Gadara east of the Galilean Sea) are occasionally mentioned. It can therefore not be concluded from the outset that Jesus never visited pagan country. How often Jesus travelled to Jerusalem must remain uncertain, since according to the Synoptic Gospels it was only once, while according to the Gospel of John he did so several times (at least three times). Jesus certainly did not

Bibliography to §8.2

Rudolf Bultmann, *Jesus and the Word* (New York and London: Scribner's, 1934; reprint, 1958). Since its first publication in German in 1926 this work has been recognized as a critical masterpiece on Jesus.

Günther Bornkamm, *Jesus of Nazareth* (translated form the 3d German ed.: London: Hodder and Stoughton, 1959; New York: Harper, 1960). This remains the outstanding work on Jesus' message and life.

Hans Conzelmann, *Jesus* (Philadelphia: Fortress, 1973).

Martin Dibelius, *Jesus* (Philadelphia: Westminster, 1949).

Morton Smith, *Jesus the Magician* (New York: Harper, 1978). Controversial, well documented with material from the religious world of antiquity.

Robert W. Funk, *Jesus as Precursor* (SBLSS 2; Philadelphia: Fortress, and Missoula: Scholars Press, 1975).

Albert Schweitzer, *The Quest of the Historical Jesus* (New York: Macmillan, 1948). The classic critique of the "life of Jesus" works from the last century.

Bibliography to §8.2: The New Quest for the Historical Jesus

James M. Robinson, *A New Quest of the Historical Jesus* (SBT 25; London: SCM, 1959).

Rudolf Bultmann, *Das Verhältnis der urchristlichen Christusbotschaft zum historischen Jesus* (3d ed.; Heidelberg: Winter, 1962). Bultmann's response to the "New Quest."

Ernst Käsemann, "Blind Alleys in the 'Jesus of History' Controversy," in: idem, *New Testament Questions,* 32–65.

Norman Perrin, *Rediscovering the Teaching of Jesus* (London: SCM, 1967).

Helmut Koester, "The Historical Jesus: Some Comments and Thoughts on Norman Perrin's *Rediscovering the Teachings of Jesus,*" in: Hans Dieter Betz (ed.), *Christology and a Modern Pilgrimage: A Discussion with Norman Perrin* (2d ed.; Missoula: Scholars Press, 1974) 123–36.

Ernst Fuchs, *Studies of the Historical Jesus* (STB 42; London: SCM, 1964).

Leander E. Keck, *A Future for the Historical Jesus* (Nashville: Abingdon, 1971).

Aureus of Augustus
This gold coin shows the wreathed head of Augustus
with the inscription AUGUSTUS DIVI F[ILIUS] =
Augustus Son of the Divinized (Caesar). A coin like this
might have been shown to Jesus when he was asked
whether one should pay taxes to Caesar.

exclude Judea from his ministry. Nothing can be said about the duration of Jesus' ministry. Calculating the years according to the different reports of the Gospels from at least one year to as many as three is not helpful, because all these calculations are based upon exclusively later, redactional materials. Early traditions do not exist. It is certain, however, that Jesus was arrested while in Jerusalem for the Passover, probably in the year 30, and that he was executed. In the context of the passion narratives some reliable data are preserved about these last days of Jesus' life. Contradictions exist solely in determining the exact day of his death and identifying those who were primarily responsible for his conviction.

According to the Johannine passion narrative, Jesus' last meal with his disciples was not a Passover meal, but took place one day before Passover; John 18:28 refers explicitly to the Passover meal which would take place on the evening after Jesus' crucifixion. The dating of the Synoptic Gospels is ambiguous. According to Mark 14:1–2, one would expect that the execution would take place before the festival, and the report of Jesus' last meal does not, in itself, contain any references to Passover (Mark 14:17ff). The impression that this was indeed a Passover meal was created by the legend about the finding of the room for the Passover meal which was added later to the older passion narrative (Mark 14:12–16), and especially by Luke's redaction (Luke 22:15). Since all the Synoptic references to Passover are secondary, the Johannine data are to be preferred, especially since the older version of Mark's passion narrative agrees with John. After all, even someone as ruthless as Pilate would probably hesitate to execute a Jew on a festival day as important to the Jews as Passover.

As for the question of identifying those primarily responsible for Jesus' execution, at least the tendentious development of the tradition is clear: it attempts to shift the major responsibility further and further onto the Jewish authorities. In Matthew, Pilate even washes his hands in innocence (Matt 27:24), and a later tradition claims that Pilate had already come to believe in Jesus in his heart, but that the Jews had forced him nevertheless to go ahead with the execution (cf. the apocryphal *Letter of Pilate*). But there are two reasons which lead to the definitive conclusion that the Roman administration was responsible for the condemnation and execution of Jesus. First, the Jewish authorities did not have the right of capital punishment, which was the exclusive reserve of the Roman prefect. The only two cases which seem to suggest that the Jewish court could sentence a person to death are the stoning of Stephen and the murder of Jesus' brother, James. But the former was a case of mob lynching (§8.3b), while the latter occurred during a vacancy in the prefect's office (§6.6e), which means that these two cases cannot prove the point. The Jewish authorities were indeed not permitted to put anyone to death (John 18:31). They certainly would never be able to do so in the presence of the Roman prefect, who regularly came from Caesarea to Jerusalem on the high holidays in order to prevent any possible unrest.

Second, the reason for Jesus' condemnation was not the blasphemy that is reported in the Synoptic Gospels (Mark 14:64). All the gospels agree in reporting the inscription on the cross: "Jesus of Nazareth, king of the Jews" (Mark 15:26; John 19:19). This inscription says only too clearly that there was a substantive reason for Jesus' condemnation by the Romans. Whatever Jesus' own claims might have been, in the eyes of Pilate he was an actual or potential political agitator—and, to be sure, not the first made short work of by Pilate (§6.6c). One may, of course, assume that the leading circles in Jerusalem were usually interested in cooperating with the governor, as they may have done in the case of the proceedings against Jesus. But Pilate would have exercised his legal authority in any case, however interested he might have been in the cooperation of the Jewish authorities. Executed by the horribly cruel method of crucifixion, Jesus died a painful death.

(b) Jesus as Prophet, Wisdom Teacher, and Exorcist

It is difficult to find categories by which the ministry of Jesus can be correctly described. There is no direct information that would communicate a vivid picture; thus we must resort to inferences from the form and content of the sayings materials. On the other hand, what we learn in this way only partially fits the known categories of the understanding of a religious office or mission at that time. But the following alternatives can be excluded from the outset: messianic or christological titles cannot be used, because not one of these titles (Messiah/Christ, Son of David, Son of Man, Son of God, Lord) is fixed firmly enough in the older tradition to be a reliable witness for Jesus' understanding of himself. Of the non-messianic religious offices, those of the priest, the philosopher, and the apocalyptic seer can also be excluded. The title of "Priest" or "High Priest" is applied to Jesus fairly late, and only in very limited circles of Christianity which do not even attempt to construct a Levitic origin for Jesus (Heb 7:11ff), although the expectation of the messianic priest from Levi played a significant role among the Essenes (§5.2c). Philosophical influences were present in Palestine as early as the Hellenistic period, and they helped to shape rabbinic Judaism. Philo of Alexandria shows how the ideal of the philosopher can be combined with that of the Jewish teacher of wisdom. But Jesus was not a wandering philosopher, nor a school philosopher; the Christian apologists were the first who tried to juxtapose Jesus' teachings with philosophical insights. Nothing indicates that Jesus was an apocalyptic seer or visionary. No visions of the future and no celestial journeys are reported about him (the Revelation of John and the gnostic revelations stepped into this breach). And in any case there is no evidence that Jesus used the written medium of communication, which is extremely important for apocalypticism.

Philosophers and apocalyptic visionaries were religious professionals who were modern and fully in keeping with that time. But the transmitted words of Jesus correspond instead to the outmoded and archaic ideals of the prophet and the wisdom teacher. Jesus' prophetic sayings lack any speculations about the timetable of future events. His interpretation of the law knows neither casuistry nor a spiritualizing leap over the literal meaning. On the contrary, they are unequivocal and indisputable proclamations of the will of God and correspond completely, therefore, to the prophetic Torah of the Old Testament. In his wisdom teaching, Jesus preferred simple wisdom sayings, proverbs, and short metaphors which were very similar to the older proverbial wisdom of Israel. The wisdom speculations of the sapiential literature of Judaism have no parallels in the older stages of the Synoptic tradition. As in the case of John the Baptist (§8.1a), these phenomena are best understood as the result of Jesus' conscious recourse to the prophetic tradition of Israel. But it is remarkable that this recourse does not have the appearance of artificiality; no archaizing tendencies can be discovered. Rather it appears as a genuine and immediate renewal.

At the same time, the typical signs of a prophetic mission are missing from the preachings of Jesus. There is not a single tradition which reports Jesus' call; there are no visions, auditions, or stories of his receiving a commission. Jesus does not introduce his words with the formula "Thus says the Lord." Nothing is said about Jesus attempting to express his prophetic mission in his external behavior or in his dress (as is indeed reported about John the Baptist; see Mark 1:6). Similarly, there is no sign in Jesus' wisdom teaching of an appeal to the antiquity and reliable transmission of his sayings nor, at least in the older traditions, of a special wisdom instruction of the disciples—not to mention the founding of a school; it is obvious that parallels to the office of the rabbi are totally lacking. The visible documentation of Jesus' authority thus remains an enigma. Whoever wants to understand Jesus' authority is referred absolutely to his words and to that which they say and announce.

But one may go even further, for there are good reasons to assume that the numerous exorcisms reported of Jesus in the Synoptic tradition have their ultimate root in Jesus' activity as an exorcist. This, however, should not prompt us to conclude that the special authority of Jesus lay in his extraordinary psychological abilities and in his wonderful supernatural powers. The significance and function of these exorcisms of demons instead becomes clear in Jesus' own statements. It is quite likely that the sayings connected with the driving out of demons contain several genuine words of Jesus (Mark 3:23–25, 26, 27; especially Matt 12:28; see also Luke 10:18). These sayings demonstrate plainly that Jesus himself saw his exorcisms as a visible sign of the victory over Satan and of the beginning of the rule of God. That, of course, clearly implies that Jesus understood himself as the decisive and active mediator of the beginning of God's rule.

(c) The Proclamation of the Rule of God

We have already mentioned that Jesus continued the eschatological proclamation of John the Baptist (§8.1c). Like the Baptist, Jesus knew no other messianic figure except God himself, and he did not announce a special figure who was designed to play a role in the coming events (the sayings which speak about the coming Son of Man are hardly genuine). But in contradistinction to the Baptist, Jesus did not primarily emphasize the coming of God for judgment. His message was the coming of God's "rule" (or "kingship," which translates the Greek *basileia* more accurately than the word "kingdom"). This rule of God begins with Jesus' words; those who hear this word can participate in that rule here and now. The conduct of the disciples is, therefore, not motivated by the threat of the coming judgment, but by the invitation to participate. It is characteristic of the difference between Jesus and John that the disciples of John fast, while the disciples of Jesus cannot find an acceptable motive for such fasting (Mark 2:18ff).

The parables are the central part of Jesus' proclamation of the rule of God. Free of any allegorical implications, each parable states a particular fact of the beginning of God's rule in the present. The parables are not illustrations of Jesus' proclamation; they are statements through which the rule of God becomes a living word spoken to the hearers. Whoever is willing to hear what the rule of God is all about will understand what the parables proclaim. The coming of God's rule is God's sovereign act (Mark 4:26–29). Human action and care do not influence its miraculous arrival in any way (Mark 4:3–8). God's acting contradicts human criteria of both moral (Luke 16:1–8) and religious values (Luke 18:9–14). God's action is also beyond the categories of the just reward (Matt 20:1–16) because love

Bibliography to §8.2c

C. H. Dodd, *The Parables of the Kingdom* (first published, 1935; rev. ed., London: Collins, 1961).

Joachim Jeremias, *The Parables of Jesus* (2d rev. ed.; New York: Scribner's, 1972).

James Breech, *The Silence of Jesus* (Philadelphia: Fortress, 1982).

cannot be limited by human expectations (Luke 15:11–32). In understanding all these parables it is important to detect the particular element
of surprise. This element appears especially in those features that do not
correspond to the normal experiences of life. What sort of farmer does
nothing at all during the entire growing season, or simply lets the weeds
grow with the wheat? Or what kind of dignified father would run down
the street joyfully to meet his misfit son and, moreover, slaughter the fatted
calf for him? Or when did a rich man ever invite the hoodlums from the
streetcorner when his distinguished guests had declined his invitation?
The miracle, mystery, and incalculability of the coming of God's rule—
these are the topics of the parables.

The prophetic-eschatological sayings of Jesus primarily proclaim the
presence of the beginning of God's rule. The blessings are pronounced as
already present to the poor, to those who weep, and to those who are
hungry (the Beatitudes, Matt 5:3ff). What Isaiah had prophesied (Isa
35:5–6; 61:1) is already here (Luke 11:20). It would be utterly futile for
the disciples to look for any signs of the rule of God and its coming in the
future, or even to calculate the times, because the rule of God is already in
their midst (Luke 17:20–21).

It is impossible to ignore the claim that is expressed in this proclamation: if one wants to get involved in the rule of God and its coming, there is
no way to avoid the person of Jesus. If those who see what he is doing are
called blessed (Luke 10:23–24), it is the condition for acceptance not to
take offence at his person (Luke 7:23). To accept Jesus as the one who
makes God present in his word, however, does not imply ascription of a
particular dignity to him, but rather self-conduct in agreement with the
extraordinary claim of his proclamation (Luke 6:46). The coming of
God's rule is exclusively the act of God, but, paradoxically, its reality is
entirely dependent upon the human response to the eschatological demand
of Jesus' proclamation.

(d) The New Human Situation

This requires a discussion of what is called the ethical proclamation of
Jesus, which has been understood in various ways: as eschatological
ethics, as ethics for the interval until God (or the messiah) comes, as an
idealistic formulation of a morality which is obtainable only in theory, as a
criterion for the recognition of human sinfulness from which there is no
escape, and finally as "evangelical" advice for the higher morality of a

Bibliography to §8.2d

Amos N. Wilder, *Eschatology and Ethics in the Teaching of Jesus* (Cambridge, MA:
Harvard University, 1958).

select group. All these interpretations presuppose that the moral demands of Jesus are normally and in principle impossible to fulfill; thus their validity is limited. But nowhere in all the proclamation of Jesus is there any indication of a limitation in his radical ethical demand. No doubt it is "eschatological ethics," but not in the sense of ethics for an interim period. The situation of human beings under the coming of the rule of God is not a provisional one. On the contrary, it is the abiding reality which brings an end to everything that is provisional. It is exactly this that is meant by "eschatological." God demands the whole person in the eschatological situation and no longer permits evasions and excuses. But it is necessary to understand that such a demand is no longer, as in the demand of the law, a criterion which requires obedience and fulfillment. Rather, the ethical preaching of Jesus describes a new situation which one must take possession of, a new horizon of life in which there is no longer room for that which was once valid ("what has been said by those of old"). This is expressed in the antitheses of the Sermon on the Mount (Matt 5:21–48). Jesus' radical demand is not a new law, but a sign of new conduct in the realm of freedom, in which love is both possible and necessary.

It has been observed that the conduct of many characters in Jesus' parables transcends the framework of conventional forms and traditional moral criteria. Thus the signposts for conduct in the face of the coming rule of God also cannot be united organically with traditional ethical rules, but can only be presented in contrasts, in radical intensifications, in hyperbolic and paradoxical formulations, and finally in parables and example stories. The story of the Good Samaritan is characteristic (Luke 10:29–37). The characters are carefully chosen: the priest, the Levite, and precisely a hated Samaritan. The first two pass by and take no notice. Why they do so is not told, and moral judgment is deliberately avoided. But the listener is expected to be surprised, perhaps even irritated. What is also missing is any attempt to expound the moral superiority of the Samaritan. He does nothing more than what was necessary in the situation, and he does it with all his heart and circumspection. To do well what is right, without regard for religious affiliation or political usefulness, is all that is demanded.

This is not situational ethics, however, without fundamental principles and basic insights. Yet these principles are not fundamental moral pronouncements; they are insights into the human situation in the face of the coming of God's rule (not into the human situation in general!). It is the situation in which human beings, as created and as children of God, recognize God as their creator and call upon him as their father. Thus the eschatological prayer for the coming of God's rule, which is transmitted as the "Lord's Prayer," begins by addressing God as "Our Father" (Matt

6:9–13). From the perspective of the situation under God's rule, the law of the Old Testament is criticized insofar as it does not correspond to the original will of the creator. Moses' law about divorce was given solely because of the hardness of the human heart (Mark 10:5), but it had not always been so from the beginning of creation (Mark 10:6). In the same way the antitheses of the Sermon on the Mount reject the provisions of the law which contradict the original will of God. Such regulations are not only a veil behind which one can hide when confronted with the will of God. They also permit human beings to build a pretext of moral security in which they can be certain of their religious rectitude. This is attacked in the words of Jesus which are collected in the speech against the Pharisees (see especially Matt 23:13, 16–19, 23, 25, 29). True justice and mercy are thus shortchanged, because righteousness according to the law permits the establishment of walls between human beings instead of the razing of those walls. God is the father and creator of all people, who lets his rain fall and his sun shine on the just and unjust alike (Matt 5:45), and under whose rule people from all nations will participate in his festive banquet (Matt 8:11–12).

The command to love one's neighbor, which already occupied a central position in Judaism (Lev 19:18), Jesus also emphasized (Mark 12:31). Love of one's neighbor as a rule of social conduct, however, is explicitly rejected (Matt 5:46-47) and replaced by the command to love one's enemies (Matt 5:44). The dignity of human beings which requires such deeds of love cannot be derived from one's membership in a particular social class or religious group (elect people of God), nor from political affiliations or common interest groups.

As for the consequences of such behavior, Jesus did not raise utopian hopes, neither for himself nor for his disciples. His call to discipleship does not promise paradise on earth as a result of fulfilling the commandment of love. Whoever wants to follow him must be prepared to suffer (Mark 8:34). The disciples must be prepared to risk their lives (Mark 8:35). Discipleship means to give up one's security (Luke 9:62; 14:26), which does not exclude intelligent and circumspect behavior. The many wisdom sayings of the Synoptic tradition which derive, at least in part, from the proclamation of Jesus demonstrate that cleverness without falsehood is part of the discipleship of Jesus. But the use of power and force is excluded because the rule of God becomes a reality exactly in the exercise of love and mercy. In his call for discipleship in suffering, that is, in taking seriously the consequences that result from a life in the new human situation, the personal authority of Jesus is paradoxically most strongly expressed. Here he is really the master whom the disciples follow. Here he is truly the example—only later did the church also picture him as the exemplar of the right exercise of virtue. Whether Jesus indeed expected his death, and what kind of effect he anticipated, cannot be known due to a lack of historically reliable information. There is no doubt, however, that the Christians in their later attempts to formulate Jesus' authority with various christological titles were forced to deal specifically with the problem of his suffering and death.

(e) Cross and Resurrection

The proclamation of Jesus did not result directly in the founding of Christian communities. Though Jesus had assembled a circle of disciples, he did not establish a church. From all that can be known of Jesus' ministry, there is no indication that he gave any kind of organization or constitution to the circle of his disciples. In extreme cases, such as in the Pauline churches, Christian communities might completely disregard the traditional words of Jesus and the narratives about his deeds in the development of their constitutional ideology. But even where the churches explicitly referred to Jesus' words and deeds, in the situation after Easter they appeared in a completely new light and in a perspective which cannot be understood as the direct result of Jesus' ministry.

What was the condition of Jesus' followers and disciples when he died on the cross? Though many suggestions have been made in answer to this question, we actually know very little. At best it is possible to say something about the composition of that circle of people. They were men and women of all walks of life, several of a somewhat questionable background. During his lifetime Jesus had been accused of eating with publicans and sinners (the authenticity of Mark 2:16 and Matt 11:19 are, however, not generally accepted). Some names are transmitted: Peter, John and James, the sons of Zebedee, Mary of Magdala. It is not entirely

Bibliography to §8.2e

Paul Winter, *On the Trial of Jesus* (2d ed. rev. T. A. Burkill and Geza Vermes; SJ 1; Berlin: De Gruyter, 1974).

François Bovon, *Les derniers jours de Jésus* (Neuchâtel: Delachaux et Niestlé, 1974).

Hans von Campenhausen, "The Events of Easter and the Empty Tomb," in: idem, *Tradition*, 42–89.

Ulrich Wilckens, *Resurrection: Biblical Testimony to the Resurrection: An Historical Examination and Explanation* (Edinburgh: Saint Andrew, 1977; Atlanta: John Knox, 1978).

Hans Grass, *Ostergeschehen und Osterberichte* (2d ed.; Göttingen: Vandenhoeck & Ruprecht, 1962).

R. H. Fuller, *The Formation of the Resurrection Narratives* (2d ed.; Philadelphia: Fortress, 1980).

Karl Martin Fischer, *Das Ostergeschehen* (AVTRW 71; 2d ed.; Berlin: Evangelische Verlagsanstalt, 1980).

certain whether Jesus himself had already selected a special circle of twelve disciples (as the representatives of the twelve tribes of Israel?). Many of them were Galileans.

Jesus had celebrated a last meal with his disciples before his arrest, but what was said during that meal eludes our knowledge. Everything that the relevant texts report about it derives from the interests of the Christian cult and has been formulated according to later interpretations of Jesus' death on the cross. It may be conjectured that this last meal was celebrated under an eschatological perspective ("messianic banquet" would be the correct term, if one could assume that the expectation of the messiah was included), i.e., in the anticipation of the future meal in the reign of God (see also Mark 14:25). But whether Jesus expected a visible demonstration of God's rule in the near future as a result of his path to the cross, whether some of the disciples (especially Judas?) tried to force this event, whether Jesus himself thought that the hour for a decisive action had come (is the entry into Jerusalem at all a historical event?)—all these are questions which merely invite speculation. Neither the historian nor the theologian should try to answer these questions.

All that is certain is Jesus' death on the cross, for which the Roman authorities bear full responsibility. We are on much firmer ground with respect to the appearances of the risen Jesus and their effect. It is not our concern here to determine whether these appearances were "objective" or "subjective" experiences, or whether they can be explained in terms of psychology or the phenomenology of religion. As far as the latter is concerned, there is at least no doubt that whatever was experienced was not without relationship to a previous direct or indirect knowledge of or about Jesus. As for the meaning and content of the appearances, we are referred to the testimonies of the witnesses. Paradoxically, our most immediate testimony comes from a man who had not known Jesus personally: Paul. However, that Jesus also appeared to others (Peter, Mary Magdalene, James) cannot very well be questioned.

The content and effect of the appearances were decisive. In the case of Paul, it is evident that this was a vision of a call, and the reports of the canonical Gospels also include this element. It is presupposed, of course, that the Jesus of Nazareth who died on the cross is now alive. But this is not a fact of any significance for Jesus and his fate. Nor is the statement that he now lives identical with a clear and unanimous explanation of the significance of Jesus' mission. The multiplicity of christological titles proves the opposite. The resurrection and the appearances of Jesus are best explained as a catalyst which prompted reactions that resulted in the missionary activity and founding of the churches, but also in the crystallization of the tradition about Jesus and his ministry. But most of all, the

Jesus Christ
From the Apse Mosaic of Osios David in Thessaloniki. One of the oldest Christian mosaics (perhaps V c.e.), it presents Christ standing in the sun and leaning against the rainbow (Genesis 9), surrounded by the four "creatures" of the divine throne (Revelation 4; the one with the face of a man is visible in the upper left corner).

resurrection changed sorrow and grief, or even hate and rejection, into joy, creativity, and faith. Though the resurrection revealed nothing new, it nonetheless made everything new for the first Christian believers.

3. THE EARLIEST CHRISTIAN COMMUNITIES

(a) The Early Community in Jerusalem

The reports in the first chapters of the Acts of the Apostles about the early church in Jerusalem are dominated by legendary and idealizing tendencies (§7.3c). But from direct reports in the Pauline letters and indirect reports in the Synoptic tradition there is enough information to reconstruct an approximate picture. Much must remain uncertain, especially since it seems that in the first years after Jesus' death the community

Bibliography to §8.3

Maurice Goguel, *The Birth of Christianity* (London: Allen and Unwin, 1953).

Hans Conzelmann, *History of Primitive Christianity* (Nashville: Abingdon, 1973) 29–77.

Martin Hengel, *Acts and the History of Earliest Christianity* (London: SCM; Philadelphia: Fortress, 1980).

Robin Scroggs, "The Earliest Hellenistic Christianity," in: Neusner, *Religions in Antiquity*, 176–206.

Nock, "Early Christianity and its Hellenistic Background," in: idem, *Essays*, 1. 49–133.

Bibliography to §8.3: On the Theology of the Earliest Churches

Bultmann, *Theology*, 1. 33–183.

Conzelmann, *Outline*, 29–93.

Oscar Cullmann, *The Earliest Christian Confessions* (London: Lutterworth, 1949).

C. H. Dodd, *The Apostolic Preaching and its Development* (New York: Harper & Row, 1951).

Werner Kramer, *Christ, Lord, Son of God* (SBT 50; London: SCM, 1966).

Ferdinand Hahn, *The Titles of Christ in Christology* (London: Lutterworth, 1969).

Philipp Vielhauer, "Jesus und der Menschensohn," and "Ein Weg zur neutestamentlichen Christologie?" in: idem, *Aufsätze zum Neuen Testament* (ThBü 31; München: Kaiser, 1965) 92–140 and 141–98.

Siegfried Schulz, "Maranatha und Kyrios Jesus," *ZNW* 53 (1962) 125–44.

Ernst Käsemann, "The Beginnings of Christian Theology," and "On the Subject of Primitive Christian Apocalyptic," in: idem, *New Testament Questions*, 82–107 and 108–37.

Hans Conzelmann, "Present and Future in the Synoptic Tradition," *JTC* 5 (1968) 26–44.

Erich Grässer, *Das Problem der Parusieverzögerung in den synoptischen Evangelien und in der Apostelgeschichte* (BZNW 22; 3d ed.; Berlin: De Gruyter, 1977).

Bibliography to §8.3a

Foakes Jackson and Lake, *Beginnings*, 1. 265–418.

Haenchen, *Acts*, 166–75, 190–96.

Robinson and Koester, *Trajectories*, 119–26, 211–16.

in Jerusalem did not possess a unified theology or a firm organization. The Jewish-Christian church of Jerusalem, as something that could be clearly distinguished from the Pauline gentile Christian communities, was created by James only during the subsequent decades.

At the time of Paul's missionary activities in Arabia and Antioch (ca. 35–50 CE; see §9.1c) the leaders of the community in Jerusalem, known as the "pillars" (Gal 2:9), were Peter (whom Paul usually calls Cephas), John, and James. Peter, however, must have left Jerusalem soon after the Apostolic Council (§9.1d), and John seems to have taken up some missionary work elsewhere, because the churches which later claimed his name as an authority had no direct relationship with Jerusalem (§10.3a). When Paul returned to Jerusalem in the middle or at the end of the 50's of I CE, Jesus' brother James was alone the uncontested leader of the church. He suffered martyrdom in the year 62. Shortly thereafter, immediately before the beginning of the Jewish War (§6.6e), the Jerusalem community emigrated, probably to Pella on the Jordan.

Many factors indicate that at first the Christians in Jerusalem understood themselves as a special group within the Jewish religious community. They participated in the temple cult, practiced circumcision, and observed the Jewish dietary laws. They were radically different, however, from other Jews in Jerusalem because of their enthusiastic consciousness of the possession of the spirit; this was the spirit of God which was to be poured out at the end of times, which brought the gift of tongues and of prophecy, worked miracles, and granted assurance to the members of the community that they belonged to God's elect people. In its original form, the story of Pentecost (Acts 2:1ff) derives from the community in Jerusalem and is the most important witness for its consciousness of possessing the spirit. The overwhelming experience of the spirit's being poured out and its interpretation as an eschatological event must have persuaded these first Christians to organize themselves through preliminary structures ("preliminary" insofar as they expected the visible coming of God's rule in the near future) which corresponded to this eschatological experience. This is evident in several pieces of information. The disciples who had fled from Jerusalem returned and established the circle of the "Twelve." These Twelve were neither apostles nor community leaders, but the representatives of the twelve tribes of eschatological Israel. (Later, in the Book of Acts, they became the "Twelve Apostles" and were seen as a kind of chief presbytery of the whole church.) The practice of eschatological baptism, known from John the Baptist—Jesus himself apparently did not baptize his followers—was soon resumed. Through baptism "in the name of Jesus" new members were sealed as belonging to the coming Lord and received the spirit as a pledge. The common meals which Jesus

had celebrated with his followers during his lifetime were regularly celebrated as eschatological meals of the community. In these meals the community reassured itself of the coming communion with Jesus when he
would return in glory. This meal, which was of course a full regular meal,
therefore became a messianic banquet, quite analogous to the meals of the
Essenes. Of the various elements that are preserved in the tradition of the
Lord's Supper, the following may derive from the early community in
Jerusalem: the eschatological saying from the report of the institution
(Mark 14:25); prayers based on Jewish meal prayers, with an eschato-
logical interpretation, probably much like the eucharistic prayers of
Didache 9–10 (§10.1c). While taking wine and bread (in this sequence!)
one looked forward to the assembly of the elect people in the kingdom of
God. The wine is the symbol of the messiah, the holy vine of David
(*Didache* 9); the bread symbolizes the community of all those who parti-
cipate (*Didache* 9; see also 1 Cor 10:16–17). The element of eschatological
jubilation and festive joy (Acts 2:46) may also derive from the Jerusalem
community, and the liturgical call "Lord, come!" (still transmitted in
Aramaic in Paul, 1 Cor 16:22, and in *Did.* 10.6; cf. Rev 22:20).

The oldest christological titles also derive from the Jerusalem community. With the title "Lord," and probably also the title "Messiah/Christ,"
Jesus is designated as the coming redeemer. In its Aramaic form *Maran,*
the title "Lord" is firmly established in the liturgy of the common meal
and there obviously designated the coming redeemer. "Messiah" must
have been used very early, because, in its Greek translation, *Christos*
became a proper name almost everywhere in the oldest early Christian
writings which are preserved. The title is also found in some very old
creedal formulations (e.g., 1 Cor 15:3; cf. 1 Cor 5:7 and elsewhere). These
particular formulas, insofar as they are concerned with an understanding
of Jesus' death, probably originated in the bilingual community of Antioch, though the church in Jerusalem was also bilingual. The title "Son of
David" also comes from the earliest period (see the old formulas in Rom
1:3f; 2 Tim 2:8; and also "for the holy vine of your servant David" and
"Hosannah to the God of David" in the eucharistic prayers of the
Didache).

On the other hand, it is doubtful whether the expectation of Jesus as the
coming "Son of Man" can be ascribed to the oldest community in Jerusalem, although this title did originate in the Aramaic-speaking church
and is in evidence in the older stages of the *Synoptic Sayings Source*
(§10.1a). The expectation of the Son of Man is not congruent with the
hope in Jesus' coming as Lord or Messiah, because the Son of Man was
seen originally as a figure of the divine court in heaven, which is pecul-
iarly distinguished from Jesus, so that Son of Man sayings ascribed to

Jesus sometimes speak about this Son of Man in the third person (Luke 17:24; Mark 8:38). These sayings are pronouncements of Christian prophets which claimed a relationship between Jesus and the heavenly Son of Man, but did not simply identify the two. If the expectation of Jesus as the Messiah belongs to the Jerusalem church, the expectation of the Son of Man must have originated in other Aramaic-speaking churches in Palestine or Syria. The words about the suffering, death, and resurrection of the Son of Man are very different; they were created by Mark as predictions of Jesus' passion (Mark 8:31; 9:31; 10:33; see §10.2b).

It is not possible to ascertain whether the theological interpretation of the death of Jesus had its beginning in the Jerusalem community. Paul, in any case, inherited from the church in Antioch a number of formulations which already presupposed such a development (§8.3c). In the attempts to understand Jesus' death, several Jewish conceptions of the cultic sacrifice were operative, including the concept of Jesus' death as a sacrifice of expiation. This lies at the root of the frequent formula "for us," which was later also connected with the Lord's Supper. Side by side with that one finds the understanding of Jesus' death as the sacrifice of the covenant (1 Cor 11:25; Heb 13:20). Jesus' death was also interpreted as a Passover sacrifice (1 Cor 5:7). If these christological developments, as also the formation of the kerygma of Jesus' death and resurrection, are ascribed to the Antiochian church, this does not mean that the Jerusalem church knew nothing about it. On the contrary, in view of the many connections between Jerusalem and Antioch, and probably also with other communities in Palestine, one would expect that the theological exchange was rather lively. Moreover, during the first two decades after the death of Jesus, until about the time of the Apostolic Council, the Christian community in Jerusalem must have included various groups and subgroups. Tensions and controversies were not lacking, which is clear from the letters of Paul and from the traditions used in the Acts of the Apostles.

(b) The Hellenists and Stephen

Jerusalem was a metropolis of worldwide significance, largely because of the Jewish dispersion, for which that city was still the true center of the

Bibliography to §8.3b

Haenchen, *Acts,* 259–308.

Henry J. Cadbury, "The Hellenists," in: Foakes Jackson and Lake, *Beginnings,* 5. 59–74.

Marcel Simon, *St. Stephen and the Hellenists in the Primitive Church* (The Haskell Lectures; London/New York/Toronto: Longmans, Green, 1958).

Martin Hengel, "Zwischen Jesus und Paulus: Die 'Hellenisten', die 'Sieben' und Stephanus," *ZThK* 72 (1975) 151–206.

cult during the early imperial period. But most Jews living in the diaspora had become assimilated to the language and culture of their various places of residence outside of Palestine, where many of them had lived for centuries (§5.1e). This had also affected Jerusalem itself, where the Greek language was as much at home among the Jews as Aramaic. "Hellenists," that is, Greek-speaking Jews, were not at all unusual in Jerusalem. The first known conflict in the Christian community of Jerusalem resulted from the differences between the adherents of Jesus, who had come mostly from Galilee, and "Hellenists" who had now become Christians. Luke has preserved older traditions about this conflict in Acts 6:1–8:3, though he has thoroughly revised them; contradictions between the older traditions and Luke's harmonizing tendencies can still be detected. The "Twelve" appear as the representatives of the whole Christian community, though they may have been the leaders of only the Aramaic-speaking Christians. Other community leaders, who perhaps claimed the title *diakonos,* are contrasted with them. Luke, however, never uses this title, but introduces them as people who were chosen for the daily "service" (*diakonia*) at the tables. The title "deacon" was used for the office of the preacher and missionary, as is evident from 2 Cor 3:6 and 11:23. Why Hellenists should have been chosen for table service is not obvious in any case. Acts 6:5 seems rather to be a traditional list of inspired Hellenist missionaries who were active among the Greek-speaking Jews of Jerusalem. Indeed, such activity by one of these Hellenists, namely Stephen, is reported immediately afterwards.

The speech of Stephen in Acts 7:2–53 is a Lukan composition and cannot be used for the reconstruction of Stephen's views or those of his Hellenist associates. But there is a chance that the tradition used by Luke gave the reason for the eruption of the persecution which led to Stephen's martyrdom. Acts 6:11 has preserved this traditional information: Stephen is accused of criticism of Moses, that is, of the law, and of blasphemy (in contrast, the Lukan verses in Acts 6:13–14 and Stephen's speech give criticism of the temple as the reason for the accusation). If the information in Acts 6:11 is reliable, the controversy centers on the question of whether the law of Moses should continue to be valid for the Christians—a question which is not entirely unmotivated in view of the proclamation of Jesus (Matt 5:3ff). This understanding of the traditional material in Acts is confirmed by the events after the persecution. The beginnings of a Christianity which is free from the obligations of the law thus belong in the Jerusalem community itself, though it was impossible for this type of Christianity to make much headway in that city. According to Luke's presentation, Stephen was brought before the Jewish court for regular proceedings against him, and even is given the opportunity to preach a long missionary sermon. What is still preserved from Luke's source, however, gives the impression instead that Stephen was lynched, not stoned in the regular fashion (Acts 7:54, 57, 58a, 59). The Jewish authorities did not possess the right of capital punishment anyway. The suggestion that Saul/Paul participated in this persecution, as Luke reports (Acts 7:58b), must be disputed on good grounds because Paul freely admits that he persecuted the Christians, but states that he was unknown to the Christian community in Judea before his conversion and even for some years afterward (Gal 1:22). But it seems to be correct that this persecution still took place before Paul's conversion, since the latter presupposes the existence of Christian churches in Damascus and Antioch—churches which were probably founded by the Hellenists once they left Jerusalem as a result of Stephen's persecution.

Nothing is said about the role of Peter, John, and James, or of the "Twelve" in the context of the persecution of Stephen. It seems that they were not affected by it. The information that is preserved says only that the Hellenists were expelled from Jerusalem, and that the persecution thus led to the founding of new Christian communities elsewhere. Philip went to Samaria (Acts 8:1ff), others to Antioch, where they were later joined by Barnabas (Acts 11:19ff), a Jew from the diaspora of Cyprus who had earlier been a member of the Jerusalem church (Acts 4:36).

c) The Christian Church of Antioch

Freedom from the law had already been demanded by the Hellenistic Jewish Christians in Jerusalem; but a city that was not under the control of the Jewish temple and its authorities, like Antioch, a major metropolis of the east, would offer a much better opportunity for the building of a Christian church that was no longer subject to the law of Moses. This in turn would open the way for a mission to the gentiles. For the later gentile Christian churches founded by the missionary activity of Barnabas, Paul, and others, Antioch and its church became the pioneer and headquarters. An older tradition about Antioch is preserved in Acts 11:19ff, and in Acts 13:1f Luke reports a list of the names of its prophets and teachers. Paul noted that he had worked as a missionary from Antioch in Syria and Cilicia for more than a decade (Gal 1:21). Since the Apostolic Council must be dated some fourteen or even sixteen to seventeen years after the conversion of Paul (the result of a calculation based on the dates of Gala-

Bibliography to §8.3c
Haenchen, *Acts*, 364–72.
Robinson and Koester, *Trajectories*, 219–29.
Eduard Schweizer, *Lordship and Discipleship* (SBT 28; London: SCM, 1960; Naperville: Allenson, 1960).

tians 1 and 2; see §9.1b, c), and since the church in Antioch must have been founded before Paul's conversion, the latest year for the founding of this church must be 35 CE, if we date the Apostolic Council in 49 or 50. Thus only a few years lie between the death of Jesus and the beginning of the gentile mission freed from the law.

For the reconstruction of the teaching and practice of the Antiochian church the Pauline letters are eminently significant, because it can be assumed that many of the traditions quoted and used by Paul are derived from this congregation, in which he had worked for so many years. If we speak about the kerygma of the Hellenistic church before Paul, we are really talking about Antioch. The center of this kerygma was the proclamation of the crucified Jesus whom God has raised from the dead. Luke's report in Acts 11:26, that the disciples called themselves "Christians" for the first time in Antioch, is certainly anachronistic because Paul did not yet know this term. But the designation of the Christian message as "gospel" (*euaggelion*) did most certainly originate in Antioch, not in Jerusalem or in the Aramaic-speaking churches, since it comes from the Greek world and language, where its general meaning is "message" or "news." There was, however, no technical usage outside of the Christian churches. The term occurs occasionally in emperor inscriptions (for the first time in 9 BCE in Priene: "The birthday of the god was the beginning of the *euaggelia* through him"), but even there various kinds of messages could be meant. Though it is possible that the Christians developed their technical use of the term in analogy or in contrast to the emperor cult, very soon they also related the term to the occurrence of the corresponding verb "to proclaim" (*euaggelizesthai*) in the Greek text of Deutero-Isaiah (see the quotation of Isa 52:7 in Rom 10:15).

The development of the oldest gospel formulas (Paul cites one such formula as "gospel" in 1 Cor 15:1ff) falls into the early years of the church in Antioch, because Paul received this "gospel" as a tradition. The gospel formulas no longer emphasize the coming of Jesus in the future, but proclaim the past event of cross and resurrection as the turning-point of the ages. Accordingly the Lord's supper is also consistently interpreted as a representation of this eschatological event of salvation. The participation in the "one bread" not only directs one's view into the future to the coming assembly of all believers in God's kingdom, but it also becomes the participation in the one body of the crucified Lord in the present. Similarly, the cup becomes the sign of one's present sharing in the new covenant which has been founded through the shedding of Jesus' blood. The formation of the "words of institution" as they are quoted in 1 Cor 11:24–25 is based upon this understanding of the eucharist. Further reflections about the death of Jesus and its significance also derive from Antioch; traditions such as those which Paul quotes in Rom 3:25f; 4:25; and Gal 1:4 are clear attestations.

As for the organization of the Antiochian church, Acts 13:1–2 tells us that there were prophets and teachers. No doubt the office of apostle was also known (in the Syrian church order of *Didache* 11–13 apostles, prophets, and teachers occur side by side). As early as his Antiochian activity Paul understood his own office as that of an apostle. The church in Antioch was clearly not dependent upon Jerusalem. It took more than a decade before Paul and Barnabas went to Jerusalem to work out an agreement on the controversial question of the law (§9.1d). The primary activity of this church, composed of both Jews and gentiles, was the gentile mission, not only in Antioch but also in other cities of Syria and Cilicia. Although Acts 13–14 is an idealized presentation of a missionary journey by Barnabas and Paul, it still demonstrates the character of the missionary efforts of this church. It is also typical that the missionary work was organized in such a fashion that it used a political and economic metropolis as administrative headquarters. Paul later followed the same pattern for his mission in Asia Minor and Greece.

(d) Other Christian Communities in East and West

At the time of the founding of the Christian community in Antioch, a number of other Christian churches must have come into existence elsewhere. Some of this missionary activity was probably the work of the Hellenists who had been driven out of Jerusalem, as in the case of Samaria (Acts 8:5). If the report Acts 9:32–43 rests on older tradition, it demonstrates that Peter worked as a missionary among Jews of other Palestinian cities, in this particular case in Joppa (today a part of Tel Aviv). But the report of the beginning of the gentile mission by Peter in Caesarea (Acts 10) is entirely legendary. Mark 16:7 could be understood as an indication that there were congregations in Galilee that claimed to be founded by appearances of the risen Lord. Luke 6:17 speaks of people who came to Jesus from the *Paralios*, i.e., the sea coast with its cities Tyre and Sidon: does this prove the existence of congregations in that area that derived the tradition of their founding from Jesus' own ministry? A church existed in Damascus before the conversion of Paul (Acts 9:1ff; cf. 2 Cor 11:32), and Paul began his missionary work in Arabia from that city (Gal 1:17).

The time of the expansion of the Christian mission beyond the areas of Syria and Palestine can be determined with certainty only for the Pauline mission and its competitors in Asia Minor, Macedonia, and Greece: the 50's. Although we know nothing about the founding of the Roman church, it existed before that date (see Paul's Letter to the Romans, which presupposes the presence of an influential Christian congregation in Rome). Most probably this church was founded by diaspora Jews who had become Christians elsewhere and then settled in Rome or travelled to that city. Diaspora Judaism had worldwide connections, which probably also served as the vehicle for the founding of churches in the Cyrenaica, on Cyprus (Acts 11:20 mentions preachers who had come from there), and in Alexandria, although our only direct information about these churches comes from a later period. Nor is there any direct information about the beginnings of Christianity in eastern Syria. But later accounts and the tradition which they use permit the hypothesis that Christian missionaries went to the east at a very early date. The writings which were later composed in eastern Syria (the *Gospel of Thomas*, the *Odes of Solomon*, as well as the *Synoptic Sayings Source*, which was written in Palestine or Syria) show no dependence upon the Antiochian-Pauline tradition. The circles that later produced the Gospel of John are equally at home in the Syrian area (§10.3a) but not dependent upon Antioch in their early period.

However fragmentary the total picture may be, it is nevertheless obvious that the mission and expansion of Christianity in the first years and decades after the death of Jesus was a phenomenon that utterly lacked unity. On the contrary, great variety resulted from these early missions. The Pauline mission is the only one about which we possess any direct information, however; although it must have been only a small segment of the early expansion, it became very important and had momentous consequences. In the following presentation I also attempt to trace the developments of those churches and groups that were initially independent of the Pauline mission.

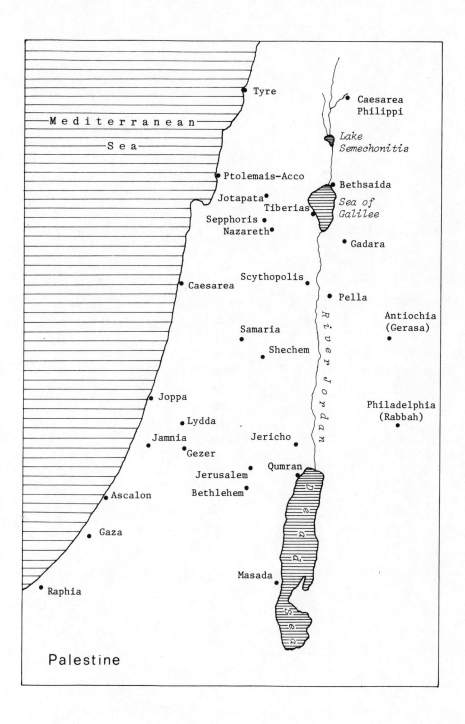

Tyre

Caesarea
Philippi

Mediterranean

Sea

*Lake
Semechonitis*

Ptolemais-Acco

Jotapata

Tiberias

Bethsaida

*Sea of
Galilee*

Sepphoris

Nazareth

Gadara

Scythopolis

Caesarea

Pella

Samaria

Shechem

River Jordan

Antiochia
(Gerasa)

Joppa

Lydda

Jamnia

Gezer

Jericho

Philadelphia
(Rabbah)

Qumran

Jerusalem

Bethlehem

Dead Sea

Ascalon

Gaza

Masada

Raphia

Palestine

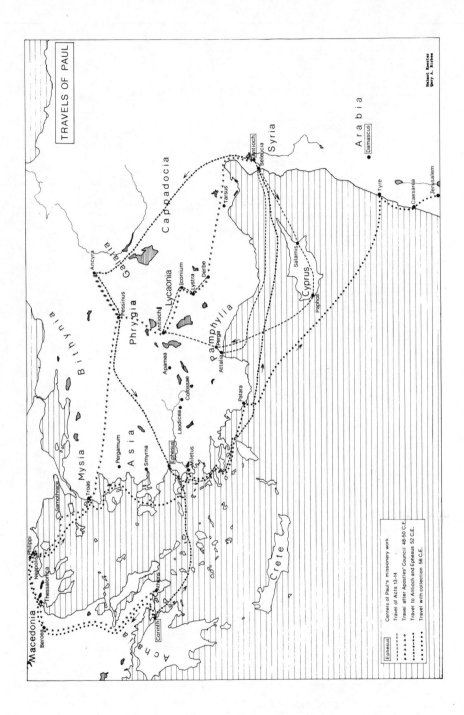

TRAVELS OF PAUL

Helmut Koester
Gary A. Bishee

Ephesus
- - - - - - - Centers of Paul's missionary work
▸ ▸ ▸ ▸ ▸ ▸ Travel of Acts 13-14
▸ ▸ ▸ ▸ ▸ ▸ Travel after Apostles' Council 48-50 C.E.
• • • • • • • Travel to Antioch and Ephesus 52 C.E.
•••••••• Travel with collection 56 C.E.

Macedonia
Beroea
Thessalonica
Philippi
Neapolis
Samothrace
Troas
Mysia
Bithynia
Pergamum
Asia
Smyrna
Ephesus
Miletus
Achaia
Corinth
Athens
Crete
Laodicea
Colossae
Apamea
Antioch
Phrygia
Lycaonia
Iconium
Lystra
Derbe
Pessinus
Ancyra
Galatia
Cappadocia
Tarsus
Patara
Pamphylia
Attalia
Perga
Cyprus
Salamis
Paphos
Seleucia
Antioch
Syria
Tyre
Caesarea
Jerusalem
Damascus
Arabia

PAUL

1. Life and Ministry to the Apostolic Council

(a) Origin and Education

In several of his letters, each time provoked by his opponents, Paul refers to his origin and life before his "conversion," most extensively in Phil 3:5–6 (see also 2 Cor 11:22; Rom 11:1; Gal 1:14; 2:15). Through such information we learn that Paul came from a Jewish family from the tribe of Benjamin, that he was circumcised on the eighth day, received a strict Jewish education, and became a member of the sect of the Pharisees. All this, no doubt, included a formal education in the interpretation of the law and of the Old Testament in general. It is also evident from his letters that Paul was a Hellenistic Jew who grew up in an environment in which Greek was the everyday language. The Pauline letters furthermore reveal such a mastery of Greek as well as knowledge of popular philosophical views and rhetorical skills that it must be assumed that Paul had received formal education in Greek schools, specifically in the tradition of the Cynic-Stoic diatribe which was popular at that time (§4.2a).

These pieces of information and conclusions from the letters are valuable but scant. It is understandable that more information has therefore customarily been sought from the Acts of the Apostles. However, this can only be done with caution. That Paul's Jewish name was "Saul" as reported in Acts 7:58; 8:1 and elsewhere is not unlikely, since diaspora Jews often chose a Greek or Roman name that sounded similar to their Jewish name. But in his letters Paul always uses his Roman name "Paulus." If Paul really had a Jewish name, the changing of his name should not be related to his "conversion." Acts also claims, which is quite conceivable, that Paul came from the Cilician city of Tarsus, an important trade center on the thoroughfare from Syria to Anatolia which must have had a high level of cultural life (Acts 9:11; 21:39; 22:3). Paul was a craftsman, however, and must have settled somewhere to pursue his trade; one may ask why, if he really came from Tarsus, he was in Damascus at the time of his conversion, and why he remained there afterwards for several years. Many typical features of his theology, such as his pronounced apocalyptic expectations, are certainly part of his Jewish inheritance and would fit much better into a milieu that was less strongly "Greek" than Tarsus.

The claim that Paul had inherited Roman citizenship from his father (Acts 22:25–29) is scarcely credible because as a Roman citizen Paul would have had no difficulty in escaping from the various punishments that he received according to his own statements (2 Cor 11:24f)—and the

Bibliography to §9

Günther Bornkamm, *Paul* (New York: Harper, 1971). The best comprehensive account of Paul's career and thought.

Wayne A. Meeks, *The Writings of St. Paul* (New York: Norton, 1972). An excellent introduction to the reading of Paul's letters.

Ferdinand Christian Baur, *Paul the Apostle of Jesus Christ* (2 vols.; Theological Translation Fund; London: Williams and Norgate, 1873). First published 1866–67; set the pattern for the debate in modern scholarship.

Rudolf Bultmann, "Paul," in: idem, *Existence and Faith,* 111–46 (first published in *RGG* IV, 2d ed., 1019–45).

Arthur Darby Nock, *St. Paul* (first published, 1938; New York: Harper, 1963).

A. Descamps, *Littérature et théologie pauliniennes* (RechBib 5; Bruges: Desclée de Brower, 1960).

Beda Rigaux, *The Letters of St. Paul* (Chicago: Franciscan Herald, 1968).

Samuel Sandmel, *The Genius of Paul: A Study in History* (2d ed.; New York: Schocken, 1970).

Ulrich Luck and Karl Heinrich Rengstorf (eds.), *Das Paulusbild in der neueren Forschung* (WdF 24; 2d ed.; Darmstadt: Wissenschaftliche Buchgesellschaft, 1969).

Bibliography to §9: Theology of Paul

Bultmann, *Theology,* 1. 185–352. Most significant interpretation of Paul's theology.

Conzelmann, *Outline,* 155–286.

Johannes Munck, *Paul and the Salvation of Mankind* (London: SCM, 1959).

Ernst Käsemann, *Perspectives on Paul* (London: SCM, and Philadelphia: Fortress, 1971). Challenging investigation of the meaning of Paul's theology for today.

Bibliography to §9: The History-of-Religions Question

Albert Schweitzer, *The Mysticism of Paul the Apostle* (New York: Macmillan, 1931). A classic in the history-of-religions approach to Paul.

Erwin R. Goodenough with A. Thomas Kraabel, "Paul and the Hellenization of Christianity," in: Neusner, *Religions in Antiquity,* 23–70.

Egon Brandenburger, *Fleisch und Geist: Paulus und die dualistische Weisheit* (WMANT 29; Neukirchen-Vluyn: Neukirchener Verlag, 1968).

Hans-Joachim Schoeps, *Paul: The Theology of the Apostle in the Light of Jewish Religious History* (Philadelphia: Westminster, 1961; reprint, 1979).

E. P. Sanders, *Paul and Palestinian Judaism: A Comparison of Patterns of Religion* (Philadelphia: Fortress, 1977).

W. D. Davies, *Paul and Rabbinic Judaism: Some Rabbinic Elements in Pauline Theology* (4th ed.; Philadelphia: Fortress, 1980).

Bibliography to §9.1

John Knox, *Chapters in a Life of Paul* (Nashville: Abingdon, n.d.).

Dieter Georgi, *Die Geschichte der Kollekte des Paulus für Jerusalem* (ThF 38; Hamburg-Bergstedt: Reich/Theologischer Verlag, 1965) 13–30 and 91–96.

Paul of Acts indeed does so (Acts 22:25ff). Paul's appeal to the emperor in his trial before Festus does not prove his Roman citizenship since every free citizen of the empire had the right to such an appeal. It should also be remembered that in the first decades of the empire Roman citizenship was much less frequently awarded than in later centuries. Finally, Acts indicates that Paul grew up in Jerusalem and studied there with the famous rabbi Gamaliel I (Acts 22:3). Since the first piece of information is not trustworthy, we can have little confidence regarding the second. One can, of course, not completely exclude the possibility that Paul was in Jerusalem before his conversion (Gal 1:22 does not necessarily exclude this), but it must remain an open question how and where Paul could have received a formal Pharisaic education outside of Jerusalem.

Thus, Acts actually contributes very little to our knowledge of Paul's origin and education. The information from the letters clearly presents a man who was a Jew from the diaspora and had received a good Greek education. But he was also a Pharisee inspired by a deep religious and moral earnestness, for whom strict observance of the law and willingness to stand up for the preservation and defense of the tradition of the fathers was a matter of course.

(b) Paul's Call

Paul's zeal for the Jewish law made him a persecutor of the Christians. He says this repeatedly (Gal 1:13, 23; 1 Cor 15:9; Phil 3:6), but we can only guess how this persecution took place. Once more the account in Acts says more than is credible. Paul's presence at the stoning of Stephen (Acts 7:58) is excluded through Gal 1:22. Acts 8:3 is unhistorical for the same reason, and consequently also Acts 26:10f. Paul's persecution of the Christians must refer to situations outside of Jerusalem, most likely even outside of Palestine. It is also unthinkable that Paul, equipped with appropriate letters from the high priest, should have taken Christians from places outside of Palestine to Jerusalem for punishment. Neither the high priest nor the Sanhedrin in Jerusalem ever had such powers of jurisdiction. Thus it must be assumed that Paul persecuted the Christians wherever he actually lived, and that this persecution followed the regular process in the local synagogues: members of the synagogue who had become Christians, and perhaps even made propaganda for the Christian message within the community, were subjected to normal synagogue pun-

Bibliography to §9.1b

Haenchen, *Acts,* 318–36.

Ulrich Wilckens, "Die Bekehrung des Paulus als religionsgeschichtliches Problem," *ZThK* 56 (1959) 273–93; reprinted in: idem, *Rechtfertigung als Freiheit* (Neukirchen-Vluyn: Neukirchener Verlag, 1974).

ishments and excluded from its religious community. Such an action might have social and economic consequences; Christians could also be maligned before the local court or the Roman authorities.

Paul experienced the vision of his call near Damascus (Acts 9:3ff; confirmed by Gal 1:17; 2 Cor 11:32f). Since it is difficult to imagine that Paul's primary profession was that of an itinerant persecutor of Christians, he must have been a resident of Damascus at that time (whether or not Damascus was also his home city). One must assume that it was in Damascus that he became acquainted with the Christian message, specifically with the Hellenists' version of a Christianity that was free from the obligations of the law (§8.3b, d). Only this type of Christian propaganda would have caused a law-abiding Jew, in this case Paul, to persecute the Christians. The question of the validity of the Jewish law was also intimately connected with the essential content of his call.

If the usual term "conversion" is used for Paul's experience, there is a danger of obscuring what was in fact essential to him in this event. Paul himself never understood his experience as a conversion, but always as a call. This is evident even in the report of Luke (Acts 9:3ff; 22:3ff; 26:9ff), which is written in the style of a legend of a prophetic call, although here the actual commission is not given to Paul directly, since it is mediated through Ananias (Acts 9:15). Luke emphasizes in this way that Paul's commissioning as a missionary to the gentiles was legitimized by the Christian church, and that Paul had first to become an ordinary baptized Christian (Acts 9:18). There is no doubt that Paul was indeed baptized because he always includes himself in the community of baptized believers. Even baptism, however, did not connote for Paul a personal experience of conversion, but meant inclusion into the community of the elect who had received the spirit, and whose life was determined by the death and resurrection of Christ (1 Cor 12:12–13; Rom 6:1ff). The decisive event in Paul's experience, as he saw it, was the fact that Christ had appeared to him and had designated him as the apostle to the gentiles. This appearance of Christ, who appointed him as an apostle (1 Cor 9:1), is described by Paul as one of Christ's resurrection appearances (1 Cor 15:5–8). He characterized it as a revelation (Gal 1:15–16), that is, he described it as an eschatological event that was part of the event of salvation through Christ's death and resurrection.

The content of this eschatological event, namely, Paul's call to be a missionary to the gentiles, also determined the turning point for this law-abiding Jew in his position toward the law. If the time of salvation began with the resurrection of Jesus, and Paul himself was called by the risen Lord to bring this message to all the nations, then the period of the validity of the law had come to an end. From now on, the work of fulfilling the law which God had once enjoined upon his people would become instead resistance to God's will. From this perspective Paul also speaks about the significance of his call for his own religious experience (Phil 3:5ff). It is clear that he by no means viewed his past under the law as a period of personal and general human inability to fulfill God's demands; on the contrary, he could say of himself that he was blameless in the fulfillment of the law! Existence under the law—by all means a law that can be fulfilled—has rather lost its meaning, because a new demand has taken its place, a demand that lays claim to the whole human being: to be "in Christ." The implications of this "being in Christ," however, are such that they cannot be reconciled with a determination of human life by the law, not only in theological terms, but also in moral, social, and cultural questions. In this way, what the call had meant for Paul personally became a fundamental insight into the new human existence established by the event of salvation in Christ: an existence in freedom from the law.

(c) The First Period of Paul's Mission; Chronology of Paul's Life

There are no direct attestations from the first period of Paul's missionary activity. Not one of his letters can be dated with any probability to the period of Paul's missionary work before the Apostolic Council. Some scholars have assumed that the Galatian mission was part of a missionary journey that Paul undertook from Antioch, and that therefore the Letter to the Galatians could have been written at an early date (provided also that the Apostolic Council be dated earlier). But this assumption has many difficulties (see below on the south-Galatian hypothesis, §9.3b). Since the report of Acts about Paul's missionary activity is legendary (Acts 13-14), all the reliable information available is the scanty narrative of Gal 1:17-2:1.

According to this report, Paul first went as a missionary to "Arabia," i.e., Damascus, its environs, and the areas to the south. After three years

---

Bibliography to §9.1c: Text of the Gallio inscription
Barrett, *Background,* 48-49.

Bibliography to §9.1c: Studies
Kirsopp Lake, "The Chronology of Acts," in: Foakes Jackson and Lake, *Beginnings,* 5. 445-74.
Haenchen, *Acts,* 60-71.
Robert Jewett, *A Chronology of Paul's Life* (Philadelphia: Fortress, 1979).
Gerd Lüdemann, *Paulus, Der Heidenapostel,* vol. 1: *Studien zur Chronologie* (FRLANT 123; Göttingen: Vandenhoeck & Ruprecht, 1980).
John C. Hurd, "Pauline Chronology and Pauline Theology," in: William R. Farmer (ed.), *Christian History and Interpretation* (Cambridge: Cambridge University, 1967) 225-48.

he travelled to Jerusalem in order to visit Peter, stayed there for two weeks, and also had a chance to see James. That was Paul's only visit to Jerusalem before the Apostolic Council. The visit mentioned in Acts 9:26–30 refers to the same event, but the sending of Paul and Barnabas to the "brothers in Judea" during the famine under Claudius (Acts 11:27–30) is legendary because it cannot be identified with the Apostolic Council. The next stage of Paul's mission was his activity in Syria and Cilicia (Gal 1:21). It is most likely that Paul had his headquarters in Antioch during this period. According to Gal 2:1 he went to the Apostolic Council in Jerusalem together with Barnabas, and according to Gal 2:11 he was in Antioch during the incident with Peter. But it must remain undecided whether it was in fact Barnabas who invited Paul to Antioch from Tarsus (Acts 11:25f), and whether Paul actually undertook missionary journeys together with Barnabas as Acts 13–14 reports. Yet the list in Acts 13:1 of the prophets and teachers of Antioch, which includes Barnabas and Paul, seems to be trustworthy. Paul gives the length of this period as "fourteen years" (Gal 2:1). It is problematic, however, whether this period should be calculated from the time of Paul's call, that is, including the three years in Arabia, or from his first visit to Jerusalem. An additional uncertainty arises from the custom of that time to count the first and last years as full years, even if only a portion of those years was included in the period in question. Thus "three years" may be only a little more than one year, and "fourteen years" could have been as little as twelve years and a few months. Depending upon the inclusion or exclusion of that "three years," we are dealing with a total period of at least twelve and not more than seventeen years. The Apostolic Council concludes this period, after which a new period of Paul's mission began. All of Paul's extant letters belong to the time after the Apostolic Council.

A discussion of Paul's chronology is indispensible at this point, although some questions which belong to the following sections must now be anticipated. It is important to realize that Acts, by describing Paul's activity in the form of sequential missionary journeys, misrepresents Paul's actual pattern of mission; he usually would stay for quite some time in a particular urban center from which he organized his work. Nevertheless, the dates which Acts gives in the context of its description of the journeys may contain some reliable information—as long as they do not contradict the information in Paul's letters. If at least some of the dates of Acts derive from the "We-Source" (§7.3c) and can thus be trusted, the following reconstruction can claim some degree of probability.

The dating of his stay in Corinth is decisive for Pauline chronology. According to Acts 18:12–18, Paul was forced by the proconsul Gallio to leave the city after he had stayed there for a year and a half. Fortunately, an inscription has been found in Delphi which permits the dating of Gallio's proconsulship to the period from the spring of 51 CE to the spring of 52 (proconsuls were appointed for just one year; see §6.2a). Thus the earliest date for Paul's expulsion from Corinth would be spring or early summer of 51, the latest the early spring of 52. For other reasons to be discussed in the next section, the latter date is to be preferred.

A second chronological point of reference may be Acts 24:1ff: Paul was imprisoned during the procuratorship of Felix; but when Felix had been recalled to Rome and was replaced by Festus (Acts 24:27 speaks about a period of two years) and Paul appealed to the emperor, Festus sent him to Rome as a prisoner for further trial. If it were possible to date the recall of Felix to a time shortly before the downfall of his brother Pallas and the murder of Britannicus, i.e., in December of 55, this would yield a date for the bringing of the collection to Jerusalem and Paul's imprisonment. The difficulty with this possible date is that neither the information from Acts nor Paul's own statements in his letters can be reconciled with such an early date for his imprisonment in Jerusalem—moreover, it is doubtful whether the recall of Felix can be dated in this way (§6.6e). It is therefore advisable to forego this date altogether, and to reconstruct Paul's chronology in both directions from the Gallio date. Uncertainties cannot be excluded, and individual dates will have to remain open to question. But if one rejects an early date for the Apostolic Council (§9.1d), which would require rather implausible constructions of the chronology, the timetable that follows can be considered as relatively certain in its basic features. For those who want to add the "three years" to the "fourteen years" rather than include them in that later period, the first dates would be moved back two or three years, thus beginning with the conversion of Paul in the year 32/33.

35: "Conversion" of Paul.
35–38: Missionary activity in Arabia (Gal 1:17).
38: Visit with Peter in Jerusalem (Gal 1:18; Acts 9:26–30).
38–48: Missionary activity in Cilicia and Syria (Gal 1:21).
48: Apostolic Council in Jerusalem (Gal 2:1ff; Acts 15).
48/49: Incident in Antioch (Gal 2:11ff).
49: Mission in Galatia (Acts 16:6).
50: Mission in Philippi, Thessalonica, and Beroea (Acts 16:11–17:14).
Autumn, 50: Travel to Corinth via Athens (Acts 17:15; 18:1); writing of 1 Thessalonians.
Autumn, 50 to spring, 52: Mission in Corinth (Acts 18:11).
Summer, 52: Travel to Antioch; then to Ephesus through Asia Minor; second visit to Galatia on the way (Acts 18:18–23; Gal 4:13).

Autumn, 52 to spring, 55: Mission in Ephesus (Acts 19:1, 8–10, 22); writing of Galatians, 1 Corinthians, and the letter preserved in 2 Cor 2:14–6:13; 7:2–4.

54: Interim visit to Corinth (presupposed in 2 Cor 13:1).

Winter, 54–55: Ephesian imprisonment; writing of correspondence with Philippi, Philemon, and the letter preserved in 2 Corinthians 10–13.

Summer, 55: Travel through Macedonia to Corinth; writing of the letter preserved in 2 Cor 1:1–2:13; 7:5–16 and of the collection letters, i.e., 2 Corinthians 8 and 9.

Winter, 55–56: Stay in Corinth; writing of the letter to the Romans.

56: Travel to Jerusalem (Acts 20); preparations for the transfer of the collection (Acts 21:15ff); imprisonment of Paul.

56–58: Imprisonment in Caesarea.

58: Replacement of Felix by Festus; Paul is sent to Rome.

58–60: Roman imprisonment (Acts 28:30).

60: Martyrdom of Paul.

(d) The Apostolic Council

The only reliable source for the Apostolic Council, which probably took place in the year 48, is Gal 2:1–10. The tradition that Luke used in Acts 15 was so thoroughly revised by him that we can learn little more from that chapter than that the council did occur. The information given in Acts 11:27–30 probably rests upon a tradition about the delivery of the collection which was inserted by Luke at the wrong place; it is useless as a source for the council.

In order to understand the Apostolic Council, it is important to reconstruct the situation in the expansion of Christianity at that time. There were two centers of Christianity, Antioch and Jerusalem, each representing a very different position and orientation. After the expulsion of the Hellenists (§8.3b), the church in Jerusalem was composed of law-abiding, Aramaic-speaking Christians. It did not apparently engage in any missionary activity among gentiles (if Acts 10 rests on an older tradition, it belongs to a later period); it expected the coming of the Lord in the place which God had designated (Jerusalem/Zion), and expressed its eschato-

Bibliography to §9.1d

Haenchen, *Acts*, 440–72.

Betz, *Galatians*, 81–103.

Martin Dibelius, "The Apostolic Council," in: idem, *Studies in the Acts of the Apostles* (London: SCM, 1956; and reprints) 93–101.

Günther Klein, *Galater 2,6–9 und die Geschichte der Jerusalemer Gemeinde: Rekonstruktion und Interpretation* (BEvTh 50; München: Kaiser, 1969) 99–128.

logical consciousness in its self-designation as the "poor" (§8.3a). On the other hand, the church in Antioch consisted for the most part of uncircumcised gentile Christians; thus the law was not considered there as binding for Christians. Greek was the language of this church and of its missionary activities, which went far beyond the boundaries of Antioch itself. If Antioch shared the eschatological expectation with Jerusalem, this did not imply that the eschatological ideal of poverty was also accepted (§8.3c).

The contrast between Jerusalem and Antioch in the question of the law certainly was the reason for the Apostolic Council. But it cannot be assumed that the authorities in Jerusalem convened the conference in order to decide this question because the apostles in Jerusalem never had such powers of jurisdiction. Furthermore, Gal 2:1f clearly shows that the initiative came from Antioch. The Christians in Antioch desired a clarification, and they apparently had a particular reason, most likely the activities of the people called "false brothers" in Gal 2:4. Jewish-Christians (not simply Jews) were raising a stir against the gentile Christians' freedom from the law and caused serious difficulties for the Antiochian mission. (Paul had to face similar Judaizing propaganda in Galatia which seriously endangered his missionary work there; see §9.3).

Paul and Barnabas, as emissaries of the Antiochian church, wanted to establish unanimity with the Christians in Jerusalem. The goal was to create an ecclesiastical unity in which Jewish and gentile Christians would be bound together in spite of their differences in the question of the law; thus, the Judaizing troublemakers could no longer appeal in defence of their cause to the faithful observance of the law among the Christians in Jerusalem. The touchstone of the agreement was the question whether the gentile Christian Titus, whom Paul had brought to Jerusalem, would be accepted as a Christian brother without being circumcised first. In spite of the opposition of the "false brothers," the leaders of the Jerusalem church, the Lord's brother James, Cephas (Peter), and John, recognized the independence of the gentile mission, its freedom from the law, and its ecclesiastical integrity. On the other hand, Paul and Barnabas assured the Christians in Jerusalem that they would remember the special eschatological role of the "poor" in Jerusalem, which included the obligation of intercession for them in prayer and a collection of money for their benefit. The careful formulations in Gal 2:1–10 demonstrate that the agreement was a contract between two equal and independent partners. Nothing is said about a recognition of the Jerusalem authorities as a kind of church government. Peter's right to be active as a missionary was explicitly recognized, but only among the Jews (Gal 2:7f). Whoever was concerned with the creation of law-abiding Christian communities—and Paul does not question their legitimacy—should stay away from missionary activity among the gentiles. Nonetheless, this agreement opened the way for future conflicts, as became clear very soon in Antioch (§9.2a). The obligation to collect money for Jerusalem would become a significant ingredient of Paul's missionary activities (§9.3f).

2. From Antioch to Ephesus

(a) The Conflict in Antioch

Soon after the Apostolic Council in Jerusalem, Paul parted company with Barnabas and the Antiochian church to begin his own independent missionary activity. Acts 15:37–39 says that the cause for this separation was a quarrel between Paul and Barnabas about the usefulness of the assistance of John Mark on their next missionary journey. But Luke does not mention the conflict which Paul reports in Gal 2:11–15. It seems that here Paul mentions the real reason for his departure from Antioch. Peter, in principle favorably disposed toward the gentile mission, had visited the church in Antioch soon after the Apostolic Council, perhaps in the context of the beginning of his own missionary activity in Palestine and Syria, for which testimonies are preserved elsewhere (§10.2a). During his visit to Antioch, Peter had at first participated in the common meals with the gentile Christians (Gal 2:12), a clear gesture of his openness and his liberal attitude with respect to the ritual law. But when messengers from James in Jerusalem arrived in Antioch, Peter withdrew from the table fellowship. Since James' people apparently were concerned about the observance of the Jewish dietary laws, Peter did not want to embarrass these guests. Other Jewish-Christian members of the community, and even Barnabas himself, also withdrew from the table fellowship with the gentile Christians, taking into consideration the presence of these guests. This might very well have been a sign of their liberal attitude; even if the observance of the ritual law was not necessary for salvation, there should still be nothing wrong with observing the law whenever it seemed opportune. But for Paul, this was a return to the life under the law which denied fellowship to the gentile Christians, unless they also made themselves subject to the law; those who compelled them to do so were by no means consistent in their own obedience (Gal 2:14). For this reason, Paul had attacked Peter in public and had taken him to task. What others might consider a liberal gesture was for Paul hypocrisy dictated by fear (Gal 2:12).

Bibliography to §9.2a
Betz, *Galatians*, 103–12.

This confrontation in Antioch had far-reaching consequences. It seems that Paul lost out in this conflict, or else he would have reported the result in Galatians 2. If so, this was probably also the reason why Paul parted with Barnabas and left Antioch to begin his own missionary work elsewhere. Furthermore, this conflict prompted Paul to formulate the question of the fulfillment of the law even more radically. The Jerusalem agreement had still granted to the Jewish Christians their privilege to take the fulfillment of the law seriously. After the conflict in Antioch, however, Paul formulated this question differently: it is especially the Jew who must recognize that nobody can be justified by works of the law (Gal 2:15–21). The controversy with Peter had made it clear that liberal tolerance of a religious convention like the Jewish ritual law could endanger the unity of the church. Henceforth Paul insisted that the constitution of the church "in Christ" abolished all traditional religious, social, and cultural particularities, and all claims based upon them (Gal 3:26–28). It is exactly in the abolition of such traditional identities that the church becomes the eschatological community. As a consequence of this new insight Paul no longer conceded a position of eschatological preeminence to Jerusalem and its law-abiding Christian community (Gal 4:24f).

(b) Mission in Anatolia and Macedonia

According to the proposed chronology (§9.1c), Paul left Antioch in 49. The next reliable information concerns the churches in Macedonia (1 Thessalonians). Acts reports a journey through Derbe and Lystra in Lycaonia, the circumcision of Timothy, and travel through Phrygia and Galatia (in this sequence!) to Mysia (Acts 16:1–8), all of which is quite unreliable. But according to 1 Thess 1:1, it is at least certain that Paul was accompanied on this journey by his co-workers Silvanus (Silas) and Timothy.

The debated problem is the time of the founding of the Galatian churches. The best solution is the hypothesis that Paul stayed in Galatia for at least several months during his travel from Antioch to Macedonia. "Galatia" designated the central highlands of Asia Minor that includes the cities Ancyra, Pessinus, and Gordion. That the Galatian churches were located here is proposed by the so-called "North Galatian hypothesis," which is preferable to the assumption that the Galatian communities were established in the south of the Roman province of Galatia, i.e., in the cities of Derbe, Lystra, and Iconium. The latter churches did preserve a tradition about Paul's missionary activity (which is the basis for

Bibliography to §9.2b
Betz, *Galatians*, 1–5.

the report in Acts 14:6ff and probably also for the place names given in the apocryphal *Acts of Paul*), but this tradition more likely derives from Paul's mission in those regions while he was still based in Antioch (§9.1c). These cities, though part of the Roman province of Galatia, were not normally considered to belong to Galatia, but rather to Lycaonia (so correctly Acts 14:6). Paul must have stayed for some time in Galatia. Gal 4:13f suggests a passage of time and alludes to Paul being ill while he was there. Furthermore, Gal 1:2 speaks of a number of Galatian communities which Paul must have founded during this stay. Thus, there are several reasons not to calculate this visit as too short a period. The departure from Galatia took place at the very earliest in the last months of 49, but more likely in the spring of 50.

Acts 16:9f reports a famous vision which Paul is said to have had in Troas: a man from Macedonia appeared to him and invited him to preach the gospel in Macedonia. Immediately after this report begins the first part of the "we-passages" (Act 16:10). Although it is disputed whether these reports told in the first person derive from an older source (diary or itinerary; see §7.3c), some of its sections contain more reliable information than other parts of Acts. Troas, or more precisely Alexandria in the region of Troas, an important trading center during the Roman period, was the natural point of departure for travel by boat to Macedonia. Paul himself reported that he travelled to Macedonia via Troas a few years later (2 Cor 2:12f), and Acts 20:6 says that Paul travelled the same route in the opposite direction on his last journey. The boat trip would take the traveller to Neapolis (today Kavalla), from where a road led a few miles inland to Philippi, an important Roman colony situated at a strategic point of the Via Egnatia, the Roman road which went from Byzantium across Macedonia and northern Greece to Dyrrhachium on the Adriatic Sea. Individual features of Paul's missionary activity in Philippi remain in the realm of legend (Acts 16:13–40). Paul suffered persecutions and was forced to leave Philippi after a short period, as is confirmed by 1 Thess 2:2. Nevertheless, Paul was successful there, and the church in Philippi maintained a close and cordial relationship with him during the following years (§9.3e).

Thessalonica, where Paul went next, was the largest and most important city of Macedonia, a port and commercial center. Here the trade routes from the north met the Via Egnatia and Aegean Sea. It is characteristic for his mission that Paul tried to establish churches in the most urban centers of commerce and industry. Like Corinth, where Paul went afterwards, Thessalonica was the seat of a Roman proconsul. Again, all the individual events of Paul's activity in this city are legendary (Acts 17:1–10). Paul's stay there should also not be calculated as too short a period, because he in fact had time to get settled and pursue his trade (1 Thess 2:9). 1 Thessalonians shows no knowledge of any persecution by the Jews (1 Thess 2:14—though this passage is probably spurious). Acts 17:10–14 reports a mission of Paul in Beroea after his expulsion from Thessalonica; the Pauline letters do not confirm this.

(c) From Thessalonica to Corinth

First Paul went to Athens, from where he sent Timothy to Thessalonica to complete the work of founding and consolidating the church he had begun but had left incomplete, having ended his work prematurely due to adverse circumstances (1 Thess 3:1f). Paul probably did not stay long in Athens, since we must assume that he arrived in Corinth no later than the autumn of 50. Luke reports the famous speech of Paul on the Areopagus while in Athens (Acts 17:22–31), which, like the other speeches of Acts, is a Lukan composition. In the tradition which Luke used, two names of Christians whom Paul converted in Athens are preserved: Dionysus the Areopagite and a woman named Damaris (Acts 17:34). These names show that Paul must have founded a Christian community in Athens at that time.

Corinth, completely destroyed by the Romans in 146 BCE, and refounded by Caesar a hundred years later as a Roman colony, was at that time the largest city in Greece. By virtue of its position between the Saronic and Corinthian Gulfs, Corinth had become the leading port of Greece as well as one of the largest industrial cities of the ancient world (pottery, metal industries, and carpet weaving). Its heterogeneous population had introduced a great variety of religions. (Pausanias reported that there were four temples of the Egyptian cult alone; the existence of a Jewish synagogue can be demonstrated by one archeological find.) The immorality of Corinth was proverbial in antiquity, but was probably no worse than that of any other major port or commercial city.

Luke seems to have used more reliable material about Paul's stay in Corinth than in other cases. The information of Acts 18:1ff can be confirmed in part by the Pauline letters. Aquila, originally from Pontus, and his wife Priscilla took Paul into their house. They were "Jews," that is, Jewish Christians, who had been driven out of Rome by the edict of Claudius. Since Paul does not mention them among the first converts of Corinth, they must have become Christians while they were still in Rome—evidence that there was indeed a Christian church in Rome at this

Bibliography to §9.2c

Gerd Theissen, *The Social Setting of Pauline Christianity: Essays on Corinth* (Philadelphia: Fortress, 1982).

early date. According to 1 Cor 16:19 (and probably also Rom 16:3), Aquila and Priscilla were later in Ephesus. As a guest of Aquila who was a tent-maker like Paul, the apostle could pursue his trade and thus earn a living. Later he also received support from Macedonia in order to devote himself fully to his missionary work (2 Cor 11:9). Crispus, converted by Paul, is also mentioned in 1 Cor 1:14; Luke claims to know that he was the leader of the synagogue (Acts 18:8). According to 1 Cor 16:15 (see also 1:16), Stephanas was the first convert of Achaea.

Paul's missionary work in Corinth lasted a year and a half (Acts 18:11), from the autumn of 50 to the spring of 52 (§9.1c). Paul's associates were Timothy and Silvanus, who are also named as co-authors of 1 Thessalonians, which was written from Corinth. Other co-workers soon joined Paul's staff, as is evident from the remark about Stephanas in 1 Cor 16:15. Apollos, a Jewish Christian from Alexandria (Acts 18:24), became one of Paul's leading associates in Corinth (1 Cor 3:4–6; later he is with Paul in Ephesus; 1 Cor 16:12 should be preferred against Acts 18:25–28). The missionary work of Paul and his associates was not limited to Corinth during this period, but included other Greek cities, which is clearly shown by the repeated mention of Achaea in Paul's letters (1 Thess 1:7–8; 1 Cor 16:15; 2 Cor 1:1; 11:10; Rom 15:26; 2 Corinthians 9 is probably a circular letter to the churches in Achaea; see §9.3d, f). Not many details about this mission are known, with one exception: Rom 16:1–2 is a letter of recommendation for the president of the church in Cenchreae, Phoebe (§9.4a).

On the whole, a picture emerges which is characteristic for Paul's missionary method. He would settle in the capital of a province, together with a few tested associates, gather any Christians already living in the city, and expand his staff; together with these co-workers he would also found congregations in other cities of the area. During his absence he would maintain contact through messengers and letters in order to influence the further building and development of these churches. Paul's missionary work, therefore, should not be thought of as the humble efforts of a lonely missionary. Rather, it was a well-planned, large-scale organization that included letter-writing as an instrument of ecclesiastical policy. It is necessary to realize this in order to understand Paul's claim that in just a few years he had completed the preaching of the gospel from Jerusalem to as far as Illyricum encompassing Syria, Asia Minor, Macedonia, and Greece (Rom 15:19). In his activity in Corinth Paul seems to have accomplished the program of missionary work for the first time on a large scale, perhaps using the model which the Antiochian church had developed.

The report about Paul's expulsion from Corinth in Acts 18:12–18 was thoroughly edited by Luke, who wanted to emphasize the correct attitude of the Roman authorities toward the Christian movement and present this

View of Corinth
In the foreground, the North Market; behind it the remaining monolithic columns of the Temple of Apollo
(built in VI B.C.E.); in the background the fortress Acro-
Corinth, rising more than 1500 feet above the ancient
city.

as a paradigm. But the report preserves the reliable information that Paul was forced to leave the city by the Roman proconsul Gallio in the spring of 52 (not later!—on the date of Gallio's proconsulship, see §9.1c). The problems of the Corinthian church, however, continued to occupy Paul for several years and required the writing of several letters and future visits (see below).

(d) The First Letter to the Thessalonians

This letter was written by Paul a few months after his visit to Thessalonica. Timothy, whom Paul had sent to Thessalonica from Athens (1 Thess 3:1f), returned to Paul after his arrival in Corinth (Acts 18:5). Since Timothy is named as co-author, the letter must have been written from Corinth, probably still in the year 50 CE. It is therefore the oldest preserved Pauline letter and as such the oldest writing of the New Testament.

We do not know whether Paul had written any letters at an earlier time; it is possible that it was the beginning of his large-scale independent missionary work which forced him to use the letter as an additional instrument in the organization of Christian communities. Since Paul had left Antioch and its missionary center, he alone carried the responsibility for the survival of the churches which he had founded. 1 Thessalonians mirrors throughout the problems that might result in a young congregation that was firm in its conviction, but would be confronted by difficulties in the exposition and defense of its new faith within a matter of a few weeks or months. These include such questions as the credibility and

Bibliography to §9.2d: Commentaries
B. Rigaux, O.F.M., *Saint Paul: Les Épitres aux Thessaloniciens* (EtBib; Paris: Gabalda, 1956).

Bibliography to §9.2d: Studies
Hendrikus Boers, "The Form Critical Study of Paul's Letters: I Thessalonians as a Case Study," *NTS* 22 (1975/76) 140–58.
Werner George Kümmel, "Das literarische und geschichtliche Problem des 1. Thessalonicherbriefes," in: idem, *Heilsgeschehen und Geschichte* (2 vols.; MThSt 3; Marburg: Elwert, 1965) 406–16.
Helmut Köster, "Apostel und Gemeinde in den Briefen an die Thessalonischer," in: *Kirche: Festschrift Bornkamm*, 287–98.
Idem, "I Thessalonians—Experiment in Christian Writing," in: F. Forrester Church and Timothy George (eds.), *Continuity and Discontinuity in Church History: Essays Presented to George Huntston Williams* (SHCT 19; Leiden: Brill, 1979) 33–44.
Birger A. Pearson, "I Thessalonians 2:13–16: A Deutero-Pauline Interpolation," *HTR* 64 (1971) 79–94.
Schmithals, "The Historical Situation of the Thessalonian Epistles," in: idem, *Paul and the Gnostics*, 123–218.

integrity of the apostle, hostilities from the outside, consequences for Christian conduct, and the significance for life in the present of the newly acquired status of salvation. Paul discusses these questions in detail, which attests to his own insights into the real problems of a newly founded church, and also testifies to the great abilities of his associate Timothy, who correctly understood the situation when he was in Thessalonica as Paul's envoy and gave a comprehensive report to Paul after his return.

Since the validity of the gospel cannot be separated from the question of the credibility of the apostle—especially in view of Paul's short stay in Thessalonica—Paul had to draw a clear line between himself and the itinerant Cynic preacher. Therefore, Paul emphasizes that his preaching was not done for personal gain, and also tries to show that the relationship of the preacher to the audience and of the audience to the subject matter is fundamentally different from the widespread philosophical and religious propaganda of his time (1 Thess 2:1–12). The obligation of the audience to the gospel rather than to the preacher is what is decisive, as well as the mutual obligations of the members to each other (1 Thess 3:11–13—no ideal of individualistic piety is involved), and the inclusion of the apostle within these ties of mutual love and care; thus Paul compares himself with the caring mother and the encouraging father (1 Thess 2:7, 12). The church is not an isolated local club, but shares in its experiences the eschatological destiny of other churches, especially in its suffering of persecution (1 Thess 1:6ff). The passage in 1 Thess 2:13–16, with its blatant anti-Judaic attitude, has been correctly identified as a later interpolation, which takes up a Jewish tradition about the official leaders of the people as the murderers of the prophets, and puts the death of Jesus as well as the experiences of the church into that context.

The first three chapters of the letter discuss these questions and make up a proem written in the style of the thanksgiving; this also includes a description of Paul's personal situation (1 Thess 2:17–3:10). All aspects of the experiences of the church and of Paul's ministry, as well as their mutual relations, are included in the thanksgiving and praise of God. Together they belong to the eschatological events of salvation that take place before God. Clearly distinguished from the thanksgiving section are the instructions and admonitions that follow in chapters 4 and 5, beginning with a parenesis with interpretations of a traditional catalogue of vices (4:1–8) and of Christian virtues (4:9–12). The concluding eschatological instructions are also based upon traditional materials, namely, on a saying of Jesus about the sequence of the events at the time of the parousia (4:13–18) and on the word of the day of the Lord which comes like a thief in the night (5:1–11; cf. Rev 3:3). These expositions are not related to the much disputed problem of the delay of the parousia; in the church that had been in existence only for a few months, this would have been absurd. Paul wants rather to explain the fundamental Christian insight that it does not matter at all for the future "being with the Lord" whether Christians "wake or sleep" (1 Thes 5:10). It is remarkable that church order materials are given only minimal space in this letter to a recently founded church (5:12–22), which is also the case in other genuine Pauline letters (in contrast to the Pastoral Epistles). But this does not imply that there was no ecclesiastical organization. Rather, the titles which occur here and occasionally elsewhere (especially Phil 1:2), and the statements in 1 Corinthians 12, demonstrate that there were church offices with clearly defined functions. Yet these authorities were not fixed in any hierarchical structure. 1 Thess 5:12–22 clearly shows that Paul has great confidence that the spirit will effect democratic teamwork which requires both mutual respect and recognition as well as critical judgment.

3. Paul's Stay in Ephesus

(a) Missionary Activity in Ephesus

After his missionary work in Corinth, Paul was active in Ephesus for some time. The statements of Acts 18:18–23 about Paul's travel route immediately after his departure from Corinth are debated: Ephesus—Caesarea—(Jerusalem?)—Antioch—Galatia—Phrygia—Ephesus. If Paul indeed went to Antioch at that time, it implies either that his relationship with that community had improved meanwhile or that he made this journey in order to reestablish good relations. It is a fact that his later remarks about Barnabas and Peter (1 Cor 9:6; 1:12; 3:22; 9:5) are not negative or even hostile. It is also possible that a second visit to Galatia, perhaps indicated in Gal 4:13f, took place during this journey. But the details of this journey must remain uncertain because the relevant statements of Acts do not seem to be very trustworthy.

In any case, Paul must have come to Ephesus during the year 52. Acts 19:1–20:1 gives only scanty information about his stay in Ephesus. Nearly everything is legendary. The unmasking of the Jewish exorcists and the burning of the magical books (Acts 19:13–20) go back to an older Christian or pagan tale. The story of the riot of the people because of the Ephesian Artemis fits Luke's time better than Paul's because it is known that the growth of the Christian churches in the post-apostolic period severely hurt both attendance at the temples and the sale of souvenirs (Acts 19:23–40; see, e.g., Pliny's correspondence with the emperor Trajan, *Epist.* 10.96). If an older tradition had really been used in the story about the encounter with disciples baptized with the baptism of

Market Gate in Miletus
(Reconstruction in the Pergamum Museum, Berlin GDR)
The Romans constructed large and elaborate entrance gates for the main markets (*agora* or *forum*) of major cities. These served not only decorative purposes, but also allowed better control of crowds in case of riots.

John, it would be located better in Syria than in Asia Minor (Acts 19:1–7; but the account is probably entirely a Lukan composition). Thus the only historically useful information is the statement about the duration of the Ephesian ministry (three months and two years; Acts 19:8, 10) and about the place of Paul's activity (the lecture hall of Tyrannus). But we hear nothing from Luke about Paul's actual missionary work in Ephesus. It most certainly involved the organization of a missionary center that would have been used as headquarters for the founding of churches in other cities of Asia by Paul and his associates. Luke says nothing about Paul's extensive correspondence during this period (most of his letters were written from Ephesus), nor about his imprisonment toward the end of his stay. But the analysis of Paul's letters with their numerous statements about travel plans, projects, and adverse circumstances gives us a rather detailed picture of this crucially important period of the Pauline mission.

Fixed points for a reconstruction of the chronology for this period and its letters and letter-fragments can be found, first, in the statements of Paul about the progress of the collection and, second, in the various stages of the controversy with the Corinthian church. Since the Letter to the Galatians only mentions the collection but does not actively promote it (Gal 2:10), this letter is best placed at the beginning of the period. 1 Corinthians belongs to a somewhat later time because here Paul has resumed his plans for the collection in earnest (1 Cor 16:1ff). After the writing of 2 Cor 2:14–7:4, Paul must have gone to Corinth for a short visit, because such a visit is presupposed in 2 Cor 10:1–13:14 (esp. 13:1). The other fragments preserved in 2 Corinthians were written after Paul's departure from Ephesus. They indicate, however, that Paul was in serious danger of death during the last months of his stay in Ephesus (2 Cor 1:8f). If this is a reference to the Ephesian imprisonment, then this imprisonment as well as the letters written from prison (Philippians and Philemon) belong to the very last part of Paul's stay in Ephesus.

(b) Judaizing Propaganda and the Letter to the Galatians

The controversy of Paul with his opponents in Galatia known from his letter to the Galatians raises the fundamenal problem about the character and origin of the various opponents whom Paul had to combat there and elsewhere (Corinth, Philippi), and who caused problems for Paul's students and successors in the next generation (Colossians, Ephesians; see also the letters of Ignatius and those in the Revelation of John). Information about these opponents is available only in indirect form through the letters written against them; and drawing conclusions from the richer materials about heretics from the following centuries is a hazardous method. Therefore, the question of the identification of Paul's opponents is one of the most difficult questions of New Testament scholarship. At the same time it is also one of the most interesting problems, and without a reconstruction of the thoughts of the opponents, many sections of the Pauline letters would remain completely incomprehensible.

Were the opponents of Paul a clearly defined unified movement with its own well-formulated doctrine and message? Were there two differnt groups (Judaizers and gnostics)? Or is it better to reckon with a whole variety of movements, perhaps not unrelated to each other? In order to answer these questions it must be understood first of all that we can presuppose neither firmly formulated doctrines nor unified organizations for the early Christian missionary movement as a whole. A fixed body of doctrines (creed and canon) and a generally accepted ecclesiastical organization (episcopate) were developed much later and over many generations, especially in the course of the ongoing controversies with the heretics. Even within contemporary Judaism, there were no equivalent structures and organizations; they were created by rabbinic Judaism during the centuries after the destruction of Jerusalem. The religious propaganda of that time employed quite varied means and was subject to conditions which did not necessarily favor the formation of a unified doctrine. The market of religious propaganda encouraged free competition; competitive instruments that could promise success therefore dominated the scene. Among these were mastery of rhetorical tricks, demonstration of one's possession of supernatural power (miracles, magic), recourse to dignified ancient tradition, and evidence for the success of religious praxis.

The first Christian missionaries were without exception Jews, that is, Jewish Christians, and the Old Testament played a role in all their

Bibliography to §9.3b: Commentaries

Hans Dieter Betz, *Galatians: A Commentary on Paul's Letter to the Churches in Galatia* (Hermeneia: Philadelphia: Fortress, 1979).

J. B. Lightfoot, *St. Paul's Epistle to the Galatians* (19th ed.; London: Macmillan, 1896). A classic, still very instructive.

Bibliography to §9.3b: Studies

James Hardy Ropes, *The Singular Problem of Galatians* (HTS 14; Cambridge, MA: Harvard University, 1929).

Hans Dieter Betz, "The Literary Composition and Function of Paul's Letter to the Galatians," *NTS* 21 (1974/75) 353–79.

Idem, "Spirit, Freedom, and Law: Paul's Message to the Galatian Churches," *SEÅ* 39 (1974) 145–60.

Wilhelm Lütgert, *Gesetz und Geist: Eine Untersuchung zur Vorgeschichte des Galaterbriefs* (BFCTh 22,6; Gütersloh: Bertelsmann, 1919).

Schmithals, "The Heretics in Galatia," in: idem, *Paul and the Gnostics*, 13–64.

Philipp Vielhauer, "Gesetzesdienst und Stoicheiadienst im Galaterbrief," in: *Rechtfertigung: Festschrift für Ernst Käsemann zum 70. Geburtstag* (Göttingen: Vandenhoeck & Ruprecht, 1976) 543–55.

missionary activities. The controversy was not over the use of the Old Testament itself (Marcion was the first to pose this question in the middle of II CE), but its interpretation. The different theological positions of the Jewish-Christians missionaries were always closely related to differences in the principles and methods of scriptural interpretation, specifically in an interpretation that was designed for propagandistic effect in religious competition. Thus, the Old Testament could appear as a book of ritual prescriptions (circumcision, dietary requirements, Sabbath observances, religious festivals); their observance would assure the true people of God of protection from the powers of the universe (the position of the opponents in Galatians and Colossians). Or the Bible could be understood as a guide to a life of perfection which would guarantee full possession of the transcendent salvation already in the present (opponents of Philippians). Or the Old Testament might be commended as a book of hidden truths: its revelation through spiritual exegesis could reveal to the hearer the divinity of the religious person (opponents of 2 Corinthians). It could also be understood as a book of ancient promises which had become a reality through Christ, through the preaching of the gospel, and through the faith of the church (Paul).

The explosion of multiple missionary efforts by Christian preachers is also related to the fact that Christian missions entered into a new phase after the Apostolic Council. The Christian message was now carried into other areas of the Roman empire and moved beyond the realm of Palestine and Syria and the immediately adjacent areas. Paul may have been the first Christian preacher who went to Asia Minor and to Greece, but others soon followed. We possess evidence about only a few of them. Most likely the gospel was also carried to eastern Syria and Egypt at this time. Testimonies preserved from a somewhat later period demonstrate again that an amazing variety was characteristic of the first beginnings in these areas.

The Galatian opponents made the first known appearance of wandering apostles who invaded a Pauline church. They are usually called Judaizers, i.e., Jewish-Christian missionaries who required the converted pagan Christians to be circumcized and observe the Jewish ritual law. These apostles were not simply representatives of traditional Jewish observance of the law, however, but were men filled with the spirit and convinced of the spiritual power and cosmic significance of the fulfillment of the law. They were not necessarily identical with the "false brothers" of Gal 2:4 who schemed against Paul in Jerusalem (§9.1d), but it can be assumed that they had connections to those people and appealed to them as the true guardians of the Jerusalem agreement. The fact that Paul gave such a careful and comprehensive exposition of his relationships to Jerusalem in Galatians 1 and 2, and that he emphasized his independence so strongly, apparently indicates that his opponents had accused him of violations of the Jerusalem agreement.

The letter that Paul wrote to the Galatian churches refuting these opponents in defense of his gospel is saturated with biting polemical remarks. This polemical style appears immediately in the letter's prescript and proem. The apostle's title is expanded to be "not by human beings and not through human beings" (Gal 1:1). The usual thanksgiving ("I give thanks to God on your part . . .") is replaced by "I am astonished that you are so quickly deserting him who called you . . ." (Gal 1:6). Hyperbolic polemical formulations appear repeatedly in the letter (such as 3:1 and 5:12). While in other instances the proem recounts the apostle's experiences and indicates his plans for the future insofar as they relate to the congregation (see 1 Thessalonians 2–3; 2 Cor 1:3ff), the proem of Galatians is a description of his call, of his relationships to Jerusalem, and of the conflict in Antioch (Gal 1:10–2:14). This report was written to demonstrate that the opponents had no right of appeal to Jerusalem for their cause; later the daring allegory in Gal 4:21ff includes the note that Jerusalem/Zion has no right to consider itself as the symbolic center of all Christendom.

To the position of his opponents that the old covenant had been renewed through Christ, Paul responds that, on the contrary, the old covenant had come to an end, that its curse had run its course, and that therefore the promises which had been given to Abraham before the law had now become valid (Gal 3:6–18). The law is by no means the guarantor of one's membership in the elect people of the covenant, but plays the role of jail-keeper and slave-master until the arrival of freedom for God's children, who include all people, Jews and Greeks, slaves and free, men and women (Gal 3:19–29). The thesis that the law as a cosmic power reconciles us with the elements and powers of the universe is rejected by Paul with the statement that this would only enslave us once more to the elements. Paul mocks the Galatians: their obedience to the law would be nothing but a return to the old idols (Gal 4:8–11). The parenetic section of the letter, once more interspersed with polemical remarks (Gal 5:1–6:10), gives a fundamental juxtaposition of conduct in the spirit (freedom and love) to the works of the "flesh," which are identical with obedience to the law. The final greetings turn into a last appeal to turn away from the opponents, who are once more accused of dishonesty and self-interest (Gal 6:11–18).

Paul was doubtlessly convinced that the work of the Judaizing missionaries in Galatia could destroy his entire missionary effort there. The letter that he wrote in this desperate situation apparently had some success. One year later, Paul was able to tell the Corinthian church that the collection had made good progress in the Galatian churches (1 Cor 16:1). Since there is nothing said in Galatians about the collection, we must assume that Paul had meanwhile had further contact with the Galatian churches through letters or messengers and was confident that his plan to make a collection for the Jewish Christians in Jerusalem would not be misinterpreted.

(c) The Spiritual People in Corinth and the First Letter to the Corinthians

Before Paul wrote the letter that is preserved as 1 Corinthians he had already written another letter from Ephesus to the church in Corinth (1 Cor 5:9). This letter has been lost. (Some have supposed that it is at least partially preserved in 2 Cor 6:14–7:1; those verses, however, were not written by Paul, but comprise a piece written by a Jewish Christian which somehow got into the collection of Paul's letters.) The occasion for the writing of 1 Corinthians was an oral report that Paul had received from Chloe's people about the situation in the Corinthian church (1 Cor 1:11) and a letter from Corinth (7:1). At the time of writing, Paul must have already been in Ephesus for quite a while; he is making plans to leave (16:5ff), but wants to stay in that city until Pentecost because of other opportunities for missionary work as well as hostilities and contro-

Bibliography to §9.3c: Commentaries

Hans Conzelmann, *1 Corinthians: A Commentary on the First Epistle to the Corinthians* (Hermeneia; Philadelphia: Fortress, 1975).

Bibliography to §9.3c: Studies

Walter Schmithals, *Gnosticism in Corinth* (Nashville: Abingdon, 1971).

Birger A. Pearson, *The Pneumatikos-Psychikos Terminology in 1 Corinthians: A Study in the Theology of the Corinthian Opponents of Paul and its Relation to Gnosticism* (SBLDS 12; Missoula: Scholars Press, 1973).

Karl-Gustav Sandelin, *Die Auseinandersetzung mit der Weisheit in 1. Korinther 15* (Meddelander från Stiftelsens för Åbo Akademi Forskninginstitut 12; Åbo: Åbo Akademi, 1976).

Gerd Theissen, "Soziale Schichtung in der korinthischen Gemeinde," *ZNW* 65 (1974) 232–72.

Hans von Soden, "Sakrament und Ethik bei Paulus," in: Heinrich Frick (ed.), *Marburger Theologische Studien: Rudolf Otto Festgruß* (vol. 1; Gotha: Klotz, 1931) 1–40; reprinted in: idem, *Urchristentum und Geschichte: Gesammelte Aufsätze und Vorträge* (ed. Hans von Campenhausen; vol. 1; Tübingen: Mohr/Siebeck, 1951) 238–76.

Bornkamm, *Experience*, 123–93.

Wolfgang Schrage, "Die Frontstellung der paulinischen Ehebewertung in 1. Kor. 7,1–7," *ZNW* 67 (1976) 214–34.

John C. Hurd, *The Origin of I Corinthians* (London: SPCK, and New York: Seabury, 1965).

versies (16:7ff). Thus, the letter must have been written in the winter months of 53–54—Paul had arrived in Ephesus in the fall of 52. It was not foreseeable then that he would have to stay in Ephesus even longer and also would have to change his plans several times (the Corinthians later accused him of doing so; 2 Cor 1:15ff).

In 1 Corinthians Paul is not dealing with opponents who had come into the church from the outside. Apollos, to be sure, had meanwhile been active in Corinth. But Paul does not accuse him nor other missionaries; rather, all his charges are directed to the Corinthians themselves. The problems must therefore have resulted from the consequences which some people in Corinth had drawn from Paul's preaching or from Apollos' instructions, as well as from the religious presuppositions that they had brought into their new existence as Christians. Two charges are especially obvious in Paul's polemical remarks: the formation of parties (1 Cor 1:11ff) and the behavior of the "strong people" (6:12 and 10:23 quote their slogan, "I am free to do anything"). Since Paul does not deal with various groups with their different opinions, but directs all his attacks to the same people, we must assume that the parties and the conduct of the "strong people" were directly related to each other. Therefore, the attempt to identify the four parties (those of Paul, Apollos, Peter, or Christ) with four different doctrinal opinions cannot work. In any case, the question never arises for Paul whether a particular doctrine of which anyone might boast is right or wrong; rather he addresses the problem of boasting as such. Thus far he is indeed dealing with a particular conviction, namely, the conviction and consciousness of religious possessions and special rights. But he does not accuse his opponents of preaching a different gospel. Therefore, 1 Corinthians is not a polemical and apologetic treatise like Galatians; rather, it resembles 1 Thessalonians, since parenesis, church order, and eschatological instruction are the basic elements. To be sure, these are saturated with basic expositions, and the first chapters introduce the letter with a discussion of fundamental issues.

It is probably not wrong to call the opponents in Corinth (the "strong people" in the church) gnostics or proto-gnostics, if by this we mean to describe their self-consciousness. But we should not look for a theoretical justification of their views in terms of a doctrine comparable to the gnostic systems of II CE. The Corinthians were convinced of their possession of divine wisdom and related its mediation to the specific apostles through whom they had been initiated into Christianity by baptism (1 Cor 1:13–17; see also Paul's emphasis upon the general significance of baptism for each and every member of the church in 1 Cor 12:13). It is also possible that they made recourse to wisdom sayings of Jesus, since words of Jesus are quoted here more frequently than in other Pauline letters (1 Cor

7:10f; 9:14; 11:23ff; 1 Cor 2:9 may also be such a saying, cf. *Gos. Thom.* 17). The missionaries, indeed even Jesus himself, thus become mystagogues, and baptism a mystery rite. Paul, however, denies the possibility of special insights of wisdom, unless such insights are directed to the event of salvation itself (2:12; cf. 2:8f). He is happy that he did not have much to do with baptizing people (1:14–17), and stresses that both he and Apollos are nothing but servants for the sake of faith (3:5). If the Corinthians did indeed accept Christ, this could not mean that they now possessed supernatural rights and extraordinary privileges, because the Crucified One is exactly the opposite: foolishness and a stumbling-block (1:18ff; 2:1ff). Consequently, the apostles are not superhuman beings, but ridiculous, persecuted, despised, and overworked fools. The Corinthians are ridiculed: in their spiritual achievements they think they are already full and rich participants in the rule of God (4:6–13; 4:8 may also allude to a saying of Jesus; cf. *Gos. Thom.* 2).

After this discussion of fundamental issues (1:10–4:21) which follows directly upon the letter's prescript and proem (1:1–3 and 1:4–9), the outline of the letter uses the traditional pattern of parenesis (interpretation of a catalogue of vices: fornication, adultery, idolatry, 5:1–11:1), church order (women in the service, eucharist, spiritual gifts and church offices, order of worship, 11:2–14:40), and eschatological instruction (15:1–52). The real topic, however, which reappears again and again, is the controversy with the "strong people" and the documentation of the gnostic self-consciousness that is destroying the community. 1 Cor 5:1–6:11 deals with grievances that are not necessarily related to the behavior of the strong people: he recommends that they excommunicate a Christian who lived in concubinage with his father's wife, and instructs them not to bring disputes between members of the congregation before secular courts. But beginning with 6:12 the parenesis explicitly addresses the strong people, since their slogan is quoted at the beginning of this section. The criticism of the consequences which they drew from their self-consciousness for their sexual and marital life offers Paul an opportunity to insert some general instructions about marriage and divorce. The first paragraph (6:12–20) leaves no doubt that the strong people believed they had the right to have intercourse with prostitutes. What kind of behavior is attacked in 7:1–40 is not as obvious and is debated among scholars. Paul is probably dealing with ascetic and misogamistic attitudes (not necessarily irreconcilable with having sex with prostitutes!). These practices could have included refusal of sex in marriage, rejection of marriage or remarriage for divorced and widowed people, and living together in spiritual marriages (*subintroductae*). Since "realized eschatology" (cf. Luke 20:34–36) also appears in other ways among the strong people (see

Cultic Dining Room in the Demeter Sanctuary at Corinth

A whole series of dining rooms was excavated in this sanctuary, each large enough to serve seven, nine, or eleven persons. The picture shows the substructures for the dining couches along the walls of the room, the offcenter door in the left, with other dining rooms in the background.

below), one can assume that they wanted to be released from all earthly
and social bonds also in matters of sex and marriage. Paul counters that
abstinence is advisable, because the end has *not* yet come (1 Cor 7:29ff).
The parenesis of Paul is otherwise distinguished by very sober and rational advice and the rejection of enthusiastic and religious motivations. In
this respect, Paul's judgment is quite different from his Jewish (Philo)
and pagan (Musonius) philosophical contemporaries, especially since he
argues without compromise for equal rights for women (e.g., 7:3–4). To
this equal status of men and women corresponds the relativizing of the
status of circumcised and uncircumcised people and of masters and slaves
(7:17–24; cf. Gal 3:28).

The discussion of the participation in the worship of the idols (1 Cor
8:1–11:1) addresses itself even more directly to the strong people than the
preceding section. Their thesis is first discussed with regard to the question of whether such behavior indeed guarantees personal freedom, and
Paul then turns to the problem of whether such conduct actually builds up
the community (10:23). Freedom and privilege, as they result from
knowledge (*gnosis*), are fully granted (8:1–13) and also exemplified with
respect to the rights of the apostle (9:1ff). But Christian conduct should
instead be documented in the renunciation of one's privileges and in the
acceptance of the weak conscience of other members of the church (8:9–
13)—even of the conscience of a pagan observer (10:28f)—as the criterion
for one's own conduct. Paul refers to the example of the renunciation of
his own privileges for the sake of the gospel (9:19–27). The analogy of the
eucharist with the "sacraments of Israel" (with typological interpretation
of passages about the exodus) is designed to demonstrate that the community as a whole must decisively understand itself as the body of Christ,
whereas the experimentation with the power and knowledge of the individual will destroy both the individual and the church (10:1–22). It must
be noted that Paul makes no attempt to regulate participation in pagan
sacrificial meals by reference to a certain minimal code of legal rules
which could regulate individual conduct. Rather, the freedom of the
Christian, which is not questioned in itself, is subordinated to respect for
weak consciences and to the building up of the community as a whole. In
his discussion of church order, Paul without exception criticizes any behavior that seeks to demonstrate advanced religious insight and possession
of religious qualities. Whether women should preach and pray in church
without a veil is not a question of emancipation, but a problem of the
general custom of the church (11:2–16). The Lord's Supper is not a
mystery meal nor a sacred dinner for the perfect, but an eschatological
meal for the whole community, which should give evidence that one really
understands what the "body of Christ" means. The "body of Christ" is the

community of all Christians who have respect and patience for each other (11:17–34). With regard to spiritual gifts, there is no rank or order; the gift of the spirit is not limited to those who have the ability to prove their special religious status by extraordinary demonstrations such as speaking in tongues, prophecy, the working of miracles, or "knowledge" (*gnosis*). The possession of the spirit is rather documented, first of all, in the confession of Jesus as Lord that is common to all Christians because they have all received the spirit in baptism. All are members of the one body, a principle which Paul explains by means of the metaphor of the body, taken not from a religious but from a secular political context (12:1–31). No single special charisma can prove the presence of God, which can be documented solely by love, as Paul explains in a didactic poem (13:1–13). His instructions for the community's services are once more directed against overemphasis on the demonstration of the possession of the spirit, as, for example, speaking in tongues, since it neither edifies the church nor can it be understood by the layperson or the unbeliever (14:1–33a and 37–40; the interpolated verses 33b–36 contradict the Pauline practice, attested several times, of the full participation of women in the church offices and in worship; they also interrupt the context and must be viewed as a later interpolation).

The question of the identity of the people attacked in 1 Corinthians 15, who deny the resurrection of the dead, is one of the most debated problems of New Testament interpretation. It is certain, however, that Paul is not speaking about members of the church who were still restrained by the misapprehensions of their former pagan unbelief. Most likely the arguments are directed against the same religious enthusiasts who are under attack elsewhere in the letter. It is difficult to say whether they championed a belief in the immortality of the soul instead of the hope in the resurrection, or whether they assumed that full participation in the salvation through Christ was already obtained before the parousia. In any case, they did not argue that death would put an end to everything because in that case they would not have practiced vicarious baptism for people who had died (15:29). The self-consciousness of these Corinthians is also evident in their claim that they had already obtained all the promised blessings of salvation. It is such a claim that 1 Cor 15:44–49 argues against, an understanding of salvation which speaks about the present achievement of return to the first spiritual Adam. Paul contrasts this with a historical perspective of salvation which reckons with a future that has not yet been fulfilled. In accordance with this view, the resurrection of Christ about which the "gospel" (15:11ff) speaks is an event established in past history and attested by historical witnesses. Resurrection is an event, not a timeless truth that can be appropriated at any time. Making recourse to an apocalyptic mystery saying (15:51f) and to a traditional apocalyptic schema (15:23ff), Paul tries to demonstrate that earthly human existence will not come to an end until the parousia of Christ, and that only this will bring the final unification with the heavenly human being through the resurrection of the dead and the transformation of the living.

In the final chapter (16) Paul discusses his travel plans. It must be noted that the collection for the "saints" (i.e., in Jerusalem) is introduced here; neither in 1 Thessalonians nor in Galatians did he make any attempt to push this matter forward. Paul also mentions the possibility that he himself might go to Jerusalem together with delegates from various churches (16:4). Paul had alrady sent his associate Timothy to Corinth before he wrote this letter (4:17; 16:10f). He is now expecting his return together with a delegation from the Corinthian church (16:11). It is possible to estimate how this letter was received in Corinth. The reaction must have been positive, because 2 Cor 12:18 (cf. 2 Cor 9:3) tells us that Paul had subsequently sent Titus and another brother to Corinth and Achaea for the organization of the collection. They did this successfully, as the Corinthians willingly admitted. On the basis of the reports received through Timothy and Titus, Paul decided to change his travel plans. He would not go to Corinth via Macedonia, but travel to Corinth first, and make his visit to the Macedonian churches from Corinth, to which he would then return for a more extended stay (2 Cor 1:15f). This itinerary met the desires of the Corinthians as is evident from the reproaches which they made when Paul did not adhere to it (2 Cor 1:17ff).

(d) New Opposition in Corinth: The Second Letter to the Corinthians

New developments in Corinth were partly responsible for Paul's not carrying out his second travel plan. As the fragments of various letters (§7.3d) now preserved in 2 Corinthians show, a new opposition against

Bibliography to §9.3d

Ernst Käsemann, "Die Legitimität des Apostels," *ZNW* 41 (1942) 33–71.

Dieter Georgi, *Die Gegner des Paulus im 2. Korintherbrief* (WMANT 11; Neukirchen-Vluyn: Neukirchener Verlag, 1964; English translation forthcoming).

Hans Dieter Betz, "Jesus as Divine Man," in: F. Thomas Trotter (ed.), *Jesus and the Historian: Written in Honor of Ernest Cadman Colwell* (Philadelphia: Westminster, 1968) 114–33.

Rudolf Bultmann, "Exegetische Probleme des zweiten Korintherbriefes," in: idem, *Exegetica*, 298–322.

Günther Bornkamm, "Die Vorgeschichte des sogenannten Zweiten Korintherbriefes," in: idem, *Geschichte und Glaube* (München: Kaiser, 1971) 2. 162–94.

Hans Dieter Betz, *Der Apostel Paulus und die Sokratische Tradition: Eine exegetische Untersuchung zu seiner "Apologie" 2. Kor. 10–13* (BHTh 45; Tübingen: Mohr/Siebeck, 1972).

Paul had meanwhile developed, instigated by foreign missionaries who had invaded the Corinthian church. In contrast to 1 Corinthians, missionaries agitating against Paul are explicitly mentioned. Furthermore, the central questions of the debate have changed. What was discussed in 1 Corinthians is mentioned only marginally; indeed Paul seems to take a more conciliatory position with respect to those previous issues (e.g., cf. 2 Cor 5:1ff with 1 Corinthians 15). Therefore the opponents of 2 Corinthians cannot be identified with the opposition of 1 Corinthians.

The opponents of 2 Corinthians were Jewish-Christian missionaries who proudly boasted that they were "Hebrews, Israelites, seed of Abraham" (2 Cor 11:22). But since the law and circumcision are never mentioned, they certainly were not the same Judaizers who had disturbed the churches in Galatia (§9.3b). However, the Jewish tradition and a theology of the new covenant played a significant role for them (2 Corinthians 3). Their message seemed to be that the Christian proclamation is the renewal of the true Jewish religion—a clear contrast to those Corinthians whom Paul attacked in 1 Corinthians! The methods employed by these new opponents originated with Hellenistic-Jewish propaganda and apologetics. Their aim was the concrete documentation of the renewal of the Jewish religion as it was worked by the spirit. This was accomplished through powerful deeds and miracles (12:11f), bragging about mystical experiences and the fulfillment of prayers (12:1–9), and spiritual exegesis (2 Cor 3:4–18). These demonstrations were intended to make it possible to repeat the possession of divine power, as it had appeared in Moses or in Jesus, and thus to become a "divine man." Paul responded that the splendor on the face of Moses was fading away (3:13), that this kind of Christ was a "Christ according to the flesh" (5:16), and that these apostles were preaching only themselves (4:5).

It is likely that the preaching of these apostles was mostly a narrative of the powerful deeds of Christ as they appear in the sources of the Gospel of Mark and in the *Semeia Source* of the Gospel of John (§7.3b). Accordingly, the letters of recommendation which these apostles were able to produce (3:1ff) were confirmations of their powerful deeds and their missionary successes. The Corinthians were impressed. Why had Paul not accomplished similar deeds among them? Why had he not at least reported some of his own religious experiences? Had Paul simply withheld from them an important dimension of religious life? He did not even use his normal apostolic right to receive payment for his missionary work (12:11ff; cf. 11:7ff). When such questions implying profound doubts about Paul's apostolic legitimacy were brought to him, he first responded with a letter which is in essence preserved in 2 Cor 2:14–6:13 and 7:2–4. The summer of 54 saw the writing of this letter, a brief visit of Paul to

Corinth shortly thereafter (the "interim" visit), and a letter written soon after the visit (2 Corinthians 10–13).

The preserved fragment of the first letter, 2 Cor 2:14–6:13; 7:2–4, is a presentation of the apostle's role as part of an eschatological event which the community also shares. Paul wants to demonstrate to the community that a visible presentation of divine power and glory in the person of the missionary is irreconcilable with the eschatological action of God, which is in fact no less than the consummation of the new creation. This much is said right away in the opening thanksgiving with a daring image: as a prisoner in the triumphal procession of God, Paul delivers his life- and death-bringing message (2:14ff). The use of impressive instruments through which one tries to peddle the gospel as successfully as possible in the religious market (2:17; cf. 4:2) is as inappropriate for this eschatological event as the employment of letters of recommendation for the successful missionary (3:1ff). Another striking image: the church is the heavenly letter administered by the apostle. The juxtaposition of this letter, written on the tablets of the heart by the spirit of God, and that which had once been written on tablets of stone (3:3), leads to a criticism of the opponents' theology of the covenant. Even an interpretation of the old covenant cannot help to visualize the glory of God, which remains hidden until today. Paul expounds this in a critical commentary on an exegesis of Exodus by his opponents (3:4–18).

The claim of the opponents that divine power can unambiguously be made tangible forces Paul to a seemingly gnostic speech about the presence of the eschatological event. To be sure, nothing less is at stake than the resplendent rise of the light of creation through the apostle's work (4:5). But it comes forth from the "heart" of the apostle; it is a treasure in earthen vessels (4:7). Paradoxically, the tribulations of the apostle are what make it really visible and tangible, because his fate is the re-experience of the dying of Jesus in order that his life might become real in the congregation (4:8ff). Only the inner human being is renewed; the outward one perishes like everything that is visible (4:16ff). Gnostic overtones are also clearly recognizable in Paul's statements about the dissolution of the earthly tent (5:1ff). Although all human actions will finally become apparent before the judgment seat of God (5:10), in the realm of earthly existence the truth of the proclamation can be revealed only in the conscience and heart of the hearer (4:2; 5:11f; 6:12; 7:3), not in any public documentation. The new creation is a present reality, and all the old things have gone (5:17); but Paul, entrusted with the office of the eschatological reconciliation (5:18–6:2), is able only to point the Corinthians to some rather paradoxical documentations of this event in his own experience and activities: "in tribulations, beatings, prisons . . . as dying, and behold, living . . ." (6:3–10).

The events following the receipt of this letter suggest that it did not remove the doubts of the Corinthians and probably only provoked his opponents' mockery. Informed about his letter's effect, Paul must have abruptly decided to go to Corinth and bring the congregation back to his side through his personal intervention. The visit was obviously a catastrophe. The Corinthians gave no indication that they were willing to submit to Paul, and what is more, someone must have offended Paul so severely (2 Cor 7:12) that the personal relationship was seriously called into question. Paul returned to Ephesus without having achieved his purpose and decided once again to write to the church in Corinth; this second letter against the foreign apostles in Corinth is at least partially preserved in 2 Corinthians 10–13, and perhaps is the letter "written with many tears" mentioned in 2 Cor 2:4. This letter is an apology for the apostolic ministry of Paul, in which he goes to the very limits of good taste in the choice of his literary and rhetorical methods. One of his most important churches was at stake. Satire and irony are employed, along with scorn and open threats.

Paul had had a chance to meet his opponents in person. He knew only too well what the Corinthians expected from him if he chose to compare himself with the opponents according to their criteria. But he could under no circumstances do the Corinthians the favor of entering into such a conversation, because the "measuring," "estimating," and "comparing," of the opponents had its basis in their own glory. Paul requested that the Corinthians not measure him according to his opponents' criteria. They should judge his letters as well as his personal appearance on the basis of the criteria appropriate to the subject in question, namely, the proclamation of the gospel (10:1–18). However, the charge that Paul had not made any use of the right which he possessed as the messenger of the gospel, namely, to receive his livelihood from the church, was a grave accusation, especially since the suspicion had been raised in this context that the collection of money sprang from ignoble motives (11:7–10; 12:11–18). If this renunciation of his apostolic right, which expressed his love for the community, could be misunderstood in such as way, Paul had to draw the conclusion that his whole work had been in vain. As an honest matchmaker, he had wanted to procure the church for Christ as a pure bride, but now if the church dallied with these "super-apostles" who were nothing but disguised messengers of Satan, then this church was indeed lost (11:1ff; 11:12ff; cf. 12:19ff).

In such a situation, Paul finally decided to accept the challenge and compare himself with his opponents according to their criteria—but in a "fool's speech." This section of the letter (11:16–12:10), carefully formulated in every detail, is a mockery of all the religious achievements of which his opponents boasted, a satire of aretalogy. Paul begins with a comparison of the titles of dignity (11:22f), but instead of the subsequent enumeration of the successful deeds of missionary activity one finds a catalogue of crises and disasters (*peristaseis*), in which he enumerates all the adverse circumstances, dangers, insults, and misfortunes which he had experienced in his work as an apostle (11:23ff). The catalogue concludes with an ironic account of his undignified flight from Damascus (11:32f). In 12:1ff Paul treats the accomplishments of his personal piety, which indicates that the opponents had also boasted of their visions and successful prayers. Paul, however, reveals that he is not quite certain about the identity of the person who was taken in rapture to the third heaven, and notes that nothing that could be communicated emerged from the whole affair in any case. With regard to his prayers, he received only a negative answer. In this way Paul makes clear that the church will learn nothing by judging the apostle in comparison with his opponents. Rather, the church has to judge itself as to whether it stands in the faith and whether Christ is present in it. If that is in fact the case, then the apostle has also stood the test. Otherwise he must use his authority to dissolve the church (13:1ff).

After the writing of this letter, some time must have gone by before the conflict's final solution. It is completely impossible to assume that 2 Corinthians 10–13 was part of the last letter written by Paul from Macedonia to Corinth, after Titus had already informed him that the church had been reconciled (2 Cor 7:6f). It is unthinkable that Paul struck his opponents with the decisive blow only after the arrival of this cheerful message. The whole tenor of 2 Corinthians 10–13, the violence of the attack, and the exhaustive use of all rhetorical devices makes it necessary to accept the hypothesis of a division of 2 Corinthians, and to assign 2 Cor 1:1–2:13; 7:4–16, as well as the two collection letters in chapters 8 and 9, to a later stage of Paul's relationship with the Corinthian church. The necessity of sending Titus to Corinth in order to accomplish a reconciliation between the church and the apostle, as well as some other unforeseen events in Ephesus again delayed Paul's anticipated visit to Corinth and forced him once more to change his travel plans.

(e) Ephesian Imprisonment; Letters to the Philippians and to Philemon

1) *The Ephesian Imprisonment.* Statements such as 2 Cor 6:5 and 11:23 show that Paul had been in prison more than once, which is also reflected in several stories in Acts. 2 Cor 1:8ff, written shortly after Paul's departure from Ephesus to Macedonia, reports an affliction in which Paul was already prepared to receive the death sentence. This report is best explained as a reference to an Ephesian imprisonment. The data of Phil

1:12–26 and the Letter to Philemon would fit this situation very well, and in that case these letters should be dated in the winter of 54–55 as letters from the Ephesian imprisonment. The traditional thesis, however, is that these letters as well as the (actually spurious) letters to the Colossians and Ephesians were written during Paul's imprisonment in Rome. A solution to the question of whether Philippians and Philemon were written in Rome or in Ephesus is difficult because, outside of the Pauline letters, we have no information whatsoever about either one of these imprisonments (Acts 28:30f at best allows the conclusion that there was a Roman imprisonment). Therefore internal information from these letters can alone be decisive.

If we follow such data, there is clearly a preponderance in favor of their composition during an Ephesian imprisonment. While in prison, Paul received a gift of money from the church in Philippi (Phil 4:10–20); Epaphroditus came to Paul from Philippi as the bearer of the gift or shortly thereafter (Phil 2:25; 4:18), and the Philippians had meanwhile heard that Epaphroditus had fallen sick while he was with Paul (Phil 2:26). Paul wants to send Timothy to Philippi as soon as possible (Phil 2:19) and, in case he receives a favorable sentence, he would like to come to Philippi in person in the near future (Phil 1:26; 2:24). Such a quick exchange of messages and messengers can be explained much more easily if Paul were in prison in Ephesus rather than Rome. Furthermore, an intention to visit Philippi soon is irreconcilable with Paul's plan to go to Spain via Rome (Rom 15:24–28). On the other hand, a visit to Philippi coincides exactly with the plans that we know from the Corinthian correspondence where he mentions a visit to Corinth by way of Macedonia—and this is precisely what Paul did after he left Ephesus. Moreover, the slave Onesimus, who had run away from the house of Philemon in Colossae, would likely have come to Ephesus, the next major port city, and it was not difficult for Paul to send him back to Colossae from Ephesus. But this would fit a Roman imprisonment very poorly, not to mention Paul's statement that he would possibly visit Colossae soon (Phlm 22; cf. Rom 15:24ff).

Bibliography to §9.3e (1)

G. S. Duncan, *Paul's Ephesian Ministry: A Reconstruction with Special Reference to the Ephesian Origin of the Imprisonment Epistles* (New York: Scribner's, 1929). Cf. idem, "Paul's Ministry in Asia—The Last Phase," *NTS* 3 (1956/57) 211–18; and idem, "Chronological Table to Illustrate Paul's Ministry in Asia," *NTS* 5 (1958/59) 43–45.

T. W. Manson, "St. Paul in Ephesus: The Date of the Epistle to the Philippians," *BJRL* 23 (1939).

Wilhelm Michaelis, *Die Gefangenschaft des Paulus in Ephesus und das Itinerar des Timotheus* (Gütersloh: Bertelsmann, 1925).

2) *The Letters to the Philippians.* Because the individual sections of Philippians reflect very different situations and moods, it is advisable to accept the hypothesis that it is a composite letter (§7.4d). The first of these letters, Phil 4:10–20, is a note of thanks directed to Philippi, and it also serves as a formal receipt for the gift of money sent from Philippi to Paul (4:18 uses the regular formula of receipt). This letter emphasizes Paul's independence and self-sufficiency (*autarkia*) (4:11–13); he does not want to understand this gift as the fulfillment of an obligation, but as an offering of thanks for God (4:18). This includes the congregation not only in a relationship of mutual give and take with the apostle, but also in the care and welfare of God (4:19).

The second letter, Phil 1:1–3:1 (perhaps also 4:4–7), reflects throughout the situation of Paul's imprisonment. The proem (1:3–26) gives a comprehensive treatment of the imprisonment and the anticipation of Paul's death in their significance for the church, for the proclamation of the gospel, and for Paul himself. With regard to the Christians in Philippi, Paul is convinced that their share in the proclamation of the gospel and the bond of love that unites them with the apostle will guarantee their continuing growth in knowledge and discernment (1:3–11). As for the gospel, Paul knows that his imprisonment has even encouraged its proclamation, but he emphasizes at the same time that both the church and the gospel are independent of his fate and of their relationship to Paul as a person (1:12–18). What happens to Paul himself, finally, is irrelevant, because Christ will be glorified whether through life or through death. Although it would be gain for Paul to die and be with Christ, he would still choose life and service on behalf of the church (1:19–26). Since Paul in this letter speaks of a direct entrance into the "being with Christ"

Bibliography to §9.3e (2): Commentaries

J.-F. Collange, *The Epistle of Saint Paul to the Philippians* (London: Epworth, 1979).

Bibliography to §9.3e (2): Studies

Günther Bornkamm, "On Understanding the Christ-hymn (Philippians 2.6–11)" in: idem, *Experience,* 112–22.

Dieter Georgi, "Der vorpaulinische Hymnus Phil. 2, 6–11," in: *Zeit und Geschichte: Dankesgabe an Rudolf Bultmann zum 80. Geburtstag* (Tübingen: Mohr/Siebeck, 1964) 262–93.

Ernst Käsemann, "Kritische Analyse von Phil. 2,5–11," in: idem, *Exegetische Versuche und Besinnungen* (Göttingen: Vandenhoeck & Ruprecht, 1960) 1. 51–95.

Schmithals, "The False Teachers of the Epistle to the Philippians," in: idem, *Paul and the Gnostics,* 65–122.

Helmut Koester, "The Purpose of the Polemic of a Pauline Fragment (Phil III)," *NTS* 8 (1961/62) 317–32.

through his death, without expressing an expectation of the parousia, it has been argued that he had developed his eschatological expectations after he wrote 1 Cor 15:51f. However, what is said in Phil 1:21ff differs in no way from Paul's statements in his earliest preserved letter (see 1 Thess 5:10). The parenesis of this letter is also closely related to the theme of the suffering of the apostle (Phil 1:27–2:18; esp. 1:29f; 2:17). But such references do not establish a relationship of dependence upon the apostle. On the contrary, the apostle is nothing more than a sacrifice poured out for the faith of the church, while the church's salvation is directly dependent upon God and Christ.

The central concept of the parenesis is, therefore, not the example of Paul, but Christ as the foundation for the new existence. This is stated in the hymn about Christ in Phil 2:6–11. This hymn is an important piece of evidence for the appropriation and modification by early Christianity of traditions from mythical wisdom theology. As the hymn is quoted by Paul, however, it no longer proclaims an individualistic understanding of salvation. It announces the cosmic rule of the crucified Christ and demands from the congregation a basic attitude that corresponds to his way of humiliation and thus requires unanimity, mutual respect, and renunciation of one's own importance. The conclusion of this letter contains recommendations for Paul's associate, Timothy, who had once spent himself selflessly for the proclamation on behalf of the church, and for Epaphroditus, who had been sent from Philippi, but was prevented from returning until now because he had fallen sick (2:19–30). It is surprising to see that it is exactly this letter, so concerned with Paul's imprisonment and his impending death, that is dominated by repeated invitations to joy (1:4, 18, 25; 2:2, 17f, 29f; 3:1; 4:4). In the face of death the eschatological joy as the festive attire of the church must demonstrate more than ever all that faith is worth.

A completely different tone predominates in Phil 3:2–4:3. Paul must have learned of a dangerous threat to the church when foreign missionaries had invaded the community in Philippi. The letter written by Paul against these missionaries is not completely preserved. But what is still extant in Phil 3:2–21 (perhaps also 4:1–3, 8f) corresponds to the literary form of the "testament." According to Jewish prototypes (see the *Testaments of the Twelve Patriarchs,* §5.3c), this genre consists of a biographical history, an ethical admonition, and an eschatological instruction, including curses and blessings (the warning about false teachers appears in this context). This literary genre was used elsewhere in early Christian literature, most obviously in the deutero-Pauline 2 Timothy (§12.2g). It is debated whether the opponents of Philippians 3 were Jewish, Jewish-Christian, or gnosticizing missionaries. They differ from the opponents of

2 Corinthians insofar as they preach circumcision and observance of the law (note especially Phil 3:3, 5f); they thus agree in this respect with the Judaizers in Galatia. But they seem to differ from those Judaizers in their proclamation of a perfection that can be obtained in the present existence by means of obedience to the law, and in their emphasis that such perfection guarantees the full possession of the heavenly blessings (3:12, 15, 19). This betrays a gnosticizing consciousness of salvation. In any case, the invectives of 3:2 and 18f cannot be understood as attacks upon libertines, but seem to be reversals of the perfectionistic slogans of the opponents.

The biographical introduction in Phil 3:5–11 is an important testimony to Paul's understanding of his "conversion" (§9.1b). The perfection extolled by the opponents parallels Paul's former possession which he surrendered in order to gain the righteousness through faith in Christ. This new existence is determined by the suffering and death of Christ, while the resurrection belongs strictly in the future; therefore the ethical admonition (3:12–16) must not encourage conduct that fulfills an ideal of perfection. Rather, ethical conduct must take into account the fact that Christian existence is an open movement toward an eschatological goal. Eschatological fulfillment cannot be achieved by one's actions in the present; those who attempt this are threatened by the curse (3:18f). The goal toward which the Christians are moving transcends earthly existence and presupposes its transformation (3:20f). Paul's arguments against the apostles of perfection in Philippi are thus similar to those he used against the enthusiasts in Corinth (1 Corinthians 15). In both cases Paul is confronted with gnosticizing opponents.

3) *The Letter to Philemon* must have been written at about the same time. It is the sole extant letter of Paul to an individual. For this reason Paul omits his title when giving his name in the prescript. He calls himself "a prisoner of Jesus Christ" (Phlm 1) and does not direct his petition to Philemon as an apostle who can demand obedience, but as "an old man

Bibliography to §9.3e (3): Commentaries

Eduard Lohse, *Colossians and Philemon: A Commentary on the Epistles to the Colossians and to Philemon* (Hermeneia: Philadelphia: Fortress, 1971) 185–208.

Richard Lehmann, *Epitre à Philémon: Le Christianisme primitif et l'esclavage* (Commentaires Bibliques; Geneva: Labor et Fides, 1978).

Peter Stuhlmacher, *Der Brief an Philemon* (EKKNT; Neukirchen-Vluyn: Neukirchener Verlag, 1975).

Bibliography to §9.3e (3): Studies

John Knox, *Philemon among the Letters of Paul: A New View of its Place and Importance* (2d ed.; Nashville: Abingdon, 1959).

Theo Preiss, "Life in Christ and Social Ethics in the Epistle to Philemon," in: idem, *Life in Christ* (SBT 13; London: SCM, 1954) 32–42.

and a prisoner" (v. 9). The addressee, Philemon, was apparently living in Colossae (cf. Col 4:9, 17). Since Philemon is also called a fellow worker, and greetings are directed to the church in his house, we can assume that the Christian church in Colossae was founded by Philemon, whom Paul must have converted in Ephesus. The letter presupposes that Philemon's slave Onesimus had run away (because of a theft?; see Phlm 18) to Ephesus and had taken refuge with Paul, who was then in prison. Onesimus had rendered useful services to Paul, who had grown fond of him; but Paul could not keep him, probably for reasons both practical and legal. Thus he sent him back, together with a letter, to his master Philemon.

It has been frequently debated whether this letter demanded that Philemon release Onesimus from slavery. But it must be noted first of all that Paul does not demand anything in this letter. He does not employ his apostolic authority and leaves all decisions to Philemon. However, the recommendation to accept the runaway slave "as a brother . . . both in the flesh and in the Lord" can hardly be understood in any other way than as a recommendation to give Onesimus his freedom. "Brother in the Lord" is something that Onesimus would be anyway as a slave; "in the flesh" must refer to his worldly status (v. 16). Instead of an apostolic command, Paul gives a personal guarantee in writing which would have been legally binding: if necessary, Paul will defray all expenses (vv. 18f). This clearly shows that the letter was written to Philemon in order to achieve Onesimus' manumission. As a whole this letter is strikingly different from a letter of the younger Pliny written in a very similar situation (*Epist.* 9.21). In this letter, Pliny appeals to his friend's magnanimity, which should make him willing to forgive a runaway servant. In contrast, the Letter to Philemon does not even so much as mention forgiveness and is meticulously concerned not to put Onesimus into a situation which would henceforth bind him in thankfulness to his master's magnanimity. On the contrary, for Paul the commandment of love requires that freedom be granted without any personal obligations, but rather on the basis of legal and business-like guarantees, which Paul himself is quite prepared to give.

(f) The Collection; Paul's Last Visit to Corinth

In the agreement at the Apostolic Council, Paul had promised to remember the "poor" in Jerusalem (Gal 2:10; see §9.1d). But in 1 Thessalonians and Galatians Paul did not make any attempt to follow up on this promise by organizing a collection of money. It can be assumed that Paul

Bibliography to §9.3f

Dieter Georgi, *Die Geschichte der Kollekte des Paulus für Jerusalem* (ThF 38; Hamburg-Bergstedt: Reich/Theologischer Verlag, 1965).

had put this enterprise aside for the time being. The tense situation in Galatia would not have been very propitious for this purpose anyway. But 1 Cor 16:1ff demonstrates that Paul had by then seriously resumed his plans to make such a collection for Jerusalem. The passage contains detailed instructions for the procedures to be followed in gathering this money, states Paul's intention to send accredited envoys to Jerusalem for the delivery of the collection, and also reports about the progress of the collection in Galatia. This shows clearly that several churches were included in the project. Titus and another brother had been sent from Ephesus to Corinth shortly afterwards in order to expedite the collection in Greece (2 Cor 12:18). The controversy with the "super-apostles" in Corinth interrupted the project, and, what was worse, in the course of this controversy, accusations had surfaced which questioned the integrity of Paul's aims with regard to the money (2 Cor 12:13–18). Paul's imprisonment in Ephesus and the fears that he might be sentenced to death ended all further plans for the collection for the time being.

As soon as Paul had been released from prison at the beginning of the year 55, his first care had to be his reconciliation with the Corinthian congregation. For this very reason he apparently changed his original plans for a direct journey from Ephesus to Corinth and a later visit to Macedonia (2 Cor 1:15f). What Paul writes in 2 Cor 1:23ff shows his concern clearly: the catastrophe of the last visit to Corinth (the "interim" visit; see §9.3d) must not be repeated. Therefore, he first sent Titus to Corinth; Titus was known to the Corinthians, and Paul had already referred to his acknowledged integrity in 2 Cor 12:18. Paul himself did not intend to come to Corinth unless Titus first brought the news that the congregation had been reconciled. Meanwhile Paul went to Troas with Timothy (it was from Troas that Paul had travelled to Macedonia for the first time five years earlier). But when Titus did not arrive in Troas as expected, Paul went on to Macedonia, probably to Philippi, even though Troas had opened some promising possibilities for missionary work (2 Cor 2:12). In Macedonia he finally met Titus, whose arrival he had longingly expected, and who brought the welcome news that the Corinthians were willing to be reconciled.

In this situation Paul wrote a letter to Corinth, of which the major part is preserved in 2 Cor 1:1–2:13; 7:5–16. Timothy is named as co-author, just as in the oldest extant letter of Paul (1 Thess 1:1; note also Phil 1:1; Phlm 1). Thus Timothy accompanied him on this last journey as well (see also Rom 16:21). In the proem Paul first speaks in general of the afflictions which he had to go through and of his experience of God's comfort (2 Cor 1:3–7). Both topics are further elucidated in the body of the letter. It is characteristic that the afflictions are not understood as isolated events concerning the personal fate of the apostle alone—in view of the threat of a death sentence in Ephesus Paul would have had sufficient reason to speak only about himself (2 Cor 1:8–10)—but as experiences which involve the church in many ways. The petitions of the church have also contributed to his rescue (1:11). The Corinthians must, therefore, also recognize that the repeated changes in Paul's travel plans did not arise from any irresoluteness on his part; his whole behavior was rooted in his unwavering commitment to the gospel which he had preached in Corinth (1:12–22). With reference to his "interim" visit, and to the letter written at that time (= 2 Corinthians 10–13; see §9.3d), Paul explains that even the offence he received in Corinth—the topic "affliction" is here continued— concerned everybody, not just Paul himself. Therefore the congregation should help to reconcile the person who caused the offence, since Paul had to change his travel plans to prevent further distress (1:23–2:11). The apostle's afflictions did not end when he had been rescued from almost certain death, nor were they ended through new opportunities for missionary work (2:12f; 7:5). They ended only when he received the news about the reconciliation with the Corinthian church (7:6–16). This last part of the letter also explains that Titus had not only earned the gratefulness of the apostle, but that the church owed him thanks too. He had accomplished what Paul himself was unable to do, namely, to change affliction into comfort, joy, and revival for all involved. These statements of Paul make it altogether clear that his mission was by no means the work of one single apostle, but the result of the successful collaboration of a number of Jewish and gentile Christian missionaries. Their greatest achievement, despite significant external difficulties and dangerous competitors, was to build and strengthen the churches they had founded, so that these churches were able to weather the storms which were still to come.

The two letters about the collection (2 Corinthians 8 and 9), which Paul sent at this time to Corinth and to Achaea respectively, indicate that he, together with the churches which were now reconciled, was now able to bring to completion the great design of the collection for Jerusalem. These short writings do more than encourage generous giving, they also measure the eschatological horizon for this work of the communities. With their gift for Jerusalem they are doing more than giving support for the poor; their giving is in itself a participation in the glorification of God on behalf of his grace, which is fully experienced in the act of giving. Because they share this experience now, the gentile Christians rank first as the recipients of the eschatological revelation of the righteousness of God.

4. Corinth—Jerusalem—Rome

(a) The Last Stay in Corinth;
Letters to the Romans and to the "Ephesians"

The stay in Corinth during the winter of 55–56 marks the conclusion of Paul's missionary work in the region of the Aegean Sea. Further strengthening of the newly founded churches, preparation for his travel to the west, and organization of the delivery of the collection must have occupied Paul during this period. Romans 16:1–23 witnesses to the first of these activities. It is a fragment

Bibliography to §9.4a: Commentaries
C. E. B. Cranfield, *A Critical and Exegetical Commentary on the Epistle to the Romans* (ICC; 2 vols.; Edinburgh: Clark, 1975–79).
Ernst Käsemann, *Commentary on Romans* (Grand Rapids: Eerdmans, 1980).

Bibliography to §9.4a: Studies
Ferdinand Christian Baur, "Über Zweck und Veranlassung des Römerbriefes und der damit zusammenhängenden Verhältnisse der römischen Gemeinde," *Tübinger Zeitschrift für Theologie* (1836) 59–113.
Robin Scroggs, *The Last Adam: Study in Pauline Anthropology* (Philadelphia: Fortress, 1966).
Dom Jacques Dupont, "Le problème de la structure littéraire de l'Epître aux Romains," *RB* 62 (1955) 365–97.
Walter Schmithals, *Der Römerbrief als historisches Problem* (Gütersloh: Mohn, 1975).
Hans-Martin Schenke, "Aporien im Römerbrief," *ThLZ* 92 (1967) 881–84.
Bornkamm, *Experience,* 47–111.
Albert Descamps, "La structure de Rom 1–11," in: *Studiorum Paulinorum Congressus* (AnBib 17; Rome: Pontifical Biblical Institute, 1963) 1. 3–14.
Ulrich Luz, "Zum Aufbau von Röm. 1–8," *ThZ* 25 (1969) 161–81.
Rudolf Bultmann, "Romans 7 and the Anthropology of Paul," in: idem, *Existence and Faith,* 147–65.
Werner Georg Kümmel, *Römer 7 und das Bild des Menschen im Neuen Testament* (ThBü 53; München: Kaiser, 1974).
Ernst Käsemann, "Principles of the Interpretation of Romans 13," in: idem, *New Testament Questions,* 196–216.
Robert J. Karris, "Rom 14:1–15:13 and the Occasion of Romans," *CBQ* 35 (1973) 155–78.

Bibliography to §9.4a: The Question of Romans 16
T. W. Manson, "St. Paul's Letter to the Romans—and Others," *BJRL* 31 (1948) 224–40.
J. J. MacDonald, "Was Romans xvi a Separate Letter?" *NTS* 16 (1969/70) 369–72.
Wolf-Henning Ollrog, "Die Abfassungsverhältnisse von Röm 16," in: *Kirche: Festschrift Bornkamm,* 221–44.
Walter Schmithals, "The False Teachers of Romans 16:17–20," in: idem, *Paul and the Gnostics,* 219–38.

of a letter that was likely written at that time and perhaps sent to Ephesus together with a copy of the Letter to the Romans (Romans 1–15). This hypothesis would also explain why this short letter to the "Ephesians" ended up in the later collection of the Pauline letters as part of the Letter to the Romans. That Romans as it is now extant was put together by a later editor is also evident from the doxology added at the end (Rom 16:25–27), which certainly is not Pauline. A number of manuscripts place this doxology at the end of chapters 14 or 15 of Romans, which proves that the letter once circulated in different versions (the one used by Marcion seems to have ended with chapter 14!). The short letter of Romans 16 allows us an interesting glance into Paul's activities as an ecclesiastical politician. He did not devise church orders, but settled individual questions in the context of fortifying personal relationships. The first part of this letter is the oldest extant letter of recommendation for a Christian minister, namely, for the "missionary" and "congregational president" Phoebe from Cenchrea (Rom 16:1–2; the traditional translations of her titles as "deaconness" and "helper" cannot be justified on linguistic grounds). In the long list of greetings a woman is also named among the apostles (Junia, Rom 16:7; we cannot read instead the male name "Junias," because this name is not attested anywhere else). Most of the persons named in this list are not simply personal friends of Paul in the church of Ephesus, but associates and co-workers. This is shown by the repeated references to their functions. The fact that such a large number of women appears in this list is clear and undeniable evidence for the unrestricted participation of women in the offices of the church in the Pauline congregations. The mention of house-churches and individual groups (Rom 16:5, 15) points to the existence of several "congregations" within the church at Ephesus. The conclusion of the letter brings a short warning of false teachers which echoes that of Philippians 3.

The writing of the letter to the church in Rome, as well as Paul's decision to deliver the collection for Jerusalem in person, demonstrates that more was at stake than just the opening up of a new missionary area after the completion of the work in the east. Both Romans as well as the collection are part of an effort to establish a new relationship between gentile and Jewish Christianity, and thus also between gentile Christianity and Judaism. Both, the collection and the Letter to the Romans, deny the authority of the law and the eschatological preeminence of Jerusalem. Instead, Paul insists upon the equal position of all people, who are united not through law, tradition, and organization, but through both their mutual care and the divine promise. Their mutual care is documented in the collection of the gentile Christians for Jerusalem; it is a service and a thanksgiving to God. The promise is universal and inclusive; it reckons with the inclusion of the full number of people from all nations, but it also remains valid as a promise to Israel. All these thoughts find expression in the Letter to the Romans.

Romans does not contain polemical controversies like so many other letters of Paul. It is also not a theoretical theological treatise. One can best characterize this writing as a letter of recommendation which Paul has written on his own behalf. But Paul does not explicitly emphasize his apostolic authority as such (cf. Rom 1:1 with Gal 1:1). His person appears only insofar as Paul is the bearer of the gospel which claims universal validity, and thus obligates its messenger to serve as a missionary for the whole inhabited world. The topic of the letter is therefore this gospel, and not the person of the apostle. The topic is explicated in terms of a dialogue with Judaism and with the law. The presence of many Jews and Jewish Christians in Rome explains this interest only very superficially. There are reasons germane to the subject itself which required that the exposition of the gospel for the gentiles entertain the question of freedom from the law, because the law is for Paul the only alternative to the freedom of the gospel, not only for the Jew but also for the gentile. Resuming the tradition of Jewish apologetics (§5.3e), Paul assigns to the law a status of universal validity, but is forced, at the same time, to enter into a discussion of the question of "Israel" and its special claim to the law and the promises.

Romans throughout reflects Paul's insights from earlier polemical controversies: for the promise to Abraham, Romans 4, compare Gal 3:16–18; for the topic of Adam and Christ, Rom 5:12ff, compare 1 Cor 15:45–49; for the question of baptism, Rom 6:1ff, compare 1 Cor 1:12ff and 15:29; on the charismata, Rom 12:1ff, compare 1 Cor 12:1ff; the relation of the strong and the weak, Rom 14:1–15:6 was extensively discussed in 1 Cor 6:12–11:1; and the doctrine of justification had been the primary topic in Philippians 3 and Galatians. The form of Romans has little in common with the other letters of Paul, however, because its general outline is borrowed from the tradition of Jewish apologetics. The apologetic schema is especially evident in Rom 1:18–3:31, though it has received some decisive modifications. According to the traditional schema, the gentiles would have been described as having a partial knowledge of God and the law, in order to commend to them the full knowledge of God and law as it is given in the biblical revelation. Paul, however, begins with the argument that both Jews and gentiles possess full knowledge of both God and the law. The law of nature which is given to the gentiles (Rom 2:12–16) is thus entirely equivalent to the law of the Bible. Of course, this is not intended to extol the law, but to show the universal predicament: just as the law makes it possible to boast of one's accomplishments, it also makes it clear that all have fallen under the power of sin. According to the protreptic interests of traditional apologetics, Paul's statement about his own proclamation (Rom 3:21ff) should be continued with expositions about right conduct in the framework of this proclamation, and with an explanation about the path on which those who aspire to follow this message can reach their aim. But the possibility of works as instruments for attaining the goal had been fundamentally questioned in Paul's criticism of the law. This goal, namely, justification, cannot be obtained by human actions. Rather, God's revelation had made justification present for all people. Faith is the realization of this presence: this is demonstrated with the example of Abraham (Romans 4). The following chapters (Romans 5–8) explain how freedom from sin and death is present as a gift through justification. To be sure, this freedom is qualified by the "eschatological reservation"—that is, the life of the resurrection cannot be enjoyed in advance, and the element of hope remains a constitutive part of faith. But this does not limit the freedom that has been obtained, it only binds this freedom to the continuing work of God's love that is present in Christ (Rom 8:31–39).

If the presence of God's freedom as a gift remains a paradoxical experience for the believer (Rom 7:7–8:30), it must be completely unintelligible to "Israel according to the flesh," because preaching and faith were not operative there. This leads Paul to an extended discussion of the question of the Jewish people (Romans 9–11). Paul is thus the first Christian writer to treat this question as a topic of Christian apologetics. But in contrast to the ideological interests of later Christian apologetics, Paul does not introduce a single argument aimed at the conversion of Israel; instead, he intensifies the concept of election. The universal validity of God's promise cannot be questioned, not even on the basis of the experience that God's act of revelation through the proclamation of the gospel has indeed failed in Israel. The promises of God remain valid in any case. They cannot be argued away from Israel, because they are determined in the counsel of God. On the other hand, Paul would never dream of abandoning the preaching of justification by faith alone in order to oblige Israel: that would destroy God's act of salvation in Christ and reestablish in its stead the vicious cycle of human righteousness and law. In this respect, Jews and gentiles fall under the same verdict (Rom 10:1–12).

The final part of the letter (Rom 12:1–15:13) is not ethical instruction in the sense of an apologetic protreptic admonition, but is written from the perspective of the giving up of one's own interests. Ethical conduct is not designed to further one's own moral perfection, but to promote the welfare of the neighbor and to build up the congregation. What is required, therefore, is a rational (not an ideological or charismatic) discernment of one's own abilities for the service of one's neighbor. This includes rejection of revenge (there are no "divine causes" Christians have to defend), rejection of political resistance (if Rom 13:1–7 is indeed Pauline and not a piece of Hellenistic-Jewish parenesis interpolated at a later date), and rejection of the realization of one's own ideal of perfection: the building up of the weak in the congregation takes precedence. In the last chapter (Rom 15:14–32) Paul returns to the occasion for his writing, namely, his intention to come to Rome so that he may be sent on from there to Spain. Paul wanted the letter as a whole to clarify to the Roman church that this was not a matter of his personal wish; in that case a letter of recommendation would have been unnecessary. Rather, the letter had to be written in order to include the Roman Christians in the universal event of the progress of the gospel, which included the delivery of the collection to Jerusalem as well as the mission in the far west: both are explicitly mentioned and joined together as a unity.

(b) The Journey to Jerusalem and the Fate of the Collection

At the end of his letter, Paul had announced his impending arrival in Rome (Rom 15:22–24), but he interrupted this announcement with the information that he had to go to Jerusalem first because of the collection for the saints. From there he would travel to Rome and then on to Spain (Rom 15:25–28). Special circumstances must have forced Paul to supervise the delivery of the collection personally, because in 1 Cor 16:3–4 he had indicated that delegates elected by the churches and accredited by letters from Paul would bring the collection to Jerusalem, while he himself would go only if absolutely necessary. Now Paul deems it advisable that he go in person, and he mentions as the reason for this decision the hostility of the nonbelievers in Judea. A welcome reception for the collection by the church in Jerusalem seems to be imperiled because of this hostility (Rom 15:31).

This is the last information which is preserved about the life and ministry of Paul from his own letters. For the course of the events after the writing of Romans, our only source is the Book of Acts, which occasionally uses reliable source material, to be sure, but on the whole shapes its narrative according to Luke's own tendencies and in fact mentions the collection only in an aside (Acts 24:17). But it is beyond doubt that the journey which is described in Acts 20–21 is indeed the journey of the delegation for the delivery of the collection. According to the Lukan re-

Bibliography to §9.4b

Henry J. Cadbury, "Roman Law and the Trial of Paul," in: Foakes Jackson and Lake, *Beginnings,* 5. 297–338.

port, Paul did not take the direct sea route from Corinth to the eastern Mediterranean because Jews travelling in the boat on which Paul had booked passage were planning an attempt on his life. Thus Paul first took the land route to Macedonia (Acts 20:3), accompanied by the delegates from the churches which participated in the collection (Acts 20:4 preserves a partial list of these delegates). The delivery of the collection by such a sizable delegation, whose travel expenses had to be paid, indicates not only the significance of the collection in Paul's view, but also proves that the sum of money brought to Jerusalem was by no means negligible. The ports of call during this trip by boat from Macedonia are given according to one of the easily accessible itineraries, but may well correspond to the actual stations of Paul's journeys: Philippi, Troas (Acts 20:6), Assus, Mitylene, Chios, Samos, Miletus (Acts 20:14–15), Cos, Rhodes, Patara, and bypassing Cyprus, Tyre in Syria (Acts 21:1–3), Ptolemais, and finally Caesarea (Acts 21:7–8).

While the narratives inserted into this itinerary are legendary, beginning with Acts 21:15 Luke seems to follow a reliable report from some source. When Paul arrives in Jerusalem, the responsible leader of the church is Jesus' brother James; Peter had long since left Jerusalem, and John is no longer mentioned. The Jewish-Christian church of Jerusalem is depicted as strictly law-abiding, while Paul had the reputation of having seduced Jews in the diaspora away from circumcision and observance of Jewish customs. Because of such widespread rumors, James persuaded Paul to give a demonstration of his faithfulness to the law: he should redeem four men who had taken a Nazirite vow and pay for the expenses of this redemption, including the necessary sacrifices. Such a demonstration of a pious and law-abiding act would end all malicious rumors about him. It has been rightly assumed that this is a direct reflection of the difficulties that resulted from the delivery of the collection from the gentile Christians for the law-abiding Jewish-Christian church in Jerusalem. Paul had indeed expected difficulties, as Rom 15:31 demonstrates. He must have known that the offer of a considerable amount of financial aid from the gentile Christians for the Jerusalem church would constitute an overexacting encumbrance on the relationship of the Jewish Christians to the other Jews in the city. But in spite of this fear, Paul had insisted on making the collection, had devoted considerable time and effort to this enterprise during his missionary activities, and had even decided to make the journey himself to Jerusalem, although his primary concern had been to go to the west as soon as possible.

All this clearly shows how highly Paul valued this demonstration of the unity of all churches. It is also the clearest proof that Paul had no interest whatsoever in documenting the unity of the churches through unified doctrines or beliefs. Unity could only come into being through mutual loving care and aid. It was exactly Paul's desire to document this concept of ecclesiastical unity that caused difficulties for the Jewish Christians in Jerusalem and finally determined Paul's personal destiny as well. The church in Jerusalem insisted that Paul visit the temple, which was necessary for the redemption of the Nazirites. Otherwise they could not have accepted the collection. While in the temple, Paul was recognized and accused of having brought a gentile into the temple (was this a false accusation?). A controversy broke out, and the Roman soldiers who appeared to break up the tumult arrested Paul. Thus the consistent pursuit of the one and most important goal of the Pauline mission, that is, the documentation of the universality of the gospel and of the unity of the church of Jews and gentiles, led to Paul's final arrest, and this in turn seems to have resulted in his martyrdom.

(c) Paul's Trial and his Journey to Rome

Although Acts devoted a total of seven chapters (Acts 22–28) to the narrative of Paul's trial and his journey to Rome, the historically reliable data about these last years of Paul's life are few. Paul's speech before the people after his arrest (Acts 22:1–21), his appearance before the Sanhedrin (Acts 22:30–23:11), the trial before Felix, Agrippa II and Festus in Caesarea, with several long speeches by Paul (Acts 24–26), and all the details of the journey to Rome, with the full account of the shipwreck (Acts 27:1–28:16), are products of the apologetic and novelistic literary activities of Luke. The "we" which is used in Acts 27 and 28 cannot be explained as the "we" of an eye-witness; it fits instead the typical style of legendary narratives in the genre of the romance very well (§12.3a). The most reliable pieces of information are the transfer of Paul to Caesarea (Acts 23:31–35), his two-year imprisonment in Caesarea until the replacement of the procurator (Acts 24:27), and his appeal to the emperor and the decision that he be transferred to Rome (Acts 25:11–12; cf. 26:32). Paul, who was at first perhaps only under protective custody, was thus arraigned before the court in Caesarea under the ill-reputed procurator Felix (see Josephus, *Ant.* 20.137–81; *Bell.* 2.247–70), who delayed his decision. When Felix was replaced by the more energetic Festus (see Josephus, *Ant.* 20.182; *Bell.* 2.271–72), the new procurator granted the appeal. The change in the procurator's office from Felix to Festus cannot be fixed with certainty; the most likely date is the year 58.

Acts is silent about the end of Paul's life. The last report speaks about

Bibliography to §9.4c
Haenchen, *Acts,* 599–732.

Paul's activity in Rome on behalf of the gospel while he was kept under house arrest (Acts 28:30–31). The next information comes from *1 Clement,* written in Rome ca. 96 CE (§12.2e): "Paul showed the way to the prize of endurance; seven times he was in bonds, he was exiled, he was stoned, he was a herald in both east and west, he gained noble fame for his faith, he taught righteousness to all the world, and when he had reached the limits of the west, he gave his testimony before the rulers, and thus passed from the world and was taken up into the holy place—the greatest example of endurance" (*1 Clem.* 5.5–7). Of course, the martyrdom of Paul is presupposed here, but neither the time nor the place of his death are identified in this eulogy. But it can be assumed that Paul was martyred in Rome (that is explicitly stated in the later legends about him; note also the parallel to the martyrdom of Peter in *1 Clem.* 5.4). One piece of information from *1 Clement* must remain uncertain, however, namely, that Paul had reached the limits of the west. Since there are no other witnesses to confirm this, it seems doubtful that Paul was set free once more before his final martyrdom so as to be able to execute his original plan of missionary work in Spain (Rom 15:28). There are no traces of any activity of Paul in the west. The Christian churches which claimed to be Pauline foundations in the later centuries are all located in the east, in Asia Minor and Greece.

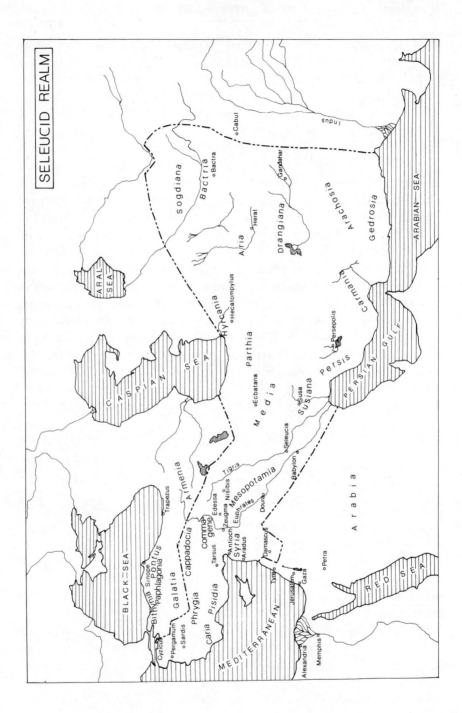

SELEUCID REALM

PALESTINE AND SYRIA

1. The Tradition of the Message of Jesus

(a) Eschatological Interpretation

The eschatological orientation of the earliest communities of Palestine has already been mentioned (§8.3a–d). In the tradition and development of the sayings of Jesus it is visible in two ways. First, the older sayings of Jesus were transformed and interpreted so that they would speak more clearly about Jesus as the future bringer of salvation and expected redeemer. Second, the prophetic proclamation of Jesus was continued in the activity of Christian prophets, who pronounced sayings of revelation about the present and future in Jesus' name and in his authority. In both instances, the development of the tradition of Jesus' sayings was aimed at the organization of the Christian community, which was thus consolidated as an eschatological sect. Attestations for this development are abundantly preserved in the Synoptic tradition. But with the exception of Jerusalem and Antioch (§8.3a, c), the communities which transmitted this tradition cannot be located with certainty, though they were certainly situated in the area of Syria and Palestine. This is clear from the fact that this tradition gives evidence for the immediate proximity of Judaism and for a direct controversy with Jewish circles. It is also attested in the transmission, collection, and recording of these sayings in Aramaic. Evidence for a translation from Aramaic, or formulations which reveal that the author's mother tongue was Aramaic, are most clearly present among the sayings of the Synoptic tradition which derive from this eschatological interpretation.

1) *The Synoptic Sayings Source.* The most important witness for the eschatological theology of these churches is the Synoptic Sayings Source ("Q"; see §7.3b). Q certainly had preliminary stages, such as occasional collections of sayings for catechetical, polemical, and homiletical purposes. But in its final composition and redaction, Q became an ecclesiastical manual which sought to bind the churches for which it was written to a particular eschatological expectation, and to conduct which was in keeping with this expectation. Its central feature was the waiting for the

coming of Jesus as the Son of Man (Luke 17:22–37). This expectation, which seems to be missing in the oldest stages of the Synoptic sayings of Jesus, is derived from Jewish apocalyptic concepts (Dan 7:13–14). In Q it has become the key christological concept for the understanding of Jesus as the redeemer of the future. In contrast, the older expectation of the coming of the rule of God recedes into the background. The outlook toward the coming of Jesus as the Son of Man on the clouds of heaven also determines the conduct of the church's members. The parousia of the Son of Man cannot be calculated in advance and is not related to the events and experiences of this world. The disciples are therefore called to constant watchfulness (Luke 12:35–46). Discipleship of Jesus implies renunciation of the world and of its social bonds (Matt 10:37–38; 8:19–22). The portions of the speeches about the sending of the disciples which derive

Bibliography to §§10–12

Rudolf Bultmann, *Primitive Christianity in Its Contemporary Setting* (New York: Meridian, 1956).

Hans Conzelmann, *History of Primitive Christianity* (Nashville: Abingdon, 1973).

Hans Lietzmann, *The Beginnings of the Christian Church* (New York: Scribner's, 1937) 171–397.

Carl Weizsäcker, *Das Apostolische Zeitalter der christlichen Kirche* (Tübingen: Mohr/Siebeck, 1902). Both Weizsäcker's and Weiss' works are classics.

Johannes Weiss, *Earliest Christianity: A History of the Period A. D. 30–150* (New York: Harper, 1959). German original first published in 1914–17.

Walter Bauer, *Orthodoxy and Heresy in Earliest Christianity* (Philadelphia: Fortress, 1971; originally published in 1934). This work is the basis of much of modern scholarship.

Robinson and Koester, *Trajectories.*

Arnold Ehrhardt, "Christianity before the Apostles' Creed," in: idem, *The Framework of the New Testament Stories* (Cambridge, MA: Harvard University, 1965) 151–99.

James D. G. Dunn, *Unity and Diversity in the New Testament* (Philadelphia: Westminster, 1977).

Conzelmann, *Outline,* 287–317.

Bibliography to §10.1a (1)

James M. Robinson, "LOGOI SOPHON: On the Gattung of Q," in: idem and Koester, *Trajectories,* 71–113.

Richard A. Edwards, *A Theology of Q: Eschatology, Prophecy and Wisdom* (Philadelphia: Fortress, 1976).

Dieter Lührmann, *Die Redaktion der Logienquelle* (WMANT 33; Neukirchen-Vluyn: Neukirchener Verlag, 1969).

Siegfried Schulz, *Q—Die Spruchquelle der Evangelisten* (Zürich: Theologischer Verlag, 1972).

David L. Dungan, *The Sayings of Jesus in the Churches of Paul: The Use of the Synoptic Tradition in the Regulation of Early Church Life* (Philadelphia: Fortress, 1971).

Heinz Eduard Tödt, *Der Menschensohn in der synoptischen Überlieferung* (Gütersloh: Mohn, 1958).

Ronald D. Worden, "Redaction Criticism of Q: A Survey," *JBL* 94 (1975) 532–46.

from Q (Matt 9:35–10:16; Luke 10:1–16) demand homelessness and renunciation of all possessions from the missionary.

In the demand for love of one's enemies and in the relinquishment of all power, the Christian church is distinguished clearly from the world, but also from those apocalyptic movements which sought to force the fulfillment of messianic hope. In the face of the allure of a messianic war against Roman rule, which other Jewish sects such as the Essenes and the Pharisees were not able to withstand, the congregations of the Synoptic Sayings Source thus made a political decision which had some significance for the separation of Christianity from Judaism within the realm of Jewish culture in Palestine. The acceptance of the originally Jewish polemic against the leaders of the people as the murderers of the prophets (Luke 11:49–51) and against Jerusalem (Matt 23:37–39) is characteristic for the position of Q towards Judaism (see also the beatitude about those who are hated because of the Son of Man; Luke 6:22–23). With such polemics Q has not cut all its ties with Judaism and the Jewish tradition, however, although the question of the law does not seem to have played a role. References to examples from the Old Testament occur in Q materials (e.g., Luke 17:26–30), as also biblical quotations (e.g., the story of Jesus' temptation, Matt 4:1–11). The relationship to John the Baptist as Jesus' predecessor is explicitly acknowledged (Matt 11:2–19) and was composed in its current form by the author of Q.

2) *The Synoptic Apocalypse.* Another important witness for the development of the prophetic words of Jesus in Palestinian Christianity is the so-called Synoptic Apocalypse of Mark 13, which is even more closely connected to the time of the Jewish War than is Q. The expectation of Jesus as the coming Son of Man also predominates in the Synoptic Apocalypse (Mark 13:26), specifically in words which clearly mirror Dan 7:13–14 (see also the allusion to Dan 9:27 and 12:11 in Mark 13:14). The connection of this eschatological expectation with contemporary historical events is explicitly rejected (Mark 13:7–8). The church which produced this document is troubled by false prophets (Mark 13:21–23) and persecuted by the Jewish authorities (Mark 13:9).

3) *Collection of Parables.* It is striking that reflections about Jesus' cross and resurrection are missing among the prophetic words which Q and Mark 13 have preserved. The entire christology is focused on the expectation of Jesus as the coming Son of Man; there is no evidence that Q ever

Bibliography to §10.1a (2)

Lars Hartmann, *Prophecy Interpreted: The Formation of Some Jewish Apocalyptic Texts and the Eschatological Discourse Mark 13 Par* (ConB NT Series 1; Lund: Gleerup, 1966).

contained a passion narrative. A third collection of traditions of Jesus' sayings is equally without relation to Jesus' cross and resurrection: the collection of parables preserved in Mark 4. This document cannot be assigned to the same circles as Q, because here Jesus is not the coming Son of Man, but the proclaimer of the coming rule of God. Yet the mystery of this rule of God is not related to the person of Jesus, but is focused upon patient waiting for God's eschatological action. God will finally establish his kingdom without any human agency or aid. It is noteworthy that the knowledge about this coming action of God is called a "mystery" which is accessible only to the disciples of Jesus. This may reveal a sectarian self-consciousness of those Christians who were the bearers of this tradition. Isolated from the world, they waited for the fulfillment of the promise. The allegorical interpretation which was added by these circles to the parable of the sower (Mark 4:13-20) indeed emphasizes explicitly that anything that happens outside of the community of the faithful will have no significance for the future. The religious attitude of these Christians is therefore comparable to those disciples of Jesus who produced Q and Mark 13; they are thus also representatives of the theology of an eschatological sect.

(b) Jesus as the Teacher of Wisdom

1) *The Gospel of Thomas.* Another tradition of interpretation of the sayings of Jesus, which also originates from the realm of Syria/Palestine, renounced the eschatological expectation which looks to the future. Characteristic for this tradition are sayings in which Jesus appears as a teacher of wisdom, or in which he speaks with the authority of the heavenly figure of Wisdom. With such words Jesus grants salvation to those who are able

Bibliography to §10.1a (3)

Willi Marxsen, *Mark the Evangelist: Studies on the Redaction History of the Gospel* (Nashville: Abingdon, 1969).

Bibliography to §10.1b: Text

A. Guillaumont, H.-Ch. Puech, G. Quispel, W. Till, Yassah 'Abd Al Masih, *The Gospel According to Thomas* (Leiden: Brill, and New York: Harper, 1959).

Helmut Koester and Thomas O. Lambdin, "The Gospel of Thomas (II,2)," *NagHamLibEngl* 117-30.

R. McL. Wilson, "The Gospel of Thomas," *NTApo* 1. 511-22.

Joseph A. Fitzmyer, "The Oxyrhynchus Logoi of Jesus and the Coptic Gospel According to Thomas," *TS* 20 (1959) 505-60.

Kurt Aland, *Synopsis Quattuor Evangeliorum* (9th ed.; Stuttgart: Württembergische Bibelanstalt, 1976) 517-30.

Cameron (ed.), "The Gospel of Thomas," in: *The Other Gospels*, 23-37.

Cartlidge and Dungan, *Documents*, 25-35.

Joannes Karavidopoulos, ΤΟ ΓΝΩΣΤΙΚΟΝ ΚΑΤΑ ΘΩΜΑΝ ΕΥΑΓΓΕΛΙΟΝ (Thessalonike, 1967). Translation of the Coptic Text into Greek.

Oxyrhynchus Papyrus 655:
Fragment of the *Gospel of Thomas*

This papyrus was found at Oxyrhynchus in Egypt in 1903 and was first labeled "Fragment of a Lost Gospel." After the discovery of the Coptic text of the *Gospel of Thomas* it was recognized that it contained the Greek text of Sayings 36–41 of that Gospel.

and prepared to hear and understand them. Similar sayings of Jesus are also preserved within the Q tradition (Matt 11:25–30; Luke 11:49–51), but they are unimportant in comparison with the dominating expectation of Jesus as the Son of Man. Through the discoveries of Nag Hammadi it has become possible to identify more clearly the interpretation of Jesus' sayings in terms of revealed wisdom, a tradition which apparently goes back to the earliest period of Christianity. The *Gospel of Thomas* (NHC II, 2), until recently known only in a few Greek fragments found in Oxyrhynchus in Egypt, is now available in its complete text in a Coptic translation. It was probably written during I CE in Palestine or Syria. The absence of any influence from the canonical gospels and the location of the Thomas tradition in Syria are strong arguments for this date and provenance (cf. the later *Acts of Thomas,* which are certainly Syrian).

In contrast to other writings from the Nag Hammadi library, the *Gospel of Thomas* shows no trace of the kerygma of the cross and the resurrection of Jesus. It is more sparing than Q in its use of christological titles; even the title of Son of Man is missing. But while there is no certain evidence for an apostolic name for the author of Q (but see below on Matthew; §10.2c), the *Gospel of Thomas* explicitly names Judas Didymus Thomas as the disciple to whom the words recorded here were spoken. Judas is doubtlessly the original name of this apostle, "Thomas" the Greek transcription of the Aramaic word for "Twin," and "Didymus" its Greek translation. This connection of names has no parallel in the canonical tradition. It is at home in the tradition of the Syrian church, where it appears in the *Acts of Thomas* and in the Syriac version of the Gospel of John (14:22). The contrast between Thomas and Jesus' brother James, which appears in Sayings 12 and 13 of the *Gospel of Thomas,* allows the conjecture that the author of this gospel belongs to Christian circles which sought to strengthen and defend the right of the tradition of Thomas against the authority of James, without denying the latter's claim

Bibliography to §10.1b (1): Studies

R. McL. Wilson, *Studies in the Gospel of Thomas* (London: Mowbray, 1960).

Ernst Haenchen, *Die Botschaft des Thomasevangeliums* (Theologische Bibliothek Töpelmann 6; Berlin: Töpelmann, 1961).

Bertil Gärtner, *The Theology of the Gospel According to Thomas* (New York: Harper, 1961).

Helmut Koester, "One Jesus and Four Primitive Gospels," in: Robinson and Koester, *Trajectories,* 158–204.

Oscar Cullmann, "Das Thomasevangelium und die Frage nach dem Alter der in ihm enthaltenen Traditionen," in: idem, *Vorträge 1925–1962,* 566–88.

Philipp Vielhauer, "ΑΝΑΠΑΥΣΙΣ: Zum gnostischen Hintergrund des Thomasevangeliums," in: idem, *Aufsätze zum Neuen Testament* (ThBü 31; München: Kaiser, 1965) 215–34.

to leadership in ecclesiastical matters. This seems to reflect a politico-ecclesiastical situation in Palestine in I CE better than a controversy from a later period.

The *Gospel of Thomas* is a collection of wisdom and prophetic sayings of Jesus, composed in the characteristic manner of a wisdom book: sayings are placed side by side, but are left unconnected; only rarely are they introduced by a question from a disciple. Wisdom sayings are in most instances formulated as general truths (e.g., 31–35; 47; 67; 94). Admonitions to recognize oneself appear repeatedly (2; 19; 49; 50; 76; 111). Parables, of which many have parallels in the Synoptic Gospels, express the significance of the discovery of one's own religious destiny (cf., e.g., *Gos. Thom.* 8 with Matt 13:47–48). In the prophetic sayings, announcements of the presence of the Father's rule in the person of Jesus, as well as in the self of the believer, predominate (see *Gos. Thom.* 3; 18; 22; 51; 111). Eschatological sayings about future events are missing, and sayings of Jesus formulated in the first-person singular (I-sayings) never speak about his future role as a redeemer, but only about the presence of salvation both in Jesus and in his words; thus Jesus speaks to the disciples in the voice of heavenly Wisdom (23; 28; 90).

In contrast to the Synoptic Sayings Source, the *Gospel of Thomas* proposes an interpretation of the sayings of Jesus which has no futuristic eschatological component, but instead proclaims the presence of divine wisdom as the true destiny of human existence. The message of the *Gospel of Thomas* is fundamentally esoteric and is directed to a limited group of elect people. A typical external sign of this orientation is the sentence "Whoever has ears to hear, let him hear," which is frequently attached to parables (8; 21; 63; 65; 96; cf. Mark 4:9). Sayings which originally had an eschatological meaning are interpreted in such as way that they point to the presence of revelation both in one's recognition of oneself (*Gos. Thom.* 3; 113) and in the person of Jesus (91). Eschatological change means nothing but insight into the divinity of the self (10; 16; 82). Wisdom sayings which once described the general human experience and exhorted people to appropriate behavior have become conveyors of the same internalized truth (6a; 26; 32–35; 39b; 45; 47; 62b; 82; 86; 93; 95; 103). Renunciation of the world is preached, just as in the Synoptic Sayings Source (*Gos. Thom.* 21c; 56), but also the liberation of the soul from the body (29; 87; 112).

Some of these interpretations may have been part of the tradition which the author inherited. The theology of the author appears most clearly in connection with the last concept. The phrases "and the two will become one," "they will not taste death," and "they will find rest" were repeatedly added to traditional sayings (4; 18; 19; 90; cf. 22; 30; 106). In such mystical and spiritualizing interpretations, the author goes beyond the traditional admonitions of wisdom theology to recognize oneself. The elect and the "single ones" know their origin and are conscious of their destiny: they come from the kingdom of the Father, and they will return to it and find rest (49; 50). This corresponds to the theme that the author has put at the beginning of the gospel: "Whoever finds the interpretation of these sayings will not experience death" (*Gos. Thom.* 1). This is further radicalized in the ascetic sayings which reject the world as well as the human body (37; 42; 56; 60; 70; 111). To be a "single one" implies participation in the unity of all those who are one with their divine origin (16; 23); only this "single one" will enter into the bridal chamber (75). The prototype is Jesus himself, "Who exists from the Undivided" (61), in whose experience as a redeemer the existence as a stranger in the world is represented (28), and in whom the rest and the new world are already present (51). To be sure, in such formulations a number of newly formed sayings of Jesus are evident. But the majority of the traditional words fit the author's theology very well. Many of these sayings are preserved in a form which is older than the forms of their parallels in the Synoptic Gospels. This is especially the case for the parables, but also for sayings which reject the claim of traditional Jewish piety (6; 14; 27; 104) and which criticize the Pharisees as the guardians of this piety (39; 102). A few sayings in the *Gospel of Thomas* reveal the influence of speculations about the biblical creation story (redemption as the rediscovery of the heavenly prototypes which are superior to the earthly Adam; *Gos. Thom.* 83–85). Such sayings appear to be later interpolations into a document of a Christian church which was interpreting the sayings of Jesus in analogy to a wisdom theology that showed clear gnostic tendencies; nonetheless, this group did not completely reject ecclesiastical authority (12).

2) *The Dialogue of the Savior.* A gnosticizing interpretation of the sayings of Jesus which searches in his words for divine wisdom, recognition of the divine self, and immortality, appears in at least one other document from the library of Nag Hammadi: the *Dialogue of the Savior* (NHC III, 5). In its original form, or in its major source, it must also be dated to I CE; because of several close relationships to the *Gospel of Thomas* and the Gospel of John, a Syrian origin is likely. In its extant form, the *Dialogue of the Savior* clearly bears the signs of a secondary

Bibliography to §10.1b (2): Text

Helmut Koester, Elaine H. Pagels, and Harold W. Attridge, "The Dialogue of the Savior (III,5)," *NagHamLibEngl* 229–38.

Cameron (ed.), "The Dialogue of the Savior," in: *The Other Gospels,* 38–48.

Stephen Emmel, "A Fragment of Nag Hammadi Codex III in the Beinecke Library: Yale Inv. 1784," *Bulletin of the American Society of Papyrologists* 17 (1980) 53–60.

compilation. The introductory gnostic sermon, prayer, and instruction (120,2–124,24) contain allusions to the Deutero-Pauline Letters, the Catholic Epistles, and the Letter to the Hebrews. There are also some other pieces which have been interpolated into the older dialogue, such as fragments of a Genesis interpretation (127,19–131,15), a cosmological list (133,16–134,24), and a gnostic interpretation of an apocalyptic vision (134,24–137,3). But the remaining parts of the writing, about sixty percent of the extant text (124,23–127,18; 131,19–132,15; 137,3–147,22), are remnants of a more original writing, which is distinguished by the form of a dialogue between Jesus, Judas, Matthew, and Mariam, and thus clearly different from the interpolated discourses cited above.

This dialogue has no relationship to the known genres of Hellenistic dialogical literature. It is instead an expanded sayings collection. Sayings are introduced by questions of the disciples; more questions lead to the addition of interpretations, which again use sayings in many instances. The underlying sayings have parallels in the Gospel of Matthew, the Gospel of John, and most frequently in the *Gospel of Thomas*. The intention of the dialogue seems to correspond to the first saying of the *Gospel of Thomas*, namely, to find the interpretation of the words of Jesus and, thus, to overcome death. The themes are arranged according to the themes of the second saying of the *Gospel of Thomas* (in the form in which it is preserved in the Oxyrhynchus Papyri): seeking-finding-marvelling-ruling-resting. The disciples are asked to recognize that they have not yet reached rule and rest, but must carry the burden of earthly labor, which Jesus himself also shares (139,6–13).

With regard to the history of early Christian literary genres, this dialogue is a significant document because it shows the further development of Jesus' sayings tradition into a new genre, which makes its appearance as the "revelation dialogue" or "revelation discourse" in the Gospel of John and in later gnostic revelation writings. In its theological themes the *Dialogue of the Savior* is also an important predecessor of the Johannine theology since it discusses the problems of a realized eschatology for the Christian church. In this tradition of the interpretation of his words, Jesus remains the teacher of wisdom and the living revealer, who challenges his disciples to discover in themselves whether and how the revelation has become a reality in their existence. Only in the recognition of the self does the revelation become effective, because here the believers become equal to Jesus insofar as they know their origin and their destiny. It is exactly at this point that we are confronted with the roots of gnostic theology. With this theology as well as this tradition of interpretation of Jesus' sayings, the Gospel of John, developing in the same context of traditional interpretation, had to come to terms.

(c) Order of Life and Organization of the Church

On the basis of the extant materials it is possible to obtain only an approximate picture of the community rules and ethical principles of the Syrian Christians who cultivated this tradition of Jesus' sayings. There were certainly wandering apostles, pledged to the ideal of poverty and frugality, who went from place to place, preaching, healing the sick—and then moving on. This is evident from the relevant sections of the Synoptic Sayings Source. Efforts to establish or found churches according to the model of the Pauline mission should not be read into this missionary activity. Even Paul had to deal with wandering Christian missionaries who had no intention to found new churches. In the *Gospel of Thomas* the ideal of the homeless disciple seems to have become the principle of Christian existence (*Gos. Thom.* 42). These Christians were wandering ascetics who rejected marriage, accepted women into their groups (61; 114), denied the world, and scorned the normal practices of piety such as fasting and almsgiving. Real church organizations developed first in Jerusalem and in Antioch. The leadership in Jerusalem consisted of the "pillar apostles" (James, Peter, John), and later James alone. The tradition of the later Jewish-Christian churches relates its authority to the name of this brother of Jesus, James the Just. The same traditional authority is also referred to in *Gos. Thom.* 12. This apparently reflects a realm of authority which included several organized local communities. One can assume that these churches were kept together not only through the sending of messengers on certain occasions, but also through writings in which the order of life for these congregations was set forth.

1) *The Epistle of James.* Under the authority of James one such writing is preserved in the canon of the New Testament: the so-called Epistle of James. The authority which is claimed for this writing is, no doubt, James, the brother of the Lord, who bears the honorary title "servant of God" in Jas 1:1 and in a fragment of Hegesippus in Eusebius (*Hist. eccl.* 2.23.7). No other person by this name ever had a comparable authority,

Bibliography to §10.1c (1): Commentaries

Martin Dibelius, *James: A Commentary on the Epistle of James* (rev. Heinrich Greeven; Hermeneia; Philadelphia: Fortress, 1976).

Bibliography to §10.1c (1): Studies

Dan O. Via, "The Right Strawy Epistle Reconsidered: A Study in Biblical Ethics and Hermeneutic," *JR* 49 (1969) 253–67.

Christoph Burchard, "Gemeinde in der strohernen Epistel: Mutmaßungen über Jakobus," in: *Kirche: Festschrift Bornkamm,* 315–28.

Roy B. Ward, "The Works of Abraham: James 2:14–26," *HTR* 61 (1968) 283–90.

Idem, "Partiality in the Assembly: James 2:2–4," *HTR* 62 (1969) 87–97.

though one should not be tempted to see this writing as a genuine product of this James. The fluent Greek style of the writing, as well as the polemic against Paul's doctrine of justification by faith (Jas 2:14–26), make this impossible because these reflect a situation which is unthinkable until sometime after James' death in the year 62. But the Epistle of James is an important witness for the continuation of the Jewish-Christian tradition of the Jerusalem church in the Greek-speaking world. This group had much in common with the Jewish-Christians of Jerusalem: emphasis upon the validity of the law (Jas 2:8–13), although the law is described in terms which had developed in Hellenistic Judaism (Jas 1:25: "the perfect law of freedom"), the ideal of poverty (2:1–7; cf. the polemic against the rich, 5:1–6), and the eschatological orientation (5:7–11). The address "To the Twelve Tribes in the diaspora" also points to a Jewish Christianity which had taken shape in the Greek world.

The Epistle of James is not, however, a true letter, but must be understood as a general circular in the form of parenesis. Traditional sayings, admonitions, instructions, and proverbial rules of conduct are loosely joined together. Thematic arrangements combine a number of sayings in each case. The material is derived largely from the parenesis of Hellenistic Judaism, and specifically Christian features are not easily detected, although it must be assumed that the "honorable name by which you are called" (2:7) refers to the name of Christ, and that the "parousia of the Lord" points to the coming of Jesus (5:7). The conclusion of the writing is a short church order (5:13–20), which at least reveals that the addressees were organized groups of Christians led by presbyters (5:14). Although the Epistle of James is a Jewish-Christian document, it should not be understood as a link between the Jerusalem church and the later Jewish-Christian sects. Still, it does continue the Jerusalem authority of James in the same way as would the later representatives of Jewish Christianity (§10.4a–c). Its purpose is to introduce the Jewish-Christian faithfulness to the law and its parenetic tradition into the developing worldwide church, without, however, emphasizing circumcision and ritual law. Paul is criticized, not because of his rejection of the law, but because of the danger of the rejection of works which might result from Paul's thesis of justification on the basis of faith alone. That such consequences had been drawn from Paul's theology may be indicated in the peculiar rejection of false wisdom in Jas 3:13–18, which is directed against the claim of the possession of heavenly wisdom that was at home in gnostic circles. The Epistle of James contrasts such claims to the validity of the inheritance of a Jewish morality that has great value in fostering a Christian life that is pious, intelligent, and responsible.

2) *The Teaching of the Twelve Apostles*. The clearest evidence for the

attempts of Christians coming from a Jewish background to erect a bar-
rier against the further spread of enthusiasm by means of the traditional
Jewish moral teachings is found in the Christianization of the Jewish
doctrine of the Two Ways. This Jewish document became a constitutive
part of the *Teaching of the Twelve Apostles* (*Didache*), the oldest Christian church order, written in Syria at the end of I CE. Although known by
name and frequently used in later Christian church orders, it was only
discovered and published about a century ago (1883). The teaching of the
Two Ways, the way of life and the way of death, forms the document's
first six chapters. This teaching of the Two Ways is independently preserved in a Latin translation; it was also used in the *Epistle of Barnabas,*
written ca. 100 CE (*Barn.* 18–20). What appears in the form of a description of the way of life is a parenesis based upon the decalogue (*Didache* 2),
admonitions based on catalogues of virtues and vices (3.1–10), rules for
the community (4.1–4, 12–14), rules about the giving and receiving of
alms (4.5–8; 1.5–6), and a table of household duties (4.9–11). The way of
death is simply an extensive catalogue of vices (5.1–2). All the materials
presented here are traditional and have numerous parallels in Jewish
literature. Much of this material was also adopted by other Christian
authors: Paul is quite familiar with the same materials, and the Epistle of
James as well as the *Shepherd of Hermas* drew numerous admonitions
from this Two Ways doctrine.

The author of the *Didache* places the teaching of the Two Ways into a
larger context. He introduces it with a quotation of the double commandment of love and the golden rule (*Did.* 1.2) and attaches quotations of
sayings of Jesus (*Did.* 1.3–4). This was a momentous step: the interpretation of the traditional sayings of Jesus is now tied to the developing
Christian catechism. Thus eschatological and gnostic enthusiasts are denied the right to use this tradition. The conclusion of the traditional Two
Ways document (6.2) is altered in such a way that the commandments

Bibliography to §10.1c (2): Text
Funk-Bihlmeyer, *ApostVät*, xii–xx, 1–9.
Lake, *ApostFath*, 1. 303–33.

Bibliography to §10.1c (2): Commentaries
Jean-Paul Audet, *La Didaché: Instructions des apôtres* (EtBib; Paris: Gabalda, 1958).
Robert A. Kraft, *Barnabas and the Didache* (Grant, *ApostFath* 3).

Bibliography to §10.1c (2): Studies
J. M. Creed, "The Didache," *JTS* 39 (1938) 370–87.
Bentley Layton, "The Sources, Date, and Transmission of Didache 1.3b–2.1," *HTR* 61
    (1968) 343–83.
Martin Dibelius, "Die Mahlgebete der Didache," in: idem, *Botschaft und Geschichte* (2
    vols.; Tübingen: Mohr/Siebeck, 1956) 2. 117–27.

cannot be understood as special instruction for the perfect, but appear as a
general teaching of morality, which everybody should follow as best as
possible. This general address of the doctrine of the Two Ways is clearly
evident in its connection with a church order (*Didache* 7–15). It contains
instructions for baptism (7; this is the first quotation of the trinitarian
formula), fasting (8.1), prayer (8.2–3; quotation of the Lord's prayer),
and celebration of the eucharistic meal (9–10).

In this context, the oldest known eucharistic prayers of Christianity are
quoted. Like the preceding moral teachings, these eucharistic prayers
were derived from Hellenistic Judaism. Even in their pre-Christian form
they seem to have contained spiritualized interpretations (bread and wine
as signs of the knowledge of life). The relationship of the full meal as
described here (10.1) to the formal Christian Lord's Supper has been
much debated. It has been asked whether the conclusion (10.4–6) was
meant to introduce the sacramental meal, whose liturgy, however, was not
quoted because of arcane discipline, for which reason the "words of institution" were not included. But this assumption is quite unfounded. There
is no reason to presuppose the same liturgy for the *Didache* which is
attested in Paul (1 Cor 11:23–26) and later in the Synoptic Gospels
(Mark 14:22–24 and parallels). Rather, the full meal which the *Didache*
describes must have been the only festive and formal common meal of the
Syrian communities for whom the *Didache* was written. The explicit
exclusion of the unbaptized (*Did.* 9.5) distinguishes this meal from other
activities of the community. The sequence "cup–bread" is peculiar, but it
is quite possible that this is an inheritance from the oldest Jewish-
Christian communities, just as the evident eschatological orientation of
this meal.

The second half of the church order deals with the Christian church
offices (*Did.* 10.7–15.4). This is essentially a compilation of early rules
about apostles, prophets, and teachers. Rules about the rights of wandering charismatic apostles and prophets are accepted on the whole, but
limited in a positive fashion. Criticism is directed not only against the
normal abuses of wandering "philosophers," but also tries to overcome the
communities' dependence upon these wandering charismatics. Thus the
order for these offices concludes with a recommendation to elect bishops
and deacons from among their own members, who could then take over
the functions of the wandering prophets and teachers, thus making the
communities independent of them.

The last chapter of the *Didache* (16) is a small apocalypse which has
many materials in common with the Synoptic Apocalypse (§10.1a), showing that the *Didache* draws upon the same traditions. But the corresponding materials appear in an older form in *Didache* 16, were still more

closely related to Jewish apocalyptic views, and were not yet influenced by the expectation of the coming of the Son of Man. On the other hand, there is no sign of a near expectation; rather, the events of the future are still distant: other events must happen first before the Lord would come. This agrees with the entire attitude of the *Didache;* the document seeks to discourage uncontrolled enthusiasm and to institute the ideal of regulated Christian conduct in firmly organized communities. Although the traditions used here are all derived from a Jewish milieu, the author does not try to advance the cause of one particular tradition. He also avoids appealing to a particular apostolic authority like Thomas or James, but instead acknowledges the general authority of the Twelve Apostles. Thus the Twelve Apostles become the normal authority for later Christian church orders (*Didascalia, Apostolic Constitutions*). Although the *Did-ache* attests the process of consolidation, signs of discussion with other Christian traditions are missing. No reference is made to those forms of Christian belief which had been developed independently of the interpretation of the sayings of Jesus. Furthermore, the *Didache* never mentions the kerygma of cross and resurrection that was first fully formulated in Antioch, became the basis of the Pauline mission, and was also associated with the further development of Christianity in western Syria, where this kerygma was closely connected with traditions under the authority of Peter.

2. From the Kerygma of the Resurrection to the Gospels of the Church

(a) Traditions under the Authority of Peter

1) *Peter*. The point of departure for the preaching of Jesus' resurrection was the Syrian capital of Antioch (§8.3c). Converted Hellenistic Jews had founded its Christian congregation, which was the first to admit uncircumcised gentiles to its table fellowship. This did not happen without conflicts, as has been discussed above (§9.2a). James and his associates in Jerusalem seem to have taken a somewhat reserved attitude about these developments. But among the leaders of the church in Jerusalem, Peter must have been more open and supportive. When Paul visited Jerusalem three years after his conversion, his primary purpose was to visit Peter

Bibliography to §10.2a (1)

Raymond Brown, Karl P. Donfried, John Reumann (eds.), *Peter in the New Testament* (Minneapolis: Augsburg; and New York: Paulist, 1973).
See also the literature for §12.2e.

and enter into discussion with him (James occurs only in a marginal reference in Gal 1:18–19). Ten years later at the so-called Apostolic Council, Peter was still one of the "pillars" in Jerusalem, but possibly even before that time he had been active as a missionary outside of Jerusalem (§8.3d). In any case, after the council Peter remained in Antioch as a member of its church composed of Jews and gentiles; during the conflict in Antioch with Paul, Peter seems to have had a stronger position than his opponent (§9.2a). During Paul's last visit to Jerusalem Peter was no longer present; only James is named as the leader of the church. Unfortunately, there is no certain information about Peter's activity during this period. The "party of Peter" in Corinth (or of "Cephas"; see 1 Cor 1:12) shows that his influence must have extended beyond Syria. According to church tradition, Peter finally came to Rome, where he suffered martyrdom shortly after 60 CE.

Although all this cannot constitute a biography of Peter, one of the most reliable data of early Christian tradition is the firm establishment of the authority of this disciple and apostle in the Christian tradition that appealed to the testimony of Jesus' resurrection. It is also undeniable that traditions under Peter's name were kept alive in Syria. In the formula from the Antiochian church that Paul quotes in 1 Cor 15:3–7, Peter appears as the first witness to the resurrection. There is abundant evidence about him in the canonical gospels. At the conclusion of the story of the road to Emmaus, we find a sentence that could be a traditional formula: "He is truly risen and has appeared to Simon [i.e., Peter]" (Luke 24:34). The following story about the appearance of Jesus before the eleven disciples (Luke 24:36–43) is quoted in an older form in Ignatius of Antioch (*Smyrn.* 3), where Jesus appears to "Peter and those with him." The first confession of Jesus as the Messiah in the canonical gospels is assigned to Peter (Mark 8:29 and parallels; John 6:68f uses the same tradition but changes the title to "Holy One of God"). The story of the call and commissioning of Peter with the old saying about the "fisher of people" is preserved in the legend of the miraculous catch of fishes (Luke 5:1–11; cf. John 21:1–14 which tells the same story, but suppresses the authority of Peter). Finally, there is the story of the transfiguration (Mark 9:2–8) which, like the story of the miraculous catch, was originally an epiphany story of the appearance of the risen Christ, that had at one time named only Peter as its witness (James and John were added by the redaction).

Peter's formal position of authority was related to this tradition. His authority is attested in the tradition of Peter as the rock on whom Jesus will found his church, and to whom the keys of the kingdom of heaven are entrusted (Matt 16:17–19). Due to its Aramaic address "Simon Bar-

Jona" and the Greek term *ekklesia*, it must have originated in a bilingual community of Syria. Matthew added this tradition to his presentation of Peter's confession (16:16), thus recognizing the disciple's authority. In the supplement to the Gospel of John (John 21:15–23) the same tradition is used (see the address "Simon son of John"); although the authority of Peter is not fundamentally questioned, it is superseded by the "disciple whom Jesus loved" (John?), in the same way that the authority of James is superseded by Thomas in the *Gospel of Thomas* (§10.1b). These passages, of course, do not reflect a personal rivalry of these apostles. They attest instead that at some time after the death of these apostles various Christian traditions were competing with each other under the authority of apostolic names. In many instances oral or written traditions under the authority of different apostles could have competed with each other in one relatively large Christian community in such major cities as Antioch.

2) *The Gospel of Peter.* Were there oral or written traditions about Jesus which were transmitted under the special authority of Peter? Though it cannot be doubted that Peter was a personal disciple of Jesus, the transmission of Jesus' sayings is never connected with his name. Beginning with Papias of Hierapolis, however, the ecclesiastical tradition for the Gospel of Mark considered this writing to be a transcript of Peter's lectures (§10.2b). The oldest writing under the authority of Peter himself is the *Gospel of Peter.* Its attestation once more points to western Syria. According to Eusebius (*Hist. eccl.* 6.12.2–6), bishop Serapion of Antioch (ca. 200 CE) had been told about a *Gospel of Peter* which was used by Christians in the church of Rhossus. At first Serapion had no objections to the use of this writing, but then studied it more closely and determined that while most of this gospel agreed with the teachings of the Savior, it also contained some later accretions that apparently revealed a docetic

Bibliography to §10.2a (2): Text

Erich Klostermann, *Apocrypha I: Reste des Petrusevangeliums, der Petrusapokalypse und des Kerygma Petri* (KlT 3; 2d ed.; Berlin: De Gruyter, 1933).

Chr. Maurer, "The Gospel of Peter," *NTApo* 1. 179–87.

Cartlidge and Dungan, *Documents,* 83–86.

Cameron (ed.), "The Gospel of Peter," in: *The Other Gospels,* 76–82.

Bibliography to §10.2a (2): Studies

Martin Dibelius, "Die alttestamentlichen Motive in der Leidensgeschichte des Petrus- und Johannesevangeliums," in: idem, *Botschaft und Geschichte,* vol. 1 (Tübingen: Mohr/Siebeck, 1953) 221–47.

Karl Ludwig Schmidt, *Kanonische und apokryphe Evangelien und Apostelgeschichten* (AThANT 5; Basel: Majer, 1944) 37–78.

Jürgen Denker, *Die theologiegeschichtliche Stellung des Petrusevangeliums: Ein Beitrag zur Frühgeschichte des Doketismus* (EHS.T 36; Bern and Frankfurt: Lang, 1975).

theology. Neither Serapion nor any of the church fathers who knew about the *Gospel of Peter* ever quoted it. Thus its contents were unknown until a fragment was discovered in 1886 in Akhmim, in Upper Egypt. It is a manuscript from VIII CE (a smaller but much earlier fragment was discovered later in Oxyrhynchus) and is generally assumed to be a copy of the same gospel that Serapion once read in Antioch. The fragment contains the major part of the passion narrative as well as the story of the empty tomb, and breaks off with the introduction to the post-Easter story of the disciples' catch of fishes (cf. John 21:1–14).

In a number of instances the *Gospel of Peter* contains features that can be traced back to a stage in the development of the passion narrative and the story of the empty tomb which is older than that known by the canonical gospels. The features of the passion narrative that are derived from the Old Testament reveal their origin still more clearly in the interpretation of Scripture. One example: *Gos. Pet.* 16 says: "Give him gall to drink with vinegar"; this was developed from Ps 68:22. But Matthew divided this passage from the Psalms between two different incidents: Matt 27:34 (gall) and 27:48 (vinegar). The day of the crucifixion is given as the day before the festival as in the Gospel of John, which is probably historically correct. In the legend of the finding of the empty tomb only Mary Magdalene is named—most likely the only name connected with this story in the early tradition (Matthew, Mark, and Luke add the names of other women). The epiphany story of Jesus' resurrection from the tomb in the *Gospel of Peter* is, to be sure, full of legendary features that go beyond the canonical gospels. But this should not mislead us into considering this story a secondary patchwork of canonical passages. Features that were secondarily added by Matthew to his presentation of the story of the empty tomb (Matt 28:2–4) and used for his apologetic legend of the guards at the tomb (Matt 27:62–66; 28:11–15) appear in the *Gospel of Peter* as natural, constitutive elements of an epiphany story of Jesus' being raised from the tomb, for which the soldiers are witnesses. Even if a number of features in the *Gospel of Peter* may be due to later legendary growth of a text unprotected by canonical transmission, its basis must be an older text under the authority of Peter which was independent of the canonical gospels. If Peter was the first and most important witness to the resurrection in the oldest tradition of Syrian churches, it is not unlikely that the old tradition about the passion and resurrection of Jesus was also written down under his authority. This is partially confirmed by the passion narrative of the canonical gospels, where Peter is the only disciple whose name appears in this context (see the story of Peter's denial).

3) *The Kerygma of Peter.* Another document under the authority of Peter, the *Kerygma of Peter* (to be distinguished from the *Kerygmata*

Petrou, one of the sources of the *Pseudo-Clementines;* see §10.4c), was probably written ca. 100 CE. Its theme is once again the interpretation of the passion of Jesus. This writing is preserved in only a few fragments (quoted by Clement of Alexandria, *Strom.* 6.5.39–41, 43, 48; 6.15.128). According to these fragments, it was a writing of apologetic character, beginning with the confession of the one invisible God and a polemic against pagan idol worship and Jewish worship of the angels. The Christians are distinguished from Greeks and Jews as the people of the new covenant (with reference to the passage in Jer 31:31–34) and a third race. As elected apostles, the twelve disciples are sent first to Israel, then to the nations. The apologetic principle of the interpretation of Jesus' death is fully developed. The disciples have recognized that Jesus is mentioned in the books of the prophets, partly in "parables," partly literally: "his coming, his death, the cross, and all the other torments which the Jews inflicted on him, his resurrection and assumption into the heavens, before Jerusalem was judged . . ." Furthermore: "For we know that God really commanded these things, and we say nothing without (the testimony of) Scripture." The employment of this principle is also clearly visible in the *Gospel of Peter,* as well as in the passion narratives of the canonical gospels. The *Kerygma of Peter* shows that the tradition developed under the authority of Peter was made fully serviceable to the purposes of the gentile mission.

4) *Other Writings under Peter's Authority.* A number of writings under the name of Peter belong to the major ecclesiastical developments that are called "early catholicism." They frequently show Pauline influences. To these writings belong the two letters of Peter in the New Testament and the *Apocalypse of Peter.* Thus, it seems that one part of the Syrian tradition of Peter merged with the larger movement of gentile Christianity. At the same time, Jewish-Christian sects of the subsequent centuries continued their claim of having preserved Peter's true teachings (§10.4c). There, Peter is closely allied with the authority of James and, together with him, he stands up for the cause of faithful observance of the law, while Paul becomes the archenemy of true Christian faith. It is quite possible that direct connections existed between the early Petrine traditions of Syria and the later anti-Pauline Jewish Christianity. In that case, Petrine literature influenced by Paul could be understood as a polemical answer to Jewish-Christian claims upon the authority of Peter.

(b) The Oldest Gospel of the Church: The Gospel of Mark

In the early postapostolic period various and independent developments in Syria resulted in the establishment of written traditions that were quite different from each other. In each instance such writings contained traditions that reflected the piety, theology, and practice of individual churches or circles of churches. The written passion narrative stems from churches in which the kerygma of the cross and resurrection of Jesus was the focus

Bibliography to §10.2a (3): Text

W. Schneemelcher, "The Kerygma Petrou," *NTApo* 2. 94–102.

Bibliography to §10.2b: Texts

Papias-Fragments: Funk-Bihlmeyer, *ApostVät*, xliv–xlvii, 133–40.
Secret Gospel of Mark: Morton Smith, *Clement*, 445–54 (with translation).
Otto Stählin (ed.), *Clemens Alexandrinus*, vol. 4: *Register* 1 (GCS; 2d ed. by Ursula Treu; Berlin: Akademie-Verlag, 1980) xvii–xviii (Greek text).
Cameron (ed.), "The Secret Gospel of Mark," in: *The Other Gospels*, 67–71.

Bibliography to §10.2b: Commentaries

Vincent Taylor, *The Gospel according to St. Mark* (2d ed.; London: Macmillan, and New York: St. Martin's, 1966). The most comprehensive scholarly commentary on Mark.
Eduard Schweizer, *The Good News according to Mark* (Richmond: Knox, 1970).
D. E. Nineham, *The Gospel of Mark* (rev. ed.; Baltimore: Penguin, 1969).
Ernst Haenchen, *Der Weg Jesu: Eine Erklärung des Markus-Evangeliums und der kanonischen Parallelen* (Berlin: Töpelmann, 1966).
C. E. B. Cranfield, *The Gospel according to Saint Mark* (CGTC; Cambridge: Cambridge University, 1959).

Bibliography to §10.2b: Studies

William Wrede, *The Messianic Secret* (Library of Theological Translation; Cambridge: Clark, 1971). First published in 1901; stimulated all research ever since.
Howard C. Kee, "Mark's Gospel in Recent Research," *Int* 32 (1978) 353–68.
Willi Marxsen, *Mark the Evangelist: Studies on the Redaction History of the Gospel* (Nashville: Abingdon, 1969).
Heinz-Wolfgang Kuhn, *Ältere Sammlungen im Markusevangelium* (SUNT 8; Göttingen: Vandenhoeck & Ruprecht, 1971).
T. Alec. Burkill, *New Light on the Earliest Gospel: Seven Markan Studies* (Ithaca, NY: Cornell University, 1972).
Paul J. Achtemeier, "Toward the Isolation of Pre-Markan Miracle Catenae," *JBL* 89 (1970) 265–91.
Thomas L. Budesheim, "Jesus and the Disciples in Conflict with Judaism," *ZNW* 62 (1971) 190–209.
George W. Nickelsburg, "The Genre and Function of the Markan Passion Narrative," *HTR* 73 (1980) 153–84.
Étienne Trocmé, *The Formation of the Gospel according to Mark* (Philadelphia: Westminster, 1975).
Georg Strecker, "Literarkritische Überlegungen zum εὐαγγέλιον-Begriff im Markusevangelium," in *Neues Testament und Geschichte: Oscar Cullmann zum 70. Geburtstag* (Tübingen: Mohr/Siebeck, 1972) 91–104.
Howard C. Kee, *Community of the New Age: Studies in Mark's Gospel* (Philadelphia: Westminster, 1977).
Norman Perrin, "Towards an Interpretation of the Gospel of Mark," in: Hans Dieter Betz (ed.), *Christology and a Modern Pilgrimage: A Discussion with Norman Perrin* (2d ed.; Missoula: Scholars Press, 1974).
Rudolf Pesch (ed.), *Das Markus-Evangelium* (WdF 411; Darmstadt: Wissenschaftliche Buchgesellschaft, 1979).

of theological reflection, and where Jesus' fate was elucidated by means of the interpretation of Old Testament passages about the suffering righteous one. A very different religious orientation appears in those communities in which the sayings tradition of Jesus was understood as the call of heavenly Wisdom. Another orientation is visible in the reference to the sayings of Jesus as apocalyptic prophecy; there, the coming of the Son of Man in the near future was proclaimed in apocalyptic propaganda writings or prophetic books of edification. Further developments in each of these different traditions and writings amplified the relevant materials, but also resulted in a narrowing of perspectives and in a sectarian isolation of such communities. On the other hand, the reception of Hellenistic-Jewish moral teachings and the development of church order led to an eventual ecumenical unification of ecclesiastical practice. But evidence for actual theological controversy between these different strands of early Syrio-Palestinian Christianity seems to be missing in the earliest available witnesses.

Yet another and quite distinct proclamation of the Christian message must have appeared rather early in Syria: the propaganda of Jewish-Christian missionaries who proclaimed a new covenant and reinforced their preaching through powerful deeds and miracles. They cultivated their own type of Jesus tradition, and it can be assumed that the earliest collections of miracles stories of Jesus were produced as missionary manuals for the activities of such preachers. In these traditions, Jesus plainly appears as the divine man, and the demonstration of supernatural power assumes the character of a binding message. A controversy with these missionaries and their message surfaced in Paul's letters now collected in 2 Corinthians (§9.3d). With reference to the kerygma of Jesus' death and resurrection, Paul had contrasted this message of Jesus as the most powerful of all divine human beings to his own thesis that Jesus was the one who had failed on the cross, and whose resurrection was power for the weak and freedom for the despised. The letters of recommendation (aretalogies) of which the opponents could boast, Paul had countered with his paradoxical apology of weakness in his missionary activity. But the controversy of the aretalogical tradition about Jesus with the proclamation of Jesus as crucified, which was meanwhile documented in written passion narratives, remained a task that the early post-Pauline and post-Petrine Christianity had still to solve.

The Gospel of Mark tried to face this problem and in doing so also incorporated some other theological traditions and writings into its new theological scheme. It is not known where the Gospel of Mark was written—probably not in Rome, where it is often located because of its Latinisms and its relationship to Peter. It is better to assume that Mark was written in a major metropolis of the east where various lines of fully developed traditions had intersected. Antioch or another city of the Syrian west coast fulfill these conditions. If the catastrophe of Jewish War was a catalyst for the composition of this gospel, the Syro-Palestinian realm would then be preferred anyway. Petrine traditions were well established in Syria, and Latinisms could occur at any place where a Roman garrison was stationed and Roman law was practiced.

The external attestation for the relationship of Mark to Peter appears in the writings of the Phrygian bishop Papias of Hierapolis (ca. 100–150). He writes that his informant, whom he calls a "presbyter," had told him that Mark had been the interpreter of Peter and that he had recorded the words and deeds of the Lord accurately, but not in the (correct) sequence, as far as he could remember them. Papias adds the remark that Mark could not be blamed for proceeding in this way, since he had never heard the Lord himself, nor did he follow him; he was dependent upon Peter's lectures, which had been composed according to existing needs (Eusebius *Hist. eccl.* 3.39.15). We should not overestimate the value of this tradition. For Papias, the trustworthiness of the oral tradition rested upon the memories of the students of the apostles ("presbyters") of everything that the apostles had transmitted from Jesus. Papias applies the same schema to the written gospels. But even for Mark, the oldest gospel, this view is not appropriate because Mark wrote on the basis of written materials, along with oral traditions that had been formed in the preaching and practice of the churches. Papias' assertion, however, of a relationship between the Gospel of Mark and Peter should not be completely overlooked, since the role of Peter in that gospel shows that Mark indeed used materials in which the authority of this apostle was expressed.

The most important source of the Gospel of Mark is the passion narrative, which presented in one continuous narrative the events from Jesus' entry into Jerusalem (Mark 11:1–10) to the finding of the empty tomb (16:1–8). The passion narrative of the Gospel of John derives from the same or a similar source. Along with this written passion narrative, Mark must have used one or several written collections of miracle stories, since these show some relationship to the "signs source" of the Gospel of John (§10.3a). Materials from this collection include the story of the miraculous feeding of the multitudes (Mark 6:32–44; John 6:1–13), the walking on the sea (Mark 6:45–52; John 6:15–21), and the healing of a blind man (Mark 8:22–26; John 9:1–7), but probably other miracle stories as well; one cannot determine the exact extent of this source. It is possible that Mark also found the characteristic exorcisms of his gospel in a written collection (Mark 1:21–28; 5:1–20; 9:14–29). The sayings of Jesus play only a minor role in the Gospel of Mark. Some of his sayings have parallels in the Synoptic Sayings Source used by Matthew and Luke (compare Mark 8:34–38 with Matt 10:33, 38–39 and Luke 14:27; 17:33; 12:8–9; the last is one of the Son of Man sayings that are characteristic for Q); but it is not possible to presuppose Mark's knowledge of this source. Such sayings, as also the apophthegms of Jesus (Mark 2:23–28; 3:1–6, 22–30; 11:27–33; 12:13–37), could have come to Mark through the free tradition, or in the form of smaller collections. Only in two cases is it possible to be sure about the use of a written source for sayings materials: in the parable chapter of Mark 4 and in the Synoptic Apocalypse in Mark 13 (§10.1a).

Attempts to reconstruct an older form of the Gospel of Mark (*Urmarkus*) that would bring us even closer to the actual life of Jesus are misguided. But one may still ask whether the gospel as it is preserved in the manuscripts of the New Testament is identical with the original work of Mark. There are a number of cases in which Matthew and Luke agree in their use of materials drawn from Mark, while Mark's extant text is different. Did Matthew and Luke preserve Mark's original text in these instances? A major section of Mark (6:45–8:26) is not reproduced by Luke at all. But precisely this section contains a number of doublets; for example, Mark 8:1–10 reports the feeding of four thousand, although 6:30–44 had already told about the feeding of the five thousand. Was this whole section missing in the original gospel?

The question of the original text of Mark is further complicated through the discovery of a previously unknown, but probably genuine letter of Clement of Alexandria, which quotes sections from a *Secret Gospel of Mark*. On the whole, this gospel, which was used by some of the Christians of Alexandria, seems to agree with the canonical Gospel of Mark. But it contained some additional materials, especially the story of the raising of a young man after the third prediction of the passion (Mark 10:32–34). Some remarks about the initiation of this young man may be later accretions, but the story itself is a variant of John 11, in fact in a form that is free of all Johannine redactional elements. Does this attest to an older edition of the Gospel of Mark containing this story of a raising from the dead which might have been drawn from the same source (closely related to the signs source in the Gospel of John), from which other Markan miracle stories were derived? An explanation is also required for the occurrence of parallels to the *Secret Gospel of Mark* in the canonical text (such as the present version of Mark 9:14–29 and the incident of Mark 14:51–52) which are not supported by the corresponding texts of Matthew and Luke: is the preserved text of Mark dependent upon the *Secret Gospel of Mark?* It is obvious that the text of this relatively old gospel was not immune to redactions, revisions, and new editions. On the contrary, it was precisely the first successful composition and distribution of a comprehensive writing comprising various types of traditions about Jesus that would necessarily lead to attempts to carry on this literary activity. Thus, Matthew and Luke did nothing other than improve Mark's work with thorough-going revisions, while John wrote a work which was in some ways analogous to Mark.

The Gospel of Mark is indeed not simply a continuation of the oral tradition in written form. Mark used various traditional materials and made them subject to a new concept. Thus, with his Gospel, Mark created a genre of literature. This new concept is not sufficiently explained by referring to the kerygma of cross and resurrection (called "gospel" in 1 Cor 15:1ff) as the backbone of this new genre. Insofar as the passion narrative takes up a comparatively large proportion of Mark, and insofar as the preceding materials are closely connected with this passion narrative, this reference is to some degree justified. But it must also be considered that this kerygma no longer designates a decisive eschatological moment, as it had in the beginning of the proclamation of the resurrection and in Paul. Death and resurrection have become the climax of a dramatic development, which is prepared in the ministry and suffering of a human life exposed to the vicissitudes of earthly existence. This insight makes it possible for Mark to write a biographical introduction to the passion narrative. He thus introduces a biographical framework as the genre of the "gospel"; this became the beginning of the writing of "biographies" of Jesus which have, of course, nothing in common with the actual course of his life. The whole biographical frame is based upon a theological concept. It is used merely to incorporate materials about Jesus' deeds and his words, derived from quite different contexts, and to relate these materials to the narrative of Jesus' passion. The genre of the Hellenistic biography provides a partial precedent, since traditional materials were also used there in a secondary biographical framework in order to present the office, mission, and teaching of a particular person.

Through his redactional work Mark from the outset related the materials transmitted in his source to the passion narrative. As early as the conclusion of the first phase of Jesus' ministry, he introduces the Herodians and the Pharisees as counselling to put Jesus to death (Mark 3:6), and he brings the scribes from Jerusalem to Galilee in order to give them the opportunity to accuse Jesus of being possessed by Beelzebul (3:22, 30). But Mark's major task was the reinterpretation of materials which contradicted his general concept. The collections of miracle stories which he used were intended to demonstrate the miraculous power present in Jesus; in other words, they were aretalogies. Their claim that Jesus' messianic dignity was present in the deeds that he did on earth is criticized by

Mark's theory of the messianic secret. This is expressed in three ways: in the commands to the demons not to reveal Jesus' identity publicly (1:34; 3:12; etc.); in the lack of understanding among the disciples (6:52; 8:16–21); and in the view that Jesus' proclamation in parables is not comprehensible to the crowds (4:10–12, 33–34; this last element, however, may have a different origin). These features put the powerful deeds of Jesus into a peculiar shadow, and the reader learns that they cannot be the key to the understanding of Jesus' true mission.

In the conception of the whole gospel, Mark made the confession of Peter at Caesarea Philippi the theological turning-point (8:29–30). The confession of Jesus as the Messiah is followed not only by a command to silence, but also by the first prediction of the passion (8:31). Peter's protest to the prediction is sharply rebuked (8:32–33). Two more passion predictions follow (9:30–32; 10:32–34). As a consequence, the section of the gospel from the confession of Peter to the entry into Jerusalem is dominated by the perspective of Jesus' suffering, death, and resurrection. From this point on, the disciples learn to understand the secret of Jesus' messiahship. Sayings materials which Mark used here speak about suffering in the discipleship of Jesus (8:34–38; 10:35–45). The disciples who follow Jesus represent the church, as is demonstrated by the occurrence of church order materials in this section of the gospel (9:33–50; 10:1–31).

It is peculiar that Mark no longer uses the title of Messiah in the predictions for the passion, but instead takes up the title Son of Man, which originally belonged to the eschatological expectation of the redeemer who is to come on the clouds of heaven. To be sure, Mark does not deny the traditional eschatological view of the sayings tradition, but he relates its primary christological title to the kerygma of Jesus' death and resurrection (9:9), even with the interpretation of Jesus' death as an expiatory sacrifice (10:45; Mark seems to have introduced the title of Son of Man into this traditional saying). Thus, the theology of the sayings tradition is also made subservient to Mark's general theological concept of the gospel. Seen from the central position of suffering, cross, and resurrection, it is no longer possible to ask whether Jesus' miracles prove his messiahship. Rather, they provoke reactions which result in Jesus' death. The completely inadequate question of the high priest, whether Jesus is the Messiah, is answered by the announcement of the coming of the Son of Man in glory (14:61–62). The resurrection—not told in Mark—cannot, therefore, be introduced as a miracle confirming Jesus' identity. It remains an open question whether the conclusion of the gospel (16:7) points to the appearance of the risen Jesus or instead to his parousia.

The various christological traditions are connected in Mark's gospel in such a way that one cannot deny the power of the earthly Jesus, nor doubt the reality of his resurrection, nor question his coming in glory at the parousia. The presentation of the biography of Jesus in the form of the gospel, however, makes it possible for the church to find its place with the disciples who follow Jesus in his suffering, though the church has no obligation to imitate Jesus' miracles (the disciples fail miserably when they try; Mark 9:14–29); nor should the church listen to a radicalized apocalyptic prophecy (not even the Son knows the exact time of the parousia; 13:31–32). The church, thus, is dependent neither upon miracle-working apostles nor upon eschatological prophets. Mark points the way into early catholicism. Its further consolidation goes hand in hand with the expansion of the biography of Jesus, a genre that Mark created as an instruction in discipleship, that is, for the life of the church and for its experience of suffering.

(c) Jesus' Teaching and Ministry as the Canon of the Church: The Gospel of Matthew

The Gospel of Mark was a work designed to unify various Christian churches and their traditions, a legacy that Matthew further developed. Mark, in creating the genre of the gospel, tried to unify conflicting traditions of a divided Syrian Christianity. Matthew's design is even more ecumenical and fully exploits the potential for ecclesiastical unification provided by the genre of the gospel: Jesus' life, teaching, ministry, and suffering would become the canon of a universal catholic church. We do

Bibliography to §10.2c: Text
Papias Fragments: Funk-Bihlmeyer, *ApostVät*, xliv–xlvii, 133–40.

Bibliography to §10.2c: Commentaries
W. C. Allen, *A Critical and Exegetical Commentary on the Gospel according to St. Matthew* (3d ed.; ICC; Edinburgh: Clark, 1912).
A. H. McNeile, *The Gospel according to St. Matthew* (London: Macmillan, 1915).
Eduard Schweizer, *The Good News according to Matthew* (Atlanta: Knox, 1975).

Bibliography to §10.2c: Studies
Günther Bornkamm, Gerhard Barth, and Hans Joachim Held, *Tradition and Interpretation in Matthew* (Philadelphia: Westminster, 1963).
Krister Stendahl, *The School of St. Matthew and its Use of the Old Testament* (2d ed.; Philadelphia: Fortress, 1968).
Jack D. Kingsbury, *Matthew: Structure, Christology, Kingdom* (Philadelphia: Fortress, 1975).
Reinhart Hummel, *Die Auseinandersetzung zwischen Judentum und Kirche im Matthäusevangelium* (BEvTh 33; München: Kaiser, 1963).
Georg Strecker, *Der Weg der Gerechtigkeit: Untersuchung zur Theologie des Matthäus* (FRLANT 82; Göttingen: Vandenhoeck & Ruprecht, 1962).
Ulrich Luz, "Die Jünger im Matthäusevangelium," *ZNW* 62 (1971) 141–71.
Joachim Lange (ed.), *Das Matthäus-Evangelium* (WdF 525; Darmstadt: Wissenschaftliche Buchgesellschaft, 1980).

not know who Matthew was, although he has been identified with the name Matthew in Matt 9:9. But it must remain uncertain whether the author really wanted to present himself in this pericope. Papias of Hierapolis, to whom we owe the information about Mark as the interpreter of Peter, says of Matthew that he "collected the sayings in the Hebrew language, and each translated them as best he could" (Eusebius *Hist. eccl.* 3.39.16). This remark is the beginning of an ecclesiastical tradition that assumed that the Gospel of Matthew was first written in Hebrew (or Aramaic) and later translated into Greek. This is out of the question, however; the Gospel of Matthew known in the canon of the New Testament was written on the basis of Greek sources (Mark!), and its most original form was a Greek document. If Papias really knew anything about a Hebrew (Aramaic) document under the authority of Matthew, this cannot have been the extant gospel of the New Testament.

We might understand Papias' remark as a reference to the Synoptic Sayings Source, which in fact existed at first in Aramaic. Since Papias indeed spoke about the "sayings," this would fit the sayings collection Q very well; it is also quite likely that different Greek translations of Q were in circulation. If this is indeed the correct understanding of Papias' remark, the author of the Synoptic Sayings Source would then have claimed the authority of "Matthew" for his writing, and in this case, the author of the Gospel of Matthew, when he incorporated the sayings into the framework of Mark, would have continued the authority of his source for his own writing. Matthew and Thomas indeed seem to be the two earliest authorities for the composition of the sayings of Jesus, and it may be no accident that these two apostles appear side by side in several lists of the twelve disciples of Jesus (Mark 3:18; Matt 10:3; Luke 6:15). In any case, the use of the Synoptic Sayings Source as well as the continuation of the tradition about Peter allow the conclusion that the author of Matthew must be located in Syria. The controversy with rabbinic Judaism as it reconstituted itself after the catastrophe of the Jewish War requires a date for the composition of the Gospel of Matthew in the last decades of I CE.

Although Matthew used the general framework of the Gospel of Mark, the composition and outline of his gospel are fundamentally different. The passion narrative no longer determines the whole conception of the writing, and the ministry of Jesus is no longer seen as simply the prelude to the passion. The external structure is changed at the beginning of the gospel with the genealogy of Jesus and the story of his birth (Matthew 1–2): the birth as the beginning and the death as the end of Jesus' life. The teaching and ministry of Jesus are enclosed by this frame. The foundation of the church is not Jesus' death, but his ministry. In this ministry the emphasis clearly lies on the discourses of Jesus, namely, on his teaching and not on his working of miracles. For these speeches Matthew fully uses the material from the Synoptic Sayings Source, but also materials drawn from Mark and from other special sources or traditions. Most of these materials are organized into five major discourses: the Sermon on the Mount (chaps. 5–7); the discourse on the sending of the twelve (9:35–11:1); the parable discourse (13:1–53); the discourse on the order of the community (18:1–19:1), and the eschatological discourse (24:1–26:1). Each of these discourses concludes with the sentence: "and it happened when Jesus had finished these words . . ." The last speech, however, is concluded with: "and it happened when Jesus had finished *all* these words." This is immediately followed by the hierarchs' council of death (26:1–2). Clearly, at this point is ended the teaching of Jesus that is the foundation of the church.

These five major discourses are compositions of Matthew. They were not written on the basis of completely unconnected individual sayings, however, but use already-existing smaller composite units of sayings. About thirty percent of the Sermon on the Mount formed a unit in Q; this older unit is essentially preserved in Luke's "Sermon on the Plain" (Luke 6:20–49). The discourse on the sending of the disciples connects the small corresponding speech from Mark 6:7–11 with several units of Q (= Luke 10:1–12; 12:2–9; 12:51–53; 14:26–27) and special materials (Matt 10:17–25). In the parables discourse most of the material is derived from Mark 4, though Matthew adds several parables. The order for the community (Matthew 18) is based upon material from Mark 9:33–48 but is mostly a Matthean composition. The eschatological discourse is a reproduction of Mark 13 in its first part; in the second part Matthew adds more material, especially eschatological parables. In addition to these five major discourses, there are a number of smaller units of sayings that Matthew usually reproduced intact from his sources: the speech about John the Baptist from Q (Matt 11:2–19 = Luke 7:18–35), the sayings about clean and unclean from Mark (Matt 15:1–20 = Mark 7:1–23), the sayings about suffering in discipleship, also from Mark (Matt 16:21–24 = Mark 8:34–9:1), and the speech against the Pharisees, mostly from Q (Matt 23:1–36 = Luke 11:37–52).

Otherwise the course of the ministry of Jesus usually follows Mark, and most of the redactional connections which Mark had introduced to join the originally isolated units together reappear in Matthew, including the information about times and places. Nevertheless, the image of Jesus' ministry is quite different. This was largely accomplished by Matthew's removal of most of the miracle stories from their original context in Mark and compilation of them in one particular section, Matthew 8–9 (including one miracle story from Q: Matt 8:5–13). Only a few miracles remained in their former context: the healing of the withered hand (Mark 3:1–6 = Matt 12:9–14), which is part of a Markan apophthegm—in Matthew it is altogether a school discussion; the Canaanite woman and the epileptic boy (Mark 7:24–30 = Matt 15:21–28; Mark 9:14–29 = Matt 17:14–21)—both have become example stories for true faith; and the healing of the blind men just before the entry into Jerusalem (Mark 10:46–52 = Matt 20:29–34). The result is obvious: Jesus is no longer a wandering miracle worker who demonstrates his divine power by his deeds. Rather, he is the Lord and redeemer in whose ministry the mercy of God becomes present, so that the prophecy of Isaiah is fulfilled: "He took our infirmities and bore our diseases" (Isa 53:4 = Matt 8:17). The miracle stories themselves were thoroughly revised by Matthew, who usually drastically shortened them (the healing of the Gerasene demoniac takes twenty verses in Mark, but only seven in Matthew) and concentrated on the central features. Only the encounters of sick people with Jesus were at times amplified: they worship Jesus and address him with honorific titles, such as "Lord" or "Son of David." The miracles are ascribed to this unique and unrepeatable mission of Jesus. On the other hand, the miracle-working disciple of Jesus may be subject to the verdict that such actions do not necessarily fulfill the will of God (Matt 7:21–23).

By establishing the passion narrative as the hermeneutical principle for the understanding of Jesus' ministry, Mark had already made sure that Jesus' miracles could no longer be measured by the criteria of Hellenistic propaganda. Although Jesus still remained the "divine man," this designation necessarily became a paradox in view of the suffering and death of the Son of Man who would one time appear on the clouds of heaven. Matthew, however, attempts to remove the entire life, teaching, and actions of Jesus from the categories of the divine man and eschatological prophet. But Matthew no longer uses the passion narrative for this purpose. Rather, within the biographical presentation itself he consistently raises Jesus above the level of human or even superhuman existence. Jesus cannot be measured with human criteria, even if they be criteria such as godlike charisma, inspiration, and power. At the same time, Matthew maintains the biographical framework and even enlarges it. In this way he insures that revelation takes place within the historical, human realm. Nevertheless, in all the things which Jesus says, does, and suffers, it is God himself who acts.

The hermeneutical principle that enables Matthew to achieve this effect comes from the thesis of Christian apologetics that the divinity of an event can be demonstrated by its agreement with ancient predictions by divine oracles. Corresponding to this principle, Matthew not only inserts occasional references to the Old Testament into traditional materials, or enlarges sayings of Jesus by the addition of sentences from the Old Testament (e.g., Matt 9:13; 12:5–7; 12:40; 21:16), but he repeatedly points explicitly to the fact that the reported event fulfills divine prophecy: "This happened in order to fulfill what had been said by the prophet . . ." (Matt 1:22; 2:15, 17, 23; 4:14–16; 8:17; 12:17–21; 13:14–15; 13:35; 21:4–5). The Old Testament quotations that are introduced by this formula result from learned scribal activity concerned with the Old Testament and its Greek translation in the interests of scriptural proof. Christian apologetics of II CE continued this work systematically. To the extent that Matthew is not isolated in this learned activity, one can speak of a "School of St. Matthew." Such scholarly endeavors played some role in the controversies of Christianity with Judaism and received important impulses there, but they were primarily addressed to the pagan world. For the world at large, the Christian revelation is presented as an event which belongs to a comprehensive world-historical and eschatological plan of God. It is particularly the effort of providing scriptural proof which makes the gospel the book of revelation of a world religion. Matthew's proximity to the Judaism of his time contributed positively to this development. This, however, presupposes that Matthew was concerned to compare Christianity with Judaism exactly at the point at which Judaism's claim to be a world religion has its roots, namely, in the question of the validity of the law.

Matthew enters into this controversy with Judaism when he interprets the sayings tradition, particularly in the Sermon on the Mount (Matthew 5–7). In 5:17–19 he quotes a traditional saying that must have been formulated by conservative Jewish Christians in their opposition to gentile Christianity that rejected observance of the law. This saying says that Jesus had not come to dissolve the law, but to fulfill it, and that "not an iota, not a dot will pass from the law until all is accomplished." Matthew uses this saying as the theme for his interpretation of the law. Thus, he claims the law of the Old Testament wholly and fully as the possession of Christianity. But he also formulates the key principle of interpretation: it must be a righteousness which is superior to that of the scribes and Pharisees (5:20). Although the concept of righteousness in Matthew is by no means exhausted by its ethical component, the immediate application of this principle appears first of all in the antitheses of the Sermon on the Mount (5:21–48): "You have heard that it was said to those of old . . . but I say to you . . ." The antithetical formulations themselves do not contain early materials. They were formulated by Matthew in order to present Jesus as the legislator of the new righteousness (not as the new Moses; this term is deliberately avoided!). What is at stake in each case is a radicalization of the demand of the law: not only murder is forbidden, even hatred and evil words are prohibited; not only is adultery sin, the design is already sinful; and finally: love of one's enemies is the radicalization of the commandment to love one's neighbor.

A number of early and probably original sayings of Jesus were employed in this context. But Matthew carefully avoids interpreting these sayings in the sense of an isolated sectarian morality. The new righteousness by all means takes account of the realities of the world; for instance, divorce is permitted in the case of adultery (cf. Matt 5:32 with Mark 10:11). The Sermon on the Mount does not proclaim eschatological ethics, but a catechism for the community. Fasting, praying, and almsgiving are required exercises of piety (note their rejection in the *Gospel of Thomas*), but they must differ from the practice of both the Jews and the gentiles in their seriousness and adequacy (Matt 6:1–18). The ethics of a higher righteousness is the order of a new and more perfect community. This "perfection" (5:48; only Matthew uses this term, which is missing in the other Synoptic Gospels) is the goal of the conduct of all Christians. Nothing indicates a special ethics for the advanced members. The Sermon on the Mount, like the other discourses of the Gospel of Matthew, is a church order (*didache;* the parallels to the *Teaching of the Twelve Apostles* are obvious). Twice Matthew refers to commandments with the remark that they comprise the whole law and the prophets, the first time with the "golden rule" (7:12), the second with the double commandment of love of God and neighbor (22:37–40). Both these commandments appear at the beginning of the way of life in the *Teaching of the Twelve Apostles* (*Did.* 1.2). All this indicates that "higher righteousness" is ethics for the community, and conduct fitting for all members of a new world religion that is just at the stage of outpacing Judaism in this role.

Matthew is also concerned to write instructions for the whole Christian community in the other discourses. The instructions to the apostles are supplemented by general instructions for all members of the church in the case of persecution (10:17–42). The church-order regulations (18:1–19:1) emphasize the election of the weak and the duty of forgiving those who have failed (emphasized by the parable of the unmerciful servant, 18:23–35). Individualistic ethical perfection is excluded (note the addition to the discussion of rank in the community, Matt 18:4). Excommunication is requested when someone scandalizes the "little ones" in the church (18:6–9). The speech against the Pharisees is not simply polemic against Judaism and its piety, it is directed against each and every pretence of individualistic fulfillment of the law. There is most probably also direct polemic against people in office in Christian communities; Matt 23:2–3 and 8–10 are clearly directed to the Christian church. This criticism of

Christian officers reveals one decisive difference with the *Didache:* Matthew forgoes any instructions for church officers. The disciples are always representative of the whole Christian community, never special officers. Although Matthew emphasizes the authority of Peter (16:17–19), there is no concept of a succession. The responsibility for the fulfillment of the new righteousness is assigned to the whole community, without any limitations.

The community, therefore, enters into a special relationship with Jesus. Jesus is not a new Moses to whom obedience is due. Rather, Jesus is "Wisdom," who invites people to take her easy burden (11:28–30). The church that accepts the obligation of the new righteousness is related not to a legislator but to a revealer (11:25–27), who himself, as a wise and righteous man, has suffered the fate of the suffering righteous. Among other changes of Mark's passion narrative, Matthew introduced the passage about Pilate's washing his hands in innocence (27:24–25), which has been called a fateful anti-Judaic polemic. This polemic, however, was not directed against "the Jews" as such, but against the leaders of the people (see Matt 27:20!) and the people who are led astray by them. Thus, Matthew continues the traditional polemic against the leaders which began in the prophetic tradition of Israel and was developed particularly in the Jewish wisdom movement. From there Matthew also ultimately drew the polemic against the murderers of the prophets (23:34–36), clearly a piece of the wisdom tradition (cf. Luke 11:49). Just as in the sect of the Essenes, "Jerusalem" is the symbol for the murder of the messengers of God (Matt 23:37–39). Matthew saw the fall of Jerusalem in the Jewish War as retribution for the acts of the official leaders of the Jewish people (see his interpretation of the parable of the wedding feast; 22:6–7).

Even though Jesus suffered the same fate as many righteous ones before him, his death has put an end to this vicious cycle: the dead saints rose when he died (27:51–53), and Jesus' resurrection is documented to the women at the tomb by an epiphany (28:2–4). Galilee (28:10, 16), not Jerusalem, is the place for the beginning of a new epoch: the mission to all the nations—and Matthew must have known that Galilee was also the starting-point of the reorganization of Judaism. But the Christians have one advantage above all others: Jesus as the Lord over all will be with them until the end of the world. How Jesus will be present is explained in the parable of the last judgment (25:31–46). It summarizes the topic of the "higher righteousness": whatever one did, whether Christian, Jew, or gentile, to the least of Jesus' brothers and sisters (the hungry, the thirsty, the naked, those in prison), was done to Jesus.

3. THE JOHANNINE CIRCLE

(a) The Development of the Special Johannine Tradition

The Gospel of John is the product of a special tradition which should be located in Syria, but it presupposes a development of communities independent of other Syrian churches and traditions, at least in its beginnings. In the course of the elaboration of this Johannine tradition, contacts with other Christian (Petrine) circles of Syria become evident, especially in the appropriation of the miracle stories and the passion narrative. A dependence upon the Synoptic Gospels may be possible in the last stage of the redaction of the Gospel of John. Characteristic for the typical Johannine developments is the material that is contained in the discourses and dialogues. The presuppositions and beginnings of Johannine christology and soteriology are concealed in these materials. The problem of a precise determination of the speeches, their traditions, and their development is the true riddle of the Gospel of John, a problem which has not yet been solved in a satisfactory way. In the large discourses of the Gospel of Matthew, the older units of the oral tradition can be determined with great accuracy through form-critical analysis, but the Johannine discourse materials have so far successfully withstood any attempts to reconstruct their earlier history. Rudolf Bultmann's hypothesis of a gnostic discourse source has found very little agreement. Indeed, this hypothesis would only shift the problem, because the origin and development of such a source and its gnostic understanding of salvation would only pose new enigmas. But new approaches to a solution may be suggested by further research into the writings of the Coptic gnostic library of Nag Hammadi, which was discovered in 1945 and is now completely published in facsimile, and also in a preliminary English

Bibliography to §10.3a

Raymond E. Brown, *The Community of the Beloved Disciple* (New York: Paulist, 1979). Most instructive recent monograph.

Oscar Cullmann, *The Johannine Circle* (Philadelphia: Westminster, 1976).

James M. Robinson, "The Johannine Trajectory," in: idem and Koester, *Trajectories,* 232–68.

Rudolf Bultmann, "Der religionsgeschichtliche Hintergrund des Prologs zum Johannesvangeliums," and "Die Bedeutung der neuerschlossenen mandäischen und manichäischen Quellen für das Verständnis des Johannesevangeliums," in: idem, *Exegetica,* 10–35 and 55–104.

Oscar Cullmann, "Das Rätsel des Johannesevangeliums im Lichte der neuen Handscriftenfunde," in: idem, *Vorträge 1925–1962,* 260–91.

George MacRae, "The Fourth Gospel and *Religionsgeschichte,*" CBQ 32 (1970) 13–24.

Haenchen, "Johanneische Probleme," in: idem, *Gott und Mensch,* 78–113.

translation (1977). Critical work with these texts has just begun. These writings include very rich material of revelation discourses and dialogues, with many analogies to the Johannine speeches.

1) *Dialogues of Jesus.* The main source of the *Dialogue of the Savior* (§10.1b) demonstrates clearly how dialogues can be developed in the process of the interpretation of the sayings of Jesus. The composition of longer discourses, only occasionally or not at all interrupted by questions of the disciples, may have proceeded along the same lines. It is not always possible to isolate the traditional sayings used in such compositions because, first, these sayings often lack parallels in the Synoptic tradition, and, second, the dialogical use of such sayings frequently implies that traditional sayings are already cited in an altered form the first time they are used in such context. Furthermore, sayings of Jesus were apparently combined with other materials, such as kerygmatic formulae, creedal sentences, and general maxims.

The discourse of John 3 (the Nicodemus dialogue) is a good example. John 3:3 quotes a saying of Jesus about rebirth which also appears in Justin Martyr in the context of his discussion of the liturgy of baptism (*Apol.* 1.61.4–5). The author of the Nicodemus dialogue thus seems to have appropriated this sentence from the baptismal liturgy. However, he changed the traditional "to be reborn" into "to be born anew = to be born from above," and he replaced the traditional "enter into the kingdom of God" with "see the kingdom of God" (the repetition of the saying in John 3:5 has preserved the original phrase). The sentence juxtaposing spirit and flesh (3:6) is a theological maxim also known to Ignatius of Antioch (*Phld.* 7.1), perhaps derived from the same liturgical context. This statement is further illustrated by a traditional wisdom saying about the wind that one can hear but whose origin one does not know (3:8). The next traditional piece can be found in 3:11, a creedal sentence of the community, clearly recognizable by the break in style: Jesus suddenly speaks in the first-person plural. John 3:14 introduces a traditional Christian allegorical interpretation of Scripture (raising of the serpent by Moses— raising up of Jesus).

Early sayings of Jesus seem especially to have been the nuclei of the development of discourses and dialogues. The Johannine speeches fre-

Bibliography to §10.3a (1)

Helmut Koester, "Dialog und Spruchüberlieferung in den gnostischen Texten von Nag Hammadi," *EvTh* 39 (1979) 532–56.

Idem, "Gnostic Writings as Witnesses for the Development of the Sayings Tradition," in: Layton, *Rediscovery of Gnosticism,* 238–61.

Heinz Becker, *Die Reden des Johannesevangeliums und der Stil der gnostischen Offenbarungsrede* (FRLANT 68; Göttingen: Vandenhoeck & Ruprecht, 1956).

quently contain sentences that can be clearly identified, with the help of the new texts from Nag Hammadi, as sayings of Jesus that were originally isolated sayings. Only a few examples can be cited here. Jesus' statement about himself, that one may seek him but will still not be able to find him (John 7:33–34), appears among the sayings of Jesus in *Gos. Thom.* 38. A parallel from *Baruch,* an unknown wisdom book, quoted in Cyprian (*Testimonia* 3.29) demonstrates that this saying was originally a statement of heavenly Wisdom about herself, saying that she would be among human beings only for a short time and then return to her heavenly abode (cf. also John 16:16ff). John 8:52, "Whoever keeps my word will not taste death," is a variant of *Gos. Thom.* 1 and is also quoted as a traditional word of Jesus in *Dial. Sav.* 147, 18–20. John 16:24 (to ask—to find—to rejoice) is attested as a word of Jesus in *Dial. Sav.* 129, 14–16. Such sayings of Jesus could be developed into dialogues in the process of interpretation through the insertion of questions and answers, as can also be demonstrated from examples in the *Dialogue of the Savior. Dial. Sav.* 132, 3–9 is a dialogue, partly composed of words of Jesus, about the heavenly place, about "seeing" and self-knowledge, which seems to be an earlier stage of the dialogue in John 14:2–12.

The *Gospel of Thomas* shows moreover that sayings of Jesus that are statements about himself (note the "I am" sayings), frequent in the Johannine discourses but rare in the Synoptic tradition, became parts of collections of Jesus' sayings at a very early stage, although in a branch of the sayings tradition that was developed in a direction different from the Synoptic Sayings Source. *Gos. Thom.* 77, "I am the light that is above the All," corresponds entirely to "Johannine" style. *Gos. Thom.* 108, "Whoever drinks from my mouth, . . ." can be compared to John 7:38. Also analogous to the Gospel of John is *Gos. Thom.* 28, in which the savior speaks about his coming and about his mission in the world in terms which are in fact analogous to Jewish wisdom literature. There, Wisdom's introduction of herself is followed by an invitation, a call to conversion or a request for faith, and a promise, to which we can compare John 6:35: "I am the bread of life; whoever comes to me shall not hunger, and whoever believes in me shall never thirst." As is clear from the *Gospel of Thomas,* such kerygmatic self-introductions of Jesus could very well have circulated as isolated sayings. For example, John 11:25f, "I am the resurrection and the life, . . ." could be a quotation of an originally independent saying of Jesus.

2) *Traditions of the Johannine Church.* If such sayings in fact represent the oldest stage of traditions of the Johannine churches, it is possible to say a few things about its christology and soteriology. As in the *Gospel of Thomas,* this sort of interpretation of sayings belongs to an early stage of

gnostic christology. Even the word of the earthly Jesus is nothing other than the voice of the heavenly revealer who calls human beings into a new existence determined by the spirit. Baptism is rebirth into this new heavenly stage by means of the spirit; an eschatological component of baptism is absent (John 3:2ff). If the words about the bread of life and the true vine (John 6:26ff; 15:1ff) are interpretations of the eucharist, bread and wine are understood as symbols for the participation in Jesus' heavenly message. Bread and wine are, therefore, not related to Jesus' coming in the future, or to his fate of suffering (as in the understanding of Paul and the Synoptic Gospels), but rather, they represent Jesus' words which give life.

It is possible that the Gospel of John has preserved information about the location in which we should look for these early Christian gnostic communities. To be sure, in John most of the statements about the places of Jesus' ministry are in redactional material, but there are some useful hints in the dialogues themselves. Jesus is known as a "Galilean," and one of the objections against him is that a prophet does not come from Galilee (John 7:52). Even if this reflects nothing more than the knowledge of his actual origin, the accusation that he is a Samaritan is striking (8:48). In the narrative and dialogue about Jesus and the Samaritan woman, the location in Samaria must also have been a part of this tradition from the beginning (John 4:4ff). The land "on the other side of the Jordan" is frequently referred to as the setting of the activities of John the Baptist and of Jesus' sojourn (John 1:28; 3:26; 10:40–41). Although it is not always possible to decide whether such information rests on older tradition, we may still be correct in assuming that the early tradition of the Johannine churches belongs to a location within the realm of Palestinian Judaism, but outside the jurisdiction of the Jerusalem sanhedrin such as Samaria, for which an early mission by Philip is attested in Acts 8:5. It is impossible to know, however, whether John the son of Zebedee, who was once one of the pillars in Jerusalem and who later left Jerusalem like Peter, is in any way related to the formation of the early "Johannine" churches because there is no early attestation for the name "John" in this tradition.

3) *Papyrus Egerton 2.* A controversy with Judaism was also part of the early experiences in this region. The result was a special terminology that uses the term "Jews" categorically as a designation for the enemies of Jesus (see below on the passion narrative in John). It is certain that this controversy led to the formation of traditions that were later used for the

Bibliography to §10.3a (2)

C. H. Dodd, *Historical Tradition in the Fourth Gospel* (Cambridge: Cambridge University, 1963).

composition of the gospel. Interpretations of Scripture dealing with the question of the authority of Abraham and Moses played a major role in these discussions. In this context, a fragment of a previously unknown gospel, which was published in 1935, has not received enough attention: *Papyrus Egerton 2.* The script of this manuscript has been dated into the beginning of II CE, which would make it a good deal older (with one exception) than the oldest manuscripts of the New Testament (§7.2b). The fragment contains, in addition to a story about the healing of a leper, a controversy about the payment of taxes and a miracle of Jesus on the Jordan (the text breaks off in this story) as well as two units that are very closely related to the Gospel of John. The first of these is a controversy of Jesus with the "rulers of the people" which contains sentences agreeing almost verbatim with John 5:39 ("Search the Scriptures . . ."), 5:45 ("there is one who accuses you, Moses . . ."), and 9:29 ("We know that God has spoken to Moses . . ."). But there are characteristic differences: although the language is "Johannine," typical expressions of the author of the Fourth Gospel are missing (e.g., *Pap. Eg. 2* says "life" instead of John's "eternal life"). The first two sentences of these parallels are part of a rather long discourse in the Gospel of John, but belong to a smaller dialogue in *Papyrus Egerton 2,* which thus contains a version that is older in formal terms. The second of these two units is a short report of an attempted stoning and arrest of Jesus, which the author of the Gospel of John seems to have known, and parts of which he used in several instances in order to create the impression of repeated attempts upon Jesus' life (the equivalent sentences appear in John 7:30 and 10:31, 39).

In view of the early date of the papyrus and the relationship of the two texts to each other, it is not possible to see the *Papyrus Egerton 2* as a later excerpt from the Gospel of John, because it is hard to imagine that its author could have patched his text together from half a dozen passages in John (there is another parallel in John 3:2) and from the three Synoptic Gospels. It must instead be a text that is older than the Gospel of John. With its language that contains Johannine elements but reveals a greater affinity to the Synoptic tradition, it belongs to a stage of a tradition that preceded the canonical gospels. If it is a text that stems from the Johannine community, it demonstrates that confessional statements about Jesus and his divine origin were formulated in the controversy with Jewish

Bibliography to §10.3a (3): Text

Goro Mayeda, *Das Leben-Jesu-Fragment Papyrus Egerton 2 und seine Stellung in der urchristlichen Literaturgeschichte* (Bern: Haupt, 1946).

J. Jeremias, "An Unknown Gospel with Johannine Elements (Pap. Egerton 2)," *NTApo* 1. 94–97.

Cameron (ed.), "Papyrus Egerton 2," in *The Other Gospels,* 72–75.

opponents, for example, "We know that you have come from God" (*Pap. Eg. 2* 1. 45), or as a critical statement of such beliefs: "As for you, we do not know where you come from" (*Pap. Eg. 2* 11. 16f; cf. John 7:27). Such a source should also be assumed for other controversies of this type about the authority of Moses (John 7:19, 22f; cf. 3:14) and the true descendants of Abraham (8:33ff). *Papyrus Egerton 2* is therefore an important testimony for the formation of controversy traditions that were later used and expanded in the Johannine discourses; these traditions also provide a reference point for the separation of these communities from Judaism.

4) *The Passion Narrative.* In the course of their history, the Johannine communities had to come to terms with other Christian churches of Syria and were deeply influenced by their traditions. This is most evident in the passion narrative. The narrative of Jesus' passion which the communities of John appropriated agrees in its outline and in many details with the source of the Gospel of Mark. In both instances the narrative begins with Jesus' entry into Jerusalem (or with the annointing in Bethany respectively; John 12 has these two stories in reversed sequence) and ends with the discovery of the empty tomb (John 20:1–18). The name of Peter is fixed even more firmly in the Johannine version of the passion than in Mark: he appears in the story of the discovery of the tomb and is not just mentioned as an afterthought as in Mark 16:7.

We are certainly dealing in both instances with the same basic narrative of the passion, which seems to have been produced by circles under the authority of Peter, and was used in John, in the *Gospel of Peter,* and in Mark (as well as indirectly in Matthew and Luke). Some of the features preserved in John's version are more original, especially the dating of Jesus' death on the day before Passover (John 18:28). Accordingly, John does not present any of the secondary interpretations of Jesus' last meal as a Passover meal (Mark 14:12–16; Luke 22:15). Other features, however, have been added by the Johannine redaction: a second disciple appears in the passion account ("the other disciple" John 18:15f; "the disciple whom Jesus loved" 19:26f), who outdoes Peter by outrunning him in the discovery of the empty tomb (20:3–10). Also secondary are the stronger martyrological coloring of the passion report, and the clearly expressed intention to put the blame for the death of Jesus on the Jews and to exonerate Pilate. An anti-Judaic tendency appears here which was already visible in some of the traditions of controversy in the earlier Johannine communities. The reason for this tendency must be found in exper-

Bibliography to §10.3a (4)

D. Moody Smith, "The Sources of the Gospel of John: An Assessment of the Present State of the Problem," *NTS* 10 (1963/64) 336–51.

iences of persecution from the side of Jews: note the mention of the exclusion from the synagogue on the basis of the confession of Christ (John 9:22; 16:2).

5) *The Source of Signs.* Another complex of source materials of John which is closely related to the sources of Mark is the tradition of miracle stories, which appears in John as the Signs Source (*Semeia Source*). The following stories are drawn from it: John 2:1–11; 4:43–5:9; 6:1–21; 9:1–7; 11:1–44; its conclusion is probably preserved in 20:30–31. This source is a collection of pieces from the Hellenistic propaganda in which Jesus is proclaimed as divine man. The language of these traditions, however, points to an Aramaic milieu. The stories were used in Christian missionary activities among Aramaic-speaking Jews and gentiles and were collected in a bilingual community. It is characteristic of religious syncretism, especially among the population of Syria and Palestine which did not use the Greek language, that one of these miracle narratives (the wine miracle at Cana, John 2:1–11) derived its main features from the cult of Dionysus. The miraculous power of Jesus is even more emphasized in John's Signs Source than in the Markan parallels. These stories proclaim Jesus as the god who walks on earth. Instead of speaking about God who raised Jesus from the dead, they preach a Jesus endowed with the divine power to call the dead to life from their tombs (John 11). This tradition is not typically "Johannine"; the author of the Fourth Gospel in fact exhibits a very critical attitude with respect to these miracles. It is not unthinkable that an even earlier stage of the tradition had already combined these miracles with certain traditions of sayings and dialogues that presented Jesus as endowed with divine knowledge. In this case, the older form of the narrative of Jesus' encounter with the Samaritan woman (John 4:4ff) could have been part of this tradition since Jesus appears here as the prophet who possesses supernatural knowledge (4:16–19).

6) *Eschatological Traditions.* The eschatological proclamation of Jesus as the coming Son of Man or Messiah was not unknown in the Johannine circles, but was critically received and appropriated. Unequivocal predictions of the future parousia, with references to the well-known apocalyptic events, are missing in the Johannine tradition (John 5:28–29 and 6:39b, 40b, 44b are later interpolations). The farewell discourses of John's gospel interpret the parousia of Jesus as the coming of the spirit. As we have already mentioned, even the eucharist does not contain an eschatological component (John 6:26ff and 15:1ff; John 13:1ff does not contain any clear reference to the eucharist). Baptism is not an act of sealing for the eschatological time, but present rebirth through the spirit (3:1ff). The christological titles of Messiah/Christ and Son of Man had become familiar in the Johannine circles, and the latter is even empha-

sized (1:51). But the sayings about the coming of the Son of Man on the clouds of heaven which are so characteristic for an important segment of the Synoptic sayings tradition are missing. Eschatological terms like "judgment" and "eternity" are current, but are always understood as gifts or events of a salvation that is taking place in the present. On the whole, there can be no question that the concepts and terminology of the eschatological expectation were well known in the Johannine tradition, but are interpreted throughout in accordance with a piety and a theology that had totally different christological and soteriological presuppositions. The author of the Gospel of John is primarily responsible for the attempt to fuse the early gnostic views of the Johannine tradition with the kerygma of the cross and resurrection. The result of this effort is a new and quite independent theological concept.

(b) Exaltation on the Cross as Gospel

The Gospel of John results from the attempt to amalgamate the special tradition of the Johannine communities with the traditions of Syrian Christianity in general. This attempt must have been made before the end of I CE since the writing can no longer be dated as late as was often assumed. The earlier dating has been established through the discovery of papyrus Rylands 457 (= $\mathfrak{P}$52). The script of this small fragment with a few verses from John 18 has been dated to ca. 125. Thus the Gospel of John was known in Egypt at the beginning of II CE. Its author, however, must be located in Syria (§10.3a).

It is doubtful whether the extant text of the gospel, attested through several papyrus manuscripts from III CE ($\mathfrak{P}$66, $\mathfrak{P}$75), gives us the original form of this writing. The narrative about Jesus and the woman taken in adultery (John 7:53–8:11) is certainly a later interpolation, since it is missing in the papyri and in most of the uncials, and the Ferrar group of minuscules places this story after Luke 21:38. The status of the last chap-

Bibliography to §10.3b: Commentaries

Rudolf Bultmann, *The Gospel of John: A Commentary* (Philadelphia: Westminster, 1971). This work and C. H. Dodd's *Interpretation of the Fourth Gospel* (see below) are the two most formidable and stimulating works on the Gospel of John in this century.

Raymond E. Brown, *The Gospel according to John* (2 vols.; AB 29; Garden City, NJ: Doubleday, 1966–70).

Ernst Haenchen, *Das Johannesevangelium: Ein Kommentar* (ed. U. Busse: Tübingen: Mohr/Siebeck, 1980; English translation forthcoming).

C. K. Barrett, *The Gospel according to St. John* (2d. ed.; Philadelphia: Westminster, 1978).

Rudolf Schnackenburg, *The Gospel according to St. John* (vols. 1–2; New York: Seabury, 1980).

ter of the gospel (John 21:1–25) is debated, although it is present in all manuscripts. John 20:30–31 is the gospel's real conclusion, which is repeated in 21:25 in an exaggerated formulation. The author of the gospel had obviously reached the goal of his presentation with the appearance of the risen Jesus before Thomas (20:24–29), which demonstrates the precedence of faith over seeing, and concludes with the final confession of Jesus as "Lord and God." The appearance of Jesus at the miraculous catch of fishes (John 21:1–14; cf. Luke 5:1–11) is quite unmotivated. Just like the following discussion about the rank of Peter in comparison to the disciple whom Jesus loved (21:15–23), it was written in the interests of adjusting competing claims of ecclesiastical authorities. A successor of the author supplemented this work in such a way that the agreement between the Petrine and the Johannine traditions, which the gospel tried to achieve, is formulated in terms of ecclesiastical polity: Peter and his tradition are confirmed in the leadership of the organization of the Christian churches ("Tend my sheep!" John 21:15, 16, 17); the authority of the disciple whom Jesus loved, on the other hand, is described with the mysterious word "If it is my will that he remain until I come, what is that to you?" (21:22). Whatever may be meant by this statement, it is clear that the author of this additional chapter wants to underline the authority of

Bibliography to §10.3b: Studies

Erwin R. Goodenough, "John a Primitive Gospel," *JBL* 54 (1945) 145–83.

Ernest Cadman Colwell, *The Greek of the Fourth Gospel* (Chicago: University of Chicago, 1931).

Rudolf Bultmann, "Untersuchungen zum Johannesevangelium," in: idem, *Exegetica*, 124–97.

Ernst Käsemann, "Structure and Purpose of the Prologue to John's Gospel," in: idem, *New Testament Questions*, 138–67.

Andreas Lindemann, "Gemeinde und Welt im Johannesevangelium," in: *Kirche: Festschrift Bornkamm*, 133–61.

Wayne A. Meeks, "The Man from Heaven in Johannine Sectarianism," *JBL* 91 (1972) 44–72.

Ernst Käsemann, *The Testament of Jesus: A Study of the Gospel of John in the Light of Chapter 17* (Philadelphia: Fortress, 1966).

F. L. Cross (ed.), *Studies in the Fourth Gospel* (London: Mowbray, 1957).

Robert Kysar, *The Fourth Evangelist and His Gospel: An Examination of Contemporary Scholarship* (Minneapolis: Augsburg, 1975).

Karl Heinrich Rengstorf (ed.), *Johannes und sein Evangelium* (WdF 82; Darmstadt: Wissenschaftliche Buchgesellschaft, 1973).

Bibliography to §10.3b: Theology of the Fourth Gospel

C. H. Dodd, *The Interpretation of the Fourth Gospel* (Cambridge: Cambridge University, 1953 and reprints).

Bultmann, *Theology*, 2. 3–92.

J. Louis Martyn, *History and Theology in the Fourth Gospel* (2d ed.; Nashville: Abingdon, 1979).

Amos N. Wilder, *New Testament Faith for Today* (New York: Harper, 1955) 142–64.

the gospel as the report of an eyewitness and thus raise it to the same level as the authority of Peter (21:24).

We may ask whether the same redactor also changed the text of the original gospel in other instances; this seems indeed to be the case. The underlining of the truth of the eyewitness report in John 19:35 closely resembles 21:24. A number of obviously interpolated remarks about the future resurrection of the dead (5:28–29; 6:39b, 40b, 44b) and the future judgment (12:48b) contradict the Johannine discourses about the presence of judgment and resurrection (5:24–26; 11:25–26). Finally, a section interpolated into the Johannine discourse about the bread of life speaks about the physical eating and drinking of Jesus' blood (6:52b–59), whereas John otherwise speaks about Jesus as the bread of life who is present in his word (6:63, 68). Obviously, a redactor speaks here who wants to insist upon a realistic sacramentalist interpretation of the eucharist, which was also advocated by Ignatius of Antioch around the turn of the first century (§12.2d). Some scholars have argued that a few sentences of the Gospel of John which agree almost verbatim with the Synoptic Gospels (e.g., John 1:27; 12:8) should be seen as interpolations, but this agreement may simply result from the use of the same sources.

A peculiar and still unsolved problem of the Johannine text results from the observation that the sequence of individual units as presented in all known manuscripts is not always meaningful. John 3:31–36 is not appropriate as spoken by John the Baptist; it should be a continuation of the discourse of Jesus that ends in 3:21. In John 6:1 Jesus is quite unexpectedly found in Galilee, though he was still in Jerusalem in 5:1ff: is it possible that John 6:1–71 originally followed immediately upon John 4:43–54? There the Galilean locale is presupposed, which must also be assumed for John 6. The conclusion of chapter 14 is quite inexplicable: with "Rise, let us go hence!" (14:31) it leads directly to the scene of the imprisonment of Jesus (18:1ff), but in 15:1–17:26 the farewell discourses are continued. Here there should be no doubt: the section 15:1–17:26 was originally placed elsewhere, probably after 13:38 and before 14:1. This particular displacement could be explained by an accidental exchange of leaves in an early copy of the gospel. This explanation, however, cannot be used as an argument for the rearrangement of small units of not more than a few verses. Thus, in such instances we cannot arrive any further than the statement that in some instances the question of a meaningful order of the gospel remains a puzzle. It seems that some sections were never drafted in final form. This is confirmed by the observation that in John 4:43–54 a miracle story is told which sets the stage for a rather long discourse about the problem of faith and miracles (note 4:48), but the author—in stark contrast to other sections of the gospel, where a discourse always follows such a miracle—never presents such a discourse. Moreover, the many disconnected fragments of discourses and dialogues in chapters 7 and 8 suggest that the gospel contains sections in which a final redaction by the author never took place.

Nevertheless, the outline of the Gospel of John as a whole is quite clear. The first part (chaps. 2–11) was composed on the basis of a source of miracle stories (the Signs Source). Longer discourses and dialogues, composed on the basis of traditional sayings and dialogue materials, follow in each case (except after 4:43–54) upon the miracle story or are inserted into the story (as in John 11). The framework for the second part (chaps. 12–20) is provided by the traditional passion narrative. It begins with the annointment in Bethany (12:1ff), but is interrupted at the scene of Jesus' last meal by a long sequence of dialogues and discourses, the so-called farewell discourses (13:31–17:26); the author returns to the passion narrative with the story of Jesus' imprisonment (18:1ff). The external frame of the entire gospel is a three-fold introduction (prologue, witness of John the Baptist, and calling of the disciples, John 1:1–51) and a conclusion with three appearances of the risen Jesus (to Mary, to all the disciples, and to Thomas; John 20:11–29).

The hymnic prologue at the beginning of the gospel (1:1–18) derives from the tradition of the Johannine churches. The author has made a number of additions to the traditional hymn in order to connect it more closely with the rest of the gospel (1:6–8, 15, cf. 1:19–34; also 1:17, cf. 5:39–47; 9:28–29; 19:7). Whether a pre-Christian hymn is the ultimate source of this section cannot be decided for certain because in the form in which is was used by the Fourth Gospel it is certainly a product of the Christian community. Its relationship to and dependence upon Jewish wisdom theology is nevertheless quite apparent (§5.3e). But the term "word" (*logos*) has replaced the older term "wisdom" (*sophia*), something which also happened with Philo of Alexandria under Greek influence. Like the Jewish figure of Wisdom, the Logos is pre-existent with God, who creates the world through him. He appears in the world as the revealing light, is not understood, but gives to those who accept him the right to become God's children. To this point nothing has been said that goes beyond the scope of wisdom theology. A typical Christian confession does not appear until 1:14, in the sentence about the Logos becoming flesh, and again in the praise of the glory of God which has appeared in the form of a human being (1:14b, 16). Since these later statements were already a part of the traditional hymn, it is apparent that while the Johannine community had appropriated the concepts of the Jewish myth of Wisdom, it also confessed the incarnation of the heavenly revealer in the earthly Jesus. It thus rejected a gnostic understanding of the event of revelation, for which the radical rejection of the earthly and human sphere would have been the criterion of salvation. This anti-gnostic position, which appears in the hymn in a programmatic formulation, is determinative for the whole Gospel of John, although the author frequently uses mythical language that is closely akin to the language of Gnosticism.

It is debated whether the description of the activity of John the Baptist in the second part of the introduction (John 1:19ff) contains a polemic against still-existing circles of John's disciples (see also John 3:22–30; 4:1). The tradition used by the gospel apparently knew about such conflicts and also reported that several of Jesus' disciples came from the circle of John the Baptist. But the primary interest of the gospel in this section, including the report of the calling of the disciples, is a discussion of traditional titles of dignity for Jesus (Prophet, Messiah/Christ, Son of God, King of Israel; see John 1:20ff, 34, 41, 49), in order to introduce the title which, provisionally, in addition to the designation "Son," describes Jesus' dignity adequately: the Son of Man (1:51).

The primary theological interest of the first major part of the gospel (chaps. 2–11) is the controversy concerning the traditional religious criteria for revelation. These criteria are introduced in the peoples' reaction to the miracles of Jesus and in the criticism of Jesus by the "Jews." Criticism of the miracles and polemic against the "Jews" are, to be sure, topics already provided by the tradition that John uses, but the author wants to discuss a more fundamental problem. Both he and his tradition see Jesus as the divinely empowered man, the Son of God walking on earth; but faith which is directed solely towards the visible documentation of the divine presence is nothing more than a demonstration of that general human attitude which accepts revelation gladly only when it confirms religious expectations and prejudices. In a similar vein, the Jews represent that attitude which rejects revelation when it does not conform with preconceived theological criteria. Both attitudes are seen by the author of the gospel as the judgment of the "world," which cannot or will not listen to the word of the revealer. What is meant by the "word" of revelation and why it is an absolute opposite to the judgment of the "world," must be understood on the basis of the gnostic concept of revelation, which the author has inherited together with the sayings and dialogues of his tradition (§10.1b; 10.3a). According to this gnostic concept, the word of revelation differs fundamentally from the language of the world, and can be understood only by those who are "from God" (John 8:47) or "from the truth" (18:37). The gnostic determinism that appears here has been modified by John insofar as the miracle that Jesus does is granted as an answer to real human need. Nor is the Johannine "I am" formula, which is used repeatedly (e.g., John 11:25: "I am the resurrection and the life"; also 6:33 and often elsewhere), the self-introduction of a divine being from another world, which can be heard only by those who are also of divine origin. Rather, it is a formula of recognition, in which the hearer recognizes the fulfillment of genuine human hope.

The word of the revealer thus does not, as it would in Gnosticism, appeal to the ultimately divine knowledge of the hearer, but to the yearnings and expectations that arise from human experience. These include the efforts to understand the religious tradition correctly. Moses is, therefore, indeed a witness of the revelation which became present in Jesus (5:46–47; cf. 8:56). Clearly the schema of gnostic revelation has been radically modified, altogether disrupted by the inclusion of the revealer in the sphere of human suffering and death. At this point, the author of the Fourth Gospel has used the church's proclamation of Jesus' suffering and death as the event of salvation and has applied it as a theological and literary bracket to bind the two parts of his work together. As early as John 2:18–20 the author refers to Jesus' death and resurrection as the key for the understanding of his message. The exaltation of the revealer no longer designates, as in Gnosticism, the return of the revealer to his heavenly abode, untouched by the sphere of earthly humanity; rather, his exaltation comes in the death on the cross (3:14; 8:28; 12:32–34). This Johannine theology of the cross is directed not only against Gnosticism, it also contradicts the theology of the divine miracle worker. It is exactly the last and greatest miracle of Jesus, the raising of Lazarus, that is the immediate cause for the decision of the sanhedrin to kill Jesus (11:46–52). If Jesus' ministry as revealer thus results in his death, the claim of his preaching, that it is the gift of the presence of judgment and eternal life for those who believe, becomes even more of a paradox. The more the author of the gospel tried to interpret the death of Jesus, the more the rejection and radical reinterpretation of the traditional eschatological expectation, which the author took over from his gnosticizing tradition of the sayings of Jesus, had to enter into ever sharper conflict with the traditional theology of the church. This question is discussed in the farewell discourses that are inserted into the framework of the passion narrative.

In its presentation of the passion narrative the Fourth Gospel agrees on the whole with the Synoptic account, although there are a number of significant differences. Most of these occur with features that are clearly secondary expansions of the older report appearing in the Synoptic Gospels and missing in John: the finding of the ass in the report of the entry into Jerusalem (Mark 11:1b–6); the preparation of the Passover meal (Mark 14:12–16); the elaborate account of the betrayal by Judas (Mark 14:10–11; see also Matt 27:3–10), Jesus in Gethsemane (Mark 14:32–42; it is doubtful whether John 12:27 shows any knowledge of this report); Jesus before Herod (Luke 23:6–12); the two criminals (Luke 23:39–43); and the guards at the tomb (Matt 27:62–66). This much already demonstrates the reliance of the Gospel of John on a more original version of the passion narrative, which is further confirmed by the preservation of the dating of the crucifixion on the day before the festival (John 18:28). Accordingly, there is no indication in John that Jesus' last meal was a Passover meal (John 13:1ff)—which is most likely historically correct.

It is quite peculiar, however, that John either knows nothing about the institution of the eucharist at Jesus' last meal, or else suppressed this information and replaced that account with the foot-washing scene (13:4ff). It is highly unlikely that John did not know the Lord's Supper at all because allusions to the eucharist are found several times in the Fourth Gospel (15:1ff; also John 6, even without the questionable verses of 6:52b–59). The terminology used in such passages has some relationship to the eucharist prayers of the *Didache* (§10.1c). It is probably better to assume that the author wanted to avoid the materialistic understanding of the sacrament, which appears, for example, in the writings of his younger contemporary Ignatius of Antioch (§12.2d), and therefore passed by the opportunity of establishing the institution of the eucharist (and of baptism!) in the life of Jesus. The Fourth Gospel is concerned with "the bread that remains for eternal life, which the Son of Man gives" (6:27), namely the word of Jesus (6:63). The author has therefore heavily revised his source in the account of the last supper. Otherwise, he redacted the traditional passion narrative, but did not change it radically, with one exception: the trial before Pilate (18:29–19:15). Only a few verses of this section are traditional (18:33, 39–40; 19:1–3, 13–14); everything else is a composition of the gospel's author. The scene does more than serve to absolve Pilate from all guilt in the death of Jesus. The tendency to exonerate the Roman authorities and assign responsibility to the Jewish sanhedrin was surely present in John's source. The scene of Jesus before Pilate primarily intends to contrast Jesus as the revelation of divine truth one more time with the "world." Jesus remains the revealer, even in his trial in the face of death, because death is nothing but his final exaltation. Therefore, John has no need to refer to the future coming of the Son of Man, which is an important element of the scene of Jesus' trial in the Synoptic account (Mark 14:62).

The farewell discourses provide the essential basis for understanding the exaltation on the cross as the consummation of Jesus' work of revelation. As he goes to the Father, so will his return as the Paraclete guarantee the lasting presence of revelation in the community. The author composed these farewell discourses, like the others, on the basis of individual gnostic interpretations of sayings and units of dialogue, which he recast into criticial discussions of the traditional eschatology of the church and, at the same time, of the gnostic concept of salvation. Gnostic theological concepts and terms appear frequently, such as the emphasis that the disciples are "not from the world" (17:14), the definition of eternal life as "recognition of the true God and of his messenger" (17:3), the interpretation of faith as the "way" to the house of the Father (14:1ff), and, especially, the characterization of Jesus as the revealer who came from the Father and is returning to the Father as he leaves the world (16:38, etc.). But there are also clear contrasts with the gnostic concept of salvation. The task of the disciples is turned toward the world; it is in the world that they must labor (17:15, 18). Discipleship of Jesus includes the experience of sorrow, suffering, and the hostility of the world, and cannot be understood as following Jesus on his way to the heavenly realms (13:36–38; 15:18–25; 16:20–24, 32–33). The request for the vision of God as the goal of salvation is rejected (14:8ff); instead the keeping of the commandments, in particular of the commandment of love, is demanded from the disciples (14:12, 15; 15:7ff).

At the same time, the author resists the obvious alternative of contrasting with the realized eschatology of Gnosticism an apocalyptic expectation that looks toward a future event of salvation. He maintains a radically realized, thus also a demythologized, eschatology. The parousia of Jesus after his exaltation is not an apocalyptic event, but is understood in ecclesiological terms as the coming of the spirit to the disciples (14:15–17, 25–26; 15:26; 16:7–15). The Paraclete, that is, the "Counselor," "Defender" (not the "Comforter"), also called the "Spirit of Truth," is originally an angelic figure, as is shown by the texts of Qumran. In John, he is identified with Jesus as he returns to his disciples. The actions of Jesus after his return are not described as the apocalyptic conquest of the powers of evil, but as the response to the prayers of the community, which is continuing in its own work the earthly work of Jesus (14:12–14); Jesus has already conquered the world (16:33). His ascension is nothing other than the assurance of peace for the community, not the introduction of the apocalyptic labor-pains (14:27–31). If the disciples have sorrow, as Jesus leaves them, this only points forward to the clarity of understanding that they will achieve after Jesus has left them (16:16ff). Jesus will appear to the world as the exalted Lord, but only insofar as the obedience of the church to his commandments demonstrates to the world who this Jesus really is (14:21–24). Accordingly, the discourse about the eucharist (apparently the theme of John 15) does not point to a future event, but emphasizes the elements of eschatological festive joy and mutual love as the bond of unity (15:9ff). It is characteristic that it is precisely in this discourse that Jesus' word (not the sacramental action) guarantees the purity of the church. Thus these farewell discourses discuss all the important topics of apocalyptic theology and relate each of them to the present experience of the community.

Therefore, the appearances of Jesus after his resurrection which are reported in the conclusion of the gospel (20:11–29) do not point forward to a future, understood in terms of apocalypticism, nor to the parousia. Their message is instead Jesus' exaltation, the gift of the spirit, and true faith which is independent of "seeing." Easter, Pentecost, and Parousia are one and the same, and ultimately nothing but the exaltation of Jesus on the cross. It was left to the further development of the Johannine tradition to show whether this radical and ingenious new interpretation of the traditional Christian concepts in the categories of gnostic language could succeed or even survive.

(c) The Ecclesiastical Reception of the Johannine Tradition

The further developments show that the writing of the Gospel of John marked an important turning point in the history of the separated Johannine communities. The gospel itself, soon after its appearance, was subjected to a revision that moved it more closely to the theology of the rest of Syrian Christianity. This was done, more specifically, through the formal recognition of the authority of Peter (John 21), and through the interpolation of a doctrine of the sacrament and eschatological views that were more in keeping with concepts of the Syrian churches (see above).

1) *The First Epistle of John* is an important witness for this devel-

Bibliography to §10.3c (1): Commentaries

Rudolf Bultmann, *The Johannine Epistles: A Commentary on the Johannine Epistles* (Hermeneia; Philadelphia: Fortress, 1973).

C. H. Dodd, *The Johannine Epistles* (The Moffat New Testament Commentary; New York: Harper, 1946).

Bibliography to §10.3c (1): Studies

C. H. Dodd, "The First Epistle of John and the Fourth Gospel," *BJRL* 21 (1937) 129–56.

Rudolf Bultmann, "Analyse des ersten Johannesbriefes," and "Die kirchliche Redaktion des ersten Johannesbriefes," in: idem, *Exegetica,* 105–23 and 381–93.

Wolfgang Nauck, *Die Tradition und der Charakter des 1. Johannesbriefes* (WUNT 3; Tübingen: Mohr/Siebeck, 1957).

Herbert Braun, "Literatur-Analyse und theologische Schichtung im ersten Johannesbrief," in: idem, *Studien zum Neuen Testament und seiner Umwelt* (3d ed.; Tübingen: Mohr/Siebeck, 1971) 210–42.

Hans-Martin Schenke, "Determination und Ethik im 1. Johannesbrief," *ZThK* 60 (1963) 203–15.

Hans Conzelmann, "'Was von Anfang an war,'" in *Neutestamentliche Studien für Rudolf Bultmann* (BZNW 21; Berlin: Töpelmann, 1954) 194–201.

opment. Its author's theological position is closely related to that of the gospel's redactor. Some have even assumed that the author of 1 John and the redactor of the Fourth Gospel were one and the same person. 1 John is well preserved and is perhaps attested even earlier than the gospel, in Papias of Hierapolis (Eusebius *Hist. eccl.* 3.39.17; perhaps Polycarp also reflects knowledge of 1 John, *Phil.* 7.1). But the trinitarian section in 1 John 5:7–8 is a later interpolation. It appears for the first time in late editions of the Vulgate and in a few very late Greek minuscules, though through the third edition of Erasmus' New Testament it also made its way into many modern translation. The final section of 1 John, 5:14–21, gives the impression of an appendix which was secondarily added after the conclusion in 5:13. If this is the case, its language and content would still argue for the same author.

1 John is not a true letter—the prescript and postscript are lacking—but a polemical treatise that seeks to intervene in the controversy about the interpretation of the Johannine tradition and of the Gospel of John. Even if the author of that gospel had clearly distanced himself from Gnosticism in theological terms, he still had not clarified his position in this matter with respect to ecclesiastical policy. 1 John tries to draw the necessary consequences for political decisions. He identifies the opponents and enters into controversy with them, explicitly quoting their opinions. According to his characterization of the opponents, it must be assumed that they were members of the Johannine churches (it is of no use to try to identify any one particular heretic who was known to the later fathers, such as Cerinthus). The opponents read the Gospel of John and appealed to it, apparently claiming that the Jesus depicted in that gospel fully supported their gnostic theology. They boasted of their knowledge of God (1 John 2:4; 4:8), of their love of God (4:20), of their sinlessness (1:8–10), and of their walking in the light (2:9). Like Jesus himself, they claimed to be "from God" and to speak with the voice of the spirit (4:2–6). But they denied that Jesus had come in the flesh (4:2) and they denied the identity of the (heavenly) Christ and the earthly Jesus (2:22).

The author of 1 John refutes this gnostic foreshortening of the Johannine gospel, to which he himself also appeals with good reason. He belongs to the same tradition, speaks the same language as the author of the gospel, and he states explicitly in the prologue of his writing that his own position agrees completely with that of the gospel (1 John 1:1–4; cf. John 1:1ff). He argues in agreement with the gospel that love of God without love of the brothers and sisters is impossible (1 John 4:16f, 20; the special reference to almsgiving, 3:17, shows a pastoral motivation). It is exactly in the mutual love of the members of the community that the overcoming of death and entering into life become a present reality (3:14).

But if the reality of salvation can be documented in the experiences of the community, it is also necessary to insist upon the identity of the Son of God with the earthly Jesus who came in "water" and in "blood," which means that he shared human experience from his baptism to his death (5:5–8). However, with the creedal formula that Jesus came "in the flesh," the author does not quite recapture the meaning of the sentence from the gospel that "the Logos became flesh" (cf. 1 John 4:2 with John 1:14).

1 John goes beyond this defense of the gospel against its gnostic opponents and expands the Johannine theology by appropriating other concepts that were current in Syrian Christianity and also in the communities dependent upon the Pauline mission. Among these are the expectation of the parousia and last judgment as part of an apocalyptic theology (1 John 4:17; 3:2), as well as the concept of the coming of the "anti-Christ," which is turned against the gnostic opponents (2:18, 22; 4:3). The understanding of Jesus' death as a sacrifice for the expiation of sin (2:2; 4:10) and the concept of purification through his blood (1:7) have no foundation in the Fourth Gospel, but correspond to widespread understandings of early catholic theology. 1 John not only emphasizes the necessity to forgive sins repeatedly (1:8–10), but also gives instructions in a church order for this forgiveness (5:16–17) and warns of the seduction of the world (2:15–17). It is clear from these interests that the author is a later church politician from the Johannine circle, who argues in this writing for the practical aspects of the continuation of the Johannine inheritance. While this inheritance is defended against the gnostics, the author at the same time strives to move the Johannine churches and their writings closer to other churches of Syria and Asia Minor. Asia Minor provides the first evidence for an acceptance of the Johannine tradition by other Christian churches.

2) *The Third Epistle of John.* The writings transmitted in the New Testament as 2 and 3 John also belong to the Johannine circle. The language and theology of the two letters clearly prove their Johannine origin. Both letters claim to be written by the "Presbyter" or "the Elder," but only 3 John is a true letter. It is not possible to reconstruct the situation to which it belongs, however, because nothing is known about the circumstances which caused the writing of the letter. We do not know who the Elder was, nor the Gaius to whom he writes, nor Diotrephes whom he accuses. Since the Elder accuses Diotrephes of love of power and lack of

Bibliography to §10.3c (2)

Ernst Käsemann, "Ketzer und Zeuge (zum johanneischen Verfasserproblem)," in: idem, *Exegetische Versuche und Besinnungen* (Göttingen: Vandenhoeck & Ruprecht, 1971) 1. 168–87.

Rudolf Schnackenburg, "Der Streit zwischen dem Verfasser des 3. Joh. und Diotrephes," *MThZ* 4 (1953) 18–26.

willingness to cooperate, but does not reproach him for any theological reasons (3 John 9–10), we must assume that the conflict was about matters of church organization or missionary activities. The Elder seems to commission and supervise wandering missionaries, while Diotrephes wants to maintain control over his own church and apparently expels whoever will not obey him. Was Diotrephes a bishop who had suspicions about the Johannine tradition being too closely connected to wandering gnostic apostles? Perhaps the letter was written at a time at which the Johannine communities had not clearly separated themselves from their gnostic fellows.

3) *The Second Epistle of John* is not a true letter, but a rather superficial compilation of Johannine sentences in the form of a catholic epistle (the "elect lady" in 2 John 1 is the church). Both 1 John and 3 John were used by this writing. From the latter, 2 John borrows the title of the "Elder," and from the former, the confession that Jesus Christ has come in the flesh (2 John 7), which is propagated as the criterion of right teaching (*didache;* 2 John 9f). 2 John is significant since it demonstrates how Johannine Christianity, following in the footsteps of 1 John, makes its appearance as the advocate of the fight against Gnosticism.

(d) The Gnostic Inheritance of John

There are indeed clear attestations for a gnostic continuation of the Johannine tradition, against which 1 and 2 John struggled at the beginning of II CE. However, these writings which were rejected by the church have been preserved in only fragmentary form or in later editions. The most important document is the *Acts of John,* a history of the apostle John in the form of a romance; a number of Greek manuscripts and translations have preserved various parts. The reconstruction of the original text, which must have been written in II CE, is burdened with difficulties and in fact is hardly possible in the present status of our knowledge. But several portions can be assigned with certainty to the original *Acts of John,* or identified as portions of the sources used by the author. The most signif-

Bibliography to §10.3d: Texts

Lipsius-Bonnet, *ActApostApoc,* 2,1. 151–216.

K. Schäferdiek, "The Acts of John," *NTApo* 2. 188–259.

Cameron (ed.), "John's Preaching of the Gospel, The Acts of John 87–105," in *The Other Gospels,* 87–96.

Bibliography to §10.3d: Studies

Karlmann Beyschlag, *Die verborgene Überlieferung von Christus* (München and Hamburg: Siebenstern, 1969) 88–116.

Walther von Loewenich, *Das Johannesverständnis im zweiten Jahrhundert* (BZNW 13; Giessen: Töpelmann, 1932).

icant piece is the so-called *Gospel Preaching of John* (chaps. 87–105) and
a long hymn (94–96), which is the oldest tradition preserved in it. This
hymn must once have been used as a liturgical song (with responses) in
the Johannine communities. Its terminology is very closely related to that
of John's Gospel, especially to its prologue. In both instances the terms
Father, Logos, grace, and spirit occur (94.1–2; cf. the trinitarian formula
Father-Logos-Spirit at the end of the hymn, 96.51), as also the contrast
light/darkness (94.3), and a number of themes that are important elements in the Johannine discourses: house, place, way (95.21f, 27; cf. John
14:1ff), door (95.26; cf. John 10:9). The sentence "Who I am, you will
recognize when I leave" (96.38) is a fitting summary of the theme of the
farewell discourses of the Gospel of John. It remains an open question
whether this hymn is dependent upon the Gospel of John, or comes from
the same circles to which the author of the Fourth Gospel also owes
another hymn that he used for his prologue. The basic gnostic position of
the hymn is obvious, although there are no signs of an elaborate gnostic
mythology. The believer recognizes himself in the person of the revealer
("If you follow my dance, you will see yourself in me who is speaking,"
96.28f), and the revealer is not the one who he seems to be (96.39).

   The docetism which appears in the hymn is further elaborated in the
Gospel Preaching of John. It is a gospel that John tells in the I-style
(possibly the author of the *Acts of John* introduced this first person; but
note the I-style of the *Gospel of Peter;* §10.2a). Its dependence upon the
Gospel of John is clear. The titles of the heavenly Jesus are predomi-
nantly Johannine, especially "Logos," but also "Door," "Way," "Resurrection," "Life," and "Truth" (98), among others. The passion narrative
refers to John 19:34 (97; 101). But other gospels are used at the same
time: Mark 1:16–20 for the calling of John, James, Peter, and Andrew;
Mark 9:2ff for the story of the transfiguration; and Luke 7:36 for the
narrative of a meal. Analogously to 1 John, the author draws on traditions
that were current in circles of the early catholic church in Asia Minor and
Syria. He also takes up the tradition from Asia Minor that identifies John
with the son of Zebedee, the brother of James, and he parallels the ecclesiastical tradition in his transfer of the locale of John's activities to western
Asia Minor. Both the gnostic and the ecclesiastical traditions have thus
moved well beyond the realm of Syria, the original home of the Johannine
communities.

   The primary purpose of this gospel section of the *Acts of John* is the
validation of docetism against the ecclesiastical attacks upon gnostic docetic christology. This proof is cast into a narrative of the earthly appearance of Jesus. Jesus appears in constantly changing shapes, sometimes as
a small boy, sometimes as a beautiful man; then again John sees him as a

bald-headed man with a long beard, while James perceives him as a youth with a pubescent beard; sometimes Jesus' body is soft or immaterial, in other instances it is as hard as a rock—and when he walks, he leaves no footprints. In the passion narrative the author emphasizes the difference between the heavenly Lord, who speaks with the voice of the revealer from the cross of light separating this world and the transcendent realms, and the earthly phantom which the people hung on the wooden cross. Such crude docetism is clearly a later development of the earlier Logos christology to which the Gospel of John was closely related. Indeed the older Logos christology appears once more at the end of the passion narrative, in a quotation of a formulated tradition: "recognize me as . . . the piercing of the Logos, the blood of the Logos, the wounding of the Logos, the hanging of the Logos, the death of the Logos. . . . First therefore recognize the Logos, then you will recognize the Lord, and third you will recognize the human being and its sufferings" (*Acts of John* 101).

In Asia Minor, the place of origin of the *Acts of John,* the early catholic tradition recognized the Gospel of John in the first half of II CE, also accepted the tradition of Jesus' disciple John and, assimilating the information from the Synoptic Gospels, identified him with the son of Zebedee. As such he received a new home in Ephesus. In the west, however, especially in Rome, John's letters and Gospel found only very hesitant acceptance. On the other hand, Egyptian Christianity accepted the Gospel of John very early, although it must be assumed that gnostic Christians were responsible for its introduction. In the gnostic schools of Egypt the Gospel of John was fully at home in II CE. The first extant commentary on the gospel's prologue (a fragment quoted in Irenaeus *Adv. haer.* 1.8.5–6) is a gnostic document, as is the oldest commentary on this gospel, written by the Valentinian Heracleon (fragments are quoted by Origen in his *Commentary on John*).

4. JEWISH CHRISTIANITY

(a) The Fate of the Jerusalem Church

One could with justification designate the whole first generation of Christians as "Jewish Christian." Almost all the Christian missionaries of this first generation were Jews, although some of them came from the diaspora (Barnabas, Paul, and others). For all of them the Old Testament

Bibliography to §10.4: Texts

A. F. J. Klijn and G. F. Reinink, *Patristic Evidence for Jewish-Christian Sects* (NovTSup 36; Leiden: Brill 1973).

was Holy Scripture. The theology of Judaism provided all the categories, terms, and concepts for the formation of Christian theology. The code for moral and pious conduct formed by Judaism (see the Two Ways, §10.1c) became binding for the Christians, and the legislation of the Old Testament was used as the basis for the development of generally valid ethical rules. Thus if we are to treat the phenomenon of Jewish Christianity in the narrower sense as the topic of this section, it is necessary to define criteria which describe more specific forms of adherence to the tradition of Judaism.

There is some specific information from the early history of Christianity which demonstrates that particular criteria for the faithfulness to the Jewish law could lead to the identification of a clearly defined group as "Jewish-Christian": the controversy of Paul with Jerusalem about the question of circumcision, and the subsequent fight against the Judaizers in Galatia (§9.1d, 3b). One specifcally Jewish-Christian element was, therefore, circumcision, as well as the observance of other portions of the Jewish ritual law. Christians who insisted on such observance could be found outside of Jerusalem at an early time, as is shown by Paul's letter to the Galatians (note also Philippians 3). We know nothing, however, about the formation of Jewish-Christian communities elsewhere in the early period. For a description of Jewish Christianity it is therefore necessary to begin with the community in Jerusalem. This community was known to have been bound to the observance of the ritual law, at least at the time of Paul.

When Paul came to Jerusalem with the collection from the gentile Christians, the Jerusalem church was obviously continuing in obedience

Bibliography to §10.4: Studies

Jean Daniélou, *The Theology of Jewish Christianity* (Philadelphia: Westminster, 1965; reprint, 1977).

Georg Strecker, "On the Problem of Jewish Christianity," in: Bauer, *Orthodoxy and Heresy*, 241–85.

Marcel Simon, *Verus Israel: Etude sur les relations entre chrétiens et juifs dans l'empire romain (135–425)* (Bibliothèque des Ecoles françaises d'Athènes et de Rome 166; Paris: Boccard, 1948).

Idem, *Recherches d'histoire Judéo-Chrétienne* (EtJ 6; Paris: Mouton, 1962).

Hans-Joachim Schoeps, *Theologie und Geschichte des Judenchristentums* (Tübingen: Mohr/Siebeck, 1949).

Bibliography to §10.4a

Roy Bowen Ward, "James of Jerusalem," *Restoration Quarterly* 16 (1973/74) 174–90.

Hans von Campenhausen, "Die Nachfolge des Jakobus," in: idem, *Aus der Frühzeit des Christentums* (Tübingen: Mohr/Siebeck, 1963) 135–51.

Marcel Simon, "La Migration à Pella: Légende ou réalité?" in *Judéo-Christianisme: volume offert au Cardinal Jean Daniélou,* = *RechSR* 60 (1972) 37–54.

to the law. There were some difficulties in the collection's delivery that were related to this attitude of the Jerusalem Christians (§9.4b). It can also be assumed that Jesus' brother James was the advocate of this church's faithfulness to the law. For the future development of Jewish Christianity, the Jerusalem community, with its adherence to ritual law and circumcision and its apparent faithfulness to the cult of the Jewish religious community, would doubtlessly have had a commanding role. Historical events, however, prevented the fulfillment of this expectation. During a vacancy in the Roman procuratorship, James was murdered in the year 62, and the Christian community of Jerusalem left the city shortly before the beginning of the Jewish War (§8.3a). Eusebius (*Hist. eccl.* 3.5.3) says that a prophecy had prompted their emigration to Pella on the east side of the Jordan (Perea).

There are a few scattered pieces of information which indicate that the community continued to exist, but they do not permit us to form a consistent picture, or to say anything about its significance. It is said that Simeon, son of Clopas, a cousin of James, was elected as James's successor (Eusebius, *Hist. eccl.* 3.11.1). But Simeon's successor Justus, a converted Jew, is called bishop of Jerusalem—did the congregation return from Pella to Jerusalem?—and Eusebius names another fifteen bishops of Jerusalem down to the time of Hadrian (*Hist. eccl.* 4.5). A tradition about the relatives of Jesus was connected with information about this Jewish-Christian community. Eusebius reports Vespasian's search for descendants of the house of David (*Hist. eccl.* 3.12.1), and he reproduces a report of Hegesippus which says that Domitian arrested two grand-nephews of Jesus, grandsons of his brother Judas, because they were from the house of David, and then released them when it appeared that, though Christians, they were nothing other than simple farmers (*Hist. eccl.* 3.19 and 3.20.1–7). We may therefore assume that even in the later history of the church that had once been based in Jerusalem, members of Jesus' family played a role after the death of James. But there is no visible connection between this church and the later history of Jewish Christianity.

The only possible relationship appears in the name *Ebionites* = "the poor," which later Jewish Christians used as their self-designation. One or several sects with this name were known in II CE. The church fathers, however, were unable to understand this name. But Paul knows the designation of "the poor" for the Jerusalem church (Gal 2:10), and it is not impossible that by this self-designation the Jerusalem community identified itself with the elected poor, the people of God who were the recipients of the promises of the messianic time. It is, therefore, likely that the designation of Ebionites for later Jewish-Christian groups preserved a memory of their ultimate origin from the church in Jerusalem. But there is no indication that these sects possessed traditions that were independent of, or older than, the writings and traditions of other Christian churches.

(b) Jewish Christianity as a Branch of the Development of the Catholic Church

1) *The Jewish-Christian Gospels.* Among the most important witnesses for Jewish Christianity are the so-called Jewish-Christian gospels. The opinion that Jewish-Christian communities still used copies of the original Gospel of Matthew in Aramaic was common already in the ancient church. One source of this assumption was the report of Papias that Matthew had composed the sayings in Hebrew (Eusebius *Hist. eccl.* 3.29.16; see §10.2c). On the basis of this and other pieces of information, Jerome produced the hypothesis of only one Jewish-Christian gospel and assigned all known quotations of Jewish-Christian gospels to this one document, the "Gospel According to the Hebrews," which, he held, was identical with the original Aramaic Matthew. This hypothesis has survived into the modern period, but has been severely challenged by a number of critical studies published during this century. It is questionable whether Jerome ever saw a copy of this gospel which he calls the original Matthew, and it is quite certain that he never translated it into Greek (and Latin) as he claims several times. A number of quotations of Jewish-Christian gospels found in other church fathers which Jerome assigns to his "Gospel According to the Hebrews" demonstrably could never have existed in a Semitic language. Furthermore, it is impossible to assign all these quotations to one and the same writing. Rather, it must be assumed that there were at least two and more likely three different Jewish-Christian gospels, only one of which actually existed in a Semitic language.

2) *The Gospel of the Nazoreans.* A gospel in Aramaic or Syriac was in use among the Jewish Christians of Syria as early as II CE, in a group that

Bibliography to §10.4b

Alfred Schmidtke, *Neue Fragmente und Untersuchungen zu den judenchristlichen Evangelien* (TU 37,1; Leipzig: Hinrichs, 1911).

Hans Waitz, "Judenchristliche Evangelien," in: Edgar Hennecke (ed.), *Neutestamentliche Apokryphen* (2d ed.; Tübingen: Mohr/Siebeck, 1924) 17–55.

Idem, "Neue Untersuchungen über die sogenannten judenchristlichen Evangelien," *ZNW* 36 (1937) 60–81.

P. Vielhauer, "Jewish-Christian Gospels," *NTApo* 1. 117–65.

R. McL. Wilson, "Jewish Christianity and Gnosticism," in: *Judéo-Christianisme: volume offert au Cardinal Jean Daniélou,* = *RechSR* 60 (1972) 261–72.

Bibliography to §10.4b (2): Texts

Erich Klostermann (ed.), *Apocrypha II: Evangelien* (KlT 8; 3d ed.; Berlin: De Gruyter, 1929) 5–15.

Cameron (ed.), "The Gospel of the Nazoreans," in *The Other Gospels,* 97–102.

called itself "Nazoreans." This gospel is best designated as the *Gospel of the Nazoreans*, since we do not know its actual name. Hegesippus is the first to report about it (ca. 180 CE; in Eusebius *Hist. eccl.* 4.22.8). It is also attested by Eusebius and Epiphanius, and was probably the only Jewish-Christian gospel with which Jerome ever had any actual contact. Furthermore, textual readings of this gospel have been preserved in a number of marginal notations in medieval manuscripts of Matthew, all of which derive from a gospel edition made in Jerusalem before 500 CE. A number of medieval quotations might also possibly be assigned to this *Gospel of the Nazoreans*. An investigation of the roughly thirty-six passages and readings quoted from this gospel demonstrates that it was an Aramaic translation of the Greek Gospel of Matthew. In the process of this translation, Matthew's text was repeatedly expanded, annotated, and illustrated; new materials were occasionally inserted. In each instance, however, the Greek Matthew holds the priority. No heretical alterations can be identified in the *Gospel of the Nazoreans*, which seems to have reproduced the whole text of Matthew, including the birth narrative. These Jewish Christians obviously did not deny the birth of Jesus from a virgin. On the contrary, they seem to have been quite in agreement with the general development of early catholic theology; in fact they were dependent on it. To be sure, it is not known whether they used other New Testament writings in addition to their Aramaic translation of Matthew. But nothing indicates that they maintained any special Jewish-Christian doctrines.

3) *The Gospel of the Ebionites.* The situation is quite different with respect to the second Jewish-Christian gospel, which is known through quotations in Epiphanius. Irenaeus already knew of the *Gospel of the Ebionites*, so named since it was used by the sect of the Ebionites. Its actual name is not known, though it was possibly called the "Gospel of the Twelve." These Ebionites were Greek-speaking Jewish Christians, and their gospel was written in Greek. It drew from Matthew and Luke, and perhaps also from Mark. In some instances, the extant quotations show a similarity to the gospel harmony of Justin Martyr (II CE). As far as the few preserved citations allow us to judge, there are no traces of independent special traditions. This fact is even more striking since the Ebionites were indeed a heretical Jewish-Christian group. They rejected the virgin birth and therefore omitted the Synoptic birth narratives. They assumed that the spirit had come down upon Jesus and entered into him at his

Bibliography to §10.4b (3): Text
Cameron (ed.), "The Gospel of the Ebionites," in *The Other Gospels*, 103–6.

Bibliography to §10.4b (3): Studies
Georg Strecker, "Ebioniten," *RAC* 4. 487–500.

baptism—a concept which has parallels in gnostic texts. They rejected the sacrificial cult (Jesus said: "I have come to do away with sacrifices, and if you do not cease to sacrifice, the wrath of God shall not cease from you."), and they practiced vegetarianism. Apart from the name "Ebionites," the position they assigned to the twelve apostles is also Jewish-Christian: they were elected as the representatives of the twelve tribes of Israel. Not much more can be learned from the extant fragments; nor do we know whether the Ebionites had any connections to other Jewish-Christian groups.

While the two Jewish-Christian gospels discussed here were at home in the area of Syria and Palestine, the third of these gospels, the so-called *Gospel of the Hebrews,* belongs to Egypt. Since there is no relationship between this and the other two Jewish-Christian gospels, it will be discussed below (§11.1c) in the treatment of early Egyptian Christianity.

(c) The Fight against Paul

The preceding discussion has shown how difficult it is to find signs of an independent and self-reliant Jewish-Christian tradition in the period of early Christianity. Indeed, it seems to be the case that the formation of later Jewish Christianity was not due to any continuing, separate tradition which had originated in the very beginning of Christian history. Rather, it was formed in the constant controversy with gentile Christianity over claims of freedom from the law, something which is evident as early as the writing of the Pauline letters. The controversies that are attested there were probably much more responsible for the formation of Jewish Christianity than the preservation of early traditions among Christians of Jewish origin living in isolated communities of Palestine. It is likely that such communities existed, but the general developments passed them by as much as any remnants of the early community of Jerusalem.

1) *The Judaizers.* The theological effort to defend the Jewish law, particularly the ritual prescriptions and the rite of circumcision, was triggered by Paul's rejection of the law. The challenge was clear: it was necessary to compete with Paul in the gentile mission. As for Paul and the authorities in Jerusalem at that time, the agreement dividing the missionary areas when they met for the Apostolic Council might have satisfied everybody involved. In view of the hope that everybody shared that the end of times would come soon, no one among the participants would have thought that by its restriction to the mission among the Jews historical developments would soon pass Jerusalem by. But other participants, whom Paul called the "false brothers" (Gal 2:4), seem to have had a clearer picture of what the future might bring. Since the real problem was the validity of the law for gentile Christians, they could not be satisfied

with an agreement that only the Jewish Christians should henceforth have permission to remain faithful to the law. The real concern was the validity and central role of the law within a missionary movement that was preparing to become a world religion. Those Jewish Christians who recognized this immediately began their own mission in the pagan world, of which several Pauline letters give a very lively, though not very appreciative, picture soon thereafter. For Paul's opponents as known from Galatians and Philippians 3, the primary question is not the law in general, but specifically the significance of the ritual commandments. Therefore, in Paul's response the question of circumcision appears as the leading issue (§9.3b, e).

Paul's refutation of his Jewish-Christian competitors did not do away with this movement. In the Letter to the Colossians, a student of Paul attacks a form of Jewish-Christian propaganda with syncretistic features, namely, that observation of the Jewish festivals and dietary regulations is understood as initiation into the cosmic realities (§12.2a). Somewhat later, Ignatius of Antioch fights against Judaizers who may in fact be closely related to the gnostics whom he also attacks in his letters (§12.2d). Ignatius gives evidence that his opponents appeal to the Old Testament, which for him carries only limited authority (*Phld.* 8). He acknowledges that his opponents use an argument that might impress many Christians much more than his own Paulinism, which stands at a considerable distance from the Old Testament and its interpretation. Around the year 100 the heretic Cerinthus was active in Asia Minor; he advocated gnostic teaching, but seems to have been a Jewish Christian who insisted upon circumcision. However uncertain our information about Cerinthus might be, considering the syncretistic development of anti-Pauline Jewish Christianity, the traditional characterization does not seem to be unlikely. Some of the opponents of the Revelation of John could also belong to this Judaizing Christian syncretism (§12.1c).

2) *The Book of Elkasai.* This excursus into the area of the Pauline mission was necessary because these are our only sources from I CE that give us any indication of the anti-Pauline position of early Jewish Christianity. The real home for the development of Jewish Christianity, however, must have been Syria; Jewish Christians could still be found in these

Bibliography to §10.4c (2): Text
J. Irmscher, "The Book of Elchasai," *NTApo* 2. 745–50.

Bibliography to §10.4c (2): Studies
Hans Waitz, "Das Buch Elchasai," in *Festgabe von Fachgenossen und Freunden Adolf von Harnack zum siebzigsten Geburtstag dargebracht* (Tübingen: Mohr/ Siebeck, 1921) 87–104.

regions in the early Byzantine period. One of the important witnesses for the formation of Jewish-Christian sects is of Syrian origin: the *Book of Elkasai*. The alleged author of this book, Elkasai, appeared in the year 101 (according to his own statement, the third year of Trajan) as a prophet and wrote his book a few years later. The sect which he founded is attested several times in the following two centuries, but received little attention until the very recent publication of an autobiography of Mani. This writing reveals that Mani's parents were Elkasaites, and that he himself had received his first religious impressions in this sect. This gives a special significance to Syrian Jewish Christianity in general and to Elkasai in particular.

The extant fragments of the *Book of Elkasai* testify to a renewal of apocalyptic prophecy. The eruption of a battle of godless angelic powers is predicted for the third year after the end of Trajan's Persian campaign. Elkasai, like the *Shepherd of Hermas* (§12.1d), connects with his message the announcement of a second repentance and the granting of a second baptism for the forgiveness of sins. The book's primary concern was the preservation of cultic purity through precepts that rely on Old Testament prescriptions and emphasize the necessity of repeated baths of purification. In such rites the "invocation of the seven witnesses" (heaven, water, holy spirits, angels of prayer, oil, salt, and earth) is syncretistic and derives, as do also the warnings of evil stars and of the moon, from speculations about cosmic powers. The command to turn one's face toward Jerusalem while praying shows Jewish influence. Elkasai is connected with the Ebionites through his rejection of sacrificial rites. Typical for the development of the heretical Jewish Christianity that appears here is the distinction between "true" and "false" pericopes in the Old Testament, use of the canonical gospels, and rejection of the Pauline letters (attested by Origen for the later Elkasaites, in Eusebius *Hist. eccl.* 6.38). The same characteristics are also found in the most important testimony to Jewish Christianity in Syria, the Jewish-Christian sources used by the *Pseudo-Clementines*.

3) *The Pseudo-Clementines and the Kerygmata Petrou.* The *Pseudo-Clementines* is a romance centering around Clement of Rome. The story tells of his religious development, especially his experiences as a disciple of Peter, whom he accompanied on his missionary journeys. The romance is

Bibliography to §10.4c (3): Texts

Bernhard Rehm (ed.), *Die Pseudoklementinen*, vol. 1: *Homilien* (GCS; 2d ed.; Berlin: Akademie-Verlag, 1969).

G. Strecker, "The Kerygmata Petrou," *NTApo* 2. 102–27.

Betz, *Galatians,* 331–33. English translation of Epistle of Peter to James and of parts of *Ps. Clem. Hom.* 11 and 17.

preserved in two recensions, the Greek *Homilies* and the Latin *Recognitions,* which were both written during IV CE. Their common source, which is lost, must have been composed early in III CE. Unquestionably this source in turn used extensive earlier written materials, but there is no agreement in scholarship about their character and extent. Nevertheless, some probability can be assigned to the hypothesis of a Jewish-Christian source, the *Kerygmata Petrou,* written in II CE. This hypothesis is the most convincing explanation of the appearance of large sections in the *Pseudo-Clementines* whose Jewish-Christian character is totally obvious. The *Kerygmata Petrou* consist of Peter's letter to James, a "Contestatio" (James's testimony about the recipients of the letter), and lectures and debates of Peter. The *Kerygmata* are doubtlessly dependent upon the general tradition of the early catholic church. The Gospel of Matthew is especially used (some quotations seem to come from a gospel harmony related to that of Justin Martyr).

This work seeks to lay claim to the authority of Peter for the law-abiding Jewish Christians. It denies the right of appeal to Peter for those who assert that Peter was Paul's successor in the gentile mission free of the law (§12.2f). Although it is recognized that Peter indeed followed Paul in the gentile mission, Peter is seen as the representative of a law-abiding Christian mission to the gentiles and he explicitly rejects the calumny that he had ever taught the abolishment of the law. Peter's true teaching, which is recorded in his lectures, is submitted to James in Peter's letter, and in the "Contestatio" it is formally entrusted to James. James is, thus, the undoubted authority for Jewish Christianity that observes the law. The appeal to James is described as an act of legal-ecclesiastical sanction (this is not a motif of the romance). In the lectures and debates of Peter, it is apparently Paul who is actually attacked wherever Peter refutes Simon Magus. The doctrine of the law that is held against Paul is Jewish, as is the emphasis upon the ritual rules of purification. Moses and Christ are connected with each other in such a way that they are both seen as revelations of the true prophet. The "gnosis" that is mediated through Jesus is said to be identical with the law of Moses. There are, however, false pericopes that have been interpolated into the Old Testament since Moses did not write the law himself, and the

Bibliography to §10.4c (3): Studies

Georg Strecker, *Das Judenchristentum in den Pseudoklementinen* (TU 70; Berlin: Akademie-Verlag, 1958).

A. Salles, "La diatribe antipaulinienne dans le 'Roman pseudoclémentin' et l'origine des 'Kérygmes de Pierre,'" *RB* 64 (1957) 516–51.

Oscar Cullmann, "Die neuentdeckten Qumrantexte und das Judenchristentum der Pseudoklementinen," in: idem, *Vorträge 1952–1962,* 241–59.

Jews did not always prove reliable in their transmission. But from the true prophet as he appeared in Jesus one can learn to understand the true pericopes.

This concept of the repeated incarnation of the true prophet shows some relationship to gnostic doctrines. Such gnostic influence becomes even more obvious in the *Kerygmata*'s teaching of the syzygies. In the creation of the world and human beings in pairs, the first member of the pair is always the stronger (Heaven and earth, man and woman). But in the history of humankind, which also proceeds in syzygies, the weaker members come first (from Cain and Abel to Paul and Peter). In this explanation of the world and history, the universalistic claims of the *Kerygmata*'s Jewish Christianity appear in clear form. The law has become the critical principle through which revelation and the world can be better understood than through the preaching of Paul, who can appeal neither to the law nor to the words of Jesus.

5. Syria, the Country of Origin of Christian Gnosticism

(a) Summary of Previous Observations

In the course of our discussion of the development of early Christianity in Syria, it has been necessary to refer repeatedly to Gnosticism. Gnostic concepts, terms, myths, hymns, and sayings traditions have been mentioned on several occasions. Not to do so would make the history of early Syrian Christianity and its literature an impenetrable puzzle. The attempt to portray the history of Syrian Gnosticism in its own right, however, is burdened with many difficulties. This is not due simply to the incompleteness of our available sources, nor to the fact that the hypothesis of Syrian origin for gnostic writings known only from Egypt is rarely fully conclusive (§10.5b). To be sure, these factors are significant, but others are more weighty.

The history of Gnosticism in its early stages during the period of early Christianity cannot be identified with the history of a tangible sociological phenomenon. "Gnostic churches" with a membership that was clearly distinguished from the early catholic churches and from the Jewish-Christian churches never existed. Especially in Syria, the authority of resident church officers was established rather slowly (§10.1c). Wherever somewhat more stable forms of organization and traditions were instituted in

Bibliography to §10.5a: Texts
See the texts under §10.1b.
John D. Turner, "The Book of Thomas the Athlete (II,7)," *NagHamLibEngl*, 188–94.

individual communities or groups of churches, they were repeatedly threatened or altered by wandering charismatic prophets and apostles. There was a certain continuity connected with the transmission of traditions under the authority of particular apostolic names, but the challenge in these cases was the new formulation and reinterpretation of such traditions and writings. Continuity in the theological position was by no means guaranteed. This is most clearly visible in the history of the traditions under the name of the apostle "John" (§10.3a–d). The history of Gnosticism in this context can be described only as the history of particular tendencies and aims which appear in the interpretation of traditional materials. Gnosticism proves its presence in the process of exegesis.

In the tradition of the sayings of Jesus, Gnosticism appears in the emphasis upon, and the predominance of, wisdom sayings, and in the spiritualizing of the eschatological sayings of Jesus. The *Gospel of Thomas* offers this interpretation of the sayings under the apostolic authority of Thomas, a tradition that seems to have continued under the name of this particular apostle in communities of Syria. In II CE this is evident in the *Book of Thomas* (NHC II, 7; falsely called the book of *Thomas the Contender*). In early III CE the same tradition reappears in the *Acts of Thomas,* which also draws the aretalogical tradition of the apostles' miraculous deeds into the process of gnostic interpretation: individual miracle stories become descriptions of the encounter of the heavenly world and its messenger with the lower world of demons and transitoriness. Within the circle of the Johannine churches, gnostic interpretation is again tied to the sayings of Jesus, which were used for the development of dialogue materials in which Jesus speaks about the presence of eschatological salvation, mediated through himself as the revealer from the heavenly world of the Father, the home of all those who are able to hear his voice. The basic concept of the hymn, used by the author of the Gospel of John for his prologue, demonstrates the intimate connection between the myth of Wisdom and the gnostic understanding of Christian revelation. A fully developed gnostic christology, however, does not appear until later among the opponents of 1 John and in the *Acts of John,* where it took shape in explicit controversy with the Gospel's attempt to amalgamate the concept of the gnostic revealer with the kerygma of the death and resurrection of the earthly Jesus.

The history of Jewish Christianity indicates how viable Gnosticism indeed was as a possiblity of interpretation within the Christian tradition. To be sure, the suggestion that the opponents of Paul in Galatia represented a gnostic position can be doubted with good reasons. But when we consider the emphasis upon perfection to be accomplished in the present which appears among the opponents of Philippians 3, we may speak of gnostic tendencies with justification. It was especially in their christology that Jewish Christians used mythological constructs that are unequivocally gnostic. This is clearly the case when the *Gospel of the Ebionites* speaks of the descent of the "person" of the spirit, and of his unification with Jesus in baptism. The *Kerygmata Petrou*, in order to defend the lasting validity of the law, used the gnostic concept of the repeated manifestations of the true prophet. The appearance of gnostic ideas in Jewish Christianity is one factor among others which has led to the suggestion that the roots of gnostic thought might be found in heretical Judaism. A suitable milieu for the development of Jewish Gnosticism may have been the area of Syria and Palestine. Further investigation of the texts from Nag Hammadi is likely to support this assumption. Indeed, it is already possible to defend the hypothesis of a Syrian origin of a number of these texts, and to show that they are attestations of a Christian Gnosticism that owes much to Jewish influence.

(b) The Texts from Nag Hammadi and Syrian Gnosticism

Speculative interpretations of the first chapters of the Book of Genesis played a decisive role in the development of gnostic cosmogonies. Allusions to the biblical story of creation are found even in the pagan Gnosticism of the *Corpus Hermeticum* (§6.5f). There was certainly a direct connection to Jewish apocalypticism, as well as to the exegesis of rabbinic Judaism, although many of the details of these relationships are yet to be clarified. Alongside this interest in the biblical creation story we find in these texts a preoccupation with the figures of the primeval history. This moves Gnosticism once more into close proximity with the Jewish apocalypticism known in Palestine until the end of i CE (§5.3c; 6.6f). It is quite apparent that several of the writings from Nag Hammadi drew a good deal of their materials from such Jewish sources in Palestine, including some gnostic writings that only occasionally exhibit Christian features.

1) Christian features are, it seems, completely lacking in the *Apoca-*

Bibliography to §10.5b: Survey and Bibliography

G. MacRae, "Nag Hammadi," *IDBSup* (1976) 613–19.

David M. Scholer, *The Nag Hammadi Bibliography 1948–1969* (NHS 1; Leiden: Brill, 1971), continued as "Bibliographia Gnostica," in *NovT* 13 (1971) and subsequent volumes.

Bibliography to §10.5b: Studies

Alexander Böhlig, *Mysterium und Wahrheit* (Leiden: Brill, 1968) 80–111; 149–61.

Carsten Colpe, "Heidnische, jüdische und christliche Überlieferung in den Schriften aus Nag Hammadi," *JAC* 15 (1972) 5–18; 16 (1973) 106–26; 17 (1974) 109–25; 18 (1975) 144–65; 19 (1976) 120–38; 20 (1977) 149–70; 21 (1978) 125–46; 22 (1979) 98–122; 23 (1980) 108–27.

Page from Codex II of the Nag Hammadi Library

Page 97 of Codex II shows the ending of the *Hypostasis of the Archons* (note the colophon in the lower middle of the page) and the beginning of the *Gospel of Philip*. The last line of the text of the *Hypostasis of the Archons* is filled up with a decoration.

lypse of Adam (NHC V, 5). Its basis is an apocalyptic interpretation of the stories of Adam, Seth, and Noah. Seth receives the revelation and knowledge of the future from his father Adam, just before Adam's death, in the form of a testament. This apocalypse has been revised by a gnostic interpreter so that it speaks, in its extant form, about the repeated acts of salvation for the children of the true transcendent God, or of the coming of the "illuminator of knowledge" (76, 9–10), who is recognized solely by the generation without a king (82, 19–20). This illuminator is a typical gnostic redeemer figure. Through him those who are redeemed receive "the words of imperishability and truth" (85, 13–14). The community from which this writing originated apparently practiced baptism with water, which was understood as rebirth through the word (85, 24ff). Since this book contains no references to specific Christian names, themes, or traditions, it should be assigned to a Jewish gnostic baptismal sect. Seth appears as the recipient of the revelation, which classifies this writing as a representative of "Sethian Gnosticism" and argues strongly for the Jewish origin of this type of gnostic theology. It is likely that other gnostic tractates of the Sethian type come from Syria, especially those which show no Christian influence, such as *Zostrianus* (NHC VIII, 1) and *The Three Steles of Seth* (NHC VII, 5).

2) The *Hypostasis of the Archons* (NHC II, 4) most certainly belongs to the same context since it also contains references to Sethian Gnosticism. In its extant form it has received a secondary Christian framework, possibly in Egypt in II or III CE. The introduction quotes "the great apostle" (Col 1:13; Eph 6:12; cf. *Hyp. Arch.* 86, 21–25), and the conclusion (96, 17ff)

Bibliography to §10.5b (1): Texts

Alexander Böhlig, *Koptisch-gnostische Apokalypsen aus Kodex V von Nag Hammadi* (Wissenschaftliche Zeitschrift der Martin-Luther-Universität. Sonderband; Halle-Wittenberg, 1963).
George W. MacRae, "NHC V,5: The Apocalypse of Adam," in: Douglas M. Parrott (ed.), *Nag Hammadi Codices V,2–5 and VI with Papyrus Berolinensis 8502, 1–4* (NHS 11; Leiden: Brill, 1979) 151–95.
Idem, "The Apocalypse of Adam (V,5)," *NagHamLibEngl*, 256–64.
"The Apocalypse of Adam," in: Foerster, *Gnosis*, 2. 13–23.

Bibliography to §10.5b (1): Studies
George MacRae, "The Coptic Gnostic Apocalypse of Adam," *HeyJ* 6 (1965) 27–35.

Bibliography to §10.5b (2): Texts
Bentley Layton, "The Hypostasis of the Archons or the Reality of the Rulers . . . edited . . . with a Preface, English Translation, Notes, Indexes," *HTR* 67 (1974) 351–425; 69 (1976) 31–101.
Roger A. Bullard and Bentley Layton, "The Hypostasis of the Archons (II,4)," *NagHamLibEngl*, 152–60.
"The Hypostasis of the Archons," in: Foerster, *Gnosis*, 2. 40–52.

alludes to Christian concepts of salvation. But the original writing lacks Christian elements completely. The first part (87,11–93,2) presents a gnostic exegesis of Genesis 1–6 which often quotes the biblical text verbatim; its point is to show that Adam and Eve actually belong to the heavenly world, while only their forms of terrestrial appearance are under the power of the archons. These earthly human beings are driven out of paradise by the archons and are tortured by the flood. But Seth and his sister Norea, "the man through God" and "the virgin whom the forces did not defile," appear as the incorporation of the true heavenly *anthrōpos* and the prototypes of salvation (91,30–92,3). The second part of the book is a discourse of the angel Eleleth to Norea, which seems to have been added on to the Genesis interpretation (93,2–96,17). This is essentially a narration of the gnostic myth of the fall of Sophia. Even if this second part were of Christian origin, it clearly reflects a milieu of Semitic language. This is shown by, among other things, the names of the evil creator of the world, Samael ("God of the blind"), Sakla ("fool"), and Yaldabaoth (which cannot be explained with certainty, but is surely Semitic). The name of his son, Sabaoth, is certainly of Old Testament origin, and his role, surprisingly, is not entirely negative. A direct connection to Jewish exegesis of Genesis is demonstrated by the name "Norea": it is composed from the Hebrew name *Na'ama* (Gen 4:22) and the Greek word *oreia* (= beautiful).

3) *The Apocryphon of John.* In some cases gnostic writings are transmitted under the name of a certain apostle, and we must at least ask whether this may imply a conscious resumption of particular apostolic traditions. This is apparently the case with the *Apocryphon of John,* a work that also belongs to Sethian Gnosticism. It was known to Irenaeus, and was thus written no later than the middle of ii CE. It is preserved in two shorter (NHC III, 1; BG 8502, 2) and two longer versions (NHC II, 1; IV, 1). The introduction reports the appearance of Jesus to John, in which Jesus first looks like a youth, then again like an old man. This is reminiscent of the *Acts of John* (§10.3d), and is in any case not unique in gnostic literature. The content of the work is a coherent narrative of the fall of Sophia, the creation of the lower world by Yaldabaoth, including the creation of the human race, and the salvation through Christ, which is accomplished through his descent to the lower world, even to Hades, and through his call. This writing drew upon an abundance of materials from

Bibliography to §10.5b (3): Texts

Martin Krause and Pahor Labib, *Die drei Versionen des Apokryphon des Johannes im Koptischen Museum zu Alt-Kairo* (ADAI.K 1; Wiesbaden: Harrassowitz, 1962).
Frederik Wisse, "The Apocryphon of John (II,1, III,1, IV,1 BG 8502,2)," *NagHamLibEngl,* 98–116.

Jewish apocalypticism and angelology, a number of mythological names (often no longer understood, and hence distorted), and also mythological and astrological lists, which probably found their way into Gnosticism and its mythology via Judaism. Citation and interpretation of the first chapters of Genesis again play an important role. But despite the use of the name "John," nothing points to a continuation of the tradition of the Johannine communities. The name of John might have been used, however, by Syrian gnostics who took the material employed in this writing as well as the Gospel of John itself to Egypt (§11.1b).

4) *The First and Second Apocalypses of James.* These two writings from the Nag Hammadi library continue the tradition of Jewish-Christian Gnosticism from Syria. The first of these books (NHC V, 3) introduces James the brother of Jesus as the recipient of a revelation of the "Lord" (addressed by James as "Rabbi"), which primarily discusses the questions of suffering and the ascent of the soul. A number of features in the work point to a Jewish-Christian origin: the name of God, "He Who Is," is derived from Exod 3:14; the discussion of the weaker female principle presupposes the same doctrine of syzygies which also appears in the *Kerygmata Petrou* of the *Pseudo-Clementines;* also related is the statement that the Old Testament contains only partial truth and requires Jesus' revelation in order to be fully understood (§10.4c). The designation of Sophia as "Achamoth" is Aramaic. A Syrian origin is also indicated by the mention of Addai, known later as the apostle of Edessa, to whom James is instructed to transfer these teachings. The theology of the writing is entirely gnostic, including the traditions used in the writing: a hymn to the revealer (28, 7–26) and a catechism of answers to the questions of the cosmic guardians (33, 11–34; cf. *Gos. Thom.* 50). The *Second*

Bibliography to §10.5b (4): Texts

William R. Schoedel, "NHC V,3: The (First) Apocalypse of James" in: Douglas M. Parrott (ed.), *Nag Hammadi Codices V,2–5 and VI with Papyrus Berolinensis 8502, 1 and 4* (NHS 11; Leiden: Brill 1979) 65–103.

William R. Schoedel and Douglas M. Parrott, "The First Apocalypse of James (V,3)," *NagHamLibEngl,* 242–48.

Charles W. Hedrick, "NHC V,4: The (Second) Apocalypse of James," in Douglas M. Parrott (ed.), *Nag Hammadi Codices V,2–5 and VI with Papyrus Berolinensis 8502, 1–4* (NHS 11; Leiden: Brill, 1979) 105–49.

Wolf-Peter Funk, *Die zweite Apokalypse des Jakobus aus Nag Hammadi Codex V, neu herausgegeben, übersetzt und erklärt* (TU 119; Berlin: Akademie-Verlag, 1976).

Charles W. Hedrick and Douglas M. Parrott, "The Second Apocalypse of James (V,4)," *NagHamLibEngl,* 249–55.

Bibliography to §10.5b (4): Studies

William R. Schoedel, "Scripture and the Seventy-two Heavens of the First Apocalypse of James," *NovT* (1970) 18–29.

Apocalypse of James (NHC V, 4) is based upon a report of the martyrdom of James which is essentially identical with the report of Hegesippus preserved by Eusebius (*Hist. eccl.* 2.23.4ff). A number of gnostic hymns have been inserted into this report. The conclusion contains a prayer of petition of James in the face of death, which completely corresponds to the form of the psalms of lamentation in the Old Testament. These two writings thus have preserved in their songs a genre which Syrian Gnosticism had especially appropriated as an expression of its piety.

(c) Gnostic Hymns and Songs

1) *Prologue of John's Gospel and Hymn of the Dance.* A large number of hymns and songs have been preserved from Syria or through the tradition of Syria that are either of gnostic origin or reveal the influence of gnostic thought and concepts. It is very difficult to determine the exact dates for the composition of such poetry, but it is reasonable to assume that many of these pieces were created in the period between 50 and 150 CE. All of these hymns and songs belong to the category of Semitic poetry; their prototypes are the psalms of the Old Testament, the *Psalms of Solomon,* and the thanksgiving hymns from Qumran. Special mythological speculations are characteristically absent from these hymns; at best one can find some rather remote allusions. Like the hymns of the churches today, these ancient Christian songs are more closely related to the piety of the typical believer than to speculative theology and exegesis. But central christological statements and theological terms are clearly recognizable, though they are frequently translated into the metaphorical language of poetry. These hymns are dominated by the first-person singular, representing the voice of either the revealer or the believer—in fact, sometimes both flow together into the voice of the redeemed redeemer. But we also find address of the savior in the second person, or the description of his coming and deeds in the third person. The "we" of the confessing community appears only occasionally.

Some of these hymns have already been mentioned. The hymn used in the prologue of the Gospel of John describes the actions and the coming of the Logos in the third person, but concludes with a confession of the

Bibliography to §10.5c: Studies

Joseph Kroll, *Die christliche Hymnodik bis zu Klemens von Alexandreia* (Verzeichnis der Vorlesungen der Akademie zu Braunsberg 1921–22; reprint: Darmstadt: Wissenschaftliche Buchgesellschaft, 1968).

Bibliography to §10.5c (1): Texts

Lipsius-Bonnet, *ActApostApoc,* 2,1. 197–99.
K. Schäferdiek, "The Acts of John," *NTApo* 2. 227–32.

community in the first-person plural. Theological terms are used abundantly: light, darkness, father, only-born son, glory, grace, and truth, while the actual description of the action recedes into the background. The *Hymn of the Dance* in the *Acts of John* (94–96) begins with the "we" of the congregation ("We praise you, Father"), but then the revealer speaks about himself in the first-person singular. Everyting he says, however, expresses the believer's hope of salvation ("I want to be saved"). Cosmological statements have been included: "The Ogdoad sings praises . . . the Twelve [the zodiac] are dancing up on high." Metaphors that are characteristic of Gnosticism dominate the language (the revealer is light, mirror, door, and way). The believer is once more included in the description of suffering. This is particularly the case in the summons to recognize the revealer, which is identical with the summons to recognize oneself.

2) *Hymns in the Apocalypses of James.* In the hymn of the *First Apocalypse of James* (28,7–27), the poet speaks to the revealer in the second person: "You have come with knowledge, that you might rebuke their ignorance." In the conclusion, the believer speaks about himself in the first person, clearly distinguished from the revealer: "There is in me a forgetfulness, yet I remember." In the hymns of the *Second Apocalypse of James* (55,15–56,14; 58,2–24), doxological predications of the revealer are used which only rarely contain gnostic terminology. In the first hymn, the revealer is called illuminator and savior, is admired for his powerful deeds, blessed by the heavens, and called the Lord. In the second part, however, the poet speaks in gnostic language about those who are to be saved: they will receive the call, find rest, rule, be kings. The second hymn is a doxology, speaking about God in the third person: he is life, light, the "one who will come to be . . . an end for what has begun and a beginning for what is about to be ended . . . Holy Spirit and the Invisible One . . . virgin." The conclusion is a typically gnostic addition: "I saw that he was naked, for there was no garment clothing him."

3) *Hymns in the Acts of Thomas.* A clear gnostic orientation is evident in the hymns of the *Acts of Thomas.* The book itself, to be sure, cannot be dated earlier than the beginning of III CE, but its hymns and songs are older. *Acts Thom.* 6–7 is a bridal song modelled upon secular prototypes.

Bibliography to §10.5c (2): Texts
See the texts under §10.5b (4).

Bibliography to §10.5c (3): Texts
Lipsius-Bonnet, *ActApostApoc,* 2,2. 109–10; 219–24.
G. Bornkamm, "The Acts of Thomas," *NTApo* 2. 445–46, 498–504.
"The Acts of Thomas," in: Foerster, *Gnosis,* 1.345–46, 355–58.
Kee, *Origins,* 253–57.
Cartlidge and Dungan, *Documents,* 37–39, 46–50.

The beauty of the bride is described, but soon interrupted by allegorical sentences ("truth rests upon her head"), although later on the "thirty-two who praise her" are nothing but her teeth. The second stanza, however, clearly speaks about the queen of heaven. The seven "best men" are the planets, the twelve servants the signs of the zodiac. The bridegroom thus becomes the corporate image of the redeemed, who are attending the heavenly wedding feast. The second song of the *Acts of Thomas,* the "Song of the Pearl" (108–113), is even less related to congregational hymns than the bridal song. It is instead an allegorical poem, based upon a fairy tale about a prince who went into far away lands in order to snatch a precious pearl from a dragon, expecting to become co-regent as a reward. This fairy tale was used by the author in order to describe the journey of the soul from its heavenly home into the foreign terrestrial realms and its subsequent salvation through the celestial call. Features alien to the original fairy tale can be easily identified: the prince leaves his shining garment in the Persian homeland, dresses in the dirty garments of Egypt, and falls into sleep and forgetfulness (in the fairy tale he apparently served the Egyptian king). A letter (this is the motif of the heavenly letter) awakens him, and he recognizes in this letter what is written in his heart; the radiant garment sent to meet him is the mirror of his own true self.

4) *The Odes of Solomon.* A whole collection of community hymns has been preserved in the *Odes of Solomon.* Until the beginning of this century nothing was known about them except their name, which occurred in ancient canon lists and in a quotation in Lactantius. The collection, originally written in Greek, was dicovered in 1909 and 1912 in two Syriac manuscripts, containing *Odes* 3–42 and *Odes* 17.7–42 respectively. *Odes* 1, 5, 6, 22, and 25 were subsequently identified in a Coptic translation as part of the gnostic writing *Pistis Sophia,* and *Ode* 11 was discovered in its

Bibliography to §10.5c (3): Studies

Alfred Adam, *Die Psalmen des Thomas und das Perlenlied als Zeugnisse vorchristlicher Gnosis* (2d ed.; FRLANT NF 33; Göttingen: Vandenhoeck & Ruprecht, 1954).

Bibliography to §10.5c (4): Texts

James H. Charlesworth, *The Odes of Solomon: The Syriac Texts* (SBLTT 13, Pseudepigrapha 7; Missoula: Scholars Press, 1977).

Walter Bauer (ed.), *Die Oden Salomos* (KlT 64; Berlin: De Gruyter, 1933).

Bibliography to §10.5c (4): Studies

Robert M. Grant, "The Odes of Solomon and the Church of Antioch," *JBL* 63 (1944) 363–77.

Michael Lattke, *Die Oden Salomos und Ihre Bedeutung für Neues Testament und Gnosis* (2 vols.; OBO 25,1–2; Fribourg: Editions Universitaires, and Göttingen: Vandenhoeck & Ruprecht, 1979).

Gerhard Kittel, *Die Oden Salomos, einheitlich oder überarbeitet?* (BWAT 16; Leipzig: Hinrichs, 1914).

original Greek text in Pap. Bodmer XI. The search for a particular author of these *Odes* is just as futile as a determination of a specific date of their composition. They may have been written at about the same time as the prologue of the Gospel of John, but a date in early II CE is just as likely. Nor is there any reason to suppose that they were all written at the same time by the same author. Many of the songs are closely modelled upon prototypes from the psalms of the Old Testament and are direct continuations of Jewish psalmic poetry. *Ode* 5 is a thanksgiving psalm for protection from persecutors; *Ode* 14 is a psalm of confidence; *Odes* 22 and 25 are hymns praising God for his victory over his enemies, especially over death and hell; and *Ode* 29 praises Christ for the gift of his word, through which the believers are victorious.

The language of the *Odes of Solomon* is rich with images and metaphors, including many that also occur in gnostic texts. The statement that the Lord is the crown of truth on the head of the believer (*Ode* 1), however, does not necessarily imply a gnostic meaning. Neither does the image of the community as the planting in paradise (*Ode* 11.18ff), or the comparison of the gift of God with milk from the breasts of the Father, who is milked by the Holy Spirit, even though the continuation (the virgin conceived in her womb from this milk) might not quite agree with our sense of good taste (*Ode* 19). Clearly gnostic are the images of the Lord as the mirror (*Ode* 13) and of *gnosis* as a mighty stream of water (*Ode* 6; cf. 11.6–7; 30). The christological statements contain many sentences that formulate generally accepted Christian beliefs. The praise of the appearance of the Lord in human form (*Ode* 7) is by no means typical for Gnosticism, nor are the hymn of praise for the eschatological victory of Christ over the lower world (*Ode* 24), the enumeration of the deeds of the Lord with the request to listen to them and to hold on to them (*Ode* 8; cf. 9), and the Hellenistic missionary sermon (*Ode* 33). It is peculiar, however, that in those *Odes* which are formulated in the I-style, the person of the revealer often flows together with the person of the believer. The possession of immortality and the activity in the world can therefore be described as referring to both believer and revealer at the same time (*Ode* 10); it sometimes becomes impossible to distinguish between the one who works the salvation and the one who receives it (*Ode* 17). Through rebirth, the redeemed becomes identical with the redeemer (*Ode* 36), is one and the same with the suffering Christ in the experience of his own suffering (*Ode* 28; cf. 31), and even becomes the redeemer as he descends with Christ into hell (*Ode* 42).

Finally, there are a number of verses and portions of these psalms which are direct reflections of gnostic piety. Sometimes individual sentences in a context not otherwise informed by gnostic thought betray a

gnostic understanding of the whole song, such as in the hymn of praise in
Ode 26: "It is enough to have *gnosis* and to find rest" (26.12). The putting
off of the earthly garment and the putting on of the heavenly garment of
light (*Ode* 11.10f; cf. 15.8) is as gnostic as the description of the heavenly
journey of the soul (*Ode* 35), the description of the lower world as an
empty illusion (*Ode* 34), the praise of the truth as the pathfinder in the
ascension (*Ode* 38), and of Christ as the guide over the abyss of the hostile
waters (*Ode* 39). It is still an open question whether the *Odes of Solomon*
should therefore be called a gnostic hymnbook. Athough the gnostic character of many of these concepts cannot be doubted, it is quite likely that
gnostic images and terms expressing the individual's hope for a future life
and resurrection were not limited to communities committed to gnostic
theology but had become much more widespread. If this was the case, this
oldest Christian hymnal attests that Gnosticism affected the language of
early Christian piety in Syria very deeply indeed.

EGYPT

1. The Beginnings of Christianity in Egypt

(a) The Problem of Sources and Evidence

Egypt was a country with unusual political, social, and economic structures. Its one major city, Alexandria, was one of the largest cities of the Mediterranean world and one of its most significant cultural and economic centers. The rest of the country was mostly rural, with a few major settlements like Oxyrhynchus, Arsinoë, and Hermopolis. These towns had some share in civic culture and offered some of the amenities of city life, but could not be compared with the major cultural and economic centers elsewhere in the Roman empire. The contrast between Alexandria and the Egyptian hinterland was sharpened by differences in language and education. Alexandria had a thoroughly Hellenized Greek-speaking population, including a large Jewish community, while the native population of the rural areas continued to speak several vernacular Egyptian dialects. It seems that the Christian mission in Egypt did not reach much of the populace of the countryside until early III CE. Thus, the beginnings of Christianity in Egypt were likely limited to Alexandria and a few settlements which had some Greek-speaking inhabitants, but would have been unlikely to develop a church life independent of the history of Alexandrian Christianity. Discoveries of Greek papyri in places like Oxyrhynchus can therefore be considered representative of Alexandrian Christianity. Alexandria, on the other hand, because of its large Greek-speaking population of various ethnic origins, would offer ample opportunity for the simultaneous development of several competing Christian groups.

Unfortunately, there is no direct evidence for the beginnings of Christianity in Egypt, although there can be little doubt that the Christian mission must have reached Alexandria during I CE. The historian must therefore attempt to draw conclusions from various pieces of later evidence. This is difficult and even hazardous, as is already evident in the case of the ancient historian Eusebius of Caesarea, who wrote in the early decades of IV CE. In agreement with later ecclesiastical tradition, Eusebius names Mark as the first Christian preacher in Egypt, founder of the church in

Alexandria, and its first bishop. In order to give more concreteness to his picture of the earliest Alexandrian Christian community, Eusebius borrows the description of the Jewish sect of the Therapeutae from the Jewish philosopher Philo of Alexandria (*De vita contemplativa;* §5.3f) and concludes, quite consistently, that the first Christians of Egypt were a group of ascetic philosophers (Eusebius *Hist. eccl.* 2.16.2). Since this information already has no real value, not much more can be learned from Eusebius' list of the bishops of Alexandria who followed upon Mark, nor from the information about their years in office: Annianus, twenty-two years; Abilius, thirteen years; Cerdo, eleven years (?); Primus, twelve years—and at this point the reader is already in the third year of Hadrian (120 CE). Surprisingly, after this year the list of bishops for the following seventy years is fragmentary (Justus, Agrippinus, Julian), until the first tangible historical figure appears with Demetrius, who became bishop of Alexandria in 189 CE.

It is indeed unthinkable that the Christian mission should have bypassed Alexandria for decades. One or several Christian communities must have existed there as early as the second half of I CE. It is understandable that attempts have been made to fill this gap in information. Acts 18:24 reports, after all, that Apollos, the fellow-worker of Paul, was an Alexandrian Jew. Among the writings of the Apostolic Fathers, there are two for which an Alexandrian origin has been claimed: the *Epistle of Barnabas,* because of its "Alexandrian" exegesis of the Old Testament (§12.2b) and *2 Clement,* because of the relationship of one of its gospel quotations to the *Gospel of the Egyptians* (§11.2b). Although such judgments are by no means completely misguided, and in the latter case even quite persuasive (§11.3a), they do not explain why the information about the early period of Christianity is so scanty, while the Christian traditions from Syria, Asia Minor, and Greece, though incomplete, are still rich and diversified enough to create difficulties for the reconstruction of a clear and coherent historical picture.

In his book *Orthodoxy and Heresy in Earliest Christianity,* first published in 1934, Walter Bauer provided an answer to this question. Seen from the perspective of the early catholic church, the beginnings of Christianity in Egypt were "heretical," and therefore Christian writings composed in Egypt in this early period were not preserved, while other pieces of information were either suppressed or not admitted to the treasure of

Bibliography to §11

Bauer, *Orthodoxy and Heresy,* 44–60.

Colin H. Roberts, *Manuscript, Society and Belief in Early Christian Egypt* (The Schweich Lectures 1977; London: Oxford University, 1979).

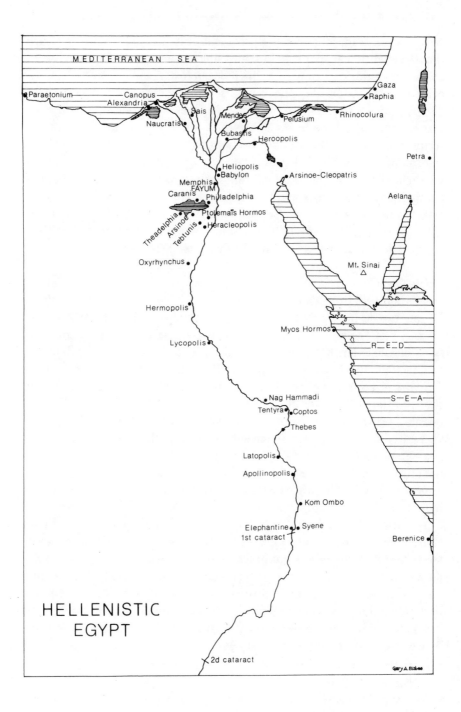

MEDITERRANEAN SEA

Paraetonium
Canopus
Alexandria
Sais
Mendes
Gaza
Raphia
Pelusium
Rhinocolura
Naucratis
Bubastis
Heroopolis
Petra
Heliopolis
Babylon
Arsinoe-Cleopatris
Memphis
FAYUM
Caranis
Philadelphia
Aelana
Theadelphia
Arsinoe
Ptolemaïs Hormos
Tebtunis
Heracleopolis
Oxyrhynchus
Hermopolis
Mt. Sinai
△
Myos Hormos
Lycopolis
R E D
Nag Hammadi
S E A
Tentyra
Coptos
Thebes
Latopolis
Apollinopolis
Kom Ombo
Elephantine
Syene
1st cataract
Berenice

HELLENISTIC
EGYPT

2d cataract

Gary A. Bisbee

ecclesiastical traditions. What Eusebius is able to report indicates clearly that the tradition available to him was silent about early Christian history in Egypt. In this case, however, the modern historian has some advantage over Eusebius. On the one hand, several church fathers, especially Clement of Alexandria and Origen, have preserved more than Eusebius was willing to include in his historical work; on the other hand, manuscript discoveries in Egypt have brought to light a great deal of valuable information. Eusebius, of course, even if he had known such writings, would not have used everything for his ecclesiastical history. In addition to a large number of Greek and Coptic papyri from Egypt (§6.2b), the most significant discovery is the Coptic Gnostic library from Nag Hammadi (§10.1b; 10.5b). It is especially these latter writings that lead us directly to the question of the Syrian origin of Egyptian Christianity.

(b) Syrian Traditions in Egypt

Missionaries from Palestine or Syria must have brought Christianity to Egypt. We do not know their names, but it is possible to form some impressions of their preaching and teachings. The two oldest manuscript finds of Christian books from Egypt point to the Gospel of John. The fragment of the Gospel of John in $\mathfrak{P}$52 and the *Unknown Gospel* of *Papyrus Egerton 2* were both written before the middle of II CE, possibly shortly after 100. Thus both the Gospel of John and a gospel which possibly provided some of its source material were known in Egypt at a very early date (§10.3a, b). Later witnesses prove that John was a favorite book among Egyptian gnostics. It is therefore likely that Christians who not much later were called "gnostics" were the first Christian preachers to appear in Egypt. There are further testimonies which seem to confirm this hypothesis. Three fragments stemming from three different copies of the Greek original of the Coptic *Gospel of Thomas* have been found in Egypt (*Pap. Oxyrh.* 1, 654, and 655; see §10.1b); at least one of these was written before 200, the others not much later. Only from the Gospel of John do we have as many as three papyri from the same period ($\mathfrak{P}$52, 66, and 75). Although the accidental nature of such manuscript discoveries has to be kept in mind, it is difficult to avoid the conclusion that these two gospels are better known in Egypt during II CE than any other Christian writing. The earliest extant manuscripts of Matthew and Luke were written at the

Bibliography to §11.b: Text

Morton Smith, *Clement,* 445–54. For further editions and translations of the *Secret Gospel,* see §10.2b.

Bibliography to §11.1b: Studies
See the literature for §10.3a and 10.5b.

beginning of III CE, although we know through Clement of Alexandria that both gospels were read in Alexandria before the end of II CE.

The evidence of a *Secret Gospel of Mark* from a recently discovered letter of Clement of Alexandria is quite peculiar (§10.2b). Toward the end of II CE not only was this gospel used among the "perfect" Christians in the church of Alexandria, but Clement reveals that the gnostic sect of the Carpocratians also used it, though in a somewhat different recension. Perhaps this apocryphal version of the gospel was brought to Egypt earlier than the Gospel of Mark which was later admitted to the canon of the New Testament. The *Secret Gospel of Mark* gives indications of a secret initiation rite: Jesus spends a night with the young man he had raised from the dead; he comes to Jesus dressed only in a linen cloth, and Jesus teaches him the mystery of the kingdom of God. This fits very well with what is otherwise known about secret rites of initiation among the gnostic sects of Egypt. Some of the writings preserved in the library of Nag Hammadi could also have been brought to Egypt from Syria as secret books, because formulae designed to guarantee secrecy occasionally occur (cf. the conclusion of the *Apocryphon of John*).

(c) Egyptian Jewish Christianity

1) *The Gospel of the Hebrews.* A number of fragments of the Jewish-Christian gospels (§10.4b) should be assigned to a gospel which was used in Alexandria and known under the name of the *Gospel of the Hebrews.* While the Jewish-Christian gospels discussed above, namely, the *Gospel of the Nazoreans* and the *Gospel of the Ebionites,* were closely related to the Gospel of Matthew, the *Gospel of the Hebrews,* to judge from the few extant fragments, must have had a different character. There are, to be sure, elements which can be called Jewish-Christian, but this gospel was composed in Greek. Nevertheless, the Spirit is called "the mother of Jesus"; this would fit a Semitic language, where the word "spirit" is a feminine noun. Mary is introduced as the earthly appearance of a heavenly power (Michael). In baptism the "whole fount of the Holy Spirit" descends upon Jesus and rests upon him, saying: "My Son, in all the prophets I was waiting for you, that you should come and I might rest in you. For you are my rest; you are my first-begotten Son who reigns forever." This concept is derived from the Jewish wisdom myth; the Spirit in this gospel speaks like personified Wisdom, who comes into the world

Bibliography to §11.1c: Text

P. Vielhauer, "Jewish-Christian Gospels," *NTApo* 1. 117–65.
Cameron (ed.), "The Gospel of the Hebrews," in *The Other Gospels,* 83–86.
See the literature for §10.4b.

repeatedly, appearing in prophets and divine messengers, seeking its rest (Wis 7:27; Sir 24:7). The *Gospel of the Hebrews* therefore uses a motif from Jewish theology, but no special relationship to the Jewish-Christian theology of the *Kerygmata Petrou* is discernable.

The authority of James is also emphasized in the *Gospel of the Hebrews*. This work contained a resurrection story in which Jesus appeared to his brother James and broke bread with him. The story implied further that James participated in Jesus' last supper, because "James had sworn that he would not eat bread from that hour in which he had drunk the cup of the Lord, until he should see him risen from among them that sleep." Extremely little is known about the content of this gospel as a whole, which, according to the stichometry of Nicephorus, was only a little shorter than the Gospel of Matthew! The saying assigned to the *Gospel of the Hebrews,* "And never shall you be joyful, save when you behold your brother with love," suggests that its sayings were of the same character as the Synoptic sayings. Clement of Alexandria assigns what we know as the second saying of the *Gospel of Thomas* to the *Gospel of the Hebrews (Strom.* 2.9.45 and 5.14.96). This gnostic catena-saying about a sequence of seeking, finding, marvelling, ruling, and resting could, of course, have circulated in the free tradition of Jesus' sayings. But if the *Gospel of Thomas* was brought to Egypt at an early date, we must assume that the *Gospel of the Hebrews* drew from that source. In other instances of parallels to the *Gospel of Thomas* in Christian writings from Egypt (§11.2b) that writing is to be considered as the most likely source.

2) *The Apocryphon of James.* The Jewish Christians in Alexandria may have used a number of other writings under the authority of James. The *1st* and *2nd Apocalypses of James* could be considered here, since both originate with the traditions of James from Syria, although they are gnostic writings (§10.5b). But in fact the *Gospel of the Hebrews* also has affinities to Gnosticism. Its readers would scarcely have objected to the theology of these two writings. The *Apocryphon of James* (NHC I, 2) from Nag Hammadi is of a somewhat different character, although in its extant form it appeals to a typically Jewish-Christian authority, since it claims to be a secret book revealed by the Lord to James and Peter, and written down by the former in the Hebrew language (*Ap. Jas.* 1,8–18). Its content is a farewell discourse of Jesus, based upon sayings that have

Bibliography to §11.1c (2): Texts

Francis E. Williams and Dieter Mueller, "The Apocryphon of James (I,2)," *NagHamLibEngl,* 29–36.

Cameron (ed.), "The Apocryphon of James," in *The Other Gospels,* 55–64.

Hans-Martin Schenke, "Der Jakobusbrief aus dem Codex Jung," *OLZ* 66 (1971) 117–30. German translation of the *Apocryphon of James.*

parallels in the Gospel of John, the *Gospel of Thomas,* and the Synoptics. But literary dependence upon these gospels is not evident; on the contrary, the blessing of those "who have not seen and yet believe" (*Ap. Jas.* 12,41–13,1) appears in a more original setting of a sequence of sayings, while John 20:29 has added this saying secondarily to the story of Jesus' appearance before Thomas. With respect to its genre, the *Apocryphon of James* is closely related to the *Dialogue of the Savior* (§10.1b; 10.3a): an interpretation of older sayings in dialogue and discourse form presents gnostic teaching as the legitimate continuation of older (Jewish-Christian?) traditions.

2. Egyptian Gnosticism

(a) The Testimony of the Writings from Nag Hammadi

The codices of the Nag Hammadi library (NHC) were written in Egypt in the Coptic language shortly after the middle of iv ce. This information is of little help in determining the place where the Greek originals were composed, however, and there is considerable uncertainty in assigning dates of composition for each of these books. Except for a very few instances, all our statements about the time and place of origin of each of those writings must remain tentative because the scholarly debate is still in progress. Nevertheless, it is important at the present stage of research at least to draw attention to several writings from the corpus of Nag Hammadi which may be significant for the reconstruction of the development of Gnosticism in Egypt until about the middle of ii ce.

Among those writings which were written in Syria, the *Gospel of Thomas* must have been known in Egypt by the middle of ii ce. The *Hypostasis of the Archons* and the *Apocryphon of John* show so many parallels to the Sophia myth of the Valentinian school that they might be considered its sources. The Sethian type of Gnosticism was also further developed in Egypt; its predecessor could have been the Syrian *Apocalypse of Adam.* In any case, if it can be assumed that certain types of Gnosticism originated in Syria, it necessarily follows that Syrian writings must have been brought to Egypt no later than at the beginning of ii ce.

1) *Pre-Christian Gnosticism in Egypt.* In addition to this Syrian influence upon the development of Egyptian Gnosticism, there may have been independent Egyptian formations of gnostic theology that reveal no

Bibliography to §11.2a

Alexander Böhlig and Frederik Wisse, *Zum Hellenismus in den Schriften von Nag Hammadi* (Göttinger Orientforschungen 6,2; Wiesbaden: Harrassowitz, 1975).

specifically Christian influence. Thus, also in Egypt a non-Christian Gnosticism preceded its Christian offspring and developed further without direct borrowings from Christianity. The writings of the *Corpus Hermeticum,* certainly native to Egypt, have already been mentioned (§6.5f). Even the library of Nag Hammadi included two Hermetic tractates, gnostic to be sure, but without traces of Christian influence (NHC VI, 6: *The Discourse of the Eighth and the Ninth;* and VI, 8: *Asclepius 21-29*). The *Paraphrase of Shem* (VIII, 1) is also without visible Christian influence. The creation myth presented in this writing, revealed by Derdekeas to Shem "who comes from an unmixed power" and is "the first being on the earth" (*Paraph. Shem* 1,18-21), is clearly different from those of the Syrian-Christian types, since its knows three principles: light, darkness, and the spirit standing between them. In order that "nature" can come into existence, Derdekeas, the son of light, has to intervene repeatedly. Although there are allusions to the creation story of the Book of Genesis, one does not find any extensive biblical exegesis, and Genesis 2-3 is not directly used. This book was apparently revised by Christians at a later time, because Hippolytus knows a *Paraphrase of Seth* which has many similarities with the *Paraphrase of Shem* of NHC VII, 1.

2) *Eugnostos the Blessed and Sophia of Jesus Christ.* There is one very interesting instance in which the library of Nag Hammadi has preserved both an original philosophical-gnostic treatise, the book *Eugnostos the Blessed,* and its later Christian adaptation, the *Sophia of Jesus Christ. Eugnostos the Blessed* (NHC III, 3; V, 1) describes in the form of a letter from "Eugnostos the Blessed to those who are his" the origin and struc-

Bibliography to §11.2a (1): Texts

Martin Krause, *Die Paraphrase des Sêem* (Christentum am Roten Meer 2; Berlin: De Gruyter, 1973) 2-105. Coptic text and German translation.

Frederik Wisse, "The Paraphrase of Shem (VII,1)," *NagHamLibEngl,* 308-28.

Bibliography to §11.2a (1): Studies

Frederik Wisse, "The Redeemer Figure in the Paraphrase of Shem," *NovT* 12 (1970) 118-29.

Bibliography to §11.2a (2): Texts

Demetrius Trakatellis, Ο ΥΠΕΡΒΑΤΙΚΟΣ ΘΕΟΣ ΤΟΥ ΕΥΓΝΩΣΤΟΥ (Athens: University, 1977). Introduction, Essays, Coptic transcription, and Greek translation of *Letter of Eugnostos.*

Douglas M. Parrott, "Eugnostos the Blessed (III,3 and V,1) and the Sophia of Jesus Christ (III,4 and BG 8502,3)," *NagHamLibEngl,* 206-28.

"The Letter of Eugnostos," in Foerster, *Gnosis,* 2. 24-39.

Bibliography to §11.2a (2): Studies

Martin Krause, "Das literarische Verhältnis des Eugnostosbriefes zur Sophia Jesu Christi," in: *Mullus: Festschrift für Theodor Klauser* (JAC.E 1; Münster: Aschendorff, 1964) 15-23.

Site of the Discovery of the Nag Hammadi Library

Twelve codices were found accidentally in a jar that was buried at the foot of the fallen boulders on the right. The site lies at the edge of the Nile Valley, not far from the oldest known Christian monastery (of Pachomius), near the ancient Chenoboskion in Upper Egypt.

tures of the transcendent divine world. Insight into the view presented by Eugnostos, which is confession of the God of Truth and gives immortality, is explicitly contrasted to the three erroneous philosophical views, which claim that the world has come into existence "by itself," "through providence," or "by fate." In his presentation of the three primary figures of the divine sphere, derived from each other through emanation, Eugnostos uses theological concepts which became significant in the following centuries for the Christian definition of God who was both Father and Son. The Christian writing *Sophia of Jesus Christ* (NHC III, 4 and BG 8502, 3), according to its narrative framework, is a revelation discourse of the resurrected redeemer with the twelve disciples and seven women. But the revelation discourse itself, including Jesus' answers to various questions of the disciples and the women, is nothing but a reproduction of the book of *Eugnostos.* Exegetical comments are occasionally added in order to explain the thoughts presented in the source. Additional material has been interpolated at the end, including the myth of the fall of Sophia and the imprisonment of the particles of light under the powerful archon of chaos Yaldabaoth, as well as a discourse about the role of the redeemer as their liberator. Thus, the gnostic philosophical writing of *Eugnostos* has been secondarily Christianized and at the same time mythologized.

3) *Gospel of the Egyptians (Sethian)*. The mythological counterpart to the book of *Eugnostos* is the *Holy Book of the Great Invisible Spirit,* also called the *Gospel of the Egyptians* (NHC III, 2 and IV, 2; it should not be confused with the completely different apocryphal *Gospel of the Egyptians;* see §11.2b). This writing is one of the most important documents of Sethian Gnosticism. It was probably originally composed in Syria and received the title "Gospel of the Egyptians" only after it had been brought to Egypt. The first part of the work treats in detail the complex evolution of the divine world through emanation from the primordial Father, whose name cannot be pronounced. In contrast to *Eugnostos,* numerous mythological names are used here (Barbelo, Ainon, Esephech, etc.), and one

Bibliography to §11.2a (3): Texts

Alexander Böhlig and Frederik Wisse (eds.), *Nag Hammadi Codices III,3 and IV,2: The Gospel of the Egyptians* (NHS 6; Leiden: Brill, 1975).

Idem, "The Gospel of the Egyptians (III,2 and IV,2)," *NagHamLibEngl,* 195–205.

James M. Robinson and Frederik Wisse, "The Three Steles of Seth (VII,5)," *NagHamLibEngl,* 362–67.

Joseph A. Gibbons, Roger A. Bullard, and Frederik Wisse, "The Second Treatise of the Great Seth (VII,2)," *NagHamLibEngl,* 329–38.

Bibliography to §11.2a (3): Studies

Hans-Martin Schenke, "Das Ägypterevangelium aus Nag-Hammadi-Codex III," *NTS* 16 (1969/70) 196–208.

finds multiple ogdoads, triads, and other groupings of divine powers. The entire process of divine evolution is characterized by an almost feverish activity rather than calm contemplation. The final outcome of the process is the birth of the great Seth, son of Adamas and father of the incorruptible seed. At this point in the mythical narrative one finds the first allusions to Genesis in the mention of Sodom and Gomorrah.

The second section begins with the installation of the ruler of chaos, Saclas, along with a description of his arrogance and the creation of his own aeons and demons. It continues with the sowing of the seed of the great Seth in the world and the institution of the guardian angels, who are charged with the protection of this seed until the time of salvation. This section concludes with the appearance of Seth in the person of Jesus, who brings rebirth through baptism. The work ends with a hymn and an elaborate self-characterization as a secret book written by Seth himself. The lack of explicit references to Christian traditions and the scanty appearance of Christian elements in these materials drawn from Syrian gnostic mythology is striking (some of the mythical names of the *Apocryphon of John* reappear in the *Holy Book of the Great Invisible Spirit*). It was only at a later time, probably towards the end of ii CE, that Sethian Gnosticism began to defend and modify its doctrine and message in a critical controversy with catholic Christianity (see the *Second Treatise of the Great Seth,* NHC VII, 2) or to accommodate it to the doctrines of emerging Neoplatonism (see the *Three Steles of Seth,* NHC VII, 5).

(b) Vernacular Gnostic Christianity:
The Gospel of the Egyptians

Most of the gnostic writings mentioned so far are esoteric books which must have had their home in Christian mystery associations rather than in congregations similar to those in Antioch and in the area of the Pauline mission. It is, of course, impossible to prove that congregations of this kind existed in Egypt during the period of early Christianity. No pertinent material survives and no conjectures are possible about their structures and ecclesiastical offices. Baptism, wherever it is mentioned (e.g., in the *Holy Book of the Great Invisible Spirit,* NHC III, 2, 66,24f), is understood as a mystery rite. Wherever Egyptian Christianity of this type appears more clearly, it is organized according to the model of a philosophical school or private association (§11.2c). Perhaps there were con-

Bibliography to §11.2b: Texts

Erich Klostermann (ed.), *Apocrypha II: Evangelien* (KIT 8; 3d ed.; Berlin: De Gruyter, 1929) 15–16.

W. Schneemelcher, "The Gospel of the Egyptians," *NTApo* 1. 166–78.

Cameron, "The Gospel of the Egyptians," in *The Other Gospels,* 49–52.

gregations on the periphery of Gnosticism which used such writings as the gospel of *Papyrus Egerton 2*, the Gospel of John, and the *Gospel of Thomas*. This suggestion seems to be confirmed by another writing possibly representing vernacular gnostic Christianity, the *Gospel of the Egyptians* (to be distinguished from the writing under the same name from NHC III and IV mentioned above). Only a few fragments are preserved, and Clement of Alexandria is its sole reliable witness. To judge from its name, there seems to have been a period during which this was the primary gospel writing used by the "Egyptians," that is, gentile Greek-speaking Christians, as distinct from the Jewish Christians who read the *Gospel of the Hebrews* (a hypothesis advanced by Walter Bauer).

Quotations from this writing are found in two passages that are closely related to each other. In the first passage, Jesus responds to Salome's question "Until when shall people die?" with the words: "So long as women bear children." Salome's further question, whether she did well not to bear children, receives the answer: "Eat every plant, but that which has bitterness do not eat." In the second passage, Salome once again is the one who asks a question, namely, when she would know what she had inquired about, and she receives the answer: "When you have trampled on the garment of shame, and when the two become one, and the male with the female (is) neither male nor female." Both sayings are clearly encratite, that is, they demand sexual asceticism so as to disrupt the cycle of birth and eliminate the sexual differences between male and female. This agrees with other gnostic writings from Egypt, which invariably include sexual asceticism as part of their religious program. The second of these two sayings of Jesus reappears in the *Gospel of Thomas* (22); it should also be noted that *Gos. Thom.* 61 introduces Salome as one who asks questions of Jesus. Since the very few fragments preserved of the *Gospel of the Egyptians* exhibit as many as two links to the *Gospel of Thomas*, it is not unreasonable to assume that the former was dependent upon the latter. It is impossible to say more about this writing, since it is highly doubtful that other materials occasionally assigned to the *Gospel of the Egyptians* ever actually belonged to it (for the relationship of this gospel to *2 Clement*, see §11.3a). But the character of the few certain quotations demonstrates that this vernacular gnostic Christianity of Egypt took its orientation from the transmitted sayings of Jesus and their interpretation, rather than from the cosmological and soteriological speculations of secret gnostic books.

(c) The Formation of Gnostic Schools

1) *The Naassenes.* The gnostic writings of Egypt mentioned so far cannot be assigned to any of the major gnostic schools that originated in

Egypt. Rather, they belong to gnostic groups or religious associations which may be designated for the time being with the phrase "Sethian Gnosticism." In addition to these groups there were the philosophically oriented circles of the *Corpus Hermeticum* (§6.5f) and of *Eugnostos the Blessed,* but also other gnostic groups. The best known of these is the sect of the Naassenes or Ophites, about whom Irenaeus and later patristic authors report. Nothing can be said with any certainty about the time of their origin, because no direct evidence is extant before the last third of II CE. The Naassenes referred to the serpent of Genesis 3 (Hebrew *naḥas,* Greek *ophis*) as the first revealer of divine knowledge. Like the early representatives of mythological Gnosticism in Syria, they drew their message from an interpretation of the first chapters of the Bible. According to Hippolytus' report about the Naassenes, their syncretistic attitude permitted them to borrow materials from other Hellenistic religions. Thus we find a pagan speech of religious propaganda based on a hymn to Attis, which surprisingly also contains some Jewish elements, but was only superficially Christianized (usually known as the "Naassene Sermon"). Hippolytus also quotes a Naassene hymn that might have been used liturgically; it is actually a pagan gnostic psalm about the spirit that redeems the soul from the chaos, composed in the customary anapestic foot of the Roman imperial period; the name "Jesus" was added only later.

2) *The Carpocratians.* While the names of Naassenes and Ophites apparently comprise a variety of related gnostic groups, the first organized gnostic sect under the name of its founder was that of the Carpocratians. Fragments of a writing about righteousness by Carpocrates' son Epiphanes are preserved: it proclaims communistic ideals (community of goods and sharing of women). This writing is dependent upon Paul and should be dated in the latter half of II CE. It was mentioned above (§11.1b) that the Carpocratians used the *Secret Gospel of Mark.* According to the information which is available, they were more a sect than a gnostic school.

3) *Basilides.* As the first founder of a gnostic school one would usually

Bibliography to §11.2c: Texts

Greek and Latin texts from the church fathers on Ophites, Carpocrates, Basilides, and Valentinus, in: Walther Völker, *Quellen zur Geschichte der christlichen Gnosis* (SQS 5; Tübingen: Mohr/Siebeck, 1932).

Bibliography to §11.2c (1): Texts

"Ophites and Ophians" and "Systems Involving Three Principles: The Naassenes," in: Foerster, *Gnosis,* 1. 84–99 and 261–82.

Bibliography to §11.2c (2): Texts

Extensive collection of Greek and Latin sources for Carpocrates and the Carpocratians in: Morton Smith, *Clement,* 295–350.

mention Basilides, whose activity may be dated to the early part of II CE. Reports about his gnostic system are preserved, but the accounts of Hippolytus, Clement of Alexandria, and others differ greatly from that of Irenaeus, who presents a typically gnostic system of emanations with an evil lower deity and a docetic christology. But Hippolytus reports a monistic theology that described the unfolding of the world through three spiritual principles or sonships; salvation would only be achieved when all the powers were brought to eternal rest in their proper positions. Followers of Basilides were still known in III CE.

4) *Valentinus.* The most important gnostic school was founded by Valentinus, who must have been active for some time in Egypt before he went to Rome in about 140 CE. In the second half of II CE branches of the Valentinian school were known in the east and the west; it was at this time that the well-known Valentinian systems were designed by Valentinus' students (Ptolemy, Heracleon, and Theodotus). These systems clearly reveal a controversy with the catholic church and a dependence upon the

Bibliography to §11.2c (3): Texts
"Basilides," in: Foerster, *Gnosis,* 1. 59–83.

Bibliography to §11.2c (3): Studies
Werner Foerster, "Das System des Basilides," *NTS* 9 (1962/63) 233–55.
H. A. Wolfson, "Negative Attributes in the Church Fathers and the Gnostic Basilides," *HTR* 50 (1957) 145–56.
Ekkehard Mühlenberg, "Wirklichkeitserfahrung und Theologie bei dem Gnostiker Basilides," *Kerygma und Dogma* 18 (1972) 161–75.

Bibliography to §11.2c (4): Texts
"Valentinianism I–VI," in: Foerster, *Gnosis,* 1. 121–243.
George W. MacRae, "The Gospel of Truth (I,3 and XII,2)," *NagHamLibEngl,* 37–49.
"The Gospel of Truth," in: Foerster, *Gnosis,* 2. 53–70.

Bibliography to §11.2c (4): Studies
Eugène de Faye, *Gnostiques et Gnosticisme: Etude critique des documents du gnosticisme chrétien aux IIe et IIIe siècles* (2d ed.; Bibliothèque de l'Ecole des Hautes Etudes, Sciences Religieuses 27; Paris: Leroux, 1925).
Werner Foerster, *Von Valentin zu Herakleon* (BZNW 7; Giessen: Töpelmann, 1928).
F. L. M. M. Sagnard, *La Gnose Valentinienne et le témoignage de Saint Irénée* (EPhM 36; Paris: Vrin, 1947).
Gilles Quispel, "La conception de l'homme dans la gnose Valentinienne," *ErJb* 15 (1948) 249–86.
G. C. Stead, "In Search of Valentinus," in: Layton, *Rediscovery of Gnosticism,* 75–102.
Idem, "The Valentinian Myth of Sophia," *JTS* 20 (1969) 75–104.
R. McL. Wilson, "Valentinianism and the *Gospel of Truth,*" in: Layton, *Rediscovery of Gnosticism,* 133–45.

canonical gospels and the Pauline letters. We cannot discuss this further in this context, nor is it possible to give even a brief summary of the Valentinian systems, with their theological interpretation of the myth of Wisdom's fall, and their hypothesis of three classes of human beings, the spiritual people (*pneumatikoi* = the true gnostics), those who merely possess a soul (*psychikoi* = the ecclesiastical Christians), and those who are made up solely of matter (*hylikoi*).

Valentinus himself, who clearly belongs to the Gnosticism of the first half of II CE in Egypt, is an elusive figure. The few fragments preserved from him seem to point to a visionary and poet rather than a systematic thinker. The question has also been raised whether the *Gospel of Truth* (NHC I, 3 and XII, 2), the most sublime and most beautiful writing of the entire Nag Hammadi corpus, was written by Valentinus. No doubt this meditation about the "gospel" (it does not pretend to be a gospel writing) must have been composed by a well-read and gifted theologian with a deep sense of true piety. Although there are no explicit quotations in the writing, the author not only knew the Old Testament very well, but also the gospels of the New Testament and the letters of Paul. It may have been Valentinus himself who introduced the interpretation of these early Christian writings into the exegetical endeavors of Gnosticism. Thus it would be no accident that the oldest commentary of a New Testament writing known to us was the commentary on John by Valentinus' student Heracleon. But such considerations cannot prove Valentinus' authorship of the *Gospel of Truth*, nor even such an early date for its writing, nor its "Valentinian" character. But no one should miss the opportunity of reading this book, or be deterred by either its possibly late date or its authorship by one of the archheretics of the Christian church. Its study is rewarding—especially after the laborious study of the documents of mythological Gnosticism.

3. The Beginnings of Catholicism

(a) Vernacular Catholic Christianity: The Second Letter of Clement

The beginnings of non-gnostic Christianity in Egypt are obscure, though they must have been related to the formation of the catholic churches in other provinces. Some information can be obtained from the so-called *Second Letter of Clement*, if this writing indeed originated in Egypt. This hypothesis is by no means certain and is maintained by only a few scholars; nonetheless there are important reasons in its favor. In the later tradition of the church, *2 Clement* was linked to *1 Clement* (§12.2e);

in extant manuscripts, they were always copied together. Thus *1 Clement* and *2 Clement* occur side by side in two manuscripts of the NT: Codex Alexandrinus from v CE and Codex Hierosolymitanus from the year 1056 (the complete text of the *Didache* also comes from this codex, see §10.1c; only in the Hierosolymitanus is the text of *2 Clement* fully preserved). The Syriac translation of the NT also transmitted both writings together.

Since *1 Clement* was written from Rome to Corinth, it has been assumed that *2 Clement* was composed in either Rome or Corinth. It is difficult, however, to find in either of these two churches or in their relations with each other any situation which would satisfactorily explain *2 Clement*'s purpose. Harnack's hypothesis that the Roman bishop Soter (165–174 CE) was the author of the writing is farfetched and assumes a date of authorship which is clearly too late. Moreover, it is highly unlikely that the connection of these two writings has its roots in ancient tradition. Eusebius states explicitly that he knew of no recognition of *2 Clement* by older authors (*Hist. eccl.* 3.28.4), while he found *1 Clement* well attested (*Hist. eccl.* 4.23.11; 5.6.3). This shows clearly that the two writings were not transmitted together in the time before Eusebius. Furthermore, *2 Clement* says nothing about its author, nor does it ever refer to *1 Clement*. The title occurs only in later colophons of the manuscripts. The writing itself contains no prescript with author and address, and no final greetings. In fact, it is not really a letter at all, but a homily or, better, a programmatic theological writing with homiletical features. Since there are no external indications as to its place of origin, we are left entirely to an interpretation of the internal evidence.

An assumption of an Egyptian origin would solve a number of prob-

Bibliography to §11.3a: Text
Funk-Bihlmeyer, *ApostVät*, xxix–xxxi, 71–81.
Lake, *ApostFath*, 1. 123–63.

Bibliography to §11.3a: Commentaries
Lightfoot, *Apostolic Fathers*, part 1, vols. 1–2.
Robert M. Grant and Holt H. Graham, *First and Second Clement* (Grant, *ApostFath* 2).
Rudolf Knopf, *Die Lehre der Zwölf Apostel, die zwei Clemensbriefe* (HNT.E 1; Tübingen: Mohr/Siebeck, 1920) 151–84.

Bibliography to §11.3a: Studies
Karl Paul Donfried, *The Setting of Second Clement in Early Christianity* (NovTSup 38; Leiden: Brill, 1974).
Hans Windisch, "Das Christentum des 2. Clemensbriefes," in *Festgabe von Fachgenossen und Freunden Adolf von Harnack zum siebzigsten Geburtstag dargebracht* (Tübingen: Mohr/Siebeck, 1921) 122–34.
Helmut Koester, *Synoptische Überlieferung bei den Apostolischen Vätern* (TU 65; Berlin: Akademie-Verlag, 1957) 62–111.

lems concerning the book's content. It is striking, on the one hand, that the writing represents a very simple and practical piety. Hans Windisch's characterization has been frequently repeated: "The theological basis of *2 Clement* is, stated briefly, a Synoptic-Gospels Christianity understood in terms of contemporary Judaism." Its central feature is the call for repentance and the demand for good works in the face of the coming judgment. Jesus is primarily a teacher; nothing points to a developed christology. Still, on the other hand, there is clear evidence that *2 Clement* cannot have been written at the earliest period of Christianity. The sayings of Jesus that are quoted in the writing presuppose the NT gospels of Matthew and Luke; they were probably drawn from a harmonizing collection of sayings which was composed on the basis of those two gospels. *2 Clem.* 8.5 refers to the written "gospel" as a well-established entity (though it is not necessary to understand the reference to the "apostles," *2 Clem.* 14.2, as a reference to writings under apostolic authority). It is also difficult to reconcile the otherwise quite simple christological statements of the writing with *2 Clem.* 14.2, where the sentence from Gen 1:27, "God created the human being as male and female," is interpreted as a statement about Christ and the church, which in turn is understood as the body of Christ. This presupposes either the deutero-Pauline Letter to the Ephesians or analogous speculations about the heavenly beings "Church" and "Christ." The latter seems more likely, especially since *2 Clement* elsewhere attests a knowledge of the Pauline letters only rarely or not at all.

This would be strange if the book was composed in Corinth, where those letters must have been well known in the first half of ii CE. But if *2 Clement* instead was written in Egypt at that time, lack of knowledge of Paul's letters and an occasional reference to a concept otherwise known from gnostic sources could be easily explained. What looks like a "Synoptic-Gospels Christianity understood in terms of Judaism" is actually the Christianity of a later period, which insisted upon the basic principles of active and practicing piety in order to strengthen its position against a more dominant gnostic faith. There can be little doubt that the author of *2 Clement* was fighting against the gnostics. This is why he states that *gnosis* is the confession of the one who has saved us: "But how do we confess him? By doing what he says, and by not disregarding his commandments" (3.2–4). The gnostic goal of salvation, the heavenly rest, is also critically interpreted: one finds rest by doing the will of Christ (6.7). The view that our flesh is the temple of God is especially emphasized, and *2 Clement* explicitly rejects the statement that "this flesh is not judged and does not rise again" (9.1–3). In the context of this anti-gnostic posture, the author also proposes a new interpretation of the gnostic speculation about Gen 1:27 concerning the heavenly aeons Christ and the church: Christ made the church manifest by appearing in the flesh, in order to demonstrate "that those of us who guard her in the flesh without corruption shall receive her back again in the Holy Spirit" (14:2–3). In the same context several pointedly anti-gnostic formulations appear: "the flesh is the copy of the spirit," and "guard the flesh that you may receive the Spirit" (14.3). *2 Clement* even presents an interpretation of a saying of Jesus that was used in gnostic gospels: *2 Clem.* 12.2 quotes: "When the two shall be one, and the outside as the inside, and the male with the female neither male nor female." This saying also appears in the *Gospel of Thomas* (22) and in the *Gospel of the Egyptians* (§11.2b). *2 Clement* interprets the first of these sentences as "speaking with one another in truth, so there is but one soul in two bodies," the second as meaning that the soul (the inside) should become visible in good works, just as the body (the outside) is visible, and the third sentence as pointing to a new rela-tionship between brothers and sisters in the faith, in which they learn to think about each other in terms other than sexual relationships (12.3–5). The author obviously wants to counteract a gnostic interpretation of this saying. The use of the saying in two gnostic gospels known from Egypt is a strong argument for an Egyptian origin of *2 Clement*.

If *2 Clement* was indeed written in Egypt, it would be the first tangible evidence for the existence of anti-gnostic Christianity in Egypt before the middle of II CE. To be sure, the beginnings of this Egyptian Christianity are no longer visible to us, but there can be no doubt that traditions of the early catholic church were coming to be established in Egypt at that time. This also laid the ground for the development of an ecclesiastical organi-zation, directed by a bishop, which clearly appears in Alexandria during the last two decades of II CE.

(b) The Controversy with Gnosticism: The Epistula Apostolorum

The *Epistula Apostolorum* can be seen as evidence for aggressive at-tacks by circles of the early catholic church upon Egyptian Gnosticism. This book was entirely unknown until the discovery of major portions of

Bibliography to §11.3b: Texts

Hermann Duensing, *Epistula Apostolorum* (KlT 152; Berlin: De Gruyter, 1925).
Idem, "Epistula Apostolorum," *NTApo* 1. 189–227.
Cameron, "The Epistula Apostolorum," in *The Other Gospels*, 131–62.
Carl Schmidt, *Gespräche Jesu mit seinen Jüngern nach der Auferstehung* (TU 43; Leipzig: Hinrichs, 1919). First edition of the *Epistula Apostolorum*.

Bibliography to §11.3b: Studies

Manfred Hornschuh, *Studien zur Epistula Apostolorum* (PTS 5; Berlin: De Gruyter, 1965).

the work in a Coptic translation in the year 1895 and the appearance of some Latin fragments and a complete Ethiopic translation in subsequent years. An Egyptian origin for the *Epistula Apostolorum* is the most likely, and although there is no external evidence for the time in which it was written, its date can be deduced on the basis of its use of those writings which later became a part of the NT canon. The gospels of the NT are freely used, but not quoted as canonical Scripture; Paul is known, especially the image of Paul presented by the Acts of the Apostles; allusions to passages from the Pauline letters occur several times, though these letters are never cited as authoritative words of the apostle. These references to the language and literature of the Pauline circles allows the conclusion that the author was dependent upon the Christian tradition of Asia Minor and Greece (§12.2a–g).

The genre and content of the *Epistula Apostolorum* clearly reveal its anti-gnostic position. Its genre imitates the literary form of the gnostic revelation discourse, in which the risen Jesus transmits heavenly wisdom and teaching to his disciples. Against the claim of various gnostic writings circulating under the name of a particular apostle, the *Epistula Apostolorum* adopts for its message the authority of all the apostles: John, Thomas, Peter, Andrew, James, Philip, Bartholomew, Matthew, Nathanael, Jude, and Cephas (!), who write to the entire church in the form of an apostolic letter. Before the section reporting the appearance of the risen Jesus to the disciples, the *Epistula Apostolorum* includes a section which corresponds to the creed of the church, speaking of God the creator and preserver of the world, and describing the earthly appearance of Jesus (materials are used from the NT gospels and the *Infancy Gospel of Thomas*). In the narrative about Jesus' resurrection the physical reality of his appearance is emphasized (*Epist. Apost.* 1–12). The second part of the book could be called an "anti-gnostic dogmatic theology," which treats the important topics of Christian theology in systematic fashion. Questions of christology are dealt with first: Jesus' way through the heavens in his coming; the incarnation; the passover as remembrance of his death; and his second coming (13–19). Questions of eschatology follow: resurrection of the flesh, together with the spirit and the soul; last judgment (21–29, including an excursus about the descent into Hades and preaching and baptism for Abraham, Isaac, and Jacob in 27); and preaching to Israel and the gentiles (30). The last topic leads to an excursus about Paul, the apostle to the nations (31–33), defending Paul as a legitimate apostle of the catholic church against the claims to Paul as the authority of gnostic theology, and against his rejection by Jewish-Christian circles. The last part of this theological disquisition deals with the tribulations of the endtime, the fate of sinners and the righteous, and their relationship to each other (34–40).

The final chapters of the *Epistula Apostolorum* are related to the genre of the church order. It first introduces the offices of the church: father (= preacher of the revelations), servant (*diakonos,* charged with baptizing), and teacher (41–42). The teaching of the Christian virtues is presented as an interpretation of the parable of the ten virgins (43–45). The anti-gnostic tendency is evident in its designation of the foolish virgins as "Insight, Knowledge, Obedience, Endurance, and Mercy" (the last three were perhaps directed against Jewish Christianity), whereas the wise virgins are called "Faith, Love, Joy, Peace, and Hope." Following this exposition are instructions about the rich, almsgiving, church discipline, and excommunication (46–49). The conclusion is formed by a warning about false teachers (50). With the description of Jesus' ascension the author returns to the framework of the genre which he had adopted.

This book is an extremely important document because it responds directly to the challenge of Gnosticism. Gnostic Christianity in Egypt had identified "revelation" with the production and transmission of secret books in which Christ (or some other revealer figure) disclosed the reality of the transcendent world, thus revealing to the spiritual persons their origin and destiny. The *Epistula Apostolorum* fully adopts this genre of gnostic discourse. But it is an open book "written for the whole world" (chap. 1). What Jesus says in this book is the discourse of the messenger from heaven, but this messenger is at the same time the one who has become flesh and whose earthly life can be described in a brief biographical sketch. The gnostics made reference to the sayings of Jesus; the *Epistula Apostolorum* refers to the narrative materials of the gospel tradition. What the believers are told in this discourse about their own true existence does not concern their heavenly origins, but their earthly life. This earthly experience is seen with respect to an eschatology that permits an explanation of the essence of Christian faith in terms of the teaching of virtue and of church order. The creed of the early catholic church, as well as the gospel writings which had been developed in accordance with this creed and later became the canonical gospels of the church, provided the materials for the forging of the revelation discourse of Jesus into an ecclesiastical weapon in the fight against Gnosticism. However, the later orthodox church did not continue the literary development of this genre, but checked the further growth of revelation mediated through the discourses of Jesus by canonizing the gospels of the New Testament. Thus, the *Epistula Apostolorum* was soon forgotten.

(c) The Establishment of an Ecclesiastical Organization

The introduction of an ecclesiastical organization which finally included Egyptian Christianity into the development of the universal catholic church of Syria, Asia Minor, Greece, and Rome lies beyond the scope of this book because it belongs to the second half of ɪɪ CE. To be sure, *2 Clement* and the *Epistula Apostolorum* are witnesses to the strengthening of non-gnostic Christianity in Egypt. They also demonstrate that, in addition to the Gospel of John, other NT writings such as Matthew and the Lukan writings became known in Egypt, and that the letters of Paul began to be read. But in this respect, catholic Christians were no different from the gnostics, since the Valentinians claimed the Pauline letters for themselves, just as they also learned to use the gospels of the churches of Syria and Asia Minor (Matthew and Luke). Thus no clear literary borderlines between orthodoxy and heresy were established; the controversies were fought especially about the interpretation of such writings. Clear decisions in this controversy became possible at the end of ɪɪ CE when the Christian church in Alexandria adopted the authorities for orthodox Christianity which had by then been developed: the canon of the NT and the monarchic episcopate. Demetrius, bishop of Alexandria after 189 CE, was the first ecclesiastical leader in Egypt to enforce episcopal authority. It is unlikely that he and his immediate successors achieved quick results in their fight against Gnosticism. Clement of Alexandria, Demetrius' contemporary and an open-minded Christian philosopher, argued against the gnostics, but maintained the ideal of the Christian as the true gnostic; he also cared little for episcopal authority. At the beginning of ɪɪɪ CE, Origen, who far surpassed the gnostics in his skills as an exegete and his insights as a theologian, was defeated in his battle with the orthodox bishop of Alexandria and had to move to Caesarea in Palestine, where he reestablished his theological school. Even a hundred years later, the monks of Pachomius, founder of Christian cenobite monasticism, read and copied gnostic writings for their own religious edification. Thanks to this Christian monastic activity, the writings of the Nag Hammadi library have been preserved: members of the Pachomian monastery hid these apparently precious books in order to protect them from the officially sanctioned heresy hunters. Thus orthodoxy and heresy continued to exist side by side in Egypt for centuries.

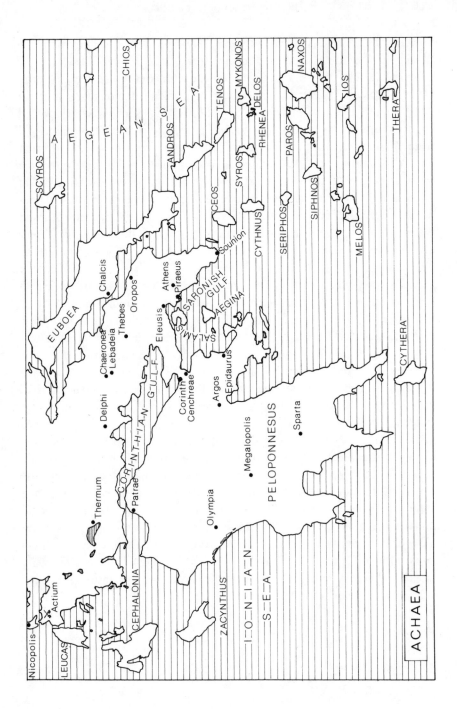

ACHAEA

ASIA MINOR, GREECE, AND ROME

1. THE RENEWAL OF APOCALYPTICISM

(a) Apocalypticism in the Pauline Churches: The Second Letter to the Thessalonians

In the period after the Pauline mission, the churches in Asia Minor and Greece developed in a direction that was quite different from the development of Christianity in Syria and Egypt. Rome was soon clearly associated with the further history of these churches, and so was Antioch, which had in fact been related to the churches of the Pauline mission from the very beginning. The particular features that characterize the history of these churches were not due exclusively to the effectiveness of Paul's missionary practice, although this must have been a significant factor. The Pauline letters demonstrate that Paul and his associates paid special attention to the consolidation of new congregations in order to insure their continuation and growth. However, the social and economic structures of the area of the Pauline mission must also be considered, since they were markedly different from Egypt and the inland areas of Syria. Greece and the western parts of Asia Minor were dominated by a large number of cities that experienced a period of considerable prosperity under Roman imperial rule. In Syria similar city cultures existed only along the Mediterranean coast, with Antioch as the largest and leading city; in Egypt, Alexandria remained the only significant city.

The domination of urban culture in the Pauline missionary areas meant that there was a comparatively large proportion of the population that enjoyed at least a modest prosperity, had access to education, and to greater personal freedom, including the freedom to travel or to settle elsewhere. Urban culture also meant a larger supply and demand on the religious market, slave labor in private houses and industry (slaves who were often better educated and had more freedom than slaves in the rural areas), a restless and unstable middle class, a dubious and insecure bourgeois morality, temples for the emperor cult, and Roman soldiers and administrators. The city of Rome, which had all these things in large measure, was within the horizon of the Christian communities of Asia

Minor and Greece as early as Paul's time. During the following decades, the Christian church in Rome participated in the development of these churches, though for a long time the leadership lay with the churches of the eastern Greek cities.

Among the various developments in the post-Pauline era until the turn of I CE, the renewal of apocalyptic expectation is particularly striking. Paul himself had maintained the expectation of Jesus' coming in the near future, but he had refused to engage in speculations about its exact time. There is no evidence from the genuine Pauline letters that the problem of the delay of parousia ever arose during Paul's lifetime (not even in 1 Thessalonians; see §9.2d). But Paul had criticized the foreshortening of the apocalyptic expectation in a realized eschatology (see 1 Corinthians, §9.3c). It is virtually certain that the expectation of Jesus' coming continued to be a vital element of Christian faith in the churches of Paul after his death. The problem was therefore unavoidable: either this eschatological expectation had to be renewed, or the delay of the parousia had to be explained. The problem came to a head exactly in this form, as is evident in the so-called Second Letter to the Thessalonians.

2 Thessalonians is accepted by many scholars as a genuine letter of Paul. In this case the letter would come from the same situation that produced 1 Thessalonians. It would be a second writing sent by Paul to Thessalonica only a few weeks after the first letter due to an unexpected change of the church's situation. The new situation is clearly characterized by the reference to opponents who proclaim that the day of the Lord is at hand (2 Thess 2:1–2). But such a situation is hardly possible just a few weeks after the writing of the first letter. It would fit much better in the time after the apostle's death, when the letters of Paul had received new significance as his legacy to the church.

Bibliography to §12.1
P. Vielhauer, "Apocalyptic in Early Christianity," *NTApo* 2. 608–42.
See also the literature under §5.2b.

Bibliography to §12.1a: Commentaries
B. Rigaux, *Les Epîtres aux Thessaloniciens* (EtBib; Paris: Gabalda, 1956).
Wolfgang Trilling, *Der Zweite Brief an die Thessalonicher* (EKKNT 14; Neukirchen-Vluyn: Neukirchener Verlag, 1980).

Bibliography to §12.1a: Studies
Schmithals, "The Historical Situation of the Thessalonian Epistles," in: idem, *Paul and the Gnostics,* 123–218.
William Wrede, *Die Echtheit des II. Thessalonicherbriefes* (TU NF 9,2; Leipzig: Hinrichs, 1902).
Braun, "Zur nichtpaulinischen Herkunft des zweiten Thessalonicherbriefes," in: idem, *Studien,* 205–9.

Early Roman Coin from Macedonia
The obverse (above) shows the head of the goddess
Artemis in a circle of Macedonian shields. The reverse
(below), a cast of the same coin, shows a club (symbol
of Heracles) in an oakwreath with the thunderbolt of
Zeus on the left. The inscription reads: ''Of the First
(Region) of the Macedonians.''

This suggestion would also explain many of the difficulties in the interpretion of 2 Thessalonians. Its frequent references to 1 Thessalonians are striking: as much as a third of 2 Thessalonians consists of sentences and phrases from 1 Thessalonians. But it is exactly in these contexts that terms and words occur which Paul never uses elsewhere, or which he employs with a different meaning. Typically Pauline thoughts, often using precisely the same words as 1 Thessalonians, are modified in a way unparalleled in genuine Pauline letters: in 1 Thess 1:6–10 the experience of tribulation is understood as a confirmation of the certainty of election; in 2 Thess 1:4–10 tribulations prove that God will give just retribution to both the persecutors and those who are persecuted. 1 Thess 3:8 speaks about the firm standing of the church "in the Lord"; 2 Thess 2:15 defines the firm standing of the church as holding on to the traditions that have been taught in the word and in the letters of the apostle. 1 Thess 1:5–7 relates the concept of imitation (of Paul and of the Lord) to the acceptance of the proclamation in much tribulation, making the congregation an example for the acceptance of the word in other congregations; and that Paul had worked day and night with his own hands was not an example to be imitated, but an expression of his love (1 Thess 2:8–9); but in 2 Thess 3:7–10 "Paul" says that he had worked day and night in the sweat of his brow so that the church would have an example to be imitated, with all the people working eagerly with their own hands: "those who do not work should not eat!" The fact that the dedicated work of the apostle to the gentiles is no longer understood as a service on behalf of the gospel but rather as an admonition against laziness should leave no doubt that 2 Thessalonians was written in a situation completely different from that of Paul's life. The proclamation of the Lord's coming in the near future has come to be a threat for a congregation whose responsible activity in the world demands that the parousia take place at some future time. This is the topic of the letter.

It is not quite clear what concepts the opponents connected with their announcement of the immediate arrival of the day of the Lord. It is not very likely that they were gnostics who proclaimed the constant presence of eschatological salvation for all believers. In that case, their refutation would not have included the presentation of a specific, though mysterious, eschatological timetable. The author of the writing seems to agree with his opponents that the parousia as an eschatological event will put an end to the course of the world. What he disagrees with is the opponents' announcement of the date; if the congregation took that announcement seriously, the entire order of the life of the church, founded in the missionary work of Paul, would be endangered. However important eschatology might have been to the author, the present time should not be understood from an eschatological perspective. The present experience of tribulation is therefore not a sign of the coming of the Lord in the near future. For this reason the author separates the discussion of the tribulations from the framework of eschatological expectations and independently relates them to future retribution and judgment (2 Thess 1:4–10). Having clarified this issue, he is ready to quote the dangerous eschatological message of his opponents (2:1–2) and to explain his own eschatological schedule in order to refute their message (2:3–12). According to this timetable, the valid sign of the parousia is the appearance of the Antichrist. He is described in traditional terms of Jewish apocalypticism as the "man of lawlessness" and the "son of perdition": he will assume the posture of divinity and seat himself in the temple of God. (This draws on traditions of Jewish apocalypticism, which means that such statements need not presuppose the existence of the temple in Jerusalem.) Furthermore, 2 Thess 2:8–12 presents a juxtaposition of the Antichrist and Jesus which, through the use of antithetical formulations and alliterations, for the first time in early Christian literature develops an "anti-christology" with exact correlations to christology.

In the exposition of the eschatological timetable an important argument is the mysterious reference to "that which (or, he who) still restrains" the adversary of Christ (2:6–7). Some have suggested that the Roman state as the ruling political power is being referred to as the restrainer of the chaos that will arise when the Antichrist arrives, but it is more likely that the author is pointing to a mythological figure from the apocalyptic tradition. The nearest analogy would be the angel who binds Satan for a thousand years (Rev 20:1–3). But the intention of such apocalyptic language should not be forgotten. The author gives no hint as to the identity of this mysterious power because he has no intention of solving the riddle for the reader: the mystery should remain mysterious. In an analogous way Mark 13:14 refers to the "desolating sacrilege set up where it ought not be." Matthew, to be sure, knew that this was a quotation from the Book of Daniel (Matt 24:15) because he was a biblical scholar. But neither the average reader of Mark 13 nor the recipient of 2 Thessalonians 2 was expected to know the exact meaning of the reference. The primary purpose of this mysterious statement was to emphasize that this future moment had not yet arrived. That alone was important, and the author had no intention of giving his readers any help in calculating the date of the parousia; it was enough to reject the radicalized eschatology of the opponents. The Christian of true belief is pointed to the present time and its duties; insights into eschatological calculations would be of no help. The future cannot be calculated—this has been good theology ever since. The author of 2 Thessalonians urges that the responsibility of the church as it exists in the world be taken seriously. This, the author argues, is the legacy of the great apostle's work. This responsibility is reinforced with the admonitions that follow upon the eschatological excursus, however these admonitions may be evaluated.

Thus a decisive step has been taken. The use of traditional apocalyptic materials serves primarily to exclude eschatological perspectives in the determination of the Christian task in the present. Only the expectation of the coming judgment remains as a factor to influence Christian conduct. At the same time, Paul is clearly designated as the originator of the Christian tradition (2 Thess 2:15), while he is freed from the suspicion of harboring radical eschatological perspectives. Apocalyptic doctrine is no doubt renewed, but it is done in such a way that eschatological expectations are transformed into doctrines about future events. Paul himself had interpreted apocalyptic traditions in order to clarify the process of salvation, of which the present life of the community and its experience was a vital factor. In 2 Thessalonians, however, the church is no longer permitted to use apocalyptic traditions in such a way; rather, the community is pointed to a morality that was acceptable to the city's bourgeois environment (2 Thess 3:6ff–with explicit reference to Paul!).

(b) Apocalypticism and Gnosticism: The Epistle of Jude

The renewed interest in apocalyptic traditions was useful not only in the struggle against a radicalized eschatology, it also proved to be an effective weapon in the controversy with Gnosticism. This is evident in the Epistle of Jude. The origin and date of this brief writing are uncertain, but its employment of apocalyptic material against Gnosticism is so obvious that it is best treated in this context. The first witness for the existence of Jude is 2 Peter, which reproduces this small letter in its entirety in chap. 2 (§7.3e). But in contrast to 2 Peter, Jude reveals a much more naive attitude in its use of apocalyptic materials. It thus belongs to an earlier period and may have been written as early as the last decades of I CE. A relatively early date is also required because of the use of the pseudonym "Jude, brother of James," meaning without any doubt not an "apostle,"

Bibliography to §11.1b: Commentaries

J. N. D. Kelly, *A Commentary on the Epistles of Peter and Jude* (Black's New Testament Commentaries; London: Black, 1969).

Walter Grundmann, *Der Brief des Judas und der zweite Brief des Petrus* (ThHK 15; Berlin: Evangelische Verlagsanstalt, 1974) 1–51.

Bibliography to §11.1b: Studies

Frederik Wisse, "The Epistle of Jude in the History of Heresiology," in *Essays on Nag Hammadi Texts in Honor of Alexander Böhlig* (NHS 3; Leiden: Brill, 1972) 133–43.

but a brother of Jesus (Mark 6:3; Matt 13:55). The use of this pseudonym would have made sense only at an early date, as long as there was still some memory of the significance of such members of Jesus' family (see Hegesippus in Eusebius *Hist. eccl.* 3.19–20). Even so, the use of this name is still somewhat curious. Considering the obviously anti-gnostic character of the writing, there is another possible explanation for the name: Judas Thomas (the twin) was recognized as an authority in gnostic circles (§10.1b) and was later also called the brother of Jesus. One may therefore ask whether the use of this authority by gnostics was the reason for the choice of this pseudonym, and whether the designation "brother of James" (rather than "brother of Jesus") was chosen for polemical reasons. In this case, however, the writing would probably belong to Syria.

The Epistle of Jude is not a real letter, but a small polemical tractate that lacks any specific addressee. It refers in general to "the faith" which has been transmitted to the saints and the authority of "the apostles of our Lord Jesus Christ" (Jude 3 and 17). Both are fixed traditional authorities that are simply presupposed and left unexplained. The author does not characterize his opponents in any detail. They were certainly gnostics, as is clear from the polemical reversal of the gnostic claim to true spirituality in Jude 19: "worldy people (*psychikoi*), devoid of the Spirit (*pneuma*)." Many of the biblical examples which are employed by the author also belong to the typical equipment of gnostic speculation: Sodom and Gomorrah (Jude 7), Cain (11), as also the fallen angels (6). But this does not exhaust the polemical material of the author, and there can be no doubt that all the exhorbitant abuse of the opponents, though written in rather good Greek, derives from Jewish apocalyptic materials, specifically written sources, of which only the *Assumption of Moses* (Jude 9) and the *Apocalypse of Enoch* (Jude 14f) can still be identified. In each case the purpose of the invective is the threat of punishment in the last judgment, interrupted several times by a disapproving characterization of the opponents, whom the author castigates unmercifully. Such uncompromising polemics can only be explained on the basis of an apocalyptic view of past history and the present which divides all humanity into two groups: the elect and the wicked. This reveals to us one of the strongest motivations for the enforcement of an increasingly sharp division in the ancient church between orthodoxy and heresy; the fundamental apocalyptic perspective that appears in Jude demands this division. But in the situation in which this letter was written, this has by no means been accomplished, since the gnostics who are attacked here still participate in the meetings and common meals of the church (Jude 12). The letter nonetheless demonstrates that the renewal of apocalyptic thought would necessarily lead to a rejection of the peaceful coexistence of various competing factions within

Christianity. The struggle for the purity of the Christian church is also visible in other testimonies of the renewal of Christian apocalypticism.

(c) Criticism of the Apocalyptic Expectation: The Revelation of John

Second Thessalonians may have been an isolated phenomenon within the continuing history of the Pauline churches, and the origin and date of Jude must remain doubtful. But the Revelation of John clearly demonstrates that the renewal of apocalypticism was a widespread phenomenon in the Pauline churches of Asia Minor at the end of I CE. The Revelation of John would be completely misunderstood if it were seen as a book of apocalyptic propaganda. Its intention is rather a critical discussion of already existing apocalyptic views and speculations. Although apocalyptic concepts and traditions are widely used in the writing, the designation "apocalypse" was poorly chosen for this Christian book which, contrary to its original intentions, has been used repeatedly throughout the history of Christianity as a source and inspiration for apocalyptic and chiliastic (millenarian) movements.

While apocalyptic books were usually written under the pseudonym of some ancient biblical authority, such as Enoch, Ezra, Daniel, and others, the Revelation of John is not pseudepigraphical, nor does it locate its

Bibliography to §12.1c: Commentaries

R. H. Charles, *A Critical and Exegetical Commentary on the Revelation of St. John* (2 vols.; ICC; Edinburgh: Clark, 1920, and reprints). Classic commentary with rich materials.

Wilhelm Bousset, *Die Offenbarung Johannis* (KEK; 6th ed.; Göttingen: Vandenhoeck & Ruprecht, 1906).

Heinrich Kraft, *Die Offenbarung des Johannes* (HNT 16a; Tübingen: Mohr/ Siebeck, 1974).

Bibliography to §12.1c: Studies

Austin Farrer, *A Rebirth of Images* (Westminster: Decre, 1949).

Günther Bornkamm, "Die Komposition der apokalyptischen Visionen in der Offenbarung Johannis" in: idem, *Studien zu Antike und Christentum* (3d ed.; München: Kaiser, 1969) 204–22.

Adela Yarbro Collins, *The Combat Myth in the Book of Revelation* (HDR 9; Missoula: Scholars Press, 1976).

Idem, "The Political Perspective of the Revelation to John," *JBL* 96 (1977) 241–56.

Elisabeth Schüssler Fiorenza, *Priester für Gott: Studien zum Herrschafts- und Priestermotiv in der Apokalypse* (Münster: Aschendorff, 1972).

J. Lambrecht (ed.), *L'Apocalypse johannique et l'apocalyptique dans le Nouveau Testament* (BETL 53; Gembloux: Duclot, and Louvain: Leuven University, 1980).

Eduard Lohse, "Die alttestamentliche Sprache des Sehers Johannes," *ZNW* 52 (1961) 122–26.

Dieter Georgi, "Die Visionen vom himmlischen Jerusalem in Apk 21 und 22," in: *Kirche: Festschrift Bornkamm,* 351–72.

August Strobel, "Abfassung und Geschichtstheologie der Apokalypse nach Kap. 17,9–12," *NTS* 10 (1963/64) 433–45.

Head and Arm of the Statue of Domitian

Found in Ephesus in the vaults of the support structure for a large temple of the "Lord and God Domitian," which was built in that city while the prophet John was in exile on the island of Patmos.

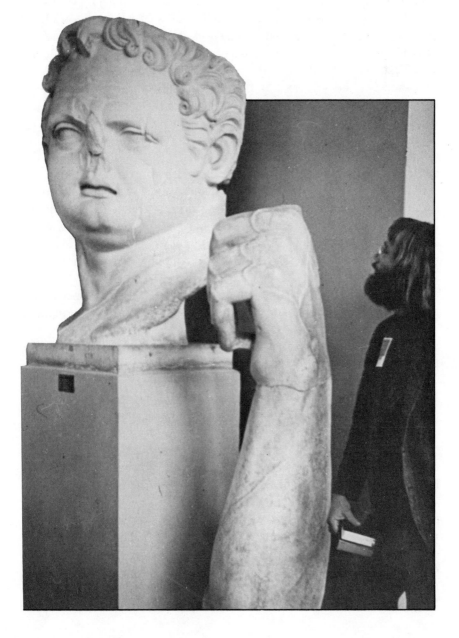

visions in some fictitious place. There is no reason to doubt that the book was written by "John" (Rev 1:1, 9) and that the place at which the book was written was indeed the Aegean island of Patmos (1:9). Unfortunately, however, we do not know anything else about the identity of this "John"; he cannot be identified with the author of the Gospel of John due to the differences in language and terminology, and the completely different mode of theological concepts and argument. The author had a very good knowledge of the situation of the churches of Asia Minor to which he directed his book. He must have been one of the leaders of those churches, and the Christians in those cities must have known quite well who "John" was. Ephesus, the address of the first of seven letters (2:1–7), may have been the city of his own church. It is therefore possible to assume that the reputation of this "John of Ephesus" led to the establishment of an Ephesian Johannine tradition which was later understood as originating from "John the son of Zebedee," and which in turn attracted the tradition of the Gospel of John and of the Johannine Epistles to this city. But the author of Revelation did not know these writings, nor any existing authority of John, and he does not make any attempt to construct a fictitious situation as the framework of his writing, whether for himself or for the churches to which he writes. The fact that he was "on the island of Patmos on account of the word of God and the testimony of Jesus" (1:9) indicates that his ministry as a Christian missionary and officer of the church had led to his exile.

The book thus had its origin in a time of persecution, more specifically in a time of persecution which seemed to threaten all Christians and whose first beginnings were already visible (see, e.g., 2:13, and especially the references to a general persecution in 3:10; 6:9, etc.). Can we be more precise as to the date of composition of the book? According to Revelation 13 and 17, the general persecution is expected to be unleashed by the Roman state: the animal from the abyss is the Roman emperor; Babylon is the city of Rome. Before the middle of II CE there were only two periods in which the Christians, as well as many other people, might have believed that the Roman emperor was indeed the destroyer of a just state order and a blasphemer of God: the second half of the reign of Nero (54–68) and the last years of the reign of Domitian (81–96). But the persecution of the Christians by Nero seems to have been limited to the city of Rome, and although Nero had a morbid desire to celebrate himself in public, he did not promote the emperor cult systematically (§6.2a). The situation which must be presupposed for the Revelation of John, therefore, can be more credibly identified as that of Domitian's religious policies and his request to be worshiped as "Lord and God" (*dominus et deus*) even during his lifetime, a demand that he cruelly enforced (§6.2b; 6.5b).

To be sure, even Domitian never ordered a worldwide persecution of the Christians. Most of the sufferings were inflicted upon people in the city of Rome, where the "philosophers" were expelled, the Christians persecuted (see *1 Clement;* §12.2e), and even members of the imperial family executed, perhaps because of their inclinations to Christianity. The effects were less strongly felt elsewhere. But Asia Minor, which increasingly became a center of the imperial cult, seems to have been concerned to a considerable degree. Domitian ordered the building of a large temple in Ephesus to serve his divine veneration. The large vaulted supports for this temple are still preserved, and the head and arm of a colossal statue of the god Domitian can still be admired in the Ephesus museum. At the same time, Asia Minor seems to have suffered considerably from the increasing economic difficulties that arose during Domitian's reign; this may be reflected in the remark in Rev 6:6. Western Asia Minor, with its quickly-growing Christian communities, would have provided the best conditions for a development in which the uncertain political situation of Christianity could deteriorate into a direct confrontation with the Roman state.

Such a situation created for the first time in the history of Christianity the alternative between "Christ or Caesar." Thus the Christians were challenged to clarify what their talk about the rule of Christ really meant in relation to a particular political situation. Domitian's claim to be a ruling deity provided that challenge. The formula about the "authority that comes from God" which Christianity had inherited from diaspora Judaism and which Paul quoted in Rom 13:1ff was called into serious question. The gnostic alternative of Christian theology could find a way around this problem because the whole visible world, and thus also its history, could be explained away as if it were just a nightmare. However terrible it might seem, it was nothing but the world of error, of the demiurge and his demons, in no way acceptable, but ultimately without reality or substance. But from the perspective of belief in a history that was directed by God and was expected to move towards a goal ordained by God, it was necessary to find an answer which could make the experiences of the deeply troubled and persecuted Christian church meaningful. The author of the Revelation of John set out to answer this question in his book.

Our difficulties in understanding this book arise from its pervasive use of apocalyptic language, images, concepts, and metaphors, which often conceal the political and historical references of the writing. The general mythological worldview of the time cannot by itself explain the extent of apocalyptic language used here. There were alternatives: Josephus, for example, a contemporary of the author of Revelation, used the medium of apologetic history. But apocalyptic language offered opportunities of linguistic expression which the Christian churches had learned to use in increasing measure. In Judaism, apocalyptic language was used as an instrument to interpret the world and its history. It put present as well as future events into a perspective of proper distance, thus allowing the community of the elect to be confident and hopeful and not disturbed by the bewildering events of the present times.

As we have seen, this was how the author of 2 Thessalonians had already used the apocalyptic schema (§12.1a). Similarly, the apocalyptic writings of Ezra (*4 Ezra*) and Baruch (*2 Baruch*) had used this schema to explain the situation of Judaism after the destruction of Jerusalem (§6.6f). On the other hand, apocalyptic concepts had also invaded the areas of religious and political propaganda. The Jewish War and the fall of Jerusalem were stark evidence of its effectiveness. The author of Revelation, himself of Jewish origin, was thoroughly trained in the tradition of this apocalyptic interpretation of history. His theological language thus forced him to explore the possibilities, consequences, and limitations of apocalyptic concepts and the apocalyptic worldview in order to find a hearing in the churches to which he wrote. The challenge arose from the confrontation of the worship of the emperor; the author wrote at a time when apocalyptic interpretations of this situation had become more and more popular. Thus, his book, which is the longest New Testament writing next to the Gospels and Acts, extensively used religious traditions of Jewish, pagan, and Christian origin, drawn primarily from materials of Jewish and Jewish-Christian apocalypticism. The Old Testament plays an important role and is frequently used, though it is never explicitly quoted. Phrasings from the Old Testament are often more closely related to the Hebrew text than to the Greek translation (the LXX).

The language of the book fits the rules of Greek prose only very poorly, while the poetic portions (hymns, doxologies, prayers) reflect the style of Semitic poetry. This fact, however, will justify neither a hypothesis of the use of written sources translated from Hebrew or Aramaic, nor the assumption of a recension of an older Jewish or Jewish-Christian writing. The temptation to make recourse to such theories is indeed great, especially since Revelation cannot be understood as a neat description of consecutive events in past, present, and future. We must take into account both the peculiarities of apocalyptic language as well as its methods of introducing new interpretations into traditional units. Apocalyptic language prefers associations within a sequence of images to a logical progression of thought; it permits individual features and metaphors to stand side by side without connections rather than composing them into a coherent picture; it repeats traditional materials without commentary and then unexpectedly indicates the direction of a new interpretation through striking omissions or additions. The special views of the author will not always find expression within the various images of the visions, but rather in their order, sequence, and numbers, in comments and interpolations, interruptions of the context, and hymnic, liturgical, and parenetic additions.

The author of Revelation uses as a primary ordering device an arrangement of seven scenes of visions in each section. The introduction (Rev 1:1–20) leads to seven letters to the churches in Ephesus, Smyrna, Pergamum, Thyatira, Sardis, Philadelphia, and Laodicea (2:1–3:22). This designates the whole book as a circular letter to the church at large. But even if we see the communities that are addressed here as representatives of generally applicable situations, the author refers to real, not fictitious, situations; the parenetic sections are specific. The seven letters are formulated according to the schema derived from the Old Testament covenant form as it was modified in the period of early Judaism. There is a basic statement in which Christ introduces himself in the authority of his saving activity, a narrative of the history of the church in question, a call for repentance, and an announcement of curses and blessings (in that order). Heretical teachers in the churches are repeatedly mentioned (2:6, 9, 14f, 20–24; 3:9) and variously identified as adherents of the teaching of Balaam, as disciples of the prophetess Jezebel, as Nicolaites, and as the Synagogue of Satan. Since the author twice refers to those "who say that they are Jews" (Rev 2:9; 3:9), and the opponents are called those who learn "the deep things of Satan" (2:24), the opponents were perhaps Jewish-Christian gnostics. But it is not possible to be certain about the character of the heresy or heresies attacked here. Apocalyptic admonition is styled as a request to separate from the heretics (cf. Jude).

The cycles of the visions are introduced by a throne vision which draws upon materials from the Old Testament, especially Isaiah 6 and Ezekiel 1 (Rev 4:1–11). The appearance of a scroll with seven seals (5:1–2), according to the pattern of a traditional vision, should point to a following scene of disclosure, including the opening of the scroll, proclamation of its content, and commissioning of the prophet. At this point, however, the author has radically revised his traditional material and introduced an interpretation that contradicts the intention of the genre of an apocalyptic book. Instead of the disclosure scene and commissioning, the author introduces a new figure, the Lion of Judah, the Lamb "as though it had been slain" (5:5f). The following hymns and doxologies reveal who this figure is: the savior, "who by his blood has ransomed humanity for God" (5:9). His task, however, is by no means—as would be expected—to disclose the content of the scroll. Rather, the authority of universal rule is transferred to him, and this is acknowledged by the entire celestial court. Everything that is said in the following chapters is not a revelation in the style of an apocalyptic book, but a description of this universal rule of Christ in historical perspective.

The following cycles of visions repeatedly demonstrate a similar procedure of the author in the revision of his traditional materials. The vision of the seven seals (6:1–8:1) is not simply a description of the course of the world until its end, but includes various subjects (four riders, sealing of the elect). But the framework has theological significance: the openings of the seals are not scenes of disclosure, but demonstrations of the authoritative rule of Christ. The first impression is misleading, that the sequence of events (war, hunger, death, cosmic catastrophe) is aimed at a final climax to be reported with the breaking of the seventh seal. The description of the final climax is omitted, and what follows upon the impressive introduction (8:1–2) is deliberately anti-climactic (8:3–5). Instead, only a new sequence of seven visions is introduced, namely, the seven trumpets (8:6–11:19). The reader is expected to learn that even the terrible events of the past and present are demonstrations of Christ's rule, and the martyrs and the elect are in his hands (6:9–11; 7:1–17). The vision of the seven trumpets is revised in an analogous fashion; but the terror of the events is intensified (8:6–9:21). Yet with the sixth trumpet the description of these events is abruptly ended without having reached its climax: the seventh trumpet, which appears in 11:15–19 like an appendix, simply grants a view of the heavenly temple. Between the sixth and the seventh trumpet the author inserts a report of the commissioning of the prophet (10:1–11) and introduces for the first time in these visions references to events of the recent past of Christian history (the fall of Jerusalem and the martyrdom of the two witnesses; we do not know who these two witnesses were; 11:1–14). This also makes it clear that so far the author had not spoken about the present at all, but only about the past and about Christ's general direction of the course of history. One striking difference from the customary apocalyptic procedure in the description of past events is the deliberate suppression of all direct references to known historical events, with the noted exception of 11:1–14.

The visions of the second part of the book (12:1–22:5) are also arranged according to the schema of "seven." With the exception of 16:1–21, however, there is no longer any explicit counting. There are three cycles: the first begins with the vision of the woman clothed with the sun (12:1ff) and ends with the vision of the sea of glass (15:2–8); the second comprises the visions of the seven bowls of wrath (16:1–21); the third begins with the vision of the enthronement of the Logos (19:11ff) and ends with the vision of the new heaven and new earth (21:1ff). The large excursus about Babylon (= Rome) appears between the second and third cycles (17:1–19:10). The contrast with the cycles of the first part of the book is obvious:

in the second part each cycle begins with the recent past, or even with the future (19:11ff); that is to say, these visions describe the events of the present time under the perspective of universal history. The reader is made to understand that the controversy of the rule of Christ with the Roman state that is now beginning is the culmination of the divinely ordained course of history. Rev 12:1–15:8, the first cycle, includes the events from the birth of the Messiah and the foundation of the Christian church (12:1–18; pagan mythological materials are used here) to the parousia (14:14–20) and the eschatological adoration (15:2–4).

The primary focus is upon the appearance of the opponent of God, namely, the Roman state (13:1–10) and its ruler (13:11–18). For the first time, the occurrence of evil in the world is ascribed to a power opposed to God. As the instrument of the exercise of this evil power, the author points to the worship of the Antichrist which perverts and destroys the life of all nations (13:6–10, 15–17). Its only alternative is faithfulness to the Lamb (14:1–5). Eschatological evil is thus reduced to the worship of Satanic power as documented in the emperor cult. The problem of Rome is the central theme, discussed fully in 17:1–19:10 and introduced by the vision of the seven bowls of wrath (15:1, 5–8; 16:1–21). Most striking are the extensive interpretations of the visions of the animals (13:1ff) and the Whore of Babylon (17:1–18). Specific historical references are included repeatedly, though not all of them are still clear to the modern reader. But it is very plausible that the number 666 (13:18) as well as the number 8 $(17:11; 1 + 2 + 3 \ldots + 8 = 36; 1 + 2 + 3 \ldots + 36 = 666)$ and the interpretation of the animal (13:3; 17:10–12) refer to the expected return of Nero. In the statements about Rome, criticism of the world-ruling power of the Roman economy and its trade is the central point. The author understands the emperor cult as an instrument devised to strengthen Rome's claim to economic domination of the world (18:11–19). The last cycle (19:11–22:4)—only at this point is the eschatological future described for the reader—resumes earlier topics with the vision of the enthronement of the Logos (19:11–16) and of Rome's military defeat (19:17–21). The concluding vision of the heavenly Jerusalem, a metropolis of huge dimensions (21:9–22:5), is the true counterpart to the vision of Babylon. The traditional apocalyptic materials used in these last visions are interpreted primarily in terms of pastoral theology, especially the vision of the binding of Satan and the thousand-year kingdom (20:1–6). The author wants to show that the martyrs and other faithful Christians will receive an immediate reward that is independent of the last judgment (20:11–15). The outline of the book itself already demonstrates that it is not an apocalyptic writing in the usual sense of the genre. John does more than reveal the future; he wants to illuminate the significance of the events of the present from the perspectives of a world history which is supported by faith in the sovereignty of God. The book does not reveal secret knowledge: its sealing as a secret apocalyptic writing is explicitly prohibited (22:10). Whatever is said about the events taking place in heaven is not directed to the wise man, who mediates knowledge of heavenly secrets, but is directed to the entire Christian community. The key for participation in the heavenly events is not the learning of divine insights, but the hymns and songs of the church which are introduced at decisive points of the composition of the book. Even the first adoration of the Lamb as ruler of the universe is explicitly designated as the offering of the "prayers of the saints," who are the Christian community (5:8). In fact, almost all of the decisive statements about the rule and victory of God or Christ are presented in the form of hymns and doxologies of the martyrs and faithful believers (see 15:2-4, and especially the invitation to praise God which is issued to "all his servants who fear him, small and great," 19:5). It is unimportant whether such hymns are real hymnic pieces that were used by the churches—which is not impossible—or compositions of the author himself. The function of the hymns in the composition of the book is what matters. They unite the announcement of Christ's victory inseparably with the confession and hymnic praise of the church.

Even though the Revelation of John is directly focused upon the problems of its own time and can only be understood within its own historical situation, the rejection or acceptance of the book in the history of the Christian churches was always based upon the understanding of the writing as a revelation that was focused exclusively upon the future and the heavenly realities. In II CE, Papias of Hierapolis, Justin, Irenaeus, and Melito of Sardis spoke about Revelation in approving terms. But in III and IV CE, the Greek-speaking eastern churches became increasingly critical (Dionysius of Alexandria, Eusebius of Caesarea). The book is even missing in several lists of canonical writings and many Greek manuscripts of the Bible. In the churches of the west, criticism began in the time of the Reformation (Luther doubted its canonicity), continued in the Enlightenment, and continues still today. On the other hand, beginning in antiquity Christian sects have employed the book with great frequency, especially for the proclamation of the coming of the thousand-year kingdom; for this expectation, and in general for the belief in an imminent end of the world and second coming of Christ, Revelation has provided both inspiration and arguments throughout Christian history. But only a critical interpretation of the writing, which pays close attention to the relationship of tradition and redaction, and to the function of the individual sections within the total composition in the light of its historical situation, is to give the Revelation of John the hearing it deserves. Especially in the discussion of the relationship of Christianity to the state and society this early Christian book is an extremely significant voice.

(d) Apocalyptic Ordering of Christian Life: The Shepherd of Hermas

The central point of the letters to the churches in the Revelation of John was the call to conversion, based upon the expectation of Christ's coming in the near future. But there is no detailed exposition of the ordering of moral conduct under this eschatological perspective in the book; the prophetic interpretation of the historical events of the present did not permit an exposition of the moral rules of conduct in the Christian life. It would require a renewal of the apocalyptic call to conversion without a prophetic interpretation of the present time to provide an opportunity to focus on the problems of morality and Christian conduct. Such tendencies are visible in the influx of Jewish moral teachings into the tradition of the words of Jesus (§10.1c). That this development could be accelerated by the renewal of the prophetic call for conversion is evident in the work which is preserved under the title of the *Shepherd of Hermas*.

In contrast to the Book of Revelation, *Hermas* provides almost no information about the time and situation of its origin. To be sure, Rome is named as the author's city of residence (*Vis.* 1.1.1), and places from the vicinity of Rome also appear (*Vis.* 1.1.3; 2.1.1; 4.1.3), although a later vision is located in Arcadia (*Sim.* 9.1.4). Information about typical Roman situations is missing. But since the *Muratorian Canon* points to a Roman origin for the writing, and since *Vis.* 2.4.3 mentions a certain Clement (see §12.2e on *1 Clement*), it is difficult to argue against a Ro-

Bibliography to §12.1d: Texts

Molly Whittaker, *Der Hirt des Hermas* (GCS, Die Apostolischen Väter 1; Berlin: Akademie-Verlag, 1956).

Lake, *ApostFath*, 2. 1–305.

Bibliography to §12.1d: Commentaries

Graydon F. Snyder, *Hermas* (Grant, *ApostFath* 6).

Martin Dibelius, *Der Hirt des Hermas* (HNT.E 4; Tübingen: Mohr/Siebeck, 1923).

Bibliography to §12.1d: Studies

Lage Pernveden, *The Concept of the Church in the Shepherd of Hermas* (STL 27; Lund: Gleerup, 1966).

J. Reiling, *Hermas and Christian Prophecy: A Study of the Eleventh Mandate* (NovTSup 37; Leiden: Brill, 1973).

Erik Peterson, "Beiträge zur Interpretation der Visionen im Pastor Hermae," "Kritische Analyse der Fünften Vision des Hermas," "Die Begegnung mit dem Ungeheuer," "Die Taufe im Acherusischen See," in: idem, *Frühkirche, Judentum und Gnosis: Studien und Untersuchungen* (Rom/Freiburg/Wien: Herder, 1959) 254–332.

man provenance for the book. The manuscript tradition shows that it was used in the western churches. The text is completely preserved only in two Latin manuscripts. The original Greek text was not known until its discovery in 1855 in a Greek manuscript from xv CE on Mt. Athos, in which the end of *Similitude* 9 and *Similitude* 10 are missing. The famous Codex Sinaiticus, discovered by Tischendorf (§7.2c), provided a second witness for a portion of the Greek text; here, however, the text breaks off with *Vis.* 4.3.6 (*Hermas* is the last writing in this manuscript of the Greek Bible). The book was known in Egypt at an early date, as is shown by a Greek papyrus fragment from the end of II CE (Pap. Michigan 130), several quotations in Clement of Alexandria, and a more extensive Greek papyrus from III CE (Pap. Michigan 129, which contains *Sim.* 2.9–9.5.1).

The external evidence for the book thus proves that it was written no later than the middle of II CE, but a more exact dating is difficult. Other early Christian writings are never quoted; but that does not mean that the author did not know them because he also does not quote the Old Testament, although there can be no doubt that he knew it well (only once does he quote anything explicitly, the lost pseudepigraphical writing *Eldad and Modad,* in *Vis.* 2.3.4). Parallels to the parables of the Synoptic Gospels (especially the parable of the good servant, *Sim.* 5.2 and 5.4–7) are best explained as reflecting a knowledge of the parables of Jesus from the oral tradition. *Hermas* knows the Christian offices of apostle, bishop, teacher, and deacon (*Vis.* 3.5.1); prophets are also mentioned (e.g., *Mandate* 11). *Sim.* 9.16.5 speaks about the descent to Hades of the apostles and teachers for the preaching and baptism of the dead. None of these elements, however, is clear enough to allow a more precise dating, though a somewhat earlier date within the period from 60 to 160 CE seems to be preferable. If the Clement who is mentioned in *Vis.* 2.4.3 is the secretary of the Roman church to whom we owe *1 Clement,* a date about the year 100 would be in order.

The dating, of course, is made more difficult by the author's use of extensive source materials and traditions for the composition of his writing. The first part, the five *Visions,* though no doubt written by a Christian author, never uses the name of Jesus Christ! The "Church," a female figure appearing in the first three visions as an old woman who becomes younger with each appearance, is borrowed from the Jewish figure of Wisdom. According to *Vis.* 2.4.1 she is the first creature of God, the one through whom the world has been created. The vision of the building of the tower (*Vision* 3) originally depicted the creation of the world; the six young men who build the tower "are the holy angels of God, who were created first, to whom the Lord delivered all his creation to make it increase, and to build it up, and to rule the whole creation" (*Vis.* 3.4.1). The interpretation of the tower as the church is therefore secondary. The animal vision (*Vision* 4) also originally had no Christian components. The animal symbolizes the coming tribulations, and its four colors symbolize this aeon, its destruction, the salvation of the elect, and the coming aeon. Finally, the "Shepherd" who appears to Hermas in order to reveal the commandments to him (*Vision* 5) has not been sent by Christ, but by the "most reverend angel," and only a very careful reader of the book can discover that this angel is identical with the "Son of God." The Christian interpretation which was secondarily attached to this basically Jewish material is closely connected with the commission to proclaim a final chance for repentance before the building of the tower (i.e., the church) is completed; note the charge to preach repentance (*Vis.* 2.2), the interpretation of the stones for the building as different categories of believers (*Vis.* 3.5–7), the presentation of the Christian virtues (*Vis.* 3.8), and the explanation of the three different appearances of the "Church" (*Vis.* 3.10–13).

The second part of the writing, the *Mandates,* is also mostly composed of traditional Jewish materials. *Mandates* 2–10 and 12 treat a series of virtues and vices, often in appropriate juxtapositions (e.g., truthfulness/lying). The material is taken from the tradition of the doctrine of the two ways and is closely related to *Didache* 1–6 and the Letter of James (§10.1c), but *Hermas* speaks about the two spirits seeking abode in the human heart, the holy and the evil spirit. This section of moral teaching is introduced by the primary commandment to believe in the one god who has created and preserves everything (*Mand.* 1). From faith comes fear of god, from fear of god comes self-control, which leads to the virtue of righteousness (*Mand.* 1.2). This terminology points to the realm of Hellenistic Jewish moral teaching. Specifically Christian issues rarely occur. *Mand.* 4.2–3 is an insertion that expresses the primary interest of the author, namely, repentance offered as a single and unrepeatable opportunity to those who have been baptized earlier in life. The instruction about the distinction between the true and the false prophet (*Mandate* 11) is also a Christian addition.

The third part of *Hermas,* the *Similitudes,* is based upon a collection of parables which certainly has a Jewish origin. The parable of the man living in a foreign city (*Similitude* 1) treats the topic of human life in the world as a sojourn in an alien world, something that is frequently discussed by the Jewish philosopher Philo of Alexandria. The parable about the elm tree and the vine that the tree supports illustrates the relationship of rich and poor in the church (*Similitude* 2); it might be a parable of pagan origin, but it nonetheless illuminates a special interest of the author. The parables of the dry trees (*Similitude* 3) and of the sprouting trees (*Similitude* 4) aid in discussing the situation of the righteous and the unrighteous in this aeon, and how the righteous who belong to the coming aeon should bear fruit. A christological interpretation appears for the first time in the book with the parable of *Sim.* 5.2, about the good servant (*Sim.* 5.4–7; the sections on fasting, *Sim.* 5.1 and 3, appear to be later interpolations and do not belong to this context). The Son of God who, together with the angels, aids the master of the vineyard in planting (and also gives the law to the people) is the Holy Spirit; the good servant who works in the vineyard is "a flesh" in whom the Holy Spirit dwells, thus making the servant the Son of God and fellow heir. The christology of this, the only passage in the whole writing which alludes to Jesus, is adoptionist. The author has once more inserted a reference to the topic of repentance: the lord of the vineyard delays his return in order to provide an opportunity for repentance. The same theme appears at the end of the parable of the evil shepherd (*Similitude* 6) by way of introducing the angel of punishment (*Sim.* 6.3–4), and through an admonition for repentance directed to the house of Hermas (*Similitude* 7).

The parable of the willow tree (*Similitude* 8) shows the Jewish origin of the material most clearly: the angel who cuts off the branches from the tree and gives them to the people is Michael, who sets the law into the hearts of the people; the tree itself is the law, which is proclaimed to all nations (*Sim.* 8.3.2–3). This is thus an eschatological parable that speaks of the general validity of the law for Israel and for the nations in the coming rule of God. A secondary Christian interpretation explains the parable in terms of repentance and conversion (*Sim.* 8.4–11). The last parable, *Similitude* 9 (10 is a final admonition of the Shepherd) has been expanded by the author into an elaborate allegory that constitutes almost a quarter of the entire writing. Older materials seem to have been used in the vision of the twelve mountains (*Sim.* 9.1), which originally referred to the twelve tribes of Israel (*Sim.* 9.17.1), and which the author then explains in a long-winded allegory as "the tribes who inhabit the world," to whom the Son of God was preached through the apostles (*Sim.* 9.17–31).

But between this parable and its interpretation the author placed a vision of the building of the tower of the church (*Sim.* 9.3–4) which is reminiscent of the vision of the tower in *Vision* 3, but departs from it in many points of detail. This parable is the central part of the book. Its allegorical interpretations are complex and repeatedly contradict each other. For example, not only the rock on which the church is built, as well as the door through which the believers enter into the kingdom of God, but finally also the lord of the building are explained as the "Son of God" (*Sim.* 9.12). On the whole, the figure of the "Son of God" is presented in such cosmic dimensions that a direct function in the process of salvation can no longer be ascribed to Christ. Even a relationship between the Son of God and the prophets who are charged with the preaching of repentance is consciously avoided; mediators are introduced instead. The highest angel sends the Shepherd, who instructs the prophet with his message of repentance. Twelve heavenly virgins are sent to the prophet on behalf of the practice of virtue: Hermas spends a night with these virgins "like a brother, not like a husband" (*Sim.* 9.11). Because of the distance to which Christ has been moved in the fullness of his power which transcends time and world, Christian existence becomes completely moralized, especially in view of the urgency of the message of repentance. To be sure, the author can use phrases that are reminiscent of Paul to describe the unity of the church: the church is "one spirit, one body" (*Sim.* 9.13.5)—but this unity rests primarily on the fact that every Christian is obligated to fulfill the same moral commandments. The order for the life and conduct of the church is related to an apocalyptic image, the building of the tower of the church, which has such fixed cosmic dimensions, transcending all earthly experience, that the thought of a historical responsibility of the Christian community cannot even arise. Consistent apocalypticism—in contrast to the Revelation of John—therefore leads to a denial of any historical responsibility of the Christian community in favor of a morality of personal sanctification.

2. The Transformation of Pauline Theology into Ecclesiastical Doctrine

(a) The Conflict with Syncretism: The Epistle to the Colossians

In the radical apocalypticism that was encountered in the *Shepherd of Hermas,* the basic theological problems showed themselves most clearly in christology. The expansion of the divine nature of the Son of God into the cosmic dimensions of the eschatological world ruler arose from the use of categories drawn from apocalyptic mythology. This is also the case for the Revelation of John; but there the process of a full mythologization of the figure of Christ is checked by the image of the Lamb that was slain, that is, by a reference to the historical event of the crucifixion. Wherever recourse to the suffering, death, and resurrection of Jesus is missing, there are no limits to the rise of cosmological speculation in christological developments. In this respect, apocalypticism and Gnosticism are united. Belief in the cosmic Christ figure also appears very early in the Pauline churches. It was not difficult to claim Paul as an authority for such views because Paul himself had presented Jesus as the eschatological ruler of the cosmos (see 1 Cor 15:25) and as a heavenly figure whose origins were that of a divine being (Phil 2:5f), in each case using apocalyptic or gnostic traditions. The controversy with such views, therefore, involved the questions of the legitimate interpretation of Paul; an important problem centered on whether the criterion of the death of Jesus on the cross, crucially important for Paul himself, would still play a central role in the further development of christological concepts.

This consideration, as well as much of the following discussion in this chapter, is part of a complex problem of early Christian history which is often called "deutero-Paulinism"; more recently some have come to call it the problem of the "Pauline school." The question of the redaction and publication of the Pauline letters is closely related. First of all, it is by no means necessarily the case that, in the generation after Paul, when one referred to "Paul" this meant the Pauline letters. On the contrary, after his death Paul was known as a missionary and martyr. As will become evident in the following discussion, the legend of the great apostle, prob-

Bibliography to §12.2

Hans von Campenhausen, *Ecclesiastical Authority and Spiritual Power in the Church of the First Three Centuries* (Stanford, CA: Stanford University, 1969).

Ernst Käsemann, "Paul and Early Catholicism," in: idem, *New Testament Questions,* 236–51.

Andreas Lindemann, *Paulus im ältesten Christentum: Das Bild des Apostels und die Rezeption der paulinischen Theologie in der frühchristlichen Literatur* (BHTh 58; Tübingen: Mohr/Siebeck, 1979).

Ernst Dassmann, *Der Stachel im Fleisch: Paulus in der frühchristlichen Literatur bis Irenäus* (Münster: Aschendorff, 1979).

Ulrich Luz, "Erwägungen zur Entstehung des 'Frühkatholizismus,'" *ZNW* 65 (1974) 88–111.

Hans-Martin Schenke, "Das Weiterwirken des Paulus und die Pflege seines Erbes durch die Paulus-Schule," *NTS* 21 (1975) 505–18. Good exposition of the problem with relevant bibliography.

Hans Conzelmann, "Die Schule des Paulus," in *Theologia Crucis—Signum Crucis: Festschrift Erich Dinkler* (Tübingen: Mohr/Siebeck, 1979) 85–96.

Bibliography to §10.2a: Commentaries

Eduard Lohse, *Colossians and Philemon: A Commentary on the Epistles to the Colossians and to Philemon* (Hermeneia; Philadelphia: Fortress, 1971).

C. F. D. Moule, *The Epistles to the Colossians and Philemon* (CGTC; Cambridge: Cambridge University, 1957).

Bibliography to §12.2a: Studies

Wayne A. Meeks and Fred O. Francis (eds.), *Conflict at Colossae: A Problem in the Interpretation of Early Christianity, Illustrated by Selected Modern Studies* (SBLSBS 4; Missoula: Scholars Press, 1973).

Hans-Martin Schenke, "Der Widerstreit gnostischer und kirchlicher Theologie im Spiegel des Kolosserbriefes," *ZThK* 61 (1964) 391–403.

James E. Crouch, *The Origin and Intention of the Colossian Haustafel* (FRLANT 109; Göttingen: Vandenhoeck & Ruprecht, 1972).

James M. Robinson, "A Formal Analysis of Colossians 1:15–20," *JBL* 76 (1957) 270–87.

ably dating back to Paul's own lifetime, certainly preceded the knowledge of the letters he had written. Secondly, Paul's letters must at first have been received and read in much the spirit in which they were written: as occasional writings. They were read by those to whom they were written, and then filed away, probably for decades.

Hypotheses about the eventual publication of the Pauline letters have been advanced, but no such suggestion has yet fully explained the beginning of the process, that is, the recourse to one or several Pauline letters in the composition of each of the deutero-Pauline letters, and the editing of the correspondence directed to one particular church into a single letter (see §7.3d on 2 Corinthians and Philippians). Such compositions reveal a desire to produce readable and instructive guides for the continuing efforts of Paul's successors to stabilize the life of their churches and to defend the Pauline legacy against attacks from opponents. It is not possible to say with any certainty when the larger collections of Pauline (and deutero-Pauline) letters were made and published. But the developments discussed in this chapter belong to the period of the editing of individual letters and various stages in their collection. The fact that the Pauline school engaged in such an endeavor is quite extraordinary in view of the continuing impact of the image of Paul as a powerful apostle and martyr. In each deutero-Pauline letter, that image is referred to in some way. But the uniqueness of the development of the Pauline legacy is found in the conscious effort to preserve and propagate Paul's thought through his correspondence, a process which is visible in the development of the deutero-Pauline letters.

The Epistles to the Colossians and Ephesians belong to this history of the Pauline churches. Many scholars presume that both epistles were written by Paul, while others agree that Ephesians is deutero-Pauline, but ascribe Colossians to Paul. There are good reasons for this position, especially since Ephesians shows many signs of literary dependence upon Colossians. The numerous, sometimes word-for-word agreements between the two letters are better explained by such a connection than by the assumption of the use of a common source. (A dependence of Colossians upon Ephesians is excluded because the latter often comments upon, corrects and expands the materials of the former.) Linguistic arguments are important, though not fully decisive, for the question of the authorship of Colossians. The letter contains a large number of words that occur in none of the genuine Pauline letters (a total of 48; 33 of these are *hapax legomena*, i.e., words which occur nowhere else in the NT). The author's style is characterized by long sequences of genitive constructions (e.g., "the kingdom of the son of his love," 1:13; "the word of the truth of the gospel that is among you," 1:5f; "putting off the body of the flesh," 2:11) and

combinations of parallel terms ("bearing fruit and growing," 1:6; "praying and petitioning," 1:9; "in all spiritual wisdom and understanding,"
1:9; "for all endurance and patience," 1:11). The author often constructs
long periodic sentences which are difficult to understand (the paragraph
1:9–20 is all one sentence!).

Those linguistic features are rare in Paul's letters, but more important
for the question of authorship is the theological intention of those statements of the letter which show very close resemblances to the terminology
of the Pauline letters. Col 1:13 says that God "has transferred us to the
kingdom of his beloved Son," using the past tense. In the genuine letters of
Paul, however, which always say "kingdom of God" (never "kingdom of
the Son"), the kingdom and one's participation in it are a matter of the
future (e.g., 1 Cor 15:50). According to Col 1:18 and 2:19, Christ is the
head of the church, which is his body. But in Paul, the concept of the head
of the body is missing; rather, in terms of a body, Christ is identical with
the church (1 Cor 12:12; also 10:16; Rom 12:4–5). In the interpretation of
baptism, Col 2:12 and 3:1 state that the Christians have already died and
have already risen with Christ. Paul, however, explicitly rejects this interpretation of baptism and consciously avoids speaking about rising with
Christ as an event of the past (Rom 6:1ff; 1 Thess 4:14ff). These are only
some examples of the most striking differences; analogous observations
can be made in the detailed exegesis of many other passages of Colossians.
We must therefore assume that one of Paul's students wrote this letter in
his name in order to avert a dangerous threat to the church in Colossae,
which had been founded by the Pauline mission.

The references of Colossians to its opponents permit us to reconstruct a
fairly good picture of their teachings. They were claiming to present a
"philosophy" based on traditions (2:8). According to the remarks which
follow, these traditions must have had a Jewish origin because the opponents recommend the observance of dietary rules, festivals of new moons
and sabbaths (2:16), as well as of circumcision (this must have been the
cause for the polemical formulation in 2:11; on the dietary laws, see 2:21).
This is reminiscent of the opponents of Galatians and Philippians (§9.3b,
e), but in the case of Colossians, the cosmic dimensions of these observances of the Jewish law are more clearly visible. The author seems to have
borrowed from his opponents the concept of Christ as the head; the opponents, however, apparently spoke about Christ as the head of the cosmic
hierarchies (principalities and powers, 2:10; cf. 1:16). In order to be
united with Christ, the mediation of angelic powers was needed so that the
believer could be in accord with the cosmic reality of the true body of
Christ ("humility" and service of the angels, 2:18). It is striking that a
term appears in this context which is otherwise attested as a designation of

the initiation into a mystery: "as he has had visions during the mystery rites" (2:18). It is therefore probable that the opponents practiced rites that were analogous to the mysteries and culminated in the "vision" of cosmic powers. It is doubtful, however, that this justifies their characterization as Jewish-Christian gnostics. Certainly the gnostics spoke about cosmic powers and angels, but in the case of the opponents of Colossians, it is more a question of a positive relationship of human beings through the powers to Christ as the head; nothing is said about overcoming those powers. But the opinion that there were such powers, and that especially religiously concerned human beings had to take them into account, was very widespread in that period. The opponents therefore were Jewish-Christian syncretists who wanted to achieve a fresh interpretation of Jewish rites and rules of cultic purity in accord with the religious thinking of their time, thus adapting the worship of Christ to the general world-view of Hellenism.

In the refutation of these opponents, the author of Colossians shows some affinity to Gnosticism. To be sure, he borrows the hymn that speaks about the creation of the powers through Christ (1:15–20), and accepts the formulation about Christ as the head of the powers (2:10), but he argues that with the death of Christ on the cross the principalities and powers were disarmed and publicly exposed in disgrace (2:15). Colossians allows a place for the powers only in the lower regions of the cosmic realm: the Christians are requested to "seek the things that are above, where also Christ is, seated at the right hand of God" (3:1). This redemption is already accomplished for the believers, and the author of Colossians can say, just as a gnostic theologian, that the Christians have already entered the kingdom (1:13). At the same time, he rejects the validity of the law, "the bond that stood against us with its legal demands" (2:14), which Christ has abolished. For the one who has been redeemed by Christ, the commands of the law are only human precepts and doctrines, related solely to the earthly body (2:22–23). Through Christ's death the church is already holy and without blemish (1:22) and needs no further purification through ritual acts because it is exactly this church that is the "body" (see 1:18; "the church" is an addition of the author to the hymn borrowed from his opponents), related directly to the head, Christ, without any mediation through powers of the cosmos (2:19).

This view of salvation that is already realized leaves open the question of the conduct of Christians in this world. Through his criticism of the powers, however, the author has exorcized the demons from the world in which the Christians now live. Christian conduct thus owes nothing to the demons and is capable of meeting the challenge of a secularized morality. Avoiding vice and accepting virtue are called in theological terms "putting on the new human being" (3:10), but there is no reference to the working of good and evil spirits (§12.1d). The table of household duties (*Haustafel,* Col 3:18–4:1) that was taken over from Stoic popular ethics had been and remained a secular instruction for conduct within the existing structures of society. Only the insertion of the phrase "in the Lord" reveals its Christian usage. The greater emphasis upon the mutuality of obligations is probably also new: husbands also have obligations to their wives, parents for their children, and masters have duties toward their slaves. But the normal ordering of society is not questioned on the basis of theological considerations; in fact, it is even defended, because in the Pauline formula "neither Jew nor Greek," and so on (Gal 3:28), Col 3:11 leaves out the phrase "neither male nor female." Tendencies toward emancipation are not supported (perhaps the opponents advocated the emancipation of women). In contrast to the doctrine of his opponents and their ritualistic and apparently ascetic ethics (2:21–22), the author of Colossians promotes an ethical behavior that takes a positive view of the world, although it is an ethics of a church whose "life is hid with Christ in God" (3:3). But the consequences of existence in the world, including the political and social components, are not theologically questioned or elaborated. Paul's eschatological and therefore critical view of existence in the world is missing (cf. 1 Corinthians 7). What the further direction of this development that eliminated both the eschatological and the general religious components of ethical thinking would be will be learned from Ephesians, which presents a new version of Pauline theology in a critical discussion of Colossians.

Colossians was probably written not very long after Paul's missionary activity. The letter continues the Pauline fight for a gentile Christianity that is free from the law and rejects a religious syncretism that would maintain the validity of the (reinterpreted) ritual law. Colossians' claim that the resurrection has already happened for the Christians in their baptism does not require a later date because the opponents of 1 Corinthians may have already spoken in similar terms; Rom 6:1ff demonstrates that Paul himself knew that understanding of baptism, though he rejected it. Nowhere does Colossians show any consciousness of a distance from the time of Paul's ministry. On the contrary, the letter speaks about the suffering of the apostle as if it were still taking place (Col 1:24f), although the concept that in his sufferings Paul completes "what is lacking in Christ's afflictions for the sake of the church" could hardly be ascribed to Paul himself. It is difficult to say how much the names that appear in Col 4:10ff relate to historical reality. Of the ten names, seven also appear in Paul's letter to Philemon and seem to be taken from that letter, which the author of Colossians used as his model. But Tychicus (Col 4:7) appears elsewhere only in the list of the members of the delegation bringing the collection to Jerusalem (Acts 20:4), which seems to be reliable and genuine. It is thus possible that at least some of the names in Colossians derive from a personal knowledge of some of Paul's fellow workers. On the whole, the author seems to depend more upon his familiarity with the Pauline proclamation and mission than upon a knowledge of Paul's letters. In fact, of all the Pauline letters known to us, the author of Colossians seems to have known only Philemon.

(b) The Struggle against Gnosticism: The Epistle to the Ephesians

The situation is quite different with the Epistle to the Ephesians. The distance of the author from the time of Paul cannot be overlooked. The author already knows a collection of the Pauline letters (including Colossians; only 2 Thessalonians is never used) and employs them repeatedly. He also looks back to the time now past of the "holy apostles" (Eph 3:5; 4:11). The preaching to the gentiles, which had been Paul's office, is part of the events of the salvation which took place in the past, and upon which the church is founded (3:1–13). These observations alone would exclude a Pauline authorship of this document. The literary dependence of Ephesians upon Colossians makes Pauline authorship of the former completely

Bibliography to §12.b: Commentaries

John A. Allan, *The Epistle to the Ephesians: Introduction and Commentary* (Torch Bible Commentaries; London: SCM, 1959).

Bibliography to §12.2b: Studies

Edgar J. Goodspeed, *The Meaning of Ephesians* (Chicago: University of Chicago, 1933).

C. Leslie Mitton, *The Epistle to the Ephesians* (London: Oliphants, 1976).

Karl Martin Fischer, *Tendenz und Absicht des Epheserbriefes* (FRLANT 111; Göttingen: Vandenhoeck & Ruprecht, 1973).

Ernst Käsemann, "Ephesians and Acts," in: Leander E. Keck and J. Louis Martyn (eds.), *Studies in Luke-Acts: Essays Presented in Honor of Paul Schubert* (Nashville: Abingdon, 1966) 288–97.

Idem, "Das Interpretationsproblem des Epheserbriefes," in: idem, *Exegetische Versuche und Besinnungen* (Göttingen: Vandenhoeck & Ruprecht, 1964) 2. 253–61.

Andreas Lindemann, *Die Aufhebung der Zeit: Geschichtsverständnis und Eschatologie im Epheserbrief* (StNT 12; Gütersloh: Mohn, 1975).

Idem, "Bemerkungen zu den Adressaten und zum Anlaß des Epheserbriefes," *ZNW* 67 (1976) 235–51.

Peter Pokorný, *Der Epheserbrief und die Gnosis* (Berlin: Evangelische Verlagsanstalt, 1965).

Idem, "Epheserbrief und gnostische Mysterien," *ZNW* 53 (1962) 160–94.

Nils A. Dahl, "Cosmic Dimensions and Religious Knowledge (Eph. 3:18)," in: E. Earle Ellis and Erich Grässer (eds.), *Jesus und Paulus* (Göttingen: Vandenhoeck & Ruprecht, 1975) 57–75.

impossible; for example, the direct quotation about the sending of Tychicus in Eph 6:21 (= Col 4:7) can be explained only on the basis of literary dependence.

Ephesians also further elaborated the theological language of the post-Pauline period, which appeared in its beginnings in Colossians. The literary style of Ephesians is even more laborious and ornate than that of Colossians. Long sequences of combinations of nouns, connected through prepositions or by the use of genitives, are even more frequent (such as, "to the sonship through Jesus Christ to him according to the purpose of his will for the praise of the glory of his grace," 1:5–6). Synonyms are often accumulated ("according to the working of the power of his greatness," 1:19; "fellow heirs and members and partakers," 3:6), and sentences become so extended that the translator is faced with great difficulties. (The following sections are made up of only a single sentence in each instance: 1:3–10; 1:15–21; 3:1–7; 3:8–12; 3:14–19; 4:11–16; the first of these contains no fewer than 130 words!) Yet it is not only the style, but also the theological terminology that is very different from that of Paul, despite many borrowings from Paul's genuine letters. This terminology shows some similarities with the writings from Qumran (§5.3c), while on the other hand there are numerous parallels with other Christian literature produced about the year 100 (such as *1 Clement* and the letters of Ignatius; see §12.2d, e). This fact also helps us find an approximate date for Ephesians' writing: not much before the year 100, but since Ignatius used Ephesians, it cannot have been written many years after the beginning of II CE.

In contrast with Colossians, Ephesians is not a true letter, though the two works otherwise have much in common. Ephesians was not written to a specific church and never alludes to a particular problem or situation of any specific church or circle of churches. It did not even include an address to one or several churches: the words "in Ephesus" do not appear in Eph 1:1 in the best and oldest manuscripts. According to Marcion, the letter was directed to the Laodiceans, but there is no evidence the "in Laodicea" ever appeared in any manuscript of Eph 1:1. The original text read "to the saints who are also faithful in Christ Jesus." But what kind of document was this book that is conventionally called "Ephesians"? Several solutions to the problem have been proposed. Some suggest that it may have been a letter written to a large number of churches, but then one would expect to find some traces of the various addressees in the extant manuscripts. It may have been a covering letter for the first collection of the Pauline letters, but Ephesians itself already presupposes such a collection, as did *1 Clement,* which was written at about the same time; furthermore, such a covering letter would normally be less weighty than Ephesians (cf. the covering letter of Polycarp for the collection of the letters of Ignatius, Pol. *Phil.* 13–14; see §12.2h). Could it have been a baptismal sermon, preached in the context of a baptismal liturgy? This hypothesis might come closer to a definition of its genre, but we know too little about the baptismal liturgy of that time, to be sure, and sermons in early Christianity probably did not employ such an ornate style.

In order to explain the intention of Ephesians we must answer the question of what the author wanted to achieve theologically. He was not trying to intervene in the specific problems of a particular church, nor did he discuss any specific ecclesiastical matter like baptism. What the author had in mind was rather a word about the general situation in the post-Pauline period in view of the churches that had grown out of the Pauline mission and that knew and used Paul's letters. The theological issue in that situation was identical with the claim to universality of the gentile Christian church that had arisen from Paul's missionary work. But these churches, more than a generation after Paul, did more than claim the authority of the great apostle to the gentiles—they had also learned to read his letters. For the author of Ephesians, the question was what could be said about the question of Jews and gentiles in view of Paul's statements in Romans. The author of Colossians was still able to solve this problem as if he were living in Paul's own time, by calling for resistance against a cosmological interpretation of the Jewish ritual law.

The author of Ephesians had learned that this solution was no longer possible. This was so, however, not because it was impossible to fight back against the Jewish-Christian propaganda on that basis, nor because of a great influx of members of the Essenic sect into the Christian church after the destruction of the monastery on the Dead Sea—though perhaps such was indeed the case. There was a much deeper reason. The Christian churches that derived from the Pauline mission had meanwhile been deeply affected by the cosmological interpretation of the Old Testament, by Jewish apocalypticism as the message of withdrawal from the world, and by syncretistic Gnosticism, which was closely related to both those theological movements. Ephesians presupposes that many theological concepts to which Paul would have raised vigorous objections had become accepted or natural: these included the understanding of Christ's death and resurrection, and of the gospel, the message of these events, as a "mystery" (Eph 3:3f); the interpretation of baptism as the accomplishment of the resurrection with Christ, so that the Christians could understand themselves as being raised already and as being transferred into the heavenly regions (2:5f); the concept of Christ as the heavenly *anthropos* to whom the church is linked as his heavenly *syzygos* (2:14ff; 5:25–32); and, finally the transformation of the eschatological expectation of the parousia into a hope for personal salvation after death (6:10ff). Colossians had already anticipated some of these developments. The concept of Christ as the head of the body, the church (Eph 5:29), had been created by Colossians as a corrective to the view of its opponents that Christ was the head of a cosmological hierarchy.

As a Pauline theologian, the author of Ephesians becomes the advocate of a new universalistic view of Christianity. Universalism entails both the cosmological perspective and involves the question of the Jews and gentiles. Both dimensions belong together and form a unity; the question of the Jewish law also plays a role in this endeavor. For Paul, the law had come to an end, since its time had run out due to the eschatological act of God; now the gentiles had access to the divine promises without the law. Ephesians resumes this Pauline concept, but changes it in such a way that the law is abolished not only as the dividing wall between Jews and gentiles, but also as the cosmic wall between the heavenly realms and the human sphere on earth. By tearing down this wall through his flesh in his death on the cross, Christ has created from both Jews and gentiles a new human being who has access to God (2:11–22). For Paul, the participation of the Jews in the promises was part of his eschatological hope (Romans 11); for Ephesians, whose author was a Jew converted to Christianity (note his use of "you" when speaking to the gentiles; Eph 2:11, 17), the direction of this statement is reversed: the pagans are included in the process of salvation that is built upon the foundation of the prophets and apostles (2:19–20). But all this is no longer the object of eschatological expectation; it is present reality—though a reality that can be described only in gnostic terms.

Ephesians does not offer a definition of the unity of the church of Jews and gentiles in sociological or ecclesiological categories. This was a different matter for Paul, who made great efforts to document the unity of the church through a collection of money from the gentile Christians for the church in Jerusalem (§9.3f). In Ephesians this unity is a divine process transcending time and space. Apostles, prophets, preachers, pastors, and teachers are appointed in order that the church might grow into this preordained unity "through faith and knowledge" (4:11–13). Insofar as the bond of Christ's body is understood as love, the church is protected from false teachers because truth documents itself not in any particular doctrines, but in the increase of love (4:14–16). But, in the end, faith is nothing but knowledge, wisdom, and insight into the divine mystery (1:8–9, 17–18; 3:3–5, 18–19). This also explains the superabundance and pleonasm in the description of the cosmic dimension of salvation. Gnostic universalism here continues Pauline theology.

There is, however, also a corrective to Gnosticism in Ephesians, namely, its moralism. Salvation is grace for the one who was "dead" in sin, and in this respect it is "being made alive together with Christ" (2:3–5), "by grace saved through faith, . . . not through works" (2:8f). To this point the formulation sounds very much like Paul's own statements, but the continuation is different: "Created in Christ Jesus for good works, which God prepared beforehand, that we should walk in them" (2:10). Through such conduct the believers show that they are worthy of the heavenly call (4:1); through works one proves that one does not belong to darkness but to the light (5:8ff). This conduct is described both in elaborately interpreted catalogues of vices and virtues that were taken over from the doctrine of the two ways (4:17–5:20) and, on the other hand, in the table of household duties which the author took from Colossians (Eph 5:22–6:9). In interpreting it the author has tried to understand the duties of married partners as a copy of heavenly realities. The relationship of husband and wife corresponds to the relationship of the heavenly figures of Christ and Church. This exposition is pointedly anti-gnostic, because Gnosticism usually understood the rejection of married life as proof of one's membership in the heavenly world. With this anti-gnostic justification of the institution of marriage, Ephesians provided a metaphysical foundation on which to sanction the social institutions of marriage, family, and slavery. This would become a significant encumbrance for Christian ethics.

Ephesians was unable to enter into a theological controversy with Gnosticism. It was from Gnosticism that the author drew the theological categories that made his universalism possible. Thus the line of demarcation between the church and Gnosticism was transferred into the area of ethics. This was a step with momentous consequences for the Pauline churches in their development toward early catholicism, which committed the church to traditional morality and commended moral defamation as an instrument in the fight against the heretics. What Ephesians said in its characterization of pre-Christian pagan morality (4:17–19) would soon reappear as a characterization of opponents in polemical writings against the gnostics (§12.2g). For the future of Pauline theology in the early catholic church, the lack of theological controversy with opponents became a heavy burden because the later gnostic theologians understood very well how to interpret the letters of Paul in the spirit of Ephesians. Indeed, Ephesians seemed to make a gnostic interpretation of Paul a legitimate enterprise. For the early catholic church, however, Paul came under the suspicion of Gnosticism. Though Paul would still be claimed as an authority, the theology documented in his letters was avoided, and it took a long time before his theology was rediscovered. During the period when Ephesians was being written, the theological effort on behalf of a contemporary reinterpretation of Paul's letters was still continuing. Our evidence for this includes the Epistle to the Hebrews and the letter of Ignatius.

(c) Apocalyptic Gnosis as Legacy of Paul

1) *The Epistle to the Hebrews* is a witness for the efforts to develop the Pauline legacy during the last decades of I CE. The writing must be dated before the end of the century, as is shown by the quotation of two passages from Hebrews in *1 Clement* (36.2–5; 17.1). At the end of II CE Hebrews is known in Egypt as a letter of Paul, and in the churches of the east it was part of the NT canon from the beginning. Hebrews was also known in the west, but Irenaeus, Tertullian, and Hippolytus did not recognize it as a letter of Paul; it was not accepted into the canon of the western churches until IV CE. The origin of the title "To the Hebrews," which was added at a later time, is unknown. The ancient theory that it was the translation of a letter that Paul had written in the Hebrew language "To the Hebrews" is impossible. The language and style of the writing prove that it was originally written in Greek, in fact in a cultivated Atticistic Greek that shows familiarity with the training of rhetorical schools (Paul was influenced by the rhetoric of the diatribe). In his scriptural interpretation the author of Hebrews follows the Alexandrian allegorical method as we know it from the writings of Philo of Alexandria (§5.3f; Paul is also acquainted with this method, but he uses it only rarely; see 1 Cor 10:1–

Bibliography to §12.2c (1): Commentaries

Jean Hering, *The Epistle to the Hebrews* (London: Epworth, 1970).

Bibliography to §12.2c (1): Studies

Ernst Käsemann, *Das wandernde Gottesvolk* (FRLANT 55; 4th ed.; Göttingen: Vandenhoeck & Ruprecht, 1961). Classic monograph which gave directions for modern research.

L. K. K. Dey, *The Intermediary World and Patterns of Perfection in Philo and Hebrews* (SBLDS 25; Missoula: Scholars Press, 1975).

Sidney G. Sowers, *The Hermeneutics of Philo and Hebrews* (Richmond: Knox, 1965).

Erich Grässer, *Der Glaube im Hebräerbrief* (MThSt 2; Marburg: Elwert, 1965).

Otto Kuss, "Der theologische Grundgedanke des Hebräerbriefes," in: idem, *Auslegung und Verkündigung* (Regensburg: Pustet, 1963) 1. 181–328.

Günther Bornkamm, "Das Bekenntnis im Hebräerbrief," in: idem, *Studien zu Antike und Christentum* (3d ed.; München: Kaiser, 1969) 188–203.

Simon Kistemaker, *The Psalm Citations in the Epistle to the Hebrews* (Amsterdam: van Soest, 1971).

Ulrich Luck, "Himmlisches und irdisches Geschehen im Hebräerbrief," *NovT* 6 (1963) 192–215.

August Strobel, "Die Psalmengrundlage der Gethsemane-Parallele Hbr. 5,7ff," *ZNW* 45 (1954) 252–66.

Helmut Koester, "'Outside the Camp,' Hebrews 13.9–14," *HTR* 55 (1962) 299–315.

13). Corresponding to the allegorical method is its Platonic world view: earthly transitoriness is the shadow and copy of the heavenly reality.

Hebrews does not even claim to be written by Paul. It does not have the prescript of a letter and thus gives no indication of its sender and addressee. It is striking that the conclusion is in the form of a letter nonetheless: here the author speaks about himself, expressing his hope to see the addressees soon (13:19) and indicating that he would come for a visit soon "together with our brother Timothy," who had been released from prison (13:23). This seems to be part of a pseudepigraphical frame that points to Paul's fellow worker Timothy and alludes to the Roman imprisonment (note the greetings from those who come from Italy, 13:24). These remarks have no bearing on the question of the author of this writing, but they do show that Hebrews belongs to the writings which resume the Pauline tradition.

The content of Hebrews is also related to the continuation of Paul's theology in his churches. The author repeatedly refers to basic theological concepts that were native to those churches that had been founded by the Pauline mission. It is a matter of course that Christian existence is based upon faith; the fundamental quotation about justification by faith from Hab 2:4 (Rom 1:17) also appears in Hebrews (10:38). The understanding of conversion as forgiveness of sins, prominent in other deutero-Pauline writings (Eph 2:1ff; Col 1:21ff; cf. Rom 3:25), is as current in Hebrews as is the emphasis upon Christ's expiatory death, especially in connection with the concept of the new covenant (Heb 1:3; chaps. 8–10; for Paul, see 1 Cor 11:24f). Also among the foundations of faith, finally, is the expectation of the resurrection of the dead and the last judgment (Heb 6:1–2). But like Ephesians, Hebrews does not speak to the situation of a specific church, nor does the treatise deal with an immediate threat from heretical teachers. Rather, Hebrews presents a theological position within the general situation of the churches after Paul's time.

Apart from the conclusion, the author does not use any part of the literary genre of the letter, and the literary form and its relationship to the content and purpose of the writing are not immediately clear. The suggestion that Hebrews was a sermon or homily is too vague in terms of literary genre; the designation "theological tractate" also needs further clarification. One striking feature of the work is the intimate connection of theological argumentation and interpretation of Scripture. Furthermore, the author states explicitly that he intends to lead the readers beyond the foundations of faith to a deeper knowledge (5:11ff). Accordingly, this "epistle" belongs to the same category as those writings of Philo of Alexandria that are esoteric and that seek to mediate deeper insight into Scripture for the initiate. The interpretation of Scripture is certainly the key for understanding Hebrews, and its outline can be explained as a sequence of scriptural interpretations under the heading of certain theological topics. The author, however, does not address himself to a limited circle of elect people, but to the whole Christian church. (There is no doubt that this is the correct understanding of the intended readership; it is highly unlikely that Hebrews was written specifically for Christians of Jewish origin.) The question of why the specific form of esoteric scriptural gnosis was chosen for this writing could perhaps be answered by looking to Gnosticism. For the continuation of the Pauline legacy Gnosticism offered the most convincing alternatives, as Ephesians had already shown.

Gnostic concepts are found frequently in Hebrews and are crucial for understanding its arguments. Hebrews not only emphasizes the preexistence of the redeemer, although using philosophical terminology related to Philo (Heb 1:3), it also speaks about the descent of the redeemer through the heavenly realms (9:11ff, 24). The common origin of the redeemer and the redeemed is presupposed (2:11). Another gnostic concept is the understanding of the believers as those who are on their way to their heavenly home, a thought that occurs repeatedly throughout the work. But in contrast to Ephesians, Hebrews enters into a critical theological controversy with Gnosticism by refuting the gnostic understanding of both the redeemer and the process of salvation. Two important elements, both basic in the Pauline proclamation, are used as criteria in this controversy: first, recourse to the suffering of the redeemer on earth, and, second, adherence to an apocalyptic view of the future (10:27). This was not an individualistic expectation (as in Eph 6:10ff), but a hope in the future that binds the whole people of God together. The instrument of this theological criticism of gnostic theology was the christological and ecclesiological interpretation of Scripture. The scriptural passages used deal mostly with the exodus, the wandering of the people of God to the promised land, and the priesthood and sacrificial cult of the tabernacle of Israel; but numerous other passages are used. For these primary scriptural passages the author was able to draw upon a long tradition of interpretation. The closest parallels for his exegetical statements and for his interpretive method are found in the writings of Philo of Alexandria, but no direct dependence on Philo can be demonstrated. Hebrews' two main themes are christological (Christ as the heavenly priest who has offered himself as a sacrifice) and ecclesiological (the church as the wandering people of God on the way to their heavenly rest).

The introduction (Heb 1:1–2:18) is based on a collection of passages from the Old Testament about the angels and polemicizes against the identification of Christ's position with that of the angels. The author obviously wants to exclude from the very beginning any mediation of salvation through angelic powers (cf. Colossians and the *Shepherd of Hermas;* §12.1d, 12.2a). The connection of salvation with the "Son" is important, because only the Son is uniquely united with God himself (1:3; 2:10) and yet was made lower than the angels through his experience of death (2:8–10), thus participating fully in humanity's fate. The first major section of scriptural interpretaion is presented under the theme of the wandering people of God (3:1–4:13) and uses Ps 95:7–11, Num 14:21–23, and Gen 2:2. The promised heavenly rest is not the goal of the celestial journey of the soul—an important theme of gnostic theology—but of the wanderings of a historical people on earth. The interpretation is therefore not allegorical, but typological. It compares the old with the new people of God as historical entities, and can thus speak about disobedience, hardness of heart, hope, and faithfulness. At the same time, the historical promises given to Israel are opened up for participation by the Christians.

The second major section discusses the christological foundation (4:14–7:28). In this part, the interpretation is based upon Psalm 110 and Gen 14:17–20, which are the two passages from the Old Testament that speak about Melchizedek. An excursus, Heb 5:11–6:20, urges progress in theological insight: at stake is a fresh approach to christology. For this endeavor, the author does not refer to the concept of cross and resurrection but to the ideas of humiliation and exaltation, which have a greater affinity to gnostic thought. (Hebrews does not mention the resurrection of Christ even once in this long tractate!) The basic thesis for the christological argument is the complete identity of Christ with human beings in the experience of temptation (4:15), in suffering, and in death (5:7–8). On the other hand, the Melchizedek typology both demonstrates the complete divinity of the redeemer (note especially 7:2–3) and also proves that the order of salvation represented by Melchizedek is superior to the order of Abraham, Levi/Aaron, and the law. In this way, Hebrews renews Paul's thesis of freedom from the law, and bases that claim on his christology: Christ as the high priest has sacrificed himself once and for all (7:27).

The third section of scriptural proof discusses the superiority of the heavenly reality over its earthly copy, thus establishing the validity of the new covenant (8:1–10:18). The basic scriptural passages are Jer 31:31–34 (promise of the new covenant), Exodus 25–26 (description of the tabernacle), and Ps 40:7–9. To the cultic dimension of the sacrificial actions of the Old Testament sacrifices, which are merely copies, Hebrews contrasts the cosmological and anthropological dimensions of the way and sacrifice of Christ. This section would be completely misunderstood, however, if it were interpreted as a criticism of the Jewish cult. To be sure, the material and temporal limitations of the sacrificial cult are pointed out (9:9–10), but the actual point of the argument as a whole is to prove that the heavenly reality of the path that the redeemer took led through his death; only for that reason does the new covenant stand (9:15–17). The author thus does not argue against Judaism, but against the gnostic denial of the salvatory significance of Jesus' death: it is no accident that Hebrews emphasizes the apocalyptic expectation of the coming judgment in the same context (9:17f).

The last major section of the writing (10:19–12:29) continues the antignostic argument with a criticism of the gnostic idea of the soul's celestial journey. The terms "freedom of entrance" and "new and living way" (10:19–20) at the beginning of the section allude to gnostic concepts. Just as the opening passage speaks of the flesh and blood of Jesus, that is, of the sacrifice that he offered through his death on earth, the "way" of the Christians is also described as the way of faith in its earthly experiences. This is accomplished by the presentation of the famous examples of faith in Hebrews 11. The chapter is introduced by a well-known definition of faith (Heb 11:1) that has become a famous *crux interpretum*. The definition explains "faith" as a "present reality" (the correct translation of the term *hypostasis*) of the things hoped for. The list of the examples of faith ends in the mention of the witnesses who were persecuted (11:35ff). In the same sense, Jesus is the forerunner of faith, because he endured the cross of shame (12:2). The final section (13:1–17), after a short parenesis (13:1–8), once more enjoins the criterion for the Christian understanding of existence: Christ died "outside of the camp," which means outside the realm of religious security. It is exactly because Christians have no abiding city in the world (in this respect the author of Hebrews agrees with the gnostics), that their place in the world is where Jesus has suffered. This offers a challenge to the pious of all times who speak only of a heavenly salvation.

2) *The Epistle of Barnabas.* Another example among the early Christian writings for an allegorical interpretation of the Old Testament in the genre of scriptural gnosis is the *Epistle of Barnabas.* Its interpretive meth-

---

Bibliography to §12.2c (2): Text

Robert A. Kraft, *Epître de Barnabé* (SC 172; Paris: Cerf, 1971).
Funk-Bihlmeyer, *ApostVät,* xx–xxiv, 10–34.
Lake, *ApostFath,* 1. 335–409.

Bibliography to §12.2c (2): Commentaries

Robert A. Kraft, *Barnabas and the Didache* (Grant, *ApostFath* 3).
Hans Windisch, *Der Barnabasbrief* (HNT.E 3; Tübingen: Mohr/Siebeck, 1920).

Bibliography to §12.2c (2): Studies

Klaus Wengst, *Tradition und Theologie des Barnabasbriefes* (AKG 42; Berlin: De Gruyter, 1971).

od is closely related to Hebrews, and *Barnabas* also strives for a scriptural understanding of the soteriological significance of Jesus' death, all the while holding to the apocalyptic expectation. Like other works of the Apostolic Fathers, *Barnabas* is transmitted in several biblical manuscripts (it is complete in Codex Sinaiticus), and is also extant in a Latin translation. The book is quoted for the first time by Clement of Alexandria. New Testament writings are never used in *Barnabas,* neither explicitly nor tacitly, which would argue for an early date, perhaps even before the end of I CE. It has been argued that *Barn.* 16.4 is a reference to the building plans for a temple of Jupiter in Jerusalem that triggered the Bar Kochba insurrection (132–135 CE); but that is just as uncertain as the recourse to *Barn.* 4.4–5 for a dating during the government of Vespasian (69–79 CE). The use of the doctrine of the Two Ways in *Barnabas* 18–20 provides no arguments for its date because it cannot be shown that there was a literary relationship between *Barnabas* and the *Teaching of the Twelve Apostles* (*Didache;* §10.1c); it is more likely that both used a common source.

We know little or nothing about the author of *Barnabas* and its place of origin. The suggestion that Barnabas, Paul's fellow missionary in Antioch, wrote this book is not entirely impossible, but highly unlikely in view of its radical rejection of the validity of the old covenant. The epistolary framework is only an external dress (this includes the greeting to the sons and daughters which lacks any indication of the sender and the addressee, and the wish of blessings at the end). Actually, the writing is not a letter, but a treatise of scriptural gnosis, just like Hebrews. *Barnabas* provides valuable insights into the techniques and results of the scriptural exegesis employed during the same period by writers such as Matthew and somewhat later by Justin Martyr.

It is the explicit intention of the work to communicate a deeper knowledge (*gnosis; Barn.* 1.5). The author maintains the connection of such basic commandments as hope, justice, and love to the last judgment (1.6), but though fear, patience, long-suffering, and self-control are helpers to faith, it is still necessary to have wisdom, insight, understanding, and knowledge (2.3). His aim is the demonstration of the deeper understanding of Scripture, as becomes evident in the repeated references to *gnosis* in the introductions to several sections of scriptural interpretation (6.9; 9.8). The basis of these interpretations is an older collection of scriptural passages that was put together according to certain topics and that may have been of Jewish origin. This older collection showed an interest in a rationalistic and allegorical-spiritual understanding of the ritual law (cf. Philo of Alexandria). This interest is still visible in several sections of *Barnabas:* sacrifice and fasting (2.4–3.6), circumcision (9.1–9), dietary and purity laws (10.1–12), sabbath (15.1–8), and temple (16.1–10). Occasionally, the author has altered his source and inserted Christian interpretations, for example, with the rationale for the sanctification of the Lord's day (15.9); but the chief contribution of the author appears in the additions that deal with the scriptural proof for the coming of Jesus, his cross and resurrection (5.1–8.7; 11.1–12.9), and for the question of the new covenant (13.1–14.9; cf. 4.6–8). He also expands the collection of testimonia for the topic of circumcision by an allegorical interpretation referring to the cross (9.8–9; the 318 servants circumcised by Abraham point to the cross of Jesus, since the Greek writing of that number is *IHT*, representing the first two letters of the name of Jesus and the letter T as the symbol of the cross). It is interesting to find in these scriptural allegories the same topics that played an important role in Hebrews.

A particular outline of the treatise as a whole is not recognizable. Much of the writing seems instead to be more of a collection of materials such as those used in the formation of the passion narrative of the gospels. *Barnabas* indeed includes material that directly influenced the formation of the passion narratives, such as the detail that Jesus was given gall to drink with vinegar (7.3, 5; see §10.2a on the *Gospel of Peter*). It cannot be shown that *Barnabas* used the gospels of the New Testament; on the contrary, what *Barnabas* presents here is material from the "school of the evangelists." The author knew about Jesus' suffering, of course (other gospels materials were also known to him; see 5.8–9 and the criticism of the titles Son of David and Son of Man, 12.10–11). This helps prove that the early Christians paid special attention to the history of the passion in order to comprehend the meaning of Jesus' suffering with the help of the interpretation of the Old Testament. A systematic new treatment of the relevant scriptural materials was made somewhat later by Justin Martyr. But Justin knew the Gospels of Matthew and Luke and used the written forms of their narratives, and was thus able to provide a certain ordering to the technique of writing scriptural proofs. The material presented by *Barnabas* represents the initial stages of the process that is continued in the *Gospel of Peter*, later in Matthew, and is completed in Justin Martyr.

The apocalyptic perspective is another concern that *Barnabas* shares with Hebrews, in addition to the scriptural proofs for the suffering of Jesus and the new covenant. The extensive scriptural proof for his suffering is introduced by an eschatological admonition (*Barn.* 4.1–14) that quotes the books of *Enoch* (*1 Enoch* 98.61–64) and Daniel (7:24; 7:7–8). The expectation of the parousia was also incorporated into the allegorical treatment of the Jewish sacrificial rite with reference to the death of Jesus (*Barn.* 7.6–9). Moreover, the final admonition of the book (21.1–3) emphasizes the parousia. With the eschatological perspective *Barnabas* connects the teaching of the Two Ways (*Barnabas* 18–20; cf. *Didache* 1–6; see §10.1c), which is called "another gnosis." While *Did.* 1.1 designates the two ways as the way of life and the way of death, they appear in *Barnabas* as the way of light and the way of darkness, which are ruled by the angel of God and by the angel of Satan. This corresponds to the source of the *Didache*, where the same designations have been preserved (cf. the Latin translation of *Didache* 1–6). In general, *Barnabas* shows fewer traces of a Christian revision of the Jewish catechism than the *Didache*, and is thus more closely related to the Jewish original. The reproduction of the teaching of the Two Ways rounds out the picture of typical representatives of the post-Pauline churches. The same basic features appeared in the other witnesses, though one or the other element may have been less clearly present in any particular case—scriptural proof for the death of Jesus, forgiveness of sins through this death, regulation of Christian conduct according to moral teachings that were taken over from Judaism, and expectation of the parousia and the last judgment. These are also the essential elements of Christian faith in *1 Clement* and 1 Peter. Such faith is recommended as true "gnosis" (see the conclusion of *Barnabas,* 21.4), which demonstrates the anti-gnostic orientation of this ecclesiastical piety.

(d) Ignatius of Antioch

We do not know the name of a single Christian from the decades that followed the deaths of the apostles of the first Christian generation, from the period of about 60–90 CE. The second Christian generation has thus become completely anonymous for us. All the Christian writings extant from this period were either anonymous or written under the pseudonym of an apostle from the first generation, although the pseudonymity may appear in a veiled form, as in Hebrews. This situation changed in the next Christian generation: several names suddenly appear, although only within the circles of the Pauline communities, in Rome, and in Antioch. To be sure, even there we still find a continuation of pseudepigraphical writing, but it is no longer the dominant phenomenon. On the other hand,

Bibliography to §12.2d: Text
Funk-Bihlmeyer, *ApostVät,* xxxi–xxxvi, 82–113.
Lake *ApostFath,* 1. 165–277.

Bibliography to §12.2d: Commentaries
Lightfoot, *Apostolic Fathers,* vol. 2, parts 1–2.
William Schoedel, *Ignatius of Antioch: A Commentary on the Epistles of Ignatius* (Hermeneia; Philadelphia: Fortress, in preparation).
Walter Bauer, *Die Briefe des Ignatius von Antiochien und der Polykarpbrief* (HNT.E 2; Tübingen: Mohr/Siebeck, 1920).
Robert M. Grant, *Ignatius of Antioch* (Grant, *ApostFath* 4).

in Syria (with the exception of Antioch) and in Egypt, pseudepigraphy
under the name of an apostle (or a figure from the Old Testament) continues unabated for at least another generation, until we learn the names
of the first gnostic founders of schools in Egypt; the first names known
from Syria are those of Tatian and Bar-Daisan (Bardesanes) from the
second half of II CE.

One factor related to the partial termination of pseudepigraphical productions, again from the areas of Asia Minor, Greece, Rome, and Antioch, was that writings began to be directed to other churches or groups of
churches with the unconcealed intention of exercising ecclesiastical-
political influence. Clement writes on behalf of the Roman church to
Corinth in order to set things right in that church. Ignatius, bishop of
Antioch, writes from Smyrna and Troas to other churches in Asia Minor
and Rome. Polycarp sends the Ignatian letters to Philippi from Smyrna,
and later writes another letter to that church to settle the case of a
presbyter who had embezzled some church money. Eusebius preserved
information about letters of the Corinthian bishop Dionysius from the
middle of II CE. He wrote to the Spartans, the Athenians, the churches in
Gortyna and Cnossus on Crete, to Nicomedia in Bithynia, to Amastris in
Pontus, and finally to Rome. In his letter to Rome, Dionysius reports that
the letter from Clement of Rome to the Corinthians was still read in their
church (Eusebius *Hist. eccl.* 4.23).

A third important factor, joined to the decrease in pseudepigraphy and
the use of the letter as a political instrument, was briefly mentioned above:
the collection of the letters of Paul, which became highly significant for the
churches treated in this chapter. Apparently Colossians and Ephesians
were part of the first somewhat complete collection of these letters, but 2
Thessalonians seems to have been missing, and also 2 Corinthians, because we can find no traces of those two letters in the first attestations of
the collection in *1 Clement* and Ignatius of Antioch. The collection may

Bibliography to §12.2d: Studies

Cyril Charles Richardson, *The Christianity of Ignatius of Antioch* (New York:
    Columbia University, 1935). Best discussion of Ignatius' thought.

Virginia Corwin, *Saint Ignatius and Christianity in Antioch* (YPR 1; New Haven:
    Yale University, 1960).

Henning Paulsen, *Studien zur Theologie des Ignatius von Antiochien* (FKDG 29;
    Göttingen: Vandenhoeck & Ruprecht, 1978).

Rudolf Bultmann, "Ignatius and Paul," in: idem, *Existence and Faith,* 267–88.

Heinrich Rathke, *Ignatius von Antiochien und die Paulusbriefe* (Berlin: Akademie-
    Verlag, 1967).

Heinrich Schlier, *Religionsgeschichtliche Untersuchungen zu den Ignatiusbriefen*
    (BZNW 8; Giessen: Töpelmann, 1929).

W. M. Swartley, "The Imitatio Christi in the Ignatian Letters," *VC* 27 (1973) 81–
    103.

have been made in Asia Minor, but it is important that it was known in Rome and in Antioch before the turn of the first century. The further history of these churches from this period is not conceivable without Paul, even for those critical of his theology, and even if his letters were no longer read in some places. We must still remember that a number of churches possessed collections of Paul's letters before anyone had the idea of referring to written gospels as authorities.

The letters of Ignatius of Antioch will be discussed first, although *1 Clement* and probably also 1 Peter were written somewhat earlier. But Ignatius presents another attempt at a theological elaboration of Pauline ideas. To that extent Ignatius belongs together with Ephesians, and especially with Hebrews. The church of Antioch, where Ignatius was bishop, seems to have been typical more of Petrine Christianity in Syria after Paul's departure from that city (§9.2a). Matthew could have been written in Antioch (§10.2c), and it is difficult to say anything about a continuing Pauline influence during that time. The gospels of Mark and Matthew, to be sure, rely upon the kerygma of cross and resurrection and agree with Christian tenets that could be subsumed under the designation of the "Pauline Gospel." But this does not necessarily mean much more than a continuation of the proclamation of Christ's cross and resurrection and the expectation of the parousia, things that were characteristic of Antiochian Christianity even before Paul's arrival there (§8.3c). However, Ignatius, bishop of Antioch in the period around the year 100, was deeply influenced as a theologian by the letters of Paul. The information of Eusebius (*Hist. eccl.* 3.22) that Ignatius was bishop during the time of Trajan seems trustworthy, especially since the report of Ignatius' martyrdom known independently of Eusebius (the *Martyrium Colbertinum*) confirms that date. Polycarp, bishop of Smyrna, to whom Ignatius wrote one of his letters, was martyred in 167 (according to Eusebius *Hist. eccl.* 4.14.10; 15.1) or perhaps already in 156 (this date derives from the less reliable information of the report of his martyrdom; see §12.3f). He was 86 years old at that time, and was therefore born in either 69/79 or 80/81. Since Polycarp was bishop when Ignatius wrote his letters, the martyrdom of Ignatius is best dated in Trajan's last years, i.e., 110–117 CE; but an earlier date is possible.

The occasion for the letters of Ignatius is clearly seen from the letters themselves. Ignatius had been arrested in Antioch and was being led to Rome by a group of Roman soldiers to be thrown to the beasts in the arena of the capital. During his travel through western Asia Minor he had the opportunity to make contact with several Christian churches or to talk with their delegations. Subsequently, he wrote letters from Smyrna to the churches in Ephesus, Magnesia, and Tralles, and also sent a letter to the

Christian community in Rome, urging the Romans not to do anything that might prevent his greatly desired martyrdom. After leaving Smyrna, and before his departure by ship to Neapolis in Macedonia, he wrote from Troas to the churches in Philadelphia and Smyrna and to Polycarp. These seven letters are preserved (for the problem of their transmission and recensions, see §7.3f). All the letters of Ignatius are true correspondence, each letter having its prescript (sender, addressee, greeting) and final greetings. The closings occasionally contain special greetings and, in the letter to Polycarp, special instructions. Ignatius sometimes will make reference to the special situation of the church to which he is writing, and will also mention individual persons. But on the whole, the content of the letters is of a more general character; like a testament, they are the instruction and bequest of someone sentenced to death. Fundamental statements about the soteriological significance of the cross of Christ, the office of the bishop, and the conduct of the members of a Christian church are repeated in each of the letters. Even the warnings about false teachers are not necessarily directed to the particular church in whose letter they occur. The writing to Polycarp, despite its personal note, is at the same time a generally valid instruction for the office of bishop. The letter to the Romans occupies a special position. It focusses upon Ignatius' personal hope of perfection through death and thus establishes the authority of his writings as a testament (see below). We are therefore justified in treating the seven letters as a unity. They were all written within the span of a few weeks, and they all refer to the same ecclesiastical and personal situation.

In his interpretation of Paul, Ignatius seems closer to Ephesians—which he knew and used—than to the post-Pauline theology that was concerned with the interpretation of the Bible and clung to the expectation of the parousia. Ignatius' eschatological expectation is reduced to the concept of martyrdom. The Old Testament does not play any role in his thinking, in fact it is scarcely referred to or used; all that is explicitly quoted are two passages from Proverbs in *Eph.* 5.3 and *Magn.* 13.1. *Phld.* 8.2 is characteristic for Ignatius' position, where he reports a debate with opponents who referred to the Old Testament in order to prove their point; but Ignatius, not willing to enter into a discussion of the problems of interpretation, simply pointed to his own decisive authority, the gospel of Jesus' cross and resurrection. Ignatius does not use concepts of time and history at all, but rather the categories of space and cosmos that have a closer affinity to gnostic thought. In this respect he also stands closer to the Gospel of John and shows many similarities to Johannine language (but it cannot be demonstrated that he knew and used this gospel). Only occasionally, however, is Ignatius willing to make mythological statements in terms of the cosmological drama. At one point (*Eph.*19), he indeed describes the ascension of the redeemer as the cosmic victory over the powers of the stars, but in general he prefers to speak about the heavenly and earthly worlds in the static rather than dynamic categories of spirit and flesh. These categories serve to describe his christology, but also his statements about the sacrament, the church, and the existence of the believer. He uses the same language in his interpretation of the traditional kerygma about the coming of the redeemer, his death, and his resurrection. His primary witness for these statements is Paul, to whom he refers frequently. Ignatius obviously considers Paul to be the theologian who had most truly understood the salvation proclaimed in Christ's cross and resurrection, although the categories of flesh and spirit were understood for Paul in the sense of a dynamic eschatology.

The kerygma of his church, repeatedly quoted and reformulated by Ignatius and referred to by the term "gospel," appears to be much expanded when compared with the Pauline gospel formula (cf. 1 Cor 15:3–4). It begins with a statement about the birth of Jesus from Mary the virgin (*Eph.* 18.2; *Trall.* 9; this reference serves to underline the humanity of Jesus!), and adds the name of Pilate to the statement about Jesus' suffering and crucifixion (*Trall.* 9; in *Smyrn.* 1.2 Herod is also mentioned). This is clearly a development of the kerygma that parallels that of the written gospels, which began with the passion narrative, were expanded by an introduction resuming the story of Jesus with his baptism (Mark), and were later expanded to include narratives about Jesus' birth (Matthew and Luke). Ignatius interprets the kerygma according to his dualistic scheme of flesh and spirit. In the coming, dying, and rising of Christ he finds the realization of the unity of the spiritual and divine world with the earthly and human world of the flesh. Christ is "nailed to the cross in the flesh and in the spirit" (*Smyrn.* 1.1); after the resurrection his disciples touch him "in the flesh and in the spirit" (*Smyrn.* 3.2). In *Smyrn.* 1 a kerygmatic formula is expanded by a phrase from Paul's letter to the Romans: "from the tribe of David according to the flesh, Son of God according to the will and power of God" (cf. Rom 1:3–4). In many instances, Ignatius simply inserts the word "truly" in order to underline the unity in Christ of the divine and earthly realities: "truly born, truly persecuted, truly crucified and dead, truly risen from the dead" (*Trall.* 9.1–2). Or he employs paradoxical juxtapositions of opposites to describe the presence of both spheres in Christ: "fleshly and spiritually, born and unborn, in the flesh becoming God, in death true life, from Mary and from God, first capable of suffering, then incapable of suffering" (*Eph.* 7.2).

That much already states the essential elements of Ignatius' christology, because for him salvation is dependent on nothing but God's presence in the human Christ. This Christ becomes effective for the congregation in the gospel and in the eucharist: as there is *one* flesh of Christ, there is also one bread, one cup, and one gospel (*Eph.* 20.2; *Smyrn.* 7.2; *Phld.* 4). The gospel itself is the arrival of the savior, his suffering, and his resurrection (*Phld.* 9.2). In the same way, the bread of the eucharist is the present Christ, the medicine of immortality (*Eph.* 20.2). This formulation, however, does not mean that Ignatius thinks that the sacrament works like an impersonal, mechanical power. On the contrary, he repeatedly emphasizes the harmony and mutual love of the living congregation, in which the gospel and eucharist are effective (*Eph.* 4.1–5.2). As the eucharist cannot be understood without the Christ who became flesh, neither can it be thought of without the Christian church; to be sure, the church in turn is inconceivable without the eucharist. The worship service is the center of the congregation's life (*Eph.* 13.1), and whoever is outside the altar is outside the bread of God (*Eph.* 5.2; *Trall.* 7.2).

The church has the same religious qualities as Christ, the gospel, and the sacrament. In this sense, the Christians are "in Christ" (*Eph.* 11.1; 20.1), or even "in God" (*Eph.* 15.3), or imitators of God or Christ (*Trall.* 1.2; *Phld.* 7.2), and everything that the church does "according to the flesh," that is, in the realm of earthly life, is "spiritual" (*Eph.* 8.2). The unity of spirit and flesh is visibly documented in the actions of the church (*Magn.* 13.2). The church is the "building of God" (*Eph.* 9.1; here Ignatius speaks of the cross as the machine for the building), but the emphasis is not, as in *Hermas* (§12.1d), upon the individual purity of the members, but upon the shaping of the life of the congregation through mutual love (*Eph.* 14; *Magn.* 1; and elsewhere). Elements from the Pauline letters are consciously adopted in these passages, and the many allusions to the Pauline correspondence demonstrate that Ignatius repeatedly returned to those letters to find guidance and instruction. Even if one may accuse him of frequent misunderstandings of Pauline terminology, what Ignatius learned from Paul's writings helped him to understand the Christian church as constantly nourished and edified by the gospel and the eucharist, and to avoid a moralizing view of Christian conduct.

Ignatius, however, moves beyond Paul in his propaganda for the church organization that is known by the name of monarchical episcopate. Ignatius calls himself "Bishop of Antioch" and presupposes that each of the churches to which he writes is headed by a bishop. This makes Ignatius the first witness for a rather novel concept of church order in which each congregation has one single leader who, at least according to Ignatius' thoughts about this office, is equipped with considerable powers. To what degree this new structure was a reality at this time is unknown. There are no earlier testimonies to the institution of the monarchical episcopate, and the assumption of appointments of bishops by the apostles of the first generation is clearly a later fiction. But it was indeed the case that the monarchical episcopate came to be accepted during the decades after Ignatius's death in the cities around the Aegean Sea and in Rome, and soon thereafter also in western Syria, at the end of II CE in Alexandria, and later in the eastern parts of Syria and beyond. Alternative solutions to the question of this system's origin cannot be discussed further in this context.

Although Ignatius equips the office of the bishop with important powers and authority, he understands himself and the office of bishop in general more in terms of charismatic than institutional functions. The bishop represents what God is thinking (*Eph.* 3.2–4); he must be received like God (*Eph.* 6). He guarantees Christ's presence in baptism and in the community meals of the church, which must therefore never be held without him (*Smyrn.* 8.2). The congregation should act only in unanimity with the bishop; unity with the thought of God presupposes unity with the bishop (*Eph.* 3.2; *Phld.* 3.2). Whoever does something without the bishop violates Christian existence (*Magn.* 4; 7; *Phld.* 7.2; *Smyrn.* 8; in *Syrn.* 9.1, actions without the bishop are even called the work of the devil). Such statements can be understood only in light of the statements about the church that represents Christ in its conduct and actions. The authority assigned to the bishop is not derived from concepts of power and control, but from the idea of Christ's unity with the church. Moreover, the bishop is not the only officer of the congregation, but shares his responsibility for it with the presbyters and deacons. All three are frequently named together (*Magn.* 13.1; *Trall.* 2; 3; 7; *Phld.* 7.1; 10.2; *Smyrn.* 8.1). Obedience toward the bishop and the presbytery stand side by side (*Eph.* 2.2; 20.2; *Magn.* 2–3; *Trall.* 2.1). The deacons should be considered as Christ, the bishop as the Father, and the presbyters as God's council (*Trall.* 3.1). Finally, the instructions for the bishop that Ignatius wrote for Polycarp demonstrate that Ignatius never thought of the office of the bishop in terms of power, but in terms of service and care for others. The bishop is asked to bear the illnesses of all people (*Pol.* 1.3), to devote his love not to the good, but to the difficult disciples (*Pol.* 2.1), to care for the widows (*Pol.* 4.1), and not to be haughty in his dealings with slaves, whether male or female (*Pol.* 4.2). Cooperation is decisive for the successful conduct of the office (*Pol.* 6.1).

The office of the bishop is especially significant in connection with the problem of heresy. When Ignatius discusses this question, he repeatedly refers to the office of the bishop (*Trall.* 7; *Pol.* 3; and elsewhere). It is difficult to get a clear picture about the character of the heretics because Ignatius makes only occasional allusions to their teachings. Several times he accuses them of "Judaism" (*Magn.* 8.1; *Phld.* 6.1); both the sabbath and circumcision are mentioned (*Magn.* 9; *Phld.* 6.1). To confess Christ and to "Judaize" are mutually exclusive for Ignatius (*Magn.* 9). In addition, in *Phld.* 8.2 Ignatius mentions the controversy about the interpretation of Scripture that was mentioned above, and immediately afterwards he contrasts, quite unexpectedly, "the priests and high priests" with Christ and the gospel (*Phld.* 9). One may ask whether his opponents offered on the basis of their scriptural interpretation a (christological?) doctrine of a priestly mediation of salvation. Were these opponents the same as those who spoke about circumcision? In any case, Ignatius alludes to a Jewish-Christian teaching that relied upon the Old Testament. It could be that the opponents of the letters to the Smyrnaeans and the Trallians were different people. Docetism is repeatedly rejected in no uncertain terms; these opponents denied the humanity of Jesus Christ (*Trall.* 10; *Smyrn.* 2; 4.2; 7.1), which means that they were gnostics. This agrees with the observation that both letters reject speculations about angels and cosmic powers: even the angels and archons will be judged if they do not believe in the blood of Christ (*Smyrn.* 6.1; see also *Trall.* 5). Should we assume that all his remarks about heretics refer to the same group? In that case, we would be dealing with Jewish-Christian gnostics.

There is a reason why Ignatius' information about the heretics is so vague. He is not interested in providing arguments to rebut his opponents—he only wants to warn and urge the church to stand together in the unanimity of faith under the leadership of their bishop. Ignatius is convinced that the problem of heresy can only be solved in this way, and also that the local congregation would thus be preserved from disintegration into splinter groups. This is a new method in the fight against heresy. The *one* local congregation is strengthened, held together through its regular worship services, mutual love, and obedience to its bishop. The criterion for the distinction between true and false belief is the "gospel" in which the human reality of Jesus' coming, death, and resurrection is clearly stated. At the same time, Ignatius uses the letter as an instrument of ecclesiastical polity, as Paul had done half a century earlier, although Ignatius does not employ the letter to give individual churches advice or admonitions for their specific problems, but rather to provide general guidelines that would serve to strengthen congregations everywhere in the same way.

Ignatius was nothing more than the bishop of a local church. Why should he feel that he was called to give this sort of instruction in letters to other churches? The answer to this question raises the topic of his self-consciousness as a martyr. Ignatius emphasizes repeatedly that he is not speaking as a bishop but as one who is on the way to martyrdom; his letters are strongly influenced by the concept of the testament. This calling to martyrdom gives him his authority. As a bishop he would be nothing more than a voice of God, while as a martyr he is the divine Logos (*Rom.* 2.1); in his martyrdom he will become like Christ and "attain to God" (*Rom.* 1.2; 4.2; 5.3; and elsewhere). This view is closely connected with his concept of the gospel and his christology. The unity of divinity and humanity is made perfect through suffering and death. Thus, only in martyrdom can one fully participate in Christ's cross and resurrection (*Rom.* 6.1). The entire eschatological expectation of early Christianity is concentrated on the idea of martyrdom—without denying that the regular members of the church are Christians in the full sense. But martyrdom, next to the gospel and sacrament, becomes the visible and tangible presence of salvation for the entire church because it accomplishes the ultimate goal of Christian existence: in it one becomes a disciple (*Eph.* 1.2; *Rom.* 5.3); it is a call to the Father (*Rom.* 7.2), freedom from slavery (*Rom.* 4.3), the bread of God (*Rom.* 7.3). Ignatius' desire to win life in his own death, "to sink to the world in order to rise towards God" (*Rom.* 2.2), "to receive the pure light" (*Rom.* 6.2), must be understood against the background of the renewal of the Pauline kerygma of cross and resurrection. For Ignatius, Paul is therefore the blessed martyr in whose discipleship he wants to go to his death. Nonetheless Ignatius does not hesitate to call all Christians the "fellow-initiates of Paul" (*Eph.* 12.2).

(e) Peter and Paul as the Authorities of Ecclesiastical Order: The First Epistle of Clement

Clement of Rome, to whom we owe the writing known as *1 Clement*, was one of the political leaders of the church who was active in that period writing letters without the pseudonym of an apostle. The text of his letter was first discovered through the biblical Codex Alexandrinus (§7.2c), where it follows upon the Revelation of John; however, one leaf is missing with the text of *1 Clem.* 57.7–63.4. The complete Greek text became accessible with the discovery of Codex Hierosolymitanus (§10.1c). In addition, two Latin, one Syriac, and two Coptic manuscripts have been published. There are also numerous quotations from *1 Clement* in Clement of Alexandria. Furthermore, the letter was used by Polycarp of Smyrna and was mentioned by Dionysius of Corinth in the middle of II CE. By this we know that the writing was distributed fairly early. It is a true letter, which mentions as its sender the Roman church and, also in the prescript, the church in Corinth as the recipient. According to well-attested ancient tradition, the letter was written by Clement, who was commissioned by the Roman church. This Clement was probably the secretary of the church in Rome, and it is possible that the reference in *Herm. Vis.* 2.4.3 speaks of the same person. There is no indication that

Clement was the bishop of the Roman church, as was claimed by later tradition, because the letter does not contain any references to the office of the monarchical episcopate, which appears at the same time or a little later in Ignatius and Polycarp. In addition, *1 Clement* 42 speaks about bishops in the plural. The most plausible date for the writing of *1 Clement* is 96–97, that is, immediately after the Domitian persecution in Rome; the letter points to persecutions that had hit the church only very recently.

The occasion for writing the letter to Corinth was the removal of the presbyters by a number of younger members of the Corinthian church (*1 Clem.* 47.6). We are told very little about the reasons for this rebellion, which the author calls foreign and unholy (*1 Clem.* 1.1). Clement reveals repeatedly that it had disturbed the church in Corinth very deeply, but he never informs the reader about its causes. It is tempting to assume that the troubles were caused by heretical teachers who had come to Corinth. We know from the Revelation of John and from Ignatius that Judaistic and gnostic teachers were active at that time in Asia Minor, and it is not too difficult to believe that these heretics also came to Corinth and were able to divide the church. In his response, Clement emphasizes traditional Jewish-Christian morality, the creation of the world by God, the resurrection

Bibliography to §12.2e: Text

Funk-Bihlmeyer, *ApostVät*, xxiv–xxviii, 35–70.
Lake, *ApostFath*, 1.3–121.

Bibliography to §12.2e: Commentaries

Lightfoot, *Apostolic Fathers*, part 1, vols. 1–2.
Robert M. Grant and Holt H. Graham, *First and Second Clement* (Grant, *ApostFath* 2).
Rudolf Knopf, *Die Lehre der Zwölf Apostel, die zwei Clemensbriefe* (HNT.E 1; Tübingen: Mohr/Siebeck, 1920) 41–150.

Bibliography to §12.2e: Studies

Adolf von Harnack, *Einführung in die alte Kirchengeschichte: Das Schreiben der römischen Kirche an die korinthische aus der Zeit Domitians* (Leipzig: Hinrichs, 1929).
Karlmann Beyschlag, *Clemens Romanus und der Frühkatholizismus: Untersuchungen zu I Clemens 1–7* (BHTh 35; Tübingen: Mohr/Siebeck, 1966).
Werner Jaeger, *Early Christianity and Greek Paideia* (Cambridge, MA: Harvard University, 1961).

Bibliography to §12.2e: Peter and Rome

Oscar Cullmann, *Peter: Disciple, Apostle, Martyr: A Historical and Theological Essay* (Philadelphia: Westminster, 1962).
Daniel Wm. O'Conner, *Peter in Rome: The Literary, Liturgical, and Archaeological Evidence* (New York: Columbia University, 1969).
Erich Dinkler, "Petrus und Paulus in Rom," *Gymnasium* 87 (1980) 1–37.
Idem, "Die Petrus-Rom-Frage," *ThR* NF 25 (1959) 189–230, 289–335; 27 (1961) 33–64.

Bronze Coin of Domitian

The inscription reads: CAES[AR] DIVI AUG[USTI] VESP[ASIANI] F[ILIUS] DOMITIANUS CO[N]S[UL] VII = "Caesar, Son of the divinized Augustus Vespasian, Domitian, consul for the seventh time." Domitian expelled the philosophers from Rome; in this context, the Christians also suffered persecution (25–96 C.E.).

of Christ, and the expectation of the future resurrection of the Christians. All these topics are appropriate in a writing directed against gnostic heretics. But it must not be overlooked that the letter does not contain any polemical remarks about false teachers, and that the author shows no interest in this question in any way. Rather, he repeats in great detail what he considers to be the foundations of Christian faith, teaching, and conduct, and he expects that careful and faithful attention to these matters will reconstitute the unity of the Corinthian church.

For the historical situation that characterizes the writing of *1 Clement*, a striking parallel with Ignatius of Antioch is significant. Both Ignatius and *1 Clement* mention Peter and Paul side by side (Ign. *Rom.* 4.3; *1 Clement* 5). In both instances, Peter and Paul are introduced as apostles, and in both passages they are referred to as martyrs. It is by no means natural that these two apostles would be named together in light of the conflict between Paul and Peter in Antioch (§9.2a) and the independent development of traditions under Peter's name in Syria (§10.2a); an anti-Pauline tradition of Peter (and James) even developed there during II CE (§10.4c). The fact that these apostles are reconciled with each other and named together reflects an important development in the ecclesiastical-political stuation. Christian churches that had at first formed their traditions independently under the name of a single apostle must have formed an alliance. The tradition about Peter certainly derives from Syria. Peter himself may have come to Rome toward the end of his life and suffered martyrdom there, but there is no certain evidence for this, because for the years from 60 to 90 CE no testimonies from the Roman church have been preserved.

The context in which both apostles are mentioned in *1 Clement* 5 is noteworthy. Clement says that he wants to add some examples from more recent times to those from the Old Testament. First, he points in general to the most righteous "pillars" (of the church) who have endured sufferings (5.2). With the remark "Let us set before our eyes the good apostles" (5.3), he introduces a short reference to the martyrdom of Peter (5.4) and continues with a long enumeration of the sufferings and martyrdom of Paul (5.5–7). In neither case does he try to establish a special relationship of these events to the Roman church. This is remarkable in view of *1 Clement* 42, where Clement says that the apostles, having preached the gospel in many countries and cities, everywhere appointed the earliest converted Christians as bishops and deacons. Since in neither passage do any references appear about the relationship of individual apostles to specific churches, it follows that Clement is not interested in the doctrine of apostolic succession, but wants to speak generally about the continuance and stability of offices in the Christian churches. Thus, Peter is not named as the founder of the legitimate church offices in Rome, nor is Paul given that same function for Corinth. Rather, both apostles together are quoted as authorities and examples for all the churches.

In terms of the character of its materials, *1 Clement* is a parenesis. The material used by the author in his parenetical passages is clearly recognizable: the teaching of the Two Ways, especially catalogues of virtues and vices, tables of household duties, and rules of the community; the Old Testament (some of its material was composed in collections of examples); from the Christian tradition, a collection of sayings of Jesus is quoted twice (13.2 and 46.8); an edition of the letters of Paul; and kerygmatic formulas and liturgical materials from his church, from which an extensive intercessory prayer is quoted (59.3–61.3). But Clement also drew from pagan traditions, most notably a description of the creation and preservation of the world through the wisdom of God (20.1–11) that may have come to him by way of diaspora Judaism, as well as popular materials of illustrations like the story of the Phoenix (25.1–5).

An analysis of the structure of this rather long writing is difficult, but the literary procedures of its composition are evident. The actual occasion for the writing is mentioned only briefly (1.1); then the formerly famous piety of the Corinthian church is described, using a catalogue of Christian virtues and a table of duties (1.2–2.8). A catalogue of vices follows (3.2), and the first vice from this catalogue (jealousy) is illustrated with materials from the Old Testament (4.1–13), from the Christian tradition (5.1–7), and from the Greek world (6). The author proceeds in a similar way in the following chapters with a series of virtues: repentance (7–8), obedience (9.2–10.6), faith and hospitality (11–12), and humility (13–17). Almost all the examples are drawn from the Old Testament, which is quoted extensively and often verbatim. A number of Old Testament names and examples of behavior appear more than once, each time to illustrate a different virtue, and many examples have parallels in Hebrews 11. This demonstrates clearly that older illustrative materials have been secondarily used for the various virtues or vices. Traditions of different origin are occasionally inserted, such as a short catechism of words of Jesus (13.2) that was not drawn from any written gospel, but shows close affinities to the Synoptic Sayings Source (that is also the case for the quotation in *1 Clem.* 46.8).

After concluding remarks (17.1–19.1), a new section is begun that follows the outline of the Christian kerygma, though it contains many digressions. The section 19.2–20.12 speaks about the creation. Upon the mention of the Lord Jesus Christ, "whose blood was given for us" (21.6), the author quotes a table of household duties (21.6–8) and an admonition of Christ in the form of a quotation of Ps 33:12–18 (*1 Clem.* 22.1–8),

warns of double-mindedness (23) and offers a discussion of the resurrection (23.4–25.5). He gives the example of the Phoenix and alludes to other
parables that are reminiscent of Matt 24:32–33 and Mark 4:3–9. A
warning of the coming judgment (*1 Clem.* 28.1) introduces admonitions
concerning sanctification and good works (29–34.6) and a reminder of the
promise (34.7–35.12). The statement "this is the way in which we found
our salvation, Jesus Christ" (36.1) looks back upon the whole first part of
the letter, which is indeed an extensive description of Christian teachings,
namely, of the "way." The special instructions begin only at this point of
the letter: material about the order of the church comes first, with many
examples and quotations. The description of the Christian offices and
their foundation is important (42). *1 Clem.* 44.1–6 finally refers to the
specific situation in Corinth. The admonition to restore unanimity, obedience, and subordination (45–58) in addition to more references to the Old
Testament, uses specifically Christian materials more widely, some of
which are drawn from the Pauline letters. The concluding intercessory
prayer (59.3–61.3) abounds with allusions to passages of the Old Testament and is clearly dependent upon Jewish prayers.

1 Clement provides important insights into the general piety of Christian churches in that period. What is found in this letter must have dominated the liturgy, teaching, and preaching of its congregation. Clement is
convinced that this kind of piety and conduct should be the foundation for
the unanimity of the individual congregation and for the unity of the
church at large, rather than specific doctrines that could be identified as
the theological position of one single Christian apostle like Paul. In the
context of this Christian piety, nobody could have understood what the
actual issues were in the showdown between Peter and Paul in Antioch.
Neither was Clement prepared to enter into a discussion of theological
issues that might have been controversial in the Corinthian church to
which he was writing. As long as the Corinthians were sincerely following
the "way" that he describes in his letter, such controversies would become
irrelevant and in any case not be important enough to cause a division in
the congregation.

(f) The Letters of Peter and the Legacy of Paul

The piety propagated by Clement made it possible to refer in general to
the authorities of the venerable martyrs Peter and Paul. The letters of
Paul, as *1 Clement* shows, could be understood as documents of this piety,
which explains how it was possible that a deutero-Pauline letter could be
written in Rome at about the same time, but be issued under the authorship of Peter: the First Epistle of Peter. Except for the name of the sender
(1 Pet 1:1), nothing in this writing points to Peter; everything is either

Pauline or general Christian tradition. The form of the prescript copies the prescripts of the Pauline letters. The beginning of the proem, "blessed be the God and Father of our Lord Jesus Christ," presupposes the identical introductory formulas of the proems in 2 Cor 1:3 and Eph 1:3. Silvanus, who is mentioned as the amanuensis of the letter in 1 Pet 5:12, is known as the co-author of a Pauline letter (1 Thess 1:1) and is otherwise attested as an apostle from Paul's staff (2 Cor 1:19; Acts 15:22ff). Mark (who sends his greetings in 1 Pet 5:13) appears in the list of greetings in Phlm 24 and Col 4:10 (note also Acts 13:5, etc., where he is mentioned as travelling with Paul and Barnabas). The author calls himself a "witness of the sufferings of Christ" (1 Pet 5:1); this does not point to an eyewitness of Jesus' crucifixion, but to a Christian who had experienced the sufferings of Christ in his own tribulations—note what was said above about the martyr Peter—and will therefore, like all other Christians, "partake in the glory that is to be revealed" (1 Pet 5:1).

Thus the letter, written in rather good Greek style, presupposes a situation in the history of the early Christian churches in which the perception of the two great apostles Peter and Paul as martyrs had been firmly fixed, just as is true in *1 Clement* and Ignatius. Models for such a pseudepigraphical letter could be found only in the collection of Pauline letters. But it was no longer a matter of much concern whether such a pseudepigraphical letter would now appear under the pseudonym of one or the other of these two great apostles and martyrs of the church. Peter was probably named as the author because the letter was written in Rome, which is hinted by the mention of "Babylon" (1 Pet 5:13), certainly a symbolic name for the capital (cf. Rev 14:8; §12.1c). If so, the letter is the first tangible evidence for Rome's claim to Peter as its special apostolic authority, a claim that was later fixed in the tradition of Peter as its first bishop. This might also explain why the author did not write under his

Bibliography to §12.2f: Commentaries

Edward Gordon Selwyn, *The First Epistle of St. Peter* (2d ed.; London: Macmillan, and New York: St. Martin's, 1947, and reprints).

Frank W. Beare, *The First Epistle of Peter* (3d ed.; Oxford: Blackwell, 1970).

Walter Grundmann, *Der Brief des Judas und der zweite Brief des Petrus* (ThHK 15; Berlin: Evangelische Verlagsanstalt, 1974).

J. N. D. Kelly, *A Commentary on the Epistles of Peter and of Jude* (Black's New Testament Commentaries; London: Black, 1969).

Bibliography to §12.2f: Studies

Rudolf Bultmann, "Bekenntnis- und Liedfragmente im ersten Petrusbrief," in: idem, *Exegetica*, 285–97.

Ernst Käsemann, "An Apologia for Primitive Christian Eschatology," in: idem, *Essays on New Testament Themes* (SBT 41; London: SCM, 1964) 169–95.

own name but made use of the name of the special Roman apostle as a pseudonym.

1 Peter was apparently written for a specific situation. The address "to the exiles of the dispersion in Pontus, Galatia, Cappadocia, Asia, and Bithynia" (1.1) is not necessarily a fiction, but reveals that the letter was sent to those churches as a circular letter in order to strengthen them in a situation of persecution. The ecclesiastical-political interest that was evident in Ignatius and *1 Clement* also appears here: leaders of the church wrote to other congregations, encouraging, counselling, and advising, in order to contribute to the building of Christian unity. The occasion and thus the date of this letter's composition may have been the Domitian persecution, which also provided our date for *1 Clement*. This persecution had consequences in the east, as is shown by the Revelation of John. But the author more likely wrote to the situation known from the correspondence of Pliny the Younger when he was governor of Bithynia (§12.3d), i.e., ca. 112. In any case, the letter shows that persecution provided the occasion for the author's concern with the strengthening of the bonds holding the church at large together.

Various hypotheses have been proposed with respect to the genre of 1 Peter. Because of the obvious allusions to baptism in 1:22f and 2:1ff (note also "having been born anew to a living hope through the resurrection of Jesus Christ from the dead," 1:3) it seems natural to suggest the baptismal liturgy as its life situation. Some scholars have even tried to find in this writing an entire baptismal liturgy that was shaped secondarily into an epistle. Another factor is the apparent ending to the letter in 4:11 and its new start in 4:12, especially since only 4:12ff seems to speak about suffering as a present reality, while the preceding chapter discussed suffering as a possibility. Is 1 Pet 4:12–5:14 an appendix that was added when the situation suddenly changed and the persecution was intensified? In order to solve such problems, we must begin with the observation that the author uses and interprets various traditional materials to a very large extent; these cannot always be reconstructed in their entirety, but are still clearly recognizable despite the author's comments and additions. 1 Pet 1:20 and 3:18–19, 22 are drawn from traditional kerygmatic formulas that describe Christ's work of salvation; 2:21–25 is a more hymnic description of Christ's suffering that draws its terminology from Isaiah 53; 1 Pet 1:3–12 uses or imitates liturgical sentences for a fundamental description of salvation, following the examples of Col 1:3–6 and Eph 1:3–14; 1 Pet 1:22–2:3 quotes an already fixed admonition for newly baptized Christians.

In addition to these liturgical materials, the author uses many parenetic traditions. 1 Pet 2:13–3:6 reproduces a table of household duties that contained not only the usual admonitions for slaves, women, and men, but was introduced by a request to be obedient to the governing authorities; 4:3–5 is based on a catalogue of vices, 4:7–11 upon a catalogue of virtues that was elaborated under the influence of passages from the Pauline letters. Eschatological admonitions like 1 Pet 1:13 (=Luke 12:35) show that the eschatological sections of the letter (1:13ff; 4:12ff; 5:6ff) draw upon traditional sentences. 1 Peter, like *1 Clement,* draws freely from the treasure of ecclesiastical liturgy, preaching, and parenesis, and uses the Old Testament, though in most cases without quoting it explicitly. All the related genres play a role in the letter, but it cannot be assigned to any one genre in particular. The language of the writing is "biblical," or is at least influenced by liturgical language that was in turn influenced by the language of the Bible and enriched with quotations from it (note especially 1 Pet 2:5–10).

The intention of the letter is beyond doubt: it was written to renew the expectation of the parousia in the face of the persecution of Christians, and it therefore calls for joyfulness in suffering (1:6f). The experience of suffering strengthens confidence in Christ's coming, though it also heightens the danger of apostasy (5:8–9). At the same time, the author enjoins regulations for Christian conduct that are not in themselves eschatological rules (cf. the table of household duties and its use in Colossians and Ephesians), but should be observed even more strictly in times of tribulation. The Christians are admonished to suffer as righteous people (3:13–17; 4:14–16). Eschatological conduct thus becomes identical to a general morality that has been tested and sharpened according to the criteria of the Bible and the gospel.

1 Peter was still written from a perspective of a genuine eschatological expectation. This, however, was no longer the case with respect to the second letter preserved under that name, 2 Peter. This letter was also written to reinforce expectation of the parousia upon the mind of its readers, but does not proclaim that expectation as a hope and consolation for those who are persecuted; rather, it tries to defend it as a theological dogma. 2 Peter is dependent upon 1 Peter and in fact refers to it explicitly (2 Pet 3:1). While many of the pseudepigraphical trappings are missing in 1 Peter, 2 Peter makes extensive use of them. The author introduces himself ceremoniously as "Symeon Petrus, servant and apostle of Jesus Christ," refers to the tradition that Jesus had predicted his martyrdom (1:14), emphasizes that he had been a witness of Jesus' transfiguration (1:16–18), and does not fail to observe that Paul is his beloved brother (3:15). The use of the Epistle of Jude (§12.1b) in chapter 2 could hardly be expected from Peter the historical disciple. Finally, the language of the writing is the written idiom of second century Christianity, a thoroughly

Hellenized literary language that uses terms such as "participants in divine nature" (1:4) that are completely alien to early Christianity, and Greek proverbs, e.g., "the sow is washed only to wallow in the mire" (2:22). Borrowings from Atticistic rhetoric clearly distinguish 2 Peter from the Greek Koine of almost all other early Christian writings.

The mention of Paul in this letter of "Peter" and the explicit reference to Paul's letters make it possible to classify 2 Peter with those early Christian writings that consider both Peter and Paul to be authorities of the church. But the situation is no longer the same as in Ignatius and *1 Clement,* because in 2 Pet 3:15–16 the author warns his readers about the difficulties in interpreting the Pauline letters and the distortions of Paul by the heretics, who were also perverting other writings. A very similar remark is found in a letter of bishop Dionysius of Corinth (quoted by Eusebius *Eccl. hist.* 4.23.12): "The apostles of the devil have filled my letters with tares by leaving out some things and putting in others. . . . Therefore it is no wonder that some have gone about to falsify even the Scripture of the Lord." Both statements presuppose that Christian writings that already had considerable authority were being edited and interpreted. The way that 2 Pet 3:2 puts side by side "the words said before by the holy prophets" and "the commandment of the Lord and Savior given through your apostles" suggests that the latter were also accessible in writings of some authority. From such documents, namely, from written gospels, the author drew his information about Peter as an eyewitness of Jesus' transfiguration (1:16–18) and the prediction of Peter's martyrdom (1:14).

There can be little doubt about the identity of the people who are said to twist the Scriptures. Even Jude was arguing against gnostic opponents. The author of 2 Peter reformulates the polemic against Gnosticism in order to aim it more directly against gnostic interpretation of Genesis (see 2 Pet 2:4–10, the remarks about Gen 6:1–4, Noah as the preacher of righteousness, Sodom and Gomorrah, and Lot the righteous), but avoids every passage in Jude that refers to apocryphal literature. With the term "cleverly disguised myths" (1:16) he attacks the gnostics, to whom he furthermore assigns the skeptical opinion regarding the expectation of the parousia that had already been quoted in *1 Clem.* 23.2–4 (cf. *2 Clem.* 11.2) and was probably derived from an unknown (Christian?) book: "Where is the promise of his coming? For ever since the fathers fell asleep, all things have continued as they were from the beginning of creation" (2 Pet 3:4). The new doctrine of the parousia of Christ, however, that the author establishes against the gnostics, is anything but renewal of the early Christian expectation. 2 Pet 3:5–13 presents an eschatological doctrine about the end of the visible world that demands recognition as a general truth, since the concept of the conflagration of the cosmos (3:12) is designed to make the Christian eschatological theories acceptable even to a Stoic. The relationship to early Christian eschatological expectations is only superficially claimed by quotations from 1 Thess 5:2 and Rev 21:1 (2 Pet 3:10, 13). The gnostic interpretation of Paul finally created a situation in which the alliance of the two authorities Peter and Paul became questionable. While the letters of Paul were still quoted and used without hesitation around the year 100, a generation later the author of 2 Peter belonged to those orthodox Christians who named Paul as an authority of the church, but secretly wished that the great apostle had not written any letters—or at least not such letters as those that were causing so many interpretive problems in the effort to defend true faith against heresy.

(g) Church Order in the Name of Paul: The Pastoral Epistles

The letters to the Colossians, Ephesians, and Hebrews, as well as Ignatius of Antioch, had been theologically engaged with Paul and with the continuation of a theology in his name. But for *1 Clement,* Paul was little more than a teacher and counselor of the right conduct that would maintain the unity of the church. *1 Clement* thus pointed the way toward an "ecclesiastical" image of Paul. The type of Pauline letters that were indirectly being requested by the author of 2 Peter were indeed being written during the first half of II CE: the letters to Timothy and Titus, usually called the Pastoral Epistles. These three letters, which form a unity in their language, theological concepts, and intention, and which were written by the same author, differ in many respects from all the other letters of the Pauline corpus. With the exception of Philemon, they are the only ones in this collection that are directed to individuals; still,

Bibliography to §12.2g: Commentaries

Martin Dibelius and Hans Conzelmann, *The Pastoral Epistles: A Commentary on the Pastoral Epistles* (Hermeneia; Philadelphia: Fortress, 1972).

Bibliography to §12.2g: Studies

Robert J. Karris, "The Background and Significance of the Polemic of the Pastoral Epistles," *JBL* 92 (1973) 549–64.

Hans von Campenhausen, "Polycarp von Smyrna und die Pastoralbriefe," in: idem, *Aus der Frühzeit des Christentums* (Tübingen: Mohr/Siebeck, 1964) 197–252.

Idem, "The Christian and Social Life according to the New Testament," in: idem, *Tradition and Life,* 141–59.

Martin Dibelius, "'Επίγνωσις ἀληθείας," in: idem, *Botschaft und Geschichte* (Tübingen: Mohr/Siebeck, 1956) 2. 1–13.

Bibliography to §12.2g: Text of *3 Corinthians*

Michel Testuz, *Payrus Bodmer X–XII* (Cologny-Genève: Bibliotheca Bodmeriana, 1959).

W. Schneemelcher, "The Acts of Paul," *NTApo* 2. 375–78.

these individuals are not addressed as private persons, but as church leaders, entrusted with the organization and supervision of the life of Christian communities. The external evidence for the Pastoral Epistles is not as good as that for the other letters of Paul since they were missing in the canon of Marcion (§12.3c) and do not appear in the oldest extant manuscript of the Pauline epistles (𝔓46). They are mentioned in the Muratorian Canon, however, and both Irenaeus and Tertullian knew them. Doubts about their authenticity were raised as early as the beginning of the nineteenth century; more recent scholarship has accumulated such a large number of conclusive arguments against authenticity that Pauline authorship can be maintained solely on the basis of tortuous hypotheses and the accumulation of historical improbabilities. I will mention only the more important arguments.

The language of the Pastoral Epistles shows many more striking departures from Pauline usage than any other letter of the Pauline corpus. Moreover, all these linguistic peculiarities are part of the Christian language of II CE that lacks analogies and parallels from the time of Paul. Particularly striking is the terminology for the description of the event of salvation. The coming of Christ is described as the "epiphany of the savior" (*soter:* Tit 2:13; cf. 2 Tim 1:10; Tit 3:4, 6, where this terminology is used for the appearance of Jesus on earth). Paul himself never uses such terms (*soter* appears only once in Paul, where it is used for the future appearance of Christ: Phil 3:20), but there are numerous parallels in Hellenistic religious usage and in the emperor cult. The title "Savior God" for Christ (Tit 2:10) would be unique in the entire theological language of first-century Christian literature. "The appearance of the goodness and loving-kindness (*philanthropia*) of our Savior, God" (Tit 3:4) is also paralleled by formulations from the emperor cult. True Christian conduct is called "religion" (*eusebeia*) throughout these epistles (1 Tim 2:2; 4:7; etc.); the Christian message is designated as "healthy doctrine" (1 Tim 1:10; 2 Tim 4:3, etc.), while the term "faith" is used mostly for the Christian creedal formula (1 Tim 3:9; 6:10; etc.). All of this is not only inconceivable for Paul, but at the same time is typical for the pagan religious language of the Roman imperial period that was increasingly adopted by Christian writers during II CE. Occasionally the Pastoral Epistles attempt to resume Pauline phrases, but especially in these instances it is most clear that the writer was not Paul himself. A characteristic phrase of this type is Tit 3:5: "saved . . . not by deeds done by us in righteousness, but by virtue of his mercy" (see also 2 Tim 1:9). Even the author's attempt to let Paul speak about his own conversion reveals the writer's deutero-Pauline theological concepts; 1 Tim 1:13 says: "I formerly blasphemed and persecuted and insulted him; but I received mercy because I had acted ignorantly in unbelief." Paul, on the other hand, speaks proudly about the fact that, although his persecution of the church was an outrage, his righteousness under the law was perfect (Phil 3:4–6; cf. Gal 1:14).

Just as important as the language of the Pastoral Epistles is the question of where in the life of Paul these letters could be placed. Strangely enough, it is exactly the instructions to Paul's personal associates, which might seem strongly to suggest the authenticity of the Pastorals, that create insurmountable problems (note especially 2 Tim 4:9–21, but also Tit 1:5; 3:12–14). When one considers the situations that are known from the Pauline letters and Acts, there is no place in the history of the Pauline mission in which the Pastoral Epistles can be accommodated. Thus, the letters to Timothy and Titus could not have been written at any time before Paul's Roman imprisonment. It is, of course, not impossible that Paul was released from imprisonment in Rome; but in that case we must assume that he made his intended missionary journey (Rom 15:28) to the west (*1 Clem.* 5.7 says that Paul had reached the limits of the west) and suffered martyrdom upon his return to Rome. There is no evidence for a return of Paul to the east, that is, to Greece and Asia Minor, which must be assumed by the defenders of the Pastorals' authenticity.

If the Pastoral Epistles were not written by Paul, the question of their date in the history of early Christianity is still to be considered. It seems that on behalf of the churches of the Pauline tradition they seek to maintain and secure Paul's authority—and thus also of the collection of his letters—against the danger of a gnostic interpretation. If one wanted to employ Paul in a pseudepigraphical letter, speaking on his own behalf and for the church as its defender against Gnosticism, several alternatives were available. One of these was chosen by the author of *3 Corinthians,* a letter now preserved in the context of the *Acts of Paul.* We can leave undecided whether the letter ever circulated independently, or was composed by the author of the *Acts of Paul* for the narrative context which related to Paul's controversy with opponents in Corinth as it was known from his Corinthian correspondence. First, a letter is sent by the Corinthian presbyters to Paul that enumerates the heretical teachings of the gnostics: one should not make recourse to the prophets; the world and human race were not created by God; Jesus was not born by the virgin and did not appear in the flesh; and there was no resurrection of the flesh. Paul, temporarily imprisoned in Philippi, responds with a letter, namely, the pseudepigraphical *3 Corinthians,* in which he repeats and confirms the ecclesiastical confession of the creation of the world by God, the birth of Jesus from the seed of David through Mary, salvation through the body of Christ, resurrection of the flesh, and punishment for all godless people. In composing this letter, the author used sentences from the Pauline epistles and proofs from the Old Testament for the resurrection of the flesh. This letter, written at about the same time as the Pastoral Epistles (though its author does not know them, or at least does not use them for his own pseudepigraphon), therefore solves the problem of the gnostic interpretation of Paul by providing a situation in Paul's own life; in the midst of his missionary work he writes on his own behalf, with sentences from the genuine letters, in order to defend those same letters against a gnostic interpretation. Paul thus presents himself as a defender of early catholic faith.

The author of the Pastoral Epistles chose a quite different alternative. He resumes the tradition of Paul the martyr (§12.2e), but in so doing does not simply continue the tradition of the "letters from prison"—a category to which even *3 Corinthians* belongs. The letters that he writes are presented rather as the testament of Paul. By choosing this literary genre that had developed in Judaism (§5.3c), a prior decision was made that gives this type of defense of Paul its peculiar character. Whoever speaks in his own testament no longer needs to be defended, because he is already one of the "ancient" people—in this case, a revered martyr—whose authority is beyond question. The testament permits a recapitulation of the past, and it demands a prospective view of the future in such a way that the experience of the past, interpreted and summarized from the perspective of the present, becomes a signpost for the future.

The genre of the testament was consciously chosen for 2 Timothy and was applied consistently in its composition. 2 Tim 1:3–18 looks back into the past of the addressee (thus the mention of Timothy's grandmother and mother by name), which leads to the situation of Paul, who is imprisoned, forsaken by all. But Paul knows that his "heritage" (*paratheke*, a term that appears only here in the NT) will be preserved. With the words "but you, my child," 2 Tim 2:1 introduces the admonition of the testament. This address is typical for testamental style and occurs in the Pastoral Epistles only here. The admonitions begin with a basic exhortation (2:1–13) that twice quotes traditional formulas of Christian faith (2:8 and 2:11–13); an admonition for behavior toward the heretics follows (2:14–21), then a personal admonition about correct conduct. Completely in accord with the genre of the testament, the next section provides a warning about the "last days" (3:1–17) that announces the coming of the false teachers (3:2–9), calls for steadfastness in persecutions (3:10–12), and refers to the Holy Scriptures as a source of strength (3:14–16). The warnings are concluded by an oath (4:1ff) and a repeated reference to Paul's situation as a martyr facing death (4:6–8). The last section of the letter demonstrates that Paul's care for the churches occupied him into his very last days (4:9ff). Forsaken by all, there is nothing left for him but to pass his legacy on to Timothy "through this testament." In contrast to Tit 3:12, Paul makes no statements about his future plans; he only expresses his confidence "that the Lord will rescue me from every evil and save me for his heavenly kingdom" (2 Tim 4:18). For this reason, we must conclude that 2 Timothy was conceived from the start as the last of these three letters.

The other two letters are closely and intricately connected with 2 Timothy. Paul's actual legacy, that is, his statements about the ordering of the church and of Christian conduct, and the procedures for the fight against heresy, is provided in more detail in 1 Timothy and in Titus; 2 Timothy had spoken about the heretics and about Christian conduct only to the extent that was called for by the eschatological admonitions and parenesis appropriate to the testamentary genre. The basic structure of 1 Timothy was provided by the genre of the church order. The schema for the arrangements of the topics stems from the traditional table of household duties, which has been modified and expanded to become a more appropriate table of ecclesiastical duties. The beginning (1 Tim 2:1–15), which follows the traditional topics, introduces the theme of the behavior to political authorities, but then leads to a discussion of prayer. The next two traditional topics also give more specifically ecclesiastical instructions about the prayer of men and the conduct of women in the worship service of the church (2:8–15). As a consequence, the subsequent instructions for the offices of the church seem to come more naturally: bishops (3:1–11) and deacons (3:12–13; 4:6). 1 Tim 5:1–2 still reveals that in the traditional table, the topics "old people" and "young people" should have been discussed. However, the author first wants to conclude his instruction about church offices, and he therefore skips those topics. Instead, 5:3–16 discusses the widows (as a church office!) and 5:17–20 the presbyters. Only at this point does the author feel free to return to some of the traditional topics of the table of household duties, namely, slaves (6:1–2) and rich people (apparently a modification of the traditional "masters," 6:17–19).

The author has interrupted this underlying schema at certain points, in part with personal information (3:14f), and in part with references to false teachers (4:1–5) and personal instruction to "Timothy"; these last, however, are actually general instructions to Christian officers in all categories (4:6–16; 6:3–16); all three elements are combined in the letter's introduction (1:3–20). The structure of the letter to Titus is similar. Instruction for the presbyters (Tit 1:5ff) is followed by admonitions for old men, young women, young men, and slaves (2:1–10), and finally a remark about obedience to the government (3:1–2). Interruptions once more offer exhortations about the false teachers (1:10–16; 3:9–11), personal information (3:12–14), and an admonition to "Titus" (2:15). In all three letters, the author has inserted kerygmatic and hymnic traditions at various occasions (e.g., 1 Tim 3:16; Tit 2:11; 3:4f).

As for the details of the instructions and admonitions, the Pastoral Epistles use catalogues of virtues and vices that are at times expanded by explanations and comments. Two features are remarkable: the same virtues are expected of the various church officers, bishops, presbyters, deacons, and widows, but also appear as general criteria for the conduct of all Christians. The virtues which are demanded throughout would have been completely acceptable for Christians, Jews, and pagans alike. The Christian moral behavior that is requested here is fully identical with the general social and moral duties and virtues that would have been expected of any upright citizen of that time. In a summary formulation it is stated thus: "renounce impiety and base desires, and live prudent and upright and religious lives in the world" (Tit 2:12). For the details of such morality, the author mentions faithfulness in marriage, care for one's children and home, hospitality, avoidance of quarrelsome behavior, care for the weak and for those in need, and satisfaction with one's worldly status and possessions. Because of this we speak of the Pastoral Epistles' ideal of a Christian citizen's morality. A specifically eschatological motivation for Christian ethical behavior is completely missing; we find instead only very general references to the Christian hope in the appearance of Christ in the future (Tit 2:13). Even if 1 Tim 6:7 says "we brought nothing into this world, and we cannot take anything out of the world," the author is simply stating something that every pagan citizen of his time would have accepted, as he would also agree with the statement that "the love of money is the root of all evil" (1 Tim 6:10). Such statements are not specifically Christian, and they have no relationship whatsoever to eschatology. The virtues requested from the Christian church officers are identical with those expected from secular professions, such as the general or the actor.

In this accommodation of Christian morality to the general moral expectations of their time, the Pastoral Epistles took a decisive step that prepared for Christian apologetics (§12.3e). Christianity no longer looked upon itself as a religious sect with a special, divine calling that required commitment to unusual ethical demands. Rather, the church had become obligated to the world and society at large and had to fulfill the general social norms in an exemplary fashion. For a group of letters found among the letters of the Pauline corpus, this is a surprising turn, because Paul himself had founded his ethics upon an eschatological perspective. In reality, however, an important element of Pauline ethics is rediscovered here and given more general significance. Paul, to be sure, had recognized a special ethical behavior as legitimate under eschatological perspectives (see, e.g., 1 Cor 7:25–35), but he had refused to make such behavior the norm for his churches' morality. On the contrary, he explicitly emphasized the legitimacy of rational moral decisions after prudent consideration of the alternatives (see 1 Cor 7:2–7; 7:36–38; Phil 4:8–9). The Pastoral Epistles resurrect this element of Paul's ethics in their fight against the gnostics, who had made Paul their chief witness of a sectarian morality that had no concern for the moral norms of the society, because the "world" of which that society was a part had no rightful claim to be taken seriously.

The identity of the heretics attacked in the Pastoral Epistles has been a difficult problem for historians. It is evident that the author makes no attempt to enter into a theological discussion with the heretics, that he instead stresses ethics and moral behavior as the only true criterion for the distinction between true and false belief. But the attempt to gather together the various scattered references about the heretics leads to a rather confusing picture. On the one hand, they seem to be Jews or Jewish Christians. The opponents want to be teachers of the law (1 Tim 1:7); they come from the "circumcision" (Tit 1:10) and preach "Jewish myths and human commands" (Tit 1:14). Their demand for abstention from certain foods would fit into this picture (1 Tim 4:3), especially since here and in Tit 1:14f the author emphasizes the purity of everything that God has created. But coupled with the dietary demand in 1 Tim 4:3 is the prohibition of marriage, and in the same chapter the author rejects the "godless old wives' tales" (*mythoi*, 1 Tim 4:7). The reference to "myths and genealogies" has a similar ring (1 Tim 1:4; cf. "genealogies," Tit 3:9). This seems to fit gnostic opponents better than Jewish Christians. Indeed, there can be little, if any, doubt that gnostics are in view, when one considers the explicit rejection of "the contradictions of the false knowledge" (*gnosis*, 1 Tim 6:20) and the quotation of the typically gnostic claim that the resurrection had already taken place (2 Tim 2:18).

The other characterizations of the false teachers do not help much because the accusation that all they wanted was money (1 Tim 6:5, 10; Tit 1:11) was raised against many political, philosophical, and religious opponents at that time. The statement that the opponents were especially eager to convert and recruit women (2 Tim 3:6–7) would fit the known tendencies toward emancipation in gnostic sects and the role women seem to have played in some of them; this is indirectly confirmed by the author's prohibition of public teaching by women (1 Tim 2:12), something that was subsequently also interpolated into a genuine letter of Paul (1 Cor 14:33b–36). But the primary difficulty in identifying the opponents remains: even though it is possible to verify each particular characterization through information from other sources, there is no way in which the various pieces of information can be fit together into a coherent picture of one single group of opponents. One may, for example, argue that the reference to the "contradictions (*antitheseis*) of the false *gnosis*" (1 Tim 6:20) indeed refers to the primary writing of the heretic Marcion (§12.3c), called the "Antitheses." But it is impossible to harmonize 1 Timothy's references to the opponents' teaching of the law with Marcion's radical criticism of the Old Testament. On the other hand, circumcision, teaching of the law, and dietary rules would be appropriate categories if the opponents were Jewish Christians or Judaizers. But can one also ascribe to the same opponents the prohibition of marriage, emancipation of women, and gnostic myths and genealogies?

Perhaps such Jewish-Christian gnostics are not completely unthinkable; gnosticizing Jewish Christianity was, to be sure, a component of the development of Christianity in Syria. This is not the place, however, to discuss the (somewhat remote) possibilities of gnostic and Jewish-Christian syncretism. After all, one would have to ascribe to one single group a number of rather contradictory heretical doctrines. Therefore, a more reasonable explanation of the references to heretics in the Pastoral Epistles strongly commends itself: the author does not intend to describe any particular group at all since he has no interest in providing materials for a proper refutation. His characterizations rather have the character of catch-words that point to typical phenomena of heresy in general. This is especially evident in the predictions of the future that "Paul" gives in 2 Tim 3:1ff, but also in 1 Tim 4:1ff. The church leader thus receives criteria for the identification of heresy, and the author has obviously crystallized his criteria from the experiences with various heresies. If this is the case, we can also understand why some of the most important criteria for the recognition of heresy are not given at all with respect to its contents, but only as formal definitions: disputations and controversies, and the refusal to submit to the demands of a healthy Christian morality. In their fight against heresies, the Pastoral Epistles are designed to be a handbook, a manual for the church leader, enabling him to identify heresies of whatever kind, and to reject them without having to enter into a discussion of subtle theological points.

Adherence to the Pauline legacy has therefore been removed from the uncertain realm of the interpretation of the Pauline letters. In theological terms, the faith has been cast into new formulations that are more appropriate to the religious language of the time. The primary accomplishment of Paul is seen to be the organization of his congregations—which was indeed a task to which Paul had once devoted considerable time and effort, and which had occupied a central place in his missionary activities! But now the offices are fixed: one bishop or presiding presbyter (who should receive twice the salary of other officers, 1 Tim 4:17); under him presbyters, deacons, and widows (the latter are to be supported by the congregation, but should be thoroughly scrutinized so that they would not constitute an unnecessary burden to the community, 1 Tim 5:3–16); ordination by the laying on of hands (1 Tim 5:22; cf. 4:14), so that the charisma of the office can be passed on in an orderly fashion (2 Tim 1:6). The Pauline concept that all members of the church have special gifts as part of their possession of the spirit, thus qualifying them for service in the church, recedes into the background. Instead, moral qualifications are required for church officers, and the members of the congregation are reminded not of their Christian charismata, but of their general moral duties as good citizens. Thus, the Christian church can claim a legitimate place as one of the religions of the society of the Roman world: their members fulfill the duties of a good citizen as well as anyone else, or even better.

There should be no question about the time and place of the writing of the Pastoral Epistles. Their own geographical information points to the realm of the countries of the Aegean Sea. Places specifically named include Ephesus, Troas, and Miletus in western Asia Minor, Thessalonica, Corinth, and Nicopolis in Greece, plus Galatia, Dalmatia, and Crete. Timothy, to whom the "testament" of Paul is entrusted, resides in Ephesus. For the date of the Pastoral Epistles we must consider the following factors: a time of relative security from persecution, of the strong growth of Christianity in the middle classes of the cities, the organization of many churches under the same church order (the Pastoral Epistles span the whole region from Galatia to the cities of western Asia Minor, across the Aegean to Greece as far as its western coast and Dalmatia), and a language that belongs to II CE and is not hesitant to borrow freely from the terminology of the imperial cult. The time of the emperors Hadrian and Antoninus Pius was a relatively long period of peace for the Christians in II CE; thus the years from 120 to 160 would be the most appropriate. The author was, no doubt, an influential and farseeing leader of the church who pointed the way toward the consolidation of Christianity as a well organized religion acceptable to the culture of its time, and strengthened its defense against the false teachers, especially the gnostics, whose propaganda sought to turn Christianity away from the world and fom the moral obligations of society. From the first half of II CE, only one such church leader is known by name: Polycarp of Smyrna. The hypothesis that Polycarp was in fact the author of these letters was proposed by Hans von Campenhausen and supported by many convincing arguments; but only a few scholars have been willing to accept this suggestion.

(h) Polycarp of Smyrna

Polycarp was bishop of Smyrna as early as the time of Ignatius, and he suffered martyrdom in the time of Marcus Aurelius (after 160 CE; §12.3e). A document which survives as his *Letter to the Philippians* is not well preserved. All the known Greek manuscripts derive from a Greek archetype in which the text of chaps. 10–13 was missing. Chap. 13 is quoted, almost complete, by Eusebius (*Hist. eccl.* 3.36.14–15), but only a rather poor Latin translation is available for the text of chaps. 10–12 and 14. It is quite likely that the letter as we have it was actually composed from two different writings to the church in Philippi. The first, consisting of chaps. 13–14, was a cover letter for the sending of the letters of Ignatius that the church in Philippi had requested. It must have been written very soon after Ignatius' visit. Polycarp does not yet know anything about the martyrdom of the Antiochian bishop, but is only concerned to carry out the instructions that he had received from him. *Phil.* 9.1, however, speaks about Ignatius in very different terms: he is now a blessed martyr whose example can be recalled. Thus, it seems that the letter to which this passage belongs, *Philippians* 1–12, was written several years or, more likely, several decades later. This is confirmed by the use of other early Christian writings in this letter. It not only knows and uses *1 Clement,* but also corrects the quotations of sayings of Jesus in *1 Clem.* 13.2 according to the text that had been established by the Gospels of Matthew and Luke (*Phil.* 2.3); a knowledge of the text of those gospels is also shown elsewhere (*Phil.* 7.2). The immediate occasion for the writing of this second letter was a case of embezzlement by the presbyter Valens in Philippi, which Polycarp discusses in chap. 11.

The language and theology of Polycarp's letter are closely related to the Pastoral Epistles. Admonitions in the style of an ecclesiastical order that was developed on the basis of the older tables for the household corres-

Bibliography to §12.2h: Text

Funk-Bihlmeyer, *ApostVät*, xxxviii–xliv, 114–20.

Lake, *ApostFath,* 1. 279–301.

Bibliography to §12.2h: Commentaries

Lightfoot, *Apostolic Fathers,* vol. 2, part 2. 897–998.

William R. Schoedel, *Polycarp, Martyrdom of Polycarp, Fragment of Papias* (Grant, *ApostFath* 5).

Bibliography to §12.2h: Studies

P. N. Harrison, *Polycarp's Two Epistles to the Philippians* (Cambridge: Cambridge University, 1936).

Hans von Campenhausen, "Polykarp von Smyrna und die Pastoralbriefe," in: idem, *Aus der Frühzeit des Christentums* (Tübingen: Mohr/Siebeck, 1963) 197–252.

pond closely to those of the Pastoral Epistles (cf. *Philippians* 4–6: women, widows, deacons, young people, presbyters); this is also the case with the catalogues of virtues and vices (*Phil.* 2.2; 4.3; 5.2; 12.2). Among the exhortations to prayer at the end of the letter we find an admonition to pray for the government (*Phil.* 12.3) that recalls 1 Tim 2:1f. The warning against avarice is given in the same words as in the Pastoral Epistles (*Phil.* 4.1 = 1 Tim 6:10). However, passages that look like quotations from the Pastoral Epistles are rare in Polycarp's writing. In most instances, he makes the same statement in independent formulations, though using the same terminology. In addition, sentences and phrases from the other letters of Paul occur frequently, and Polycarp also knew 1 Peter; although he never refers to Peter by name, he appeals to the authority of Paul several times (*Phil.* 3.2; 9.2; 11.3). For Polycarp there is no apostolic authority other than Paul, and the letter demonstrates how a bishop could conduct his office of directing and ordering the affairs of the Christian churches in the spirit of Paul, namely, in the spirit of the Pastoral Epistles.

Polycarp is also concerned with the fight against the false teachers although, like the Pastoral Epistles, he does not enter into a discussion of their arguments. References to Jewish-Christian heretics are absent in Polycarp's letter. The criteria that he establishes for the recognition of false teachers one finds solely in sentences directed against the gnostics: "For everyone who does not confess that Jesus Christ has come in the flesh is an anti-Christ; and whoever does not confess the testimony of the cross is of the devil; and whoever perverts the sayings of the Lord to benefit his own desires and says there is neither resurrection nor judgment, that one is the first-born of Satan" (*Phil.* 7.1). Irenaeus, himself from Asia Minor and acquainted, as he reports, with the great bishop while still a child, tells an anecdote about the encounter of Polycarp with Marcion (on Marcion, see §12.3c): Marcion had said to Polycarp, "Recognize me!" whereupon Polycarp had answered: "I recognize you as the first-born of Satan" (Irenaeus *Adv. haer.* 3.3.4). Inasmuch as Irenaeus knew Polycarp's letter to the Philippians it is quite doubtful whether this anecdote, as well as others that Irenaeus tells about him, can be used as historical evidence. But the possibility should be considered that when this letter (as well as the Pastoral Epistles) was written, Polycarp knew Marcion and included him in the polemic against false teachers. Marcion's first appearance must be dated in the middle of Polycarp's tenure as bishop of Smyrna; it is thus not impossible that the second letter of Polycarp, including *Phil.* 7.1, refers to Marcion with the remark about perverting the sayings of the Lord, since the Gospel of Luke, which Polycarp knew, had been published by Marcion in a thoroughly revised edition. As with the

Pastoral Epistles, it could not be expected that all remarks about heretics would refer to the same heretical group. Thus, even if various other statements about heretics were formulated with reference to Jewish Christians or to gnostics, the warning of 1 Tim 6:20 against the "antitheses of the false gnosis" could still owe its formulation to Marcion's primary work, the *Antitheses*—whether or not the author of 1 Timothy was Polycarp, who was doubtlessly the most significant ecclesiastical leader of the first half of II CE.

3. CHRISTIANITY IN ITS ENCOUNTER WITH ITS SOCIAL WORLD

(a) Gospel and History as Victory in the World

Nearly all the early Christian writings mentioned thus far were written for use within the Christian community. Apologetic motifs occur occasionally, such as in the passion narrative of the Gospel of John. But Christianity could not turn toward the Roman world in its literary activity until it had become more positive about that world and the place of the church within the society of the imperial period. Such a development required an order for the church and for the life of its members that agreed with the generally recognized principles of a good-citizens' morality, a general diminution of the eschatological expectation of Christ's coming in the near future, and an unequivocal rejection of Gnosticism with its denial of the world and of its order. All these requirements are displayed in the Pastoral Epistles in an exemplary fashion, though still in writings exclusively designed for internal Christian use. The first Christian writings written from the perspective of apologetics that also consciously appealed to pagan readership were those of Luke. Therefore, we have delayed our discussion of these New Testament books until now, although they could perhaps be dated somewhat earlier than the Pastoral Epistles.

1) *The Lukan Writings.* The Gospel of Luke and the Acts of the Apostles were written by the same author. Both writings are characterized by their prologues as two parts of one major literary work (Luke 1:1–4; Acts 1:1–2). They are uniform in language and literary style; differences

Bibliography to §12.3a (1)

Henry J. Cadbury, *The Making of Luke-Acts* (2d ed.; London: SPCK, 1958).

Hans Conzelmann, *The Theology of St. Luke* (New York: Harper, 1961).

Gerhard Lohfink, *Die Sammlung Israels: Eine Untersuchung zur lukanischen Ekklesiologie* (StANT 39; München: Kösel, 1975).

C. K. Barrett, *Luke the Historian in Recent Study* (London: Epworth, 1961).

François Bovon, *Luc le Théologien: Vingt-cinq ans des Recherches (1950–1975)* (Le Monde de la Bible; Neuchâtel and Paris: Delachaux & Niestlé, 1978).

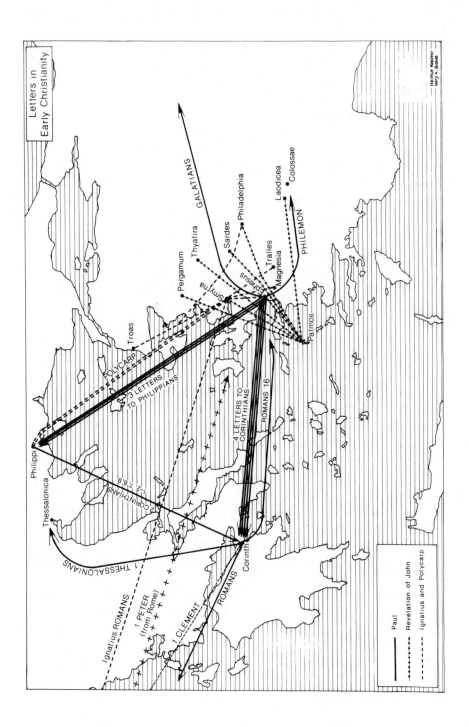

Letters in
Early Christianity

Paul
Revelation of John
Ignatius and Polycarp

Helmut Koester
Gary A. Bisbee

GALATIANS

Thyatira
Sardes
Philadelphia
Pergamum
Laodicea
Colossae
PHILEMON
Tralles
Smyrna
Magnesia
Ephesus
Patmos

Troas
POLYCARP
3 LETTERS
TO PHILIPPIANS

4 LETTERS TO
CORINTHIANS
ROMANS 16

Philippi
Thessalonica
2 CORINTHIANS
1.2.7.8.9

1 THESSALONIANS

Ignatius ROMANS
1 PETER
(from Rome)
1 CLEMENT
ROMANS
Corinth

arise from the usage of quite distinct source materials. It is unlikely that this work ever existed as a single book that was later divided, in view of the technical aspects of book production. Each of the two parts—we are dealing with the two longest writings of the New Testament—corresponds approximately to the largest size of a standard scroll. Neither of the two books gives the name of its author. Ecclesiastical tradition beginning with the end of II CE reports that "Luke" was the author and identifies him with the associate of Paul to whom Phlm 24 refers under this name, and whom Col 4:14 calls a physician (see also 2 Tim 4:11). But it is hardly conceivable that the author of Acts was a member of Paul's missionary staff. It is hard to believe that a person who was once closely connected with Paul's missionary work would suppress any mention of the letters of Paul (or even be unaware of them) and present a picture of Paul that conforms to some degree with the ideal of the missionary propagated by Paul's opponents in 2 Corinthians. It cannot be demonstrated from the language of his writings that the author was a physician anyway. Either the name of the author was indeed Luke, but the author was not the Luke mentioned as Paul's fellow worker, or the name "Luke" was added to the writings at a later date on the basis of 2 Tim 4:11 ("only Luke is still with me").

Nonetheless a bit more can be said about the author. He was a gentile Christian who had received a good education and who wrote Greek in good style. His acquaintance with the Greek Bible (the LXX) was thorough, and his language was deeply influenced by it; what he writes is "Biblical Greek." He was certainly raised and educated as a Christian. For him Peter and Paul are the two great men from the period of earliest Christianity. This fact points to those segments of the early catholic church in which these two apostles were together considered as an authority (§12.2d) and thus to a place of origin somewhere in the geographical realm of those churches, namely, Antioch, Ephesus, or Rome. But it is also apparent that Luke does not belong to the first or second generation of Christianity, but rather to its third. For the second generation, it could not be expected that these two apostles would belong together; that concept only developed during this later period. However, about the year 150, such men as Justin Martyr and Marcion, and perhaps a little earlier Polycarp of Smyrna as well, knew the Gospel of Luke (Polycarp may also have known Acts; cf. *Phil.* 1.2 with Acts 2:24). The time of the gospel's writing, therefore, cannot have been any later than ca. 125; Acts could have been written a decade later.

It is impossible to describe the purpose of the Lukan work in a single formulation. To be sure, Luke writes as if he was speaking primarily to the pagan world, yet he is always mindful of his Christian readers. This was indeed the case with all apologetic writers, because they consciously conceived of Christianity as an integral part of the entire world to which they directed their literary works. Luke intends to describe a development that comprises all of history (this does not imply that he was a historian). This development was predetermined from its primordial beginnings by the will of God, is announced in the Old Testament, and was proclaimed by John the Baptist. The life of Jesus, however, is the story of its foundation in the realm of history. From here it made its way from Jerusalem to Rome. Thus Luke wants to describe how the gospel, attested by wonderful deeds, conquered the whole world. But he intends to demonstrate at the same time that Christianity, not Judaism, was the legitimate heir of the promises of the Old Testament. To this another, more specifically apologetic thesis is added: Christianity is a religion without any elements that could possibly constitute a political problem; it has been unjustly persecuted, as Jesus' execution on the cross was already an act of injustice. And finally–here the intentions, though apologetic, are simultaneously aimed at the edification of the church—Luke wants to demonstrate the presence of divine power through the spirit of God, which had directed the course of this history until now, as indeed God is the master of all history until its very end. Each part of the Lukan work has its peculiar character. This was partly caused by the Lukan concepts that assign distinct places to Jesus and to the church within the total scheme of the history of salvation; but it is also due to the fact that Luke was able to use very extensive source materials for his gospel, a situation quite different from the less readily available sources which he employed in Acts.

2) *The Gospel of Luke.* For the composition of the gospel, Luke used as a basis the outline of the Gospel of Mark, but added materials from the Synoptic Sayings Source as well as numerous stories, sayings, and parables from a special source (see §7.3b on the synoptic question). The gospel's introduction is the prologue, which was written for both parts of Luke's work and is resumed in Acts 1:1-2. This prologue reveals Luke's relationship to traditions and writings from an earlier period of Christianity. "Those who were eyewitnesses and ministers of the word," namely, the men from the first Christian generation of the apostles, transmitted everything; then there were many who "have undertaken to compile a

Bibliography to §12.3a (2): Commentaries

Joseph A. Fitzmyer, *The Gospel according to Luke, I-IX* (AB 28; Garden City, NY: Doubleday, 1981).

Bibliography to §12.3a (2): Studies

Georg Braumann (ed.), *Das Lukas-Evangelium* (WdF 280; Darmstadt: Wissenschaftliche Buchgesellschaft, 1974).

narrative"; now Luke endeavors to compose his writing for Theophilus, "having followed all things closely for some time past." In this way Luke clearly reveals his distance from the time of the apostles and to the writings composed before him. This fits the situation of an author of the third Christian generation, that is, somewhere most likely in the beginning of II CE.

Luke uses the Gospel of Mark from Luke 3:1 to 9:50 (= Mark 1:2–9:41), from the ministry of the Baptist to about the second prediction of the passion. In doing so, he relocates a few passages from Mark in a very significant way (see below); the section Mark 6:45–8:26 is not reproduced by Luke, either because it was missing in his copy of Mark, or it was left out deliberately due to its many doublets (§10.2b). But with Luke 9:51 the author departs from his Markan framework and begins the so-called Lukan "travel narrative." He returns to Mark's outline only in Luke 18:15, and more or less follows Mark to the story of the finding of the empty tomb (Luke 24:12 = Mark 16:8), though he often treats his source rather freely. In addition to the long travel narrative, another new element in Luke's gospel is the birth narrative, which begins with the announcements of the births of John the Baptist and Jesus, reports the birth of both men, the circumcision of Jesus, and ends with the story of the twelve-year-old Jesus in the temple (Luke 1:5–2:51). New materials at the end of the gospel include the appearances of the risen Jesus (on the Emmaus road and to the Eleven) and Jesus' ascension (24:13–53). Luke inserted the materials drawn from the Synoptic Sayings Source at various points, usually in the form of major compositions of sayings found in his source. These include the "Sermon on the Plain" (6:20–49), the speech about the Baptist (7:18–35), the discourse about the sending of the missionaries (9:56–10:16), the speech against the Pharisees (11:37–52), and various sayings materials combined with special Lukan traditions in the travel narrative. Luke did not make any attempt comparable to that of Matthew in composing the sayings into major speeches of Jesus according to specific themes (§10.2c).

There is much special material in Luke's gospel that has no parallel in the other two synoptics and seems to be derived from one or several special sources. It is not likely that Luke's major special source was a complete gospel. The character of these special materials is easily recognizable from the following survey listing the most important units (including a small selection of sayings unique to Luke):

Miracle stories:
   The miraculous catch of fishes, 5:1–11
   Raising of the young man of Nain, 7:11–17

Healing of a women with a spirit of infirmity, 13:10–17
Healing of a man with dropsy, 14:1–6
Healing of the ten lepers, 17:11–19

Apophthegmata:
The woman that was a sinner, 7:36–50
Mary and Martha, 10:38–42
    Cf. the serving women, 8:1–3
Blessedness of Jesus' mother, 11:27–28
Zacchaeus, 19:1–10

Sayings:
Social teaching of John, 3:10–14
Woes of the Sermon on the Plain, 6:24–26
Eschatological sayings, 10:18; 12:49f; 17:20f
Sayings about the destruction of Jerusalem, 19:39–44
The call to repentance, 13:1–5
The two swords, 22:35–38

Similitudes, parables, example stories (all within the Lukan travel narrative):
Good Samaritan, 10:29–37
Friend at midnight, 11:5–8
Rich fool, 12:13–21
Servant's wages, 12:47–48
Figtree without fruit, 13:6–9
Building a house and waging a war, 14:28–33
Lost coin, 15:7–10
Prodigal son, 15:11–32
Unjust steward, 16:1–13
Dives and Lazarus, 16:19–31
Servant's reward, 17:7–10
Unjust judge, 18:1-8
Pharisee and publican, 18:9–14

Insertions into the passion narrative:
Words for Peter, 22:31–32
Jesus before Herod, 23:6–16
The women of Jerusalem, 23:27–31
The two crucified criminals, 23:32, 33b, 39–43

Most striking is the large number of parables, which obviously derive from a trustworthy tradition, several pericopes concerning questions of rich and poor, and apophthegmata in which women play a role.

For Luke, Jesus is the center of time, a view that Luke expressed in the very composition of his gospel. The time of prophecy is recapitulated before Jesus' public ministry begins and finds its conclusion in the birth narratives and the ministry of John the Baptist. Here the history of Israel's salvation reaches its climax and merges immediately into the history of Jesus. This is shown by Luke by the close interrelationship of the two predictions of the births of John and Jesus, with their careful formulations of the prophecies defining their different functions (John fulfills the prophetic office of Israel, 1:15–17; Jesus, as the king on the throne of David over the house of Jacob, fulfills the expectation of Israel, 1:32–33), the summary of the hope of Israel in the two eschatological psalms (1:36–55, 67–79), and the birth stories themselves (1:57–80; 2:1–20). The announcement of Jesus' birth by the angel refers to Israel's expectation (in the town of David), but also opens it to a much more universal perspective ("Savior" is here a Hellenistic concept, 2:11). This is emphasized once more in the stories of Jesus' circumcision and of the child Jesus in the temple (2:21–40, 41–52). The moment of the termination of Israel's history of salvation is fixed with precision: John the Baptist is imprisoned *before* the public appearance of Jesus (3:19–20), and the mention of his name is consciously avoided in the following story of Jesus' baptism (3:21–22). After the temptation of Jesus the devil leaves him "until a certain time" (4:13); that time is indicated in 22:2 with the return of Satan into the traitor. This makes the ministry of Jesus a special period without Satan.

Luke gives a programmatic statement about the significance of this period as the center of all time in Jesus' first preaching in Nazareth (4:16–30; this pericope was composed by Luke using Mark 6:1–6, Jesus' rejection in Nazareth, and transferred to this new context). Jesus' path and locales during this special segment of time are given specific meanings: Galilee is the place of Jesus' ministry, Samaria and Judea the places of Jesus' travel, Jerusalem the city of Jesus' suffering. The mountain is set aside as the place of prayer (even in the story of the transfiguration; note 9:28), the lake for secret revelations to the disciples; thus, there is no Sermon on the Mount in Luke, nor a parable speech on the lakeshore. Luke does not portray a realistic geographical concept of Palestine, but depicts it as the "Holy Land," full of places that have religious significance. While Mark had critically reinterpreted the motif of Jesus as the divine man from his tradition by subjecting this tradition to the criterion of the passion narrative (§10.2b), Luke gives this motif new importance. Jesus is indeed the divine man who, empowered by the spirit, accomplishes miraculous deeds and preaches the kingdom of God. With the beginning of Jesus' travel (9:51) his ministry enters a new phase. While the Twelve had still been sent "to preach the kingdom of God and to do miracles of healing" (9:2), the Seventy are sent to preach the "nearness" of the kingdom (10:9), though not in power, but "like sheep among the wolves" (10:3). On the whole, the eschatological "now" becomes more prominent. Luke 12:2–59 and 17:20–37 are eschatological speeches, each concluding a segment of Jesus' travel narrative. The travel narrative also includes instructions to the disciples and Jesus' parables.

In the last part of the gospel, Luke resumes his earlier source, the Gospel of Mark, and treats Jesus' ministry in the temple. Instead of Mark's story of Jesus' entry into Jerusalem (Mark 11:1–11), Luke describes Jesus' entry into the temple and avoids the mention of Jerusalem (cf. Luke 19:45 with Mark 11:11). Every day Jesus teaches in the temple (Luke 20:8; 21:37–38), but seemingly never enters the city, whose destruction he predicts upon his entry to the temple (19:41–44). The temple is not only the place of the debates about the census, the resurrection, and the question about the Son of David (20:29–44), but also of the apocalyptic discourse (21:5–36). Luke has used the apocalyptic discourse from Mark 13, but has thoroughly revised it so that it has become essentially a prediction of the fall of Jerusalem; into this Luke even introduced details from the siege of Jerusalem by Titus—long since past history by Luke's time (21:20–24). Only at the end of the speech does one find some eschatological admonitions, reminiscent of Pauline terminology (21:34–36), that speak about the day of the Lord that will come upon the entire circle of the earth. When compared to that future event, the destruction of Jerusalem is nothing but a past event; it is significant in the history of salvation, however, because it marks the end of Israel as a bearer of the promise. In the Christian perspective, Jerusalem is, in the first instance, the place of Jesus' suffering, death, and resurrection—events which conclude the "center of time" and set the stage for the time of the church. To be sure, the disciples return once more to the temple after the ascension (24:53; cf. Acts 2:46; 3:1), but the geographical horizon of the events to come is no longer bound to the Holy Land.

3) *The Acts of the Apostles.* In his gospel, Luke was able to use readily available sources and other materials; he also was able to concentrate his presentation, supported by the framework provided by Mark, upon the biography of one central figure. However, in writing the Acts of the Apostles, Luke was confronted with an entirely different challenge. Though

Bibliography to §12.3a (3): Commentaries

Foakes Jackson and Lake, *Beginnings,* vols. 3–5.
Ernst Haenchen, *The Acts of the Apostles: A Commentary* (Philadelphia: Westminster, 1971).

sources and traditional materials were available, they were not uniform in character, nor did they provide the structure for a coherent historical picture. Moreover, they gave only scanty information at certain points. An attempt to portray the biography of one central figure was not suggested by the character of his sources, nor would it have accorded with Luke's intention to portray the victorious course of the Christian proclamation from Jerusalem to Rome. Since biography was thus excluded as the genre for the continuation of his work, Luke might have attempted to write a historical account that could also have aided in the presentation of his apologetic interests. This, however, would have involved another problem: Luke intended to describe the activities of the Holy Spirit, an enterprise that is hardly reconcilable with the requirement that the historian critically investigate the causes behind the events he reports.

Luke, indeed, seems to have understood his work as that of a historian, but he was repeatedly forced to make recourse to aretalogy as the genre of his narrative, that is, to a form of narrative in which it was possible to demonstrate the presence of divine power in the actions and fate of the primary agents of the story. Since the Hellenistic romance had already employed the aretalogical genre for the description of divine guidance in the fate of its heroes (§3.4e), Luke was able to use this genre as a prototype for his work. This also made it possible for him to compensate for the relative scarcity of the materials available to him, and to include tradition-

Bibliography to §12.3a (3): Studies

Martin Dibelius, *Studies in the Acts of the Apostles* (London: SCM, 1956, and reprints).

Leander E. Keck and J. Louis Martyn (eds.), *Studies in Luke-Acts: Essays Presented in Honor of Paul Schubert* (Nashville: Abingdon, 1966).

Charles H. Talbert (ed.), *Perspectives on Luke-Acts* (Macon, GA: Mercer University, 1981).

Jacob Kremer, *Les Actes des Apôtres: Tradition, rédaction, théologie* (BEThL 48; Gembloux: Duclot, and Louvain: Leuven University, 1979).

J. C. O'Neill, *The Theology of Acts in Its Historical Setting* (London: SPCK, 1961).

David L. Tiede, *Prophecy and History in Luke-Acts* (Philadelphia: Fortress, 1980).

Christoph Burchard, *Der dreizehnte Zeuge: Traditions- und kompositionsgeschichtliche Untersuchungen zu Lukas' Darstellung der Frühzeit des Paulus* (FRLANT 103; Göttingen: Vandenhoeck & Ruprecht, 1970).

Charles H. Talbert, "The Redaction Critical Quest for Luke the Theologian," in *Jesus and Man's Hope: Pittsburgh Festival on the Gospels* (Pittsburgh: Pittsburgh Theological Seminary, 1970) 171–222.

Rudolf Bultmann, "Zur Frage nach den Quellen der Apostelgeschichte," in: idem, *Exegetica*, 412–23.

Petr Pokorný, "Die Romfahrt des Paulus und der antike Roman," *ZNW* 64 (1973) 233–44.

A. J. Mattill and Mary Bedford Mattill, *A Classified Bibliography of Literature on the Acts of the Apostles* (Leiden: Brill, 1966). Includes works published through 1961.

Areopagus Speech of Paul

This bronze plaque inscribed with the Greek text of the so-called Areopagus Speech of Paul (Acts 17:22–31) was placed on the rock of the Areopagus Hill of Athens in modern times to commemorate the wedding of Greek culture and the Pauline mission.

al miracle stories without expressing in each instance a historian's doubt about the reliability of such materials as sources of information. Travel reports, and even a story of a shipwreck—rarely missing in a romance—could thus find a more natural place. Of course, this does not mean that Luke freely invented such narratives. On the contrary, the stories of miraculous events, healings, visions, and dreams which occur in Acts were usually traditional stories. On the other hand, wherever Luke did write as a historian, he often had to compose the required information himself. This is particularly true in the summary accounts and the speeches.

The summary accounts (Acts 2:42–47; 4:32–37; 5:12–16; cf. 9:31), and thus also the information about the ideal life of the Christian community in Jerusalem, are Lukan compositions. The technique of inserting these accounts was known to Luke from Mark, the source for such material in Luke's gospel (cf. Luke 6:17–19 with Mark 3:7–12). The speeches of Acts were all composed by Luke as well, although traditional materials (such as christological formulas, fixed units of scriptural proof) were frequently employed. There are no substantial theological differences between the speeches of Peter, Stephen, and Paul, which in itself is a historical improbability. Moreover, the content of Paul's speeches in Acts cannot be harmonized with the theology of Paul as we know it from his letters. Paul would hardly have given a speech like that on the Areopagus (Acts 17:22–31), in which he ascribes divine origin to all human beings in the sense of Stoic philosophy (17:28f; this does not mesh with Rom 1:18ff). Neither is it credible that he affirmed repeatedly in his trial that he had always lived as a law-abiding Jew, nor that he had proclaimed nothing in his missionary activities other than the recognized Pharisaic doctrine of the resurrection (Acts 22:1ff; 26:2ff).

In short, in his speeches the author of Acts followed a widely used practice in the writing of history, which was to clarify the significance of the events in question by composing speeches; these are presented as if they had been delivered by one of the main actors. This does not exclude the possiblity of the preservation of valuable information embedded in the narratives of Acts. Such materials include a number of individual pieces of information, for instance, about Barnabas (Acts 4:36–37) and Stephen 6:8–9; 7:54, 57–58a); the list of the Hellenistic missionaries (6:5) and the prophets and teachers in Antioch (13:1–2); the report of the dispersion of the Hellenists and the mission of Philip in Samaria (8:1–2, 5) and of the church in Antioch (11:19ff); the martyrdom of James son of Zebedee (Acts 12:1–2); and the Apostolic Decree (15:28–29). In Acts 13–14 and 16–21 (also 27–28?) Luke seems to have used one or several travel diaries that may have ultimately derived from associates of Paul. The character and extent of these sources cannot be determined with any certainty, however, and the question of whether or not their author was the Luke of Phlm 24 cannot be answered in any helpful way (§7.3c).

All the materials available to him were revised by Luke according to his projected plan for the whole book. He was thus able to present a picture of the total historical development that could not have been derived from the sources he used, and this often contradicted the intentions of those sources. Since he wanted to describe the victorious course of the proclamation from Jerusalem to Rome, he needed a circle of persons who could guarantee the reliability of that proclamation. For this purpose he used the fiction of the Twelve Apostles, something that must have been traditional by this time, though for 1 Cor 15:5–7, the "Twelve" is not identical with the apostles. He introduces them as the eyewitnesses of the revelation in Jesus "beginning from the baptism of John until the day when he was taken up from us" (1:22; cf. 1:8; 10:37–41; 13:23–31). Because Judas the traitor no longer belonged to the circle chosen by Jesus, Luke reports a story about the election of a new twelfth witness (1:15–26). The avoidance of the title "apostle" whenever Luke speaks about Paul is a consequence of this fiction (the only exception is 14:14, where the title seems to have slipped in inadvertently from Luke's source). The horizon of the new events is indicated by the story of Pentecost (2:1–13). The enthusiastic event of the speaking in tongues thus received a new interpretation by Luke: it was a language miracle of universal significance and corresponded to the universal confusion of tongues in Babylon (Gen 11:1–9). The event concerns the whole world; therefore all peoples are represented in the list of nations (2:9–11). On the other hand, Luke also resumes older traditions of the interpretation of Pentecost when he describes it as an event in which the promise of Joel is fulfilled (Joel 3:1–5 = Acts 2:17–21). The speech of Peter which follows is of course directed to the reader of the book (2:14–36). The reader is given to understand that everything that will be described in the Book of Acts is the eschatological work of the Spirit in the world. The time of the church is the time of the Holy Spirit.

Luke closely interwove a number of apologetic motifs within this general conception. One of his special interests was to show that the activities of the Christian missionaries were in fact the actions of God. The trial before the Jewish sanhedrin demonstrates this point. The apostles must preach because they "must obey God rather than human beings" (5:29), and Gamaliel says explicitly what Luke wanted to emphasize for his pagan audience: "For if this plan or this undertaking is merely human, it will fail; but if it is of God, you will not be able to overthrow them. You might even be found to be opponents of God" (5:38–39). To oppose the proven presence of the divine—every pagan and every Roman knew this—was not only impious presumption, but also dangerous folly. The proof for the presence of God is given through the stories of the apostles' divinely empowered miraculous deeds (3:2ff; 6:8; etc.); the story of Ananias and Sapphira belongs to the same category (5:1–11; note that a summary of miraculous healings follows this story, 5:12–16).

Another apologetic motif appears in the repeated emphasis upon the unity and unanimity of the Christian congregation, exemplified in the accounts of the church in Jerusalem (see 2:36 and 4:32). The traditional report about the conflict between the apostles and the Hellenists was, therefore, rewritten by Luke into a story of the election of persons to serve at table (6:1–6). To be sure, Luke has not completely suppressed the information provided by his source, since it is quite evident from Acts 6:8 that Stephen, one of the elected deacons, was not a waiter but a preacher and faith-healer. Luke preserved this information as part of his report of Stephen's martyrdom, which he intended to show how the Christians had gotten into a conflict with an established, traditional religion. The speech of Stephen (7:1–53) is an extensive interpretation of Scripture, demonstrating that the entire history of Israel from Abraham to Solomon justifies the Christian proclamation: the almighty God does not live in temples made by hands (7:48–50). A third apologetic motif makes its appearance here. The Christian concept of God—with which even an educated pagan could not possibly disagree—corresponds entirely to the ancient and venerable tradition of Israel. Thus the Christians are not scornful despisers of the ancient tradition, but its legitimate heirs. They are persecuted only by those people whose fathers have already persecuted the prophets (7:51–52) and who do not even observe the law to which they appeal (7:53). From this perspective it is understandable that Luke reports only those Christian martyrdoms for which he can ascribe responsibility to the Jewish authorities (note also Acts 12:1–2). He was careful not to raise equivalent accusations against the Roman authorities, or even to give them the responsibility for the death of Jesus. The guilt is exclusively that of the Jewish authorities (see, e.g., 13:27–28; incidentally, not of the Jews in general!).

From the beginning of Acts to the martyrdom of Stephen, the central figure in the narrative has been Peter. At this point, however, Paul is introduced for the first time, still under the name of "Saul" (7:58; 8:3). The fact that Luke positioned Peter and Paul in the center of his work reveals his dependence upon the ecclesiastical tradition, for which these two apostles and martyrs were the guarantors of the church's beliefs, as we see in *1 Clement* and the letters of Ignatius. But the way in which these two apostles appear in Acts is curious. Peter is always presented as an apostle, since he belongs to the circle of the Twelve. But in Acts 15 Peter is mentioned for the last time, and Luke has nothing to report about his journey to Rome or his martyrdom. Even more peculiar is the presentation of Paul. He is neither an apostle nor a martyr, and in many other respects Luke's picture of Paul has no relationship to the Paul known from his letters. It has been suggested that Luke did not know Paul's letters, or that the original ending of Acts reporting Paul's martyrdom has been lost. But such speculations do not really remove this embarrassment. Certainly Luke should also have known that Paul was an apostle. This ignorance is just a unlikely as that of the letters, considering that Luke must have belonged to the circle of churches that claimed Peter and Paul as their authorities.

Luke's image of Paul (as also his image of Peter!) must be explained as a conscious construction in the interest of his own apologetical arguments. A "Pauline" Christianity would have been an impossible concept for him; he knows only one united Christianity—Luke is the first Christian writer to use the term "Christians" (11:26)—which has one approved proclamation. The fiction of the Twelve Apostles who guarantee the validity of that proclamation is maintained by Luke just long enough to demonstrate that the Hellenists and Paul, as the missionary of the gentiles, are also dependent upon this original proclamation (6:1–7; 9:26–28); but at Paul's last visit to Jerusalem, the Twelve were apparently no longer there (21:17ff)—Luke's sources did not mention them, nor did Luke himself show any more interest in them. But in Acts 9, contrary to Gal 1:10ff, the calling of Paul is described in such a way that the dependence of his commission upon the church (the command to preach to the gentiles is given to him through Ananias, Acts 9:10–19) and upon the Twelve is beyond question: after "some days" Paul goes to Jerusalem (9:23–30; but cf. Gal 1:17!; see §9.1c). Furthermore, Luke takes great care to demonstrate that the originator of the proclamation to the gentiles was not Paul (or Barnabas), but Peter (10:1–11:18). Paul does not begin his missionary work in Antioch until Peter has successfully defended the gentile mission in Jerusalem (Acts 11:1–18 is deliberately placed before 11:25–26).

It is not surprising, then, that the image of Paul's missionary activity also had to fit the Lukan concept; after all, in Luke's narrative Paul is the one who is designated to represent the continuation of the victorious course of the Christian gospel to Rome. For this purpose, the Pauline letters, with their emphasis upon the presence of Christ's death in the apostle's fate, would have been useless. Nor could Luke have made any use of the reports of Paul's various controversies with his opponents, because he wanted to demonstrate the unity of early Christianity, something that could not be disturbed by a controversy between the law-abiding Jewish Christians and the freedom from the law of the gentile believers. That controversy was no longer a real problem for Luke anyway. The fact that gentile Christians also abide by the law is demonstrated for Luke by their abstention from sacrifices to idols, blood, and unchastity. The Apostolic Decree (15:29) makes this clear, which is quoted once more in the context of the accusation raised against Paul that he was no longer observing the law (21:25). Luke also suppresses the information about Paul's collection for Jerusalem, although he doubtlessly knew about it (§9.3f). Acts 20:4 seems to preserve from Luke's source the list of the members of the delegation that brought the collection to Jerusalem. Instead of reporting this collection, Luke has inserted a fictional trip to Jerusalem at an earlier point (11:27–30) in which Paul and Barnabas bring a collection from Antioch to Jerusalem.

Luke has thus gained the necessary independence for a description of the Pauline mission that can serve the purposes of his work. Paul is the great itinerant preacher, endowed with the divine spirit, accomplishing great signs and miracles, as Peter had done before him, and in this way continuing the victorious course of the gospel. An exemplary presentation for this activity is found in the missionary journey of Paul and Barnabas in Acts 13–14. Like Peter in his earlier speeches, so too Paul, in his speech in Pisidian Antioch (13:17–41), refers to the tradition of Israel and positions Jesus into a series of salvific acts that God has done in Israel. But Luke was also able to present Paul as making a speech that has connections with the tradition of Greek religion and philosophy (the Areopagus speech, Acts 17:22–31). Luke knew from Christian missionary practice that either point of departure could be impressive and convincing for a pagan audience. Of course, Luke also knew that Paul did not require circumcision from gentile converts. Since this was no longer a problem in Luke's churches, a theological rationale for rejecting circumcision was no longer needed. In his presentation of the Apostolic Council (15:1ff), where the question of circumcision was raised, it was enough to point out that the Holy Spirit had already solved this problem by purifying the hearts of the gentile believers (15:8–9); the signs that God has accomplished through Barnabas and Paul serve as further proof (15:12).

Throughout Luke remains faithful to his view that the time of the church is the eschatological event determined by the activity of the Holy Spirit. Under that perspective, Paul's troublesome toil over many years in the building of his churches is transformed into an almost breathtaking travel adventure (15:40–21:14). A somewhat longer stay in one of the cities Paul visits is mentioned only occasionally—information that derives from Luke's sources (18:11; 19:10)—but travels and miracles, interrupted by an occasional stay in prison, fill most of the pages. The novelistic and aretalogical elaboration of the source, which apparently was a rather dry travel report, makes it difficult to distinguish between reliable information and legendary expansion.

This same Paul, the greatest of the early Christian missionaries, was the chosen vessel to carry the gospel to Rome, the capital of the world. Luke knew from his source that Paul had been arrested during his last stay in Jerusalem, information that enabled him to treat the position of Christianity toward the Roman authority at some length. On the one hand, Paul points out that his entire activity, the founding and establishment of a worldwide Christian church among the gentiles, is due to divine initiative and direction. For this purpose, the readers of Acts see Paul repeat the story of his calling twice (22:3–21; 26:9–20). On the other hand, Paul's speeches in these last chapters of the book leave no doubt that Christianity is by no means a novel invention designed to disturb the religious peace of the Roman empire. Luke is here defending Christianity against accusations of disrespect for ancient and venerable religious traditions. Paul has to emphasize repeatedly in his defense that he is indeed a Pharisee, which is to say, a Jew who had never done anything against the religion of his fathers (22:1ff; 23:1, 6; 24:14ff; 25:8; 26:2ff). In Luke's presentation, Paul is doing more than appealing to the emperor on his own behalf (25:10), he is also making a general appeal to the official Roman position in matters of religious policy, since he can portray himself as the prototype of the pious Roman citizen who has never offended "against the law (of the Jews), nor against the temple, nor against Caesar" (25:8). Paul's trial is designed to demonstrate that his conviction (and thus the conviction of any Christian) would be a violation of the principles of Rome's policies in matters of religion. This also explains why Luke was not interested in describing the conviction of either Paul or of Peter, both of whom were executed at the time of Nero by a Roman tribunal. Rather, Luke takes great care to point out that Paul, a Roman citizen, is treated with the necessary respect by the Roman officials and soldiers (22:24–29), that he remains in the full possession of his miraculous powers during his eventful travel to Rome, even though a prisoner (27:1–28:16), and that he is able to "preach the kingdom of God and teach about the Lord Jesus Christ quite openly and unhindered" in the capital (28:31).

(b) The Miracle-Working Apostles in Conflict with the World: The Acts of Paul and the Acts of Peter

Luke intended to create a book that would serve apologetic purposes as well as the edification of the church. We may wonder whether he was successful in the latter respect. There are two books from the middle of II CE that were not satisfied with a view of Peter and Paul that presents them solely as preachers of the gospel and miracle workers, but not as fighters against heresy or as venerated martyrs. The *Acts of Peter* and the *Acts of Paul* were probably written several decades after Luke's Acts, though both books still used traditions that date from an earlier period. But, like the Lukan work, though to a considerably larger extent, both works used the Hellenistic romance as a model. This meant a reduction in the apologetic element, while the aretalogical features, used by Luke within certain limits, became predominant.

The transmission of these two books of apostolic acts has been scanty; though reconstruction is possible to a certain degree, lacunae and uncertainties remain. There are two manuscripts of the *Acts of Paul* that can witness to the entire work: a Greek papyrus written about 300 CE and a Coptic papyrus from VI CE. Both manuscripts are fragmentary, but allow conclusions about the composition of the whole. In addition, several Greek and Coptic fragments survive. Three parts of the *Acts of Paul* were transmitted separately and are therefore better attested: (1) the *Acts of Paul and Thecla,* (2) the *Martyrdom of Paul,* and (3) additional correspondence between Paul and the Corinthians (*3 Corinthians*). Of the first two parts, there are several Greek manuscripts and translations. *3 Corinthians* became part of the Bible of the Armenian church and was probably also included in the corpus of the Pauline letters in the first Syrian canon, because the Syrian father Ephrem wrote a commentary on it. Recently, the original Greek text of *3 Corinthians* was discovered in Papyrus Bodmer X. Of the *Acts of Peter,* a manuscript from Vercelli contains a Latin translation of the last part of the book, the *Actus Vercellenses.* They report the controversies of Peter with the magician Simon in Rome and the martyrdom of Peter. The latter, like the report of the martyrdom of Paul, has also been transmitted independently and is preserved in a large number of Greek manuscripts and numerous translations. But there are

---

Bibliography to §12.3b: Texts

Lipsius-Bonnet, *ActApostApoc,* 1. 1–111, 235–72. Latin and Greek texts of *Acts of Peter* and *Acts of Paul.*

Coptic text and English translation of fragment of *Acts of Peter:* James Brashler and Douglas M. Parrott, "BG, 4: The Acts of Peter," in: Douglas M. Parrott (ed.), *Nag Hammadi Codices V,2–5 and VI with Papyrus Berolinensis 8502, 1 and 4* (NHS 11; Leiden: Brill, 1979) 473–93.

W. Schneemelcher, "The Acts of Peter," *NTApo* 2. 259–322.

Idem, "The Acts of Paul," *NTApo* 2. 322–90.

Bibliography to §12.3b: Studies

Rosa Söder, *Die apokryphen Apostelgeschichten und die romanhafte Literatur der Antike* (Stuttgart: Kohlhammer, 1932; reprint, 1969).

only two fragments of the first part of the *Acts of Peter:* the narrative of Peter's daughter from a Coptic papyrus, and a summary of a story called "The Daughter of the Gardener" in the apocryphal *Letter of Titus*. It is therefore difficult to get a clear picture of the first part of the book, which was probably located largely in Jerusalem, since *Act. Verc.* 5 reports that Peter stayed in Jerusalem for a period of twelve years.

It seems that the *Acts of Paul* is dependent upon the *Acts of Peter*. The famous "Quo vadis" episode from the martyrdom of Peter is used in the *Acts of Paul*. In *Act. Verc.* 35 Peter is persuaded to leave Rome in order to escape martyrdom; on the way he meets Jesus, who is on his way to Rome. Upon Peter's question, "Where are you going, Lord?" Jesus answers: "I am going to Rome to be crucified." In the *Acts of Paul* (chap. 10) Jesus appears to Paul, who is on a boat travelling to Rome, and tells him the same thing; but this makes little sense, since Paul was not fleeing martyrdom anyway. If this dependence is correctly recognized, both apostolic acts must have been written before the end of II CE because Tertullian (*De baptismo* 17) knew of the *Acts of Paul* and reports that it was written by a presbyter from Asia Minor "out of love for Paul." It is not possible to give a more precise date. Passages from the gospels are occasionally used, and at least the *Acts of Paul* reveals a knowledge of the Pauline letters; yet neither writing seems aware of a canon of the New Testament.

Their relationship to the canonical Acts of the Apostles is peculiar. If they indeed knew Acts—and this possiblity cannot be excluded—they still tried to create a completely different image of Peter and Paul on the basis of the great store of legends about them that Luke had also used for his work. For the authors of both books, the two apostles belong together, as was true for Luke's Acts. The *Acts of Peter* reports that Paul had worked in Rome before Peter's arrival; and the *Acts of Paul* introduces the captain of the ship that brought Paul to Rome as a Christian who had been baptized by Peter (*Act. Verc.* 1; *Act. Paul.* 10; cf. *Act. Verc.* 2). But the two apostles stand together as martyrs. The older tradition of the two martyrs Peter and Paul that Luke had suppressed, and that had appeared for the first time in *1 Clement* and Ignatius (§12.2d–e), was thus brought back into use by these two books. The composition of the reports of these martyrdoms seems to have drawn on older traditional narratives. We know that such reports existed in written form in an earlier period, as is evident in Acts 6–7, where Luke uses a written source containing a report of the martyrdom of Stephen. We should be careful, in any case, not to view such stories about the death of the apostles, and legends about the miraculous deeds, as merely the products of the pious interests of a later period. On the contrary, their origin is best explained on the basis of the immediate reaction to the martyr's death. The *Martyrdom of Polycarp* was written immediately after the bishop's death, yet it by no means lacks miraculous features (§12.3f). We could go even one step further. Not only did such stories circulate early as isolated narratives, they were soon composed into cycles of written stories. Luke's Acts already presupposes this situation, for we cannot assume that Luke himself was the first one to collect the stories of Peter and Paul that he used in his work. The existence of such collections is equally evident in the *Acts of Peter* and the *Acts of Paul;* these were their primary sources, not the canonical Acts.

The *Acts of Peter* employs a cycle of legends about the competition between Peter and Simon Magus. It does not fit very well into the *Acts of Peter,* since the story ends with Peter's victory in a contest on the Roman forum at which the prefect of the city presides: Simon Magus dies in a crash while demonstrating his magical power of flight, and Peter is recognized by all present. Thus, the author has to go to great lengths to find a reason for the subsequent execution of Peter by the prefect of Rome. Since the magical stories of the originally independent cycle include a talking dog, a dried fish that swims as though alive, and a flying magician, it is not surprising that they abound with stories of healing of the blind and resurrections from the dead. They may have been in part popular folktales before they were incorporated into the cycle of Peter and Simon the Magician. The treasure of freely circulating stories, especially with magic as a theme, was very rich during the Roman period, and the romances drew their materials especially from this source (see, e.g., the *Metamorphoses* of Apuleius).

In the *Acts of Paul,* the author used an older cycle of legends about Thecla. Although he attempts to introduce his hero Paul into this cycle, he is only partially successful. The narrative about Paul's martyrdom also existed independently before it was incorporated into this work; the introduction added by the author, with a motif borrowed from the *Acts of Peter,* in which Jesus tells Paul that he was again to be crucified (see above), does not fit the following narrative of Paul's decapitation. Thus, these apocryphal acts give numerous indications for the formation of Christian legends at an early date that were not limited to the primary apostolic figures, but also included such figures as the virgin Thecla. It is therefore highly improbable that these legends were developed primarily or exclusively on the basis of the canonical writings. To be sure, Luke also tells about the Samaritan magician Simon (Acts 8:9–24), but this Lukan report already presupposes the existence of the Simon legend that the *Acts of Peter* used. The encounter with Simon in Acts 8:14ff names Peter and John, who meet Simon in Samaria; according to *Act. Verc.* 8, Peter and Paul meet Simon in Jerusalem. This was probably what Luke had also found in his source, and it is easily understandable why he replaced Paul with John, because the conversion of Paul would not be told until the next chapter (Acts 9:1ff).

But it is not only the legends and martyrdoms of the apostles that these apocryphal acts seek to preserve, while Luke suppressed the martyrdoms. Both the *Acts of Paul* and the *Acts of Peter* show an interest in encratism, especially sexual abstinence. This was a Christian lifestyle and attitude toward existence that was either played down or opposed in the early catholic literature, but must have been rather widespread in the Christian churches of II CE. Even Luke reveals that he inclined toward sexual encratism because he introduced a significant alteration in his reproduction of Jesus' answer to the question of the Sadducees: those who are worthy of the age to come do not marry (cf. Luke 20:34–36 with Mark 12:25). But Luke did not elaborate this perspective in Acts, and the Pastoral Epistles explicitly reject false teachers who forbid marriage (§12.2g). But the *Acts of Peter* as well as the *Acts of Paul,* both by no means "heretical" writings, repeatedly emphasize the ideal of virginity. They are not interested in an accommodation of Christian morality to the general morality of the citizen. With such an attitude, they were probably closer to the religious outlook of many earnest Christians of their time than were the Pastoral Epistles. This must not be overlooked, if we choose to call this attitude "encratite." It was not the moral conviction of a special heretical group, but the widespread morality of Christians in churches that also insisted upon the other typical Christian responsibilities such as mutual help and care, providing for the poor, and communal responsibility for the widows. They were in complete agreement with early catholic writings about the need to reject Gnosticism and to preserve the "faith" handed down by the apostles. This is especially evident in the *Acts of Paul,* which includes a detailed report on the correspondence of Paul with the Corinthians about the false teachers in *3 Corinthians* (*Act. Paul.* 8), thus taking a position against Gnosticism that was completely in accord with the Pastoral Epistles (§12.2g).

It has been argued that these apocryphal acts are more closely related to the Hellenistic romances because they succumbed more than the canonical Acts to the desire for edification and entertainment. But this judgment is only partially justified and does not clearly state the difference. Edification is certainly an equally strong feature in Luke's Acts; what is missing in the apocryphal acts of Peter and Paul is the apologetic motif. They are not prepared to sacrifice the early Christian ideal of ethical rigorism to apologetic interests, and the great example of the martyred apostles has a greater significance for them than the argument that Christianity was a religion that did not threaten the Roman state. To be sure, the flowers of pious fantasy bloom more richly in these writings—which are not lacking in Luke, though he refrained from introducing baptized lions and talking dogs—but the *Acts of Paul* and the *Acts of Peter* still express a Christian vision that is not satisfied with the limitations of a society determined by the prudent morality of the average citizen. "Blessed are those who for the love of God have departed from the fashion of the world, for they shall judge angels and shall be blessed at the right hand of the Father" (*Act. Paul.* 3.6). The divinely sanctioned protest against the existing world order is thus renewed with an explicit reference to the macarisms of Jesus.

(c) The Pauline Gospel as Renunciation of the World: Marcion

After the end of the Domitian persecution, the heirs of the churches that had been founded by Paul had developed a theological position that not only made it possible for Christianity to establish itself in the world and culture of its time as a morally respectable religious community, but that also opened up the opportunity to conquer that world through its propaganda and the example of its communal life. This Christian position was based upon the Old Testament; the Christians understood themselves to be the legitimate heirs of the promises given to Israel, which had been fulfilled in the coming of Jesus, in his resurrection, and in the founding of the church by the workings of the Holy Spirit. They could look back proudly to Paul as one of the founders of this church, and it was also possible to quote and use his letters in parenesis and for the further establishment of church order. But Paul's letters were no longer significant as a norm of theology; Luke was even convinced that the church would do better without them. To be sure, there were false teachers, but nothing indicates that any other Christian group, gnostic or Jewish-Christian, possessed an organization that could seriously threaten the unity of the early catholic churches from Antioch to Rome, which were led by bishops and maintained close connections with each other through letters and personal visits. While the false teachers propagated theological teachings that promised deeper religious insights to the initiate, the strength of early catholicism was not to be found in the appeal and unity of its theology. In fact, a unified theology did not exist, and there was no ideological coercion. Rather, the pillars of faith were adherence to the Old Testament and to the gospel of Jesus' cross and resurrection, as well as the commandments to participate in the life and worship of the church, to

Bibliography to §12.3c

Adolf von Harnack, *Marcion: Das Evangelium vom fremden Gott* (TU 45: 2d ed.; Leipzig: Hinrichs, 1924; reprint: Darmstadt: Wissenschaftliche Buchgesellschaft, 1960).

submit to the bishop, to care for the poor, the widows, and the orphans, and to strive for respectable conduct in one's life and affairs.

In this situation, a theologian who was deeply influenced by Paul's theology called the foundations of this ecclesiastical position into question and caused a crisis for the church that was overcome only through a theological renewal, and finally through the creation of a new Scripture, namely, the New Testament. Marcion would later become the arch-heretic of the catholic church. None of his writings are preserved. The earliest testimony to his appearance may be the anecdote about Marcion's encounter with Polycarp that is told by Irenaeus (§12.2h). Marcionite churches existed in many places all over the Mediterranean world as early as the middle of II CE, as is attested by Justin Martyr (*Apol.* 1.26.5; 58.1–2); he had already written a treatise against Marcion, which is lost, before he wrote his *Apology* ca. 150 CE. Later witnesses include a large number of anti-heretical authors of the following centuries. Adolf von Harnack was the first scholar who accomplished a critical examination of all the relevant materials and reconstructed Marcion's career and theology (1920). All further research is based on Harnack's work.

Marcion was probably born shortly after the year 100 in the province of Pontus, in the northern part of Asia Minor. Thus, he was a somewhat younger contemporary of Polycarp, and a little older than the apologist Justin Martyr. He grew up in a Christian home and was educated in the church. It is also known that he was quite wealthy and owned a shipping business. This information about the occupation and social position of a Christian of that period demonstrates that the legends about wealthy women and men who made major donations to Christian churches were by no means the result of wishful thinking. Marcion seems to have been active at first in Asia Minor as a church member. (The story that he was excommunicated by his own father because he had seduced a virgin was a malicious polemical invention; its symbolic meaning should not be over-looked.) In any case, between the years 135 and 138 he came to Rome, joined the Christian church there, and donated the sum of 200,000 sesterces; according to Tertullian's report, this money was returned to him when he was excommunicated. The date of his departure from the Roman church has been preserved in the tradition of the Marcionite churches as 144 CE. It is not possible to know whether Marcion was excommunicated or left of his own free will. His two major works must have been written in Rome before he left the church, that is, between 135/138 and 144. They became the basis for the organization of a new church that rapidly spread. When Justin wrote his *Apology* about a decade later, there were numer-ous Marcionite congregations in east and west. Marcion probably died after 160; thus, his activity coincides almost precisely with the peaceful years of the rule of Hadrian and Antoninus Pius.

Marcion's point of departure was Paul, more specifically, the Paul of the letters. He was particularly interested in the theological statements of these letters, most of all Galatians. It was there that Marcion discovered the insurmountable and radical opposition of law and gospel as described by Paul. But then Paul was the sole true disciple of Jesus because Jesus had also broken the law. But what had the church made of this Paul? It had falsified Paul into a teacher of legalistic morality, into an interpreter of the law and the prophets who had used allegorical tricks to show that there was no difference between the actions of the God of the Old Testament and the Father of Jesus Christ. But if such statements could indeed be found in the Pauline letters themselves, it was evident to Marcion that the church had not preserved their original text.

From the gnostics, Marcion could receive neither aid nor advice, though of course he must have known gnostic teachings. His own view that the God of love, the Father of Jesus Christ, could not be identical with the God of the law who had created the world could scarcely be explained without the assumption of gnostic influences. But this does not make Marcion a gnostic theologian, because Marcion rejected the use of the speculative method of interpretation employed by the gnostics, as well as the gnostic formation of mythological constructs that claimed to derive from special revelations. Marcion did not want to be a prophet proclaiming a new revelation, nor did he ever try to publish his thoughts in a pseudepigraphical book under the pseudonym of Paul. He did not even understand his own office as that of an exegete in the sense of that time; in that case he would have engaged in the allegorical and typological methods of exegesis. It was exactly that method, however, that Marcion blamed for the terrible obfuscation of the fundamental opposition of law and gospel. Thus, there was only one path open to him: he had to attempt a reconstruction of Paul's original writings as a textual critic, philologian, and reformer. The result of that work was Marcion's canon, the first Christian canon of Scripture (§7.1b). Marcion's canon was not new in the sense that it replaced a canon of New Testament writings that the church already possessed—there is nothing to indicate that such a canon existed at his time—rather, it was new because it was designed to replace the generally recognized canon of the church, the Old Testament.

Marcion had to make a selection from among the many Christian writings that were in circulation under the names of apostles. That the Pauline letters would be included was obvious. Among the gospels, his choice fell upon Luke. He also knew Matthew, but this writing had to be rejected because of its position with respect to the law. The Gospel of

John, never quoted or referred to by Polycarp of Smyrna, was apparently not yet known in Rome at that time (Justin never quotes it). For his edition of the Pauline letters, Marcion established an order not attested anywhere else: Galatians stands at the head of the collection, followed by 1 and 2 Corinthians, Romans, 1 and 2 Thessalonians, Ephesians (called "Laodiceans" by Marcion), Colossians, Philippians, and Philemon. The Pastoral Epistles are missing; apparently Marcion did not know them—an appropriate redaction would not have presented him with major difficulties. There is no trace of Hebrews; if Marcion knew that writing, it would be no surprise that he did not use it.

The basis of the Marcionite edition of Paul's letters was the so-called "Western Text" (§7.2a), which was the most widespread popular text of II CE. A number of peculiar features that later writers noticed in Marcion's text were not the result of his own redaction, but part of the text that he used. Marcion's method must be called philological, and he never claimed that the result of his work should be sacrosanct or final. The vast majority of all the textual changes that Marcion introduced are deletions, ranging from the omission of a single word to the elimination of entire paragraphs. Additions are rare, but in a number of cases Marcion modified the text through transpositions in order to restore what he thought must have been the original sense. Among the deletions we find quotations from the Old Testament or sentences that speak positively about the relationship of Christ or the Christians to the world and history created and ruled by the creator God of the Old Testament. Marcion revised the Gospel of Luke in the same way: among other passages, he eliminated the birth narratives, the baptism of Jesus and his genealogy (Luke 1:1–4:15), all quotations from the Old Testament, the parables of the fig tree (13:6–9) and the prodigal son (15:11–32), and the entry into Jerusalem and cleansing of the temple (19:29–46).

Marcion's second major work, the *Antitheses,* is lost and cannot be reconstructed. Tertullian, Irenaeus, Origen, and Ephrem still knew it, but nothing is preserved apart from quotations and polemical references. The book apparently contained a number of antitheses about the fundamental difference between the creator God of the Old Testament and the Father of Jesus Christ. But its main content was exegetical, presented in the form of commentaries on individual passages from Luke and the Pauline letters. Passages from Matthew are occasionally referred to, but Marcion never mentions apocryphal writings. In these exegetical antitheses, Marcion regularly quotes and critically interprets passages from the Old Testament and juxtaposes passages from Luke or Paul; for example, Exod 12:11 ("your loins girded, your sandals on your feet, and your staff in your hand") and Luke 9:3 ("take nothing for your journey, no staff, no bag . . ."); or Exod 21:24 ("eye for eye, tooth for tooth") and Luke 6:29 ("to him who strikes you on the cheek, offer the other also"). The radical opposition between law and gospel was thus demonstrated even in small details.

On the basis of the information about the *Antitheses,* as well as from the way that Marcion revised the text of Luke and Paul, it is possible to reconstruct a rather clear picture of his theology. Its central concept was the sharp contrast between the "foreign" God and the creator God of the Old Testament. Marcion's message has rightly been called "the gospel of the foreign God." The foreign God is the highest God and the Savior, but he has no relationship whatsoever to the creation of the world. His essence is goodness; he shows love and mercy. The creator God, on the other hand, is not evil—in this respect Marcion's thought is clearly distinguished from Gnosticism—but he is utterly just and thus punishes transgressions. Salvation is therefore identical with the dissolution of the power of this creator God. Insofar as he wields his power by means of the law and the prophets, his power has already come to an end for the believer through the rejection of the Old Testament. This in fact was the purpose of Jesus' coming. Jesus is the son of the foreign God and indeed God himself, distinguished from the Father solely by name. Therefore, Jesus accepted the human body in appearance only, which had its origin in the inferior creation; it would have been impossible for Christ to be united in reality with the Creator's material world. In the technical language of christology, such a concept would be called "modalistic docetism," since Marcion considered Jesus to be completely identical with God in all respects, who took human form only in appearance but not in reality. It was also in appearance only that Jesus bore the name of Christ, which is taken from the Old Testament, because he wanted to deceive the creator God. Marcion's modalism was related to a Christian belief that was very widespread at his time, which saw Christ as the full and replete presence of God, particularly in the eucharist. This view was not really challenged until later, when Tertullian and other fathers began to criticize the propagation of this sort of modalistic christology. On the other hand, the explicit docetism of Marcion must have been suspicious from the outset and meant that Marcion could be accused of being a gnostic (see Ignatius' attacks against his docetic opponents, §12.2d). In his understanding of Jesus' message, Marcion followed the kerygma of the church: Jesus preached the gospel for the salvation of sinners; out of his pure and inexplicable love for humanity, God sent his Son as a sacrifice through which he purchased them from the creator. In agreement with the kerygma of the church, Marcion also spoke of Jesus' descent into hell, though not to redeem the righteous of Israel, but rather to save Cain and the Sodomites. Modifications of the church's beliefs were necessary in his eschatology because the good foreign God does not punish and judge anyone. Marcion assumed that he simply would remove the nonbelievers from his sight. Simultaneously with the final salvation of all believers, the creator God would destroy himself and his whole creation.

This salvation, however, has not yet been accomplished in the present, and there is no trace in Marcion's thought of a renewal of the early Christian expectation of an immediate end to the world. But in contrast to the catholic church's morality of the pious citizen, Marcion emphasizes the tension arising from the believers' existence in a world in which they have no share: as long as they are in the flesh, they will suffer and experience persecutions. Although even these ideas have their roots in Pauline theology, Marcion goes beyond Paul in his prohibition of marriage and his demand for abstention from meat and wine, thus clearly accepting the encratite tendencies of his time (cf. the *Acts of Paul* and the *Acts of Peter*, §12.3b). Teachings of this kind, however, could be found elsewhere, and need not have posed a threat to the catholic church. The real threat to the church arose for a very different reason: Marcion was not only a theologian and exegete, he was also a gifted and successful organizer who systematically created a firmly established religious community, designed to stand as the sacred new creation of the foreign God in this world. In that respect, Marcion had learned much from the early catholic church. His own church had bishops, deacons, and presbyters. Each office was open to all members, women as well as men, because the new creation had made distinctions of gender irrelevant. Sanctification and renunciation of the world had thus found a stable form of ecclesiastical organization, and the Marcionites possessed a powerful weapon: they had a sacred book that was a Christian creation, the first canon of the New Testment, which contained the pure words of Jesus and the unadulterated teachings of Paul. For the first time in its history, Christianity was divided into two churches. The Marcionite church indeed survived for many centuries, and it was decades before the defenders of early catholic Christianity understood how they could meet Marcion's challenge. It is not impossible that the Pastoral Epistles were a first answer to Marcion (§12.2g). That sort of response did not grasp the real issues, however, because it simply reinforced the same understanding of Paul that Marcion had so vehemently criticized. In order to defend itself against Marcion, the church first had to create its own canon of New Testament writings, and to rediscover the Pauline inheritance in the attempt to define the relationship between Christianity and world; this endeavor did not begin until Irenaeus and Tertullian. Meanwhile, the situation of the Christian churches changed drastically, as the time of relative peace between church and state came to an end, and the catholic Christians were forced to compare themselves with the Marcionites in their readiness to suffer martyrdom.

(d) The Position of the Roman Authorities

No official decision of the Roman authorities about Christianity is known from I CE, and it cannot be assumed that during this period Christians were ever persecuted or punished because of their Christian faith as such. Convictions of Christians were apparently based upon such accusations as causing public unrest, forming illegal and secret associations, and refusing to sacrifice to the emperor (the latter is first attested by the Revelation of John, §12.1c; for the problem as a whole, see §6.5a–b). The Acts of the Apostles, however, reveals a situation in which even the official Roman authorities began to show an explicit interest in the question of the existence and character of this new religious movement, an interest to which Luke responds, especially in his description of the trial of Paul (§12.3a). The same situation is attested in the first extant report of a Roman administrator about the Christians, namely, a letter of the younger Pliny to the emperor Trajan which is preserved, together with Trajan's answer, in Pliny's published correspondence. Pliny had been sent by Trajan as governor to Bithynia in order to settle the affairs of that difficult province in the northwestern part of Asia Minor. He arrived in Bithynia

Bibliography to §12.3d: Text of the Letter of Pliny

Betty Radice (ed. and trans.), *Pliny: The Letters* (LCL; 2 vols.) 2. 284–93. Pliny's letter about the Christians and Trajan's rescript: 10.96.

J. Stevenson, *A New Eusebius: Documents Illustrative of the History of the Church to 337 A.D.* (London: SPCK, 1947, and reprints) 13–16.

Kee, *Origins,* 51–53.

Bibliography to §12.3d: Studies

Henry J. Cadbury, "Roman Law and the Trial of Paul," in: Foakes Jackson and Lake, *Beginnings,* 5. 297–338.

W. H. C. Frend, *Martyrdom and Persecution in the Early Church* (Oxford: Blackwell, 1965) 104–235.

P. Keresztes, "The Imperial Roman Government and the Christian Church, I: From Nero to the Severi," *ANRW* II, 23. 247–315.

Antonie Wlosok, "Christliche Apologetik gegenüber kaiserlicher Politik," in: Heinzgünter Frohnes and Uwe W. Knorr, *Die alte Kirche* (Kirchengeschichte als Missionsgeschichte 1; München: Kaiser, 1974) 147–65. Excellent summary with comprehensive bibliography.

Kurt Aland, "Das Verhältnis von Kirche und Staat in der Frühzeit," *ANRW* II, 23. 60–246.

Rudolf Freudenberger, *Das Verhalten der römischen Behörden gegen die Christen im 2. Jahrhundert* (München: Beck, 1967).

Richard Klein (ed.), *Das frühe Christentum im römischen Staat* (WdF 267; Darmstadt: Wissenschaftliche Buchgesellschaft, 1971).

Cuirass of the Emperor Hadrian
(from a statue found in the Athenian agora)

In upper center the goddess Athena, flanked by her symbols, snake and owl, and crowned by two Nike figures (Victories). She is standing on the back of the symbol of Rome, the she-wolf nursing Romulus and Remus. Below, the horned image of Zeus-Ammon, recalling the divinity of Alexander the Great.

in the year 111 and remained there until he died in 113. As his correspondence demonstrates, and as he himself says, he wrote to Trajan
whenever he was faced with difficult cases in order to obtain the emperor's
decision. In one of these letters (10.96) he described the Christians and
gave an account of his method of conducting trials whenever accusations
were submitted against them.

As Pliny tells us, the number of Christians in the province of Bithynia
had increased dramatically; the "contagious disease of this false religion"
(*superstitio*) had spread not only in the cities, but also in the villages, and
included people of all ages and social classes; as a consequence many
temples had already become deserted, regular sacrifices had been largely
discontinued, and it had become difficult to sell sacrificial meat. Pliny had
not taken measures against the Christians in his capacity as governor until
several people had been denounced as Christians and even an anonymous
accusation listing many names had come to his attention. Pliny had not yet
come to a clear understanding as to whether the name "Christian" as such
was in itself sufficient cause for a conviction, or whether it was necessary
to find evidence "of crimes connected with the name." In any case, in the
trial he had sentenced those people to death who insisted even after
repeated interrogation that they were Christians, "because in any case
obstinacy and unbending perversity deserve to be punished." There is no
question that Pliny considered being a Christian a punishable crime. On
the other hand, those who denied that they were Christians or said that
they had only formerly been Christians were requested to make a suppli-
cation to the gods, an offering to the emperor's statue, and to curse Christ,
and were then freed; a statue of the emperor had been brought into the
courtroom just for this purpose.

In his answer, Trajan confirms Pliny's procedures, but notes that nothing final should be laid down with regard to a regular procedure in this
matter. He adds two extremely important instructions: first, Christians
should not be sought out, but should only be convicted and punished if
accused; second, anonymous accusations should not be admitted in court
because "this is not worthy of our time" (*non nostri saeculi est*). Of course,
we do not know how closely these instructions were followed elsewhere,
but it can be assumed that Trajan answered similar inquiries by other
governors in the same way. In other words, Christians would be safe as
long as they were not denounced by someone bearing ill will against them.
It is clear that this is the situation presupposed by the Pastoral Epistles'
admonition to lead a blameless life and to apply strict standards regarding
the moral qualifications of people in ecclesiastical office.

The Christians, however, were far from able to convince a Roman
governor of their innocence simply by leading a morally irreproachable

life; this is evident from Pliny's letter. He readily recognizes that in their meetings—as reported by some "former" Christians—the Christians bound themselves by an oath "not to commit theft or robbery or adultery, not to break their word, and not to disavow a debt when repayment was demanded." This clearly reflects the catalogue of vices of the Christian letters! Yet, there remained too much that the Roman governor had to view as potentially dangerous: the formation of private associations (*hetaeria*)—this Pliny had forbidden on the basis of earlier instructions from Trajan. Private meetings at night (before sunrise) were always suspicious, no matter how many "hymns to Christ as a god" (*Christo quasi deo*) the Christians sang, and no matter how harmless and ordinary the food that the Christians ate together. For Pliny, Christianity still remained a movement that lacked all the elements appropriate for true religion and piety. This was clear in the Christian refusal to sacrifice to the gods and the emperor—not because of the Romans' opinion that emperor cult and Christ's cult were irreconcilable opposites, but because it was obvious that there could be no true and useful religion unless its public character and the worship of the gods of the Roman people were part of its observances. But the Christians did not want to hear of that; they were thus not really "pious." Pliny found this judgment confirmed in his questioning of two maid-servants who were deacons of a church (the instructions of 1 Tim 2:11–12 were obviously not observed in this church!). In their statements made under torture, he found nothing but "a perverse and extravagant false religion" (*superstitio prava, immodica*). Pliny, in his measures against Christians, was not trying to punish criminals; his intention was rather to convert people who had gone astray. He hopes to achieve a reformation of the people and wants to give "an opportunity for repentance" (*penitentiae locus*). Trajan confirms this approach in his saying that those who are converted should receive "pardon on the basis of their repentance" (*venia ex penitentia*). But the Romans did not know what to make of the Christians' determination to confess their faith so courageously. Therefore, it seemed advisable to them to stay out of their way rather than to spy them out.

This policy remained in effect under Trajan's successors. A document from Hadrian (117–138) discussing the treatment of the Christians is extant. There are some doubts about its authenticity, though these seem to be unfounded. The document was preserved in its original Latin text in Justin Martyr *Apol.* 1.68, according to Eusebius; however, in the known manuscripts of Justin's works, the document appears in the Greek translation, which Eusebius provided in *Hist. eccl.* 4.9.1–3. The governor of Asia had written to Hadrian to learn what he should do about the Christians (that letter is not preserved). Hadrian directed the answer to the next governor, Minucius Fundanus, instructing him that the only accusations of Christians to be permitted were those that could be brought into court in a public trial, and that Christians should be punished whenever they had done something illegal. Those who accused Christians, however, intending solely to slander them without being able to prove any crimes, should themselves be subject to punishment. Doubts about this document's authenticity have been raised because it does not mention that a stubborn insistence upon the confession of Christ is in itself punishable. This was the position of the correspondence between Pliny and Trajan, and it would reappear later in the trials against Christians from the time of Marcus Aurelius (according to the witness of later Christian reports of martyrdoms; note also the repeated statements by Tertullian). However, the apparent fact that there were very few, if any, martyrdoms during the reigns of Hadrian and Antoninus Pius affirms the authenticity of Hadrian's rescript. The political situation of the Roman empire in this period, in both its domestic and external affairs, did not warrant the persecution of a religious group that otherwise observed the rules of public peace and order and that was eager to prove its fulfillment of a good citizen's morality. In this respect, the Pastoral Epistles were absolutely correct in their admonition. However, once the time of peace and relative prosperity ended after the middle of II CE, the Roman authorities were repeatedly forced to take measures against the Christians because public opinion blamed them for several misfortunes and catastrophes. Under Marcus Aurelius, the time of the martyrs began. The battle between church and state that was fought out on the basis of fundamental controversial issues belongs, however, to III and IV CE.

(e) The Earliest Christian Apologists

The time of the emperors Hadrian and Antoninus Pius is the period of the formation of Christian apologetic literature. The work of Luke already demonstrated an apologetic interest (many scholars would date this work somewhat before this period; see §12.3a); another apology already mentioned is the *Kerygma of Peter* (§10.2a). In both instances, the exposition of scriptural proof appeared as a central element of the apologetic argument, and this would also play a considerable role in other apologetic literature. In order to understand the importance of this type of writing, it is necessary to refer to the model that ultimately influenced all apologetic literature. The apologists were not primarily interested in the defense of Christianity against accusations that had been raised by the pagan world and by the Roman state—although this motive plays a considerable role. The primary model of apologetic works was instead the Greek *protrepticus,* that is, a literary genre designed as an invitation to a philosophical

Pergamum: Altar of Zeus

The Altar of Zeus was excavated by a team of German archeologists before World War I and reassembled in Berlin. The picture shows the flanked staircase leading to the entrance through the stoa at the top of the staircase. The altar itself was situated behind that stoa in an open peristyle court.

way of life, directed to all those who were willing to engage in the search for the true philosophy and make it the rule for their life and conduct. The *Protrepticus* of Aristotle was most influential for the formation of this genre; although it is now lost, its influence extended as far as Augustine's *City of God* (by way of Cicero's dialogue *Hortensius,* which is also lost).

To be sure, in the earliest apologetic writings we do not find literary standards that are comparable to these protreptic writings. Moreover, they do not depend upon them directly, but take their immediate point of departure from Jewish apologetics (§5.3e). But the motif of invitation to the true philosophy was still determinative for Christian apologetics. Therefore, the following themes were dominant: (1) Christianity is a philosophy, that is, a doctrine of correct living and conduct that can be taught; (2) this philosophy serves not only to build the individual moral personality, but also the community and thus the state; (3) since Christianity is the true philosophy, its truth can be documented on the basis of the wisdom of ancient traditions; (4) the philosophical doctrine of Christianity is superior to all other philosophies and exceeds by far all the superstitions of the traditional religions and beliefs in divinities. All these themes, though to a different degree in each case, played an essential role in Christian apologetic writings.

Unfortunately, the works of the oldest Christian apologists, Quadratus and Aristides—both directed to the emperor Hadrian—are preserved only very poorly. From the apology of Quadratus only a single sentence is known, quoted by Eusebius (*Hist. eccl.* 4.3.2). Nevertheless, even this meager evidence reveals that Quadratus discussed Jesus' miracles of healing and raising people from the dead. As for the *Apology* of Aristides, Eusebius says merely that it was addressed to Hadrian and was still read by many at his time (*Hist. eccl.* 4.3.3). But a Syriac translation has been discovered (where the writing is addressed to Antoninus Pius) and subse-

Bibliography to §12.3e: Texts

Edgar J. Goodspeed (ed.), *Die ältesten Apologeten* (Göttingen: Vandenhoeck & Ruprecht, 1914).

D. Ruiz Bueno (ed.), *Padres Apologistas Griegos* (BAC 116; Madrid: La Editorial Catolica, 1954).

A. Lukyn Williams (trans.), *Justin Martyr: The Dialogue with Trypho* (Translations of Christian Literature, Series 1: Greek Texts; London: SPCK, and New York: Macmillan, 1930).

Bibliography to §12.3e: Studies

Hans von Campenhausen, "Justin," in: idem, *The Fathers of the Greek Church* (New York: Pantheon, 1959) 12–20.

Erwin R. Goodenough, *The Theology of Justin Martyr* (Amsterdam: Philo, 1968).

E. F. Osborn, *Justin Martyr* (BHTh 47; Tübingen: Mohr/Siebeck, 1973).

J. Geffcken, *Zwei griechische Apologeten* (Leipzig and Berlin: Teubner, 1907).

quently also the Greek text in a speech of the medieval monastic romance of *Barlaam and Josaphat*. These texts exhibit considerable differences, causing substantial difficulties in any attempt at a detailed reconstruction of the original.

On the whole, however, the apologetic arguments are still clearly recognizable. The author begins with a proof for the existence of God that tries to reflect philosophical arguments and, in fact, shows influence from Aristotle: God is the one who moves everything, but is himself without beginning, the one who encompasses everything, but is not contained in anything. A list of the nations introduces a refutation of the various conceptions of gods. The division into the polytheistic nations of Chaldeans, Greeks, and Egyptians, who are contrasted to the Jews as the monotheists, is traditional and derived from Jewish apologetics. This division, however, has been revised by the author. He assumes three peoples: Jews, Christians, and polytheists; the last are then divided into those three polytheistic nations (*Arist.* 2). Against the Chaldeans, the author argues that the elements heaven, earth, water, and sun are not gods because they can be explained as natural phenomena. Therefore, human beings are also not gods since they are composed of these elements (*Arist.* 3–7). The arguments in these chapters are derived from the popularized natural sciences of the Hellenistic period. In the next section, Aristides repeats arguments of philosophy, both traditional and popular, against traditional religious beliefs (8–11). For the Egyptians, he uses the widely favored arguments against the Egyptian worship of animals as if they were gods (12). To this point, Aristides' apology is nothing more than a collection of arguments against polytheism that would find immediate agreement from nearly any educated Jewish or pagan reader. Quite different is the polemic against the Jews, however, who are, of course, recognized as a nation that knows the one true God. The arguments here are drawn from the Christian polemic against Jewish-Christian syncretism. For Aristides (14), the incorrect worship of God among the Jews is clear because their observation of the sabbath, the festivals, and the circumcision is nothing but service of the angels (cf. the opponents of Colossians; see §12.2a). The teaching of the Christians and the true worship of the one God are described in terms of the Christian creed. It comprises the confession of Jesus as the Son of God, his coming from heaven, his birth by the virgin, crucifixion (by the Jews!), his death, burial, resurrection on the third day, and ascension, and finally the proclamation to the nations. Thus, Aristides simply quotes "the faith" without feeling any need for further explanations (15.1–2). This Christian creed is followed by the quotation of *Didache* materials (15.3–9): the decalogue, golden rule, the command to love one's enemies, even loving of one's slaves (this last borrowed from the table of household duties), care for the widows, orphans, and the poor. The conclusion stresses the Christian preparedness for martyrdom. In the final remarks (16–17) occurs the statement that the prayer of the Christians is what maintains the continued existence of the world.

While the apology of Aristides was a clearly arranged composition of traditional materials and established arguments, the apologist Justin, writing in the middle of II CE, thoroughly reworked the traditional materials of philosophical and Jewish apologetics in the interests of Christian theology. Justin came from the eastern regions of the Roman empire, established his school in Rome, and was martyred between 163 and 167. In the extensive *Corpus Justinum,* only three writings can be claimed as genuine writings of Justin: two apologies and a dialogue with Trypho the Jew. The *First Apology* is directed to Antoninus Pius and his two adopted sons Lucius Verus and Marcus Aurelius. It must have been written soon after 150. The *Second Apology* may have been written at the same time, the *Dialogue with Trypho,* Justin's most extensive writing, not long thereafter. All three writings are preserved in only two manuscripts, written in 1364 and 1541 CE, the latter being a copy of the former. Their text must be corrected in a number of instances, but it is more reliable than formerly believed, especially in its biblical quotations.

The *First Apology* and *Dialogue* are not of one piece, but include several smaller tractates composed by Justin previously for different purposes. One example is the commentary on Psalm 22 in *Dialogue* 98–106. The psalm is first quoted in its entirety, then interpreted sentence by sentence, while in each instance corresponding texts from the gospels are quoted verbatim. In such works, Justin discloses valuable information about the activities of early Christian schools. Their work apparently included not only the detailed interpretation of passages from the Old Testament, but also critical work on its Greek text. It has been demonstrated recently that the numerous special readings in Justin's quotations from the Old Testament derive from a Jewish tradition of textual revision in which the Greek text was brought into closer agreement with the further developments of the Hebrew text. In resuming this tradition, Justin was a predecessor of the extensive text-critical work on the Greek Old Testament in Origen's *Hexapla* (§5.3b). The beginnings of scholarly work are clearly visible here, as well as in Justin's treatment of the written gospels, of which Justin certainly knew Matthew and Luke, and perhaps Mark (but not John). Justin usually calls them the "Memoirs of the Apostles," and sometimes also "Gospels." He was the first Christian writer to treat the gospels as historical records (but not yet as "Holy Scripture"), and he used and revised them accordingly. His primary interest was the systematic work of creating a harmonized text of the gospels that would agree as closely as possible with the words of the prophecies from the Old Testament. It is no accident that it was Justin's student Tatian who later composed a harmony of the four canonical gospels, the *Diatessaron,* which was widely used and was translated into many languages.

The systematic theological work of Justin's school is equally evident in a fundamental reconception of the specifically apologetic literary productions. In philosophical terms, Justin was a Platonist and represented a position that is generally called "Middle Platonism" (§4.1a). He was a gentile convert to Christianity who had worn the mantle of the philosopher even before his conversion. To be sure, the description he gives at the beginning of the *Dialogue* of his philosophical development from the Stoics via the Peripatetics and Pythagoreans to the Platonists closely follows a traditional scheme and cannot be understood as a personal biographical report. Justin's Middle Platonic concepts are particularly evident in his doctrine of the Logos. Christ as the divine Logos was a power which existed with God from the primordial beginnings; this power then appeared in the world through its birth by Mary. This "dynamistic christology," developed under Middle Platonic influence, and shared by other apologists, stands in sharp contrast to the "modalism" of the more widespread beliefs of the Christian churches (also found in Marcion; see §12.3c).

Justin also made a decisive step forward in his development of the traditional polemic against pagan belief in many gods. For him the pagan belief in gods was neither foolish nor ridiculous, but a deliberate imitation of the Old Testament prediction of Christ's coming, inspired by evil demons to lead people astray into the worship of false gods (see, e.g., *Apol.* 1.21ff). The proofs that Justin adduces for this theory show that his school had systematically collected pagan reports about the appearances of gods and religious cults and had matched them with appropriate passages from the Old Testament. But how can it be demonstrated that the fulfillments of these predictions created by the evil demons are merely delusions? And how are they to be distinguished from the true fulfillment? In order to answer these questions, Justin was able to draw on the accomplishments of his exegetical school. The basis for his demonstration is his principle of the apologetic scriptural proof: "It is the work of God to speak before something takes place, in order to show that it (the true fulfillment) happens exactly as it was predicted" (*Apol.* 1.12.6). The detailed demonstrations follow the legitimate and established principles of the allegorical method, which are handled with precision, as is evident in Justin's clear distinctions between "type," "symbol," and "parable." But Justin is also able to employ trustworthy historical records, namely, the "Memoirs of the Apostles," in order to establish in detail that the fulfillment in Christ indeed corresponds exactly to the prophecies.

Justin, however, by no means sought to prove the truth of the written gospels—that is simply presupposed. Rather, he wanted to demonstrate the truth of the Christian creed, "the faith." After a reference to the trustworthiness and inspiration of the Greek translation of the Old Testament (*Apol.* 1.31.1–5), this Christian creed is quoted in full: "in the books of the prophets have been predicted the coming of our Lord Jesus Christ, his birth through the virgin, his growing up, his healing of all diseases and raising of the dead, that he would be mocked, his crucifixion and death, resurrection and ascension, that he would be called the Son of God, and the proclamation to all nations." A comparison of the creed of Justin with that of Aristides shows that it has been expanded in its middle section in a manner revealing the influence of the story of Jesus as told in written gospels. The following chapters of the *Apology* (1.32ff) provide the evidence in detail. Isa 7:14 predicted the birth; Justin shows the fulfillment by quoting sentences from Luke 1:31–35; Matt 1:21, and the *Protevangelium of James* 11. Jesus' birthplace was predicted in Micah 5:2 (Bethlehem); the fulfillment is reported in Matt 2:1 and Luke 2:2 (*Apol.* 1.33–34). In the same way Justin argues the case for almost every sentence of the Christian creed in the remaining chapters of the *Apology,* and even more extensively in his *Dialogue.* Though the latter is ostensibly directed against the Jews, it becomes clear that the apologetic argument from Scripture, once it was fully developed, was suited for a work against the Jews just as much as for a writing against the gentiles.

It is important to note that this method of demonstrating the truth, despite the seeming artificiality of its arguments, is not just a clever trick. It is rather the expression of a new consciousness of history that had deep roots in Justin's Christian worldview. He believed that there are indeed visible actions of God in the world and its history, and that it is both possible to understand these actions of God and necessary to respond to them in faith. The inclusion of Greek philosophy and religion into this view of history as the story of salvation is extremely significant. It may be difficult to accept Justin's assurance that Plato learned from Moses; but it was exactly that view which made it possible to include the entire Greek tradition—which had become so important in the Roman world—into the dimension of God's saving history. Justin here also begins to distinguish critically in the Greek tradition between opportunities for the true recognition of God and pseudo-religious falsification (i.e., through the actions of the evil demons).

This sort of apologetic literature, though ostensibly addressed to the pagan world, had a profound effect upon the Christian church and its theology that should not be underestimated. It enabled the church to leave the horizon of a history of salvation that was exclusively informed by the Old Testament and the history of Israel, and to renew the process of Hellenization by including the Greek world and its tradition. Retaining the Old Testament as a book of revelation at the same time opened the way to appropriate the entire cultural tradition of the ancient world. In this process, the words of Jesus also received new significance. In order to illustrate the demands for Christian conduct, Aristides had still used *Didache* materials, but Justin discontinued this traditional dependence upon the teaching of the two ways and substituted a catechism composed of sayings of Jesus. Jesus thus assumes a new role: his words establish him as the true teacher of right philosophy, since in brief words full of rich meaning he explained how one should conduct one's life (Justin says that his words were brief since he was not a sophist; *Apol.* 1.14.5). Jesus' words commend temperance, love for all people, care for others, serving everyone, avoidance of oaths, and the doing of good works as philosophical virtues (*Apol.* 1.15–16). Thus, Justin uses the Sermon on the Mount as part of a philosophical protreptic, the invitation to a philosophical life. It is noteworthy, however, that Justin does more than quote words of Jesus that demonstrate that the Christians are good citizens and reliable tax-payers (*Apol.* 1.17.1–2); he also reminds the emperors that Jesus had exhorted the Christians to be prepared to suffer or even die for their faith (*Apol.* 1.19.6–8). Justin himself earned martyrdom through his willing-ness to confess his faith publicly. The report of the martyrdom of Justin and of his friends is extant, and it quotes the answers that Justin gave in the interrogation and that brought his death upon him.

(f) Martyrs: The Martyrdom of Polycarp

The end of the "golden age" shortly after the middle of II CE not only forced the Christians to defend their faith publicly in Roman courts, it also demanded that they ponder the destiny of Christian existence as they preserved the memory of their leaders, sisters, and brothers who had suffered martyrdom. The oldest and most famous independent written report of a Christian martyrdom is a letter of the church of Smyrna reporting the martyrdom of their bishop Polycarp. This writing, drawn up immediately after Polycarp's death, is still a moving testimony to the early Christian courage in public witness. But it also raises numerous questions about the desires and thoughts of those who repeatedly revised this report in the following centuries. The *Martyrdom of Polycarp* is pre-served in six Greek manuscripts, all deriving from the *Corpus Polycarp-ianum,* which was written at the beginning of V CE. But Eusebius also copied almost the entire text available to him (*Hist. eccl.* 4.15.3–45). This text was the basis of numerous translations preserved in several languages. On the whole, Eusebius' text is more reliable, while the *Corpus Polycarpianum* contains several passages, sentences, and phrases not included in Eusebius' text. But the text must have been revised even before Eusebius, as Hans von Campenhausen has demonstrated in a convincing analysis. The following picture of the historical development of this venerable text thus emerges.

The letter of the church in Smyrna originally ended with *Mart. Pol.* 20. Chap. 21 was added because of an interest in the hagiographical calendar—evidence that a special festival in memory of the martyrdom was being instituted. But a criticism of such veneration of martyrs has also been interpolated: "Christ we worship as the Son of God, but the martyrs we love as disciples and imitators of the Lord" (*Mart. Pol.* 17.3). Nevertheless, biographical curiosity and interest in the memorial celebration for the dead led to the addition of several names (17.2), a note that it was not possible to obtain the body and the relics (17.1), and information about the memorial celebration (18.3). In order to exalt the famous martyr, his holiness was augmented in the description of his behavior and experience: 9.1 contains an interpolated reference to a voice from heaven encouraging Polycarp, but it interrupts the context unnecessarily; from his mortal wound emerges not only blood, but even a dove (16.1—Eusebius did not read this in his text). A polemical interpolation is also recognizable: 4.1 directly continues what was said in 3.2; but chap. 4 offers a remark about a Phrygian, i.e., a Montanist (a movement that did not yet exist at the time of Polycarp's death!), who first volunteers for martyrdom, but is then persuaded to sacrifice.

The development of the text also shows an increasing interest in inter-

Bibliography to §12.3f: Text

Funk-Bihlmeyer, *ApostVät*, xxxviii–xliv, 120–32.

Herbert Musurillo (ed.), *The Acts of the Christian Martyrs* (Oxford: Clarendon, 1972) xiii–xv, 2–21.

Lake, *ApostFath*, 2. 307–45.

Bibliography to §12.3f: Commentaries

Lightfoot, *Apostolic Fathers*, vol. 2, part 2. 935–98.

William R. Schoedel, *Polycarp, Martyrdom of Polycarp, Fragment of Papias* (Grant, *ApostFath* 5).

Bibliography to §12.3f: Studies

Hans von Campenhausen, "Bearbeitungen und Interpolationen des Polykarpmartyriums," in: idem, *Aus der Frühzeit des Christentums* (Tübingen: Mohr/ Siebeck, 1963) 253–301.

Hans Conzelmann, "Bemerkungen zum Martyrium Polykarps," *NAWG.PH* 1978,2 (Göttingen: Vandenhoeck & Ruprecht, 1978).

polating features from the passion narratives of the gospels into the description of the martyrdom. Even before Eusebius, a reader who knew the Gospel of John added the phrases "the hour had come" (John 17:1) in *Mart. Pol.* 8.1, that "they sat him on an ass" (John 12:14), and that everything happened "on a Great Sabbath" (John 19:31)—but in *Mart. Pol.* 8.3 the ass is forgotten and Polycarp walks humbly on foot. Influence from the passion narratives is especially evident in the recension of the writing that took place after Eusebius. Eusebius did not read in his copy that Polycarp's martyrdom happened "according to the Gospel" (1.1b–2.1), that martyrs do not really feel any pain (2.2b–3), that there were traitors in Polycarp's house, and that the police captain had "the same name, being called Herod" (6.2–7.1). The concept of the imitation of Jesus in 19.1b–2 is also missing in Eusebius' text; the reference to the "Gospel" in 22.1 belongs to the same redactor.

But the original letter written by the church in Smyrna is no less impressive. It also described the suffering of the other martyrs who died with Polycarp (Eusebius *Hist. eccl.* 4.15.4). After Germanicus had been thrown to the wild beasts (*Mart. Pol.* 3.1), the crowd cried out: "Away with the atheists! Let Polycarp be searched for!" (3.2). Polycarp had been persuaded against his will to leave the city and was staying with friends not far away (5.1). While there, he had a dream in which he saw the pillow under his head burning with fire, and told his friends that he would be burned alive (5.2)—quite remarkable, since beforehand the Christians had been thrown to the wild beasts. He decides not to flee any further (7.1); thus, the police find him and bring him to the stadium. Despite his advanced age, Polycarp refuses to swear by the genius of the emperor (9.2): "For eighty-six years I have served Christ, and he has done me no wrong. How can I now blaspheme my king who saved me?" (9.3). Since the interrogation was in vain, and Polycarp steadfastly continued to confess his faith, he was condemned to death by fire (chaps. 10–11), and was finally stabbed with a dagger since the fire miraculously did not touch him (16.1). The Jews, together with the pagans, cried out in wrath: "This is the teacher of Asia, the father of the Christians, the destroyer of our gods!"—something not forgotten by the Christian writer (12.2), the continuation of a sorrowful history. Polycarp died because he refused to deny what the governor of the Roman province called "atheism," and because, looking at the crowd that fanatically called for his death, he waved his hand at them and said: "Away with the atheists!" (9.2).

Agora: The central square of the Greek city, surrounded by the public buildings, temples, and open halls with stores (stoas). People went here for business, leisure, and shopping. It also served for assemblies of the people and was considered a sacred place. See I 71.

Amanuensis: A secretary who would draft letters and take dictation. It is likely that the apostle Paul used an amanuensis for the composition of his correspondence.

Anacoluthon: Construction of sentences that are incomplete (e.g., without a predicate), either intentionally or accidentally.

Anthropos: The Greek word for "human being." It is often used to describe the celestial or spiritual and divine prototype for the creation of human beings. The *Anthropos* is thought of as bisexual or asexual and is sometimes considered as the redeemer, thus identified with the heavenly Christ.

Apocalypticism: Belief in the disclosure of the events of the future (restitution of Israel, cosmic catastrophe and creation of a new heaven and earth) through prophets who have received special revelations (visions). Such revelations are usually propagated through books, often considered mysterious and secret. Apocalypticism implies that the course of future events can be calculated. See I 230-34.

Apophthegma: A brief story, usually transmitted orally, in which a traditional saying of a famous person (Diogenes, Jesus, and others) forms the conclusion. In most cases, the saying is more original, while the narrative part of the apophthegma is subject to variation.

Aretalogy: The enumeration of the great deeds of a god or of a divinely inspired human being (a "divine man"). An aretalogy can appear in the form of a sequence of brief sentences, each describing a different *arete* ("powerful act" or "virtuous quality"), or in the form of a series of stories, such as miracle stories.

Colophon: A subscript to a work often found in ancient books; it gives the title of the work, sometimes also information about the author or the place of composition. Colophons are not original parts of such works but have been added by the scribe.

Cosmogony: Mythical descriptions of the birth or creation of the whole universe, either by a process of divine evolution or through interaction of various divine powers or substances, usually ending in the creation of heaven and earth.

Covenant formula: The genre visible in the presentations of the making of the covenant between God and Israel. It consists of a historical introduction (e.g., story of the Exodus), a basic command, individual stipulations (e.g., the decalogue), and curses and blessings. See I 256.

Diaspora: Part or all of a nation living away from its homeland in various other cities and countries. Especially used of Israelites living in the many cities of the Hellenistic world and the Roman Empire. See I 219-28.

Divine Man: Human beings endowed with special divine powers, thus transcending in their accomplishments the range of normal human abilities. Poets (e.g., Homer), philosophers, rulers, and miracle workers were considered divine men; sometimes also called "Son of God." See I 173.

Docetism: The belief that Christ could not really become human because of the insurmountable difference between the divine and the human world. It was therefore thought that Christ only "seemed" (Greek: *dokei*) to be human, but actually never gave up his divine nature and essence. See II 197.

Encratism: Abstention from sex, marriage, certain foods and drinks for religious reasons in order to avoid contamination from natural and earthly things. See II 122f. and the General Index under "Asceticism."

Eudaemonia: Usually translated "happiness." But the term expresses much more: the status of complete peace and imperturbability in this life. It is often commended as the ultimate goal of a philosophical and religious life.

Eschatology: The belief that there will be a divinely guided renewal of the world and society in the near future, often seen as beginning in the present time (realized eschatology). Eschatological beliefs may be connected with apocalyptic mythology, but can also be expressed in political terms or in terms of individualistic piety. See the General Index.

Etymology: The method used to explain the meaning of a term or word on the basis of its assumed original literal sense rather than on the basis of the context of its actual usage.

Form: The structure of units that are transmitted orally, such as sayings, miracle stories, and apophthegms.

Forum: The central square in a Roman city. Like the Greek agora, it is surrounded by administrative buildings and also serves as a market place. But it is usually built as an enclosed rectangular square with access gates allowing easy control of entry.

Genre: The structure of particular types of literature, such as letters, gospels, biographies.

Gymnasium: Special building units in Greek (and Roman) cities, normally large peristyle courts, surrounded by stoas, various rooms, small temples, and lecture halls. The gymnasia served as places of athletic training and competition as well as places of school and education.

Ithyphallic: "with raised phallus," i.e., with erect penis. Satyrs and donkeys in the company of the god Dionysus are usually presented in this way as well as some other gods like Priapus.

Kerygma: "Proclamation." Technical term for fixed formulations of the early Christian proclamation, such as the "kerygma of the death, resurrection, and exaltation of Jesus."

Leitourgia: The term for certain public offices in Greek cities, such as "president of the gymnasium." A *leitourgia* was considered a special honor, but also involved the expenditure of considerable amounts of money, e.g., endowing or paying for an athletic contest.

Manumission: The legal procedure for the freeing of a slave. It required the supervision of a public official or of a temple, the payment of certain sums of money, and the filing of the appropriate documents, which were sometimes published in the form of an inscription.

Modalism: A christological belief that fully identified God and Christ in their divine nature so that Christ became a certain "mode" of the being or presence of God himself. Later modalists were accused of saying that God the Father suffered on the cross.

Onomasticon: A method used in the composition of psalms, hymns, or wisdom lists: the first letter in each succeeding line or verse would be made to correspond to the order of the letters in the alphabet or in certain sacred names.

Parenesis: "Admonition." Used to designate certain traditional types of admonition and exhortation aimed at a proper religious and moral life. Most early Christian letters contain parenetical sections.

Parousia: Originally "coming" or "presence" of a divine being or of God. Later it was specifically used to designate the expected (second) coming of Jesus.

Pericope: Technical term for a segment of a biblical text, as it was "cut out" for liturgical reading in worship service. Pericopes are usually small, self-contained units, comprising not more than a part of the chapter of a biblical book.

Prescript: The opening of a letter, comprising the name of the sender and of the addressee as well as a greeting. See II 54-56.

Proem: The second section of a letter, following upon the prescript. It is formulated either as a thanksgiving prayer or as a doxology and may include more lengthy descriptions of the situation of the sender and of the status of the addressee. See II 54-56.

Protreptic: The invitation to enter upon a truly philosophical or religious life, to defend the qualities and virtues of such a life, and to describe the basic philosophical concepts by which it should be guided. See II 338-40.

Stichometry: A list in which the number of lines in each of the books in question is given. Ancient stichometries help us to estimate the length of writings that are lost or only preserved in fragments.

Stoa: Public buildings in ancient cities: a hall with a single or double colonnade, open on one side and often with a line of shops on the other side. But stoas did not only serve as shopping malls; they were also used as courthouses, picture galleries, lecture halls (like the Painted Stoa in Athens where Zeno, the founder of the "Stoic" philosophy, gave his lectures), and as places for general business and leisure. Often of large dimensions (several hundred feet long), they lined many squares, streets, and courts.

Syzygy: Mostly used with respect to mythical speculations in which the celestial, divine world is described as consisting of pairs, e.g., of a male and female in each cosmic aeon; it is also sometimes applied to the reconstruction of history. See II 207, 213.

Technitai: "Craftsmen." The term is used for the members of any profession that required a skill, be it bakers or actors or shipbuilders. They were usually organized in associations, such as the "Dionysiac Technitai" (the association of professional actors and dancers related to the theater under the protection of the god Dionysus).

Testament: A genre of literature. It is a modification of the covenant formula in which the historical introduction is replaced by the biographical description of an individual (patriarch or apostle). This individual, who may already be dead at the time of writing, then gives instructions and pronounces curses and blessings. See I 258.

Theogony: Mythical description of the evolution of the world of the gods in a primordial time, describing their origin, function, and power. Theogonies often recount dramatic celestial struggles, and they precede cosmogonies in many ancient myths.

Thiasos (pl. *thiasoi*): Term for an association with a particular religious commitment. The term is also used for secular associations organized under the protectorate of a deity.

Index

Early Christian Writings

This index lists only those page numbers where these writings are treated in detail. For other references, see the General Index. All page numbers refer to Volume II.

General Index

All writings are normally listed under the name of their assumed authors (except for the Pauline letters). Bold Roman numerals refer to volumes.

Apostolic Council **II** 104–6, 322
Apostolic Decree **II** 322
Apostolic Fathers **II** 12, 67–70
Apuleius **I** 139, 188–90
Aqiba, Rabbi **I** 408–10
Aquila (Associate of Paul) **II** 109f
Aquila (Judaeus) **I** 254, 408
Aramaic **I** 6, 111, 250f; **II** 73f, 147, 172, 184, 210f
Aramaisms **I** 111
Arcesilaus **I** 141f
Archelaus (Herod) **I** 394
Archimedes of Syracuse **I** 116f
Architecture **I** 337f
Aretalogy **I** 134–37, 174, 188f, 264; **II** 4, 47, 129f, 166, 316
Aretas **I** 395
Aristarchus of Samos **I** 117
Aristarchus of Samothrace **I** 118
Aristeas, Letter of **I** 252, 270f
Aristides **II** 340–42
Aristobulus I (Hasmonean) **I** 271f
Aristobulus II (Hasmonean) **I** 219, 390
Aristobulus (Jewish philosopher) **I** 271
Aristonicus of Pergamum **I** 61f
Aristotelians, see Peripatos
Aristotle **I** 9, 115, 133, 144f
Aristoxenus **I** 116, 133
Armenia **I** 22, 29
Army, Roman **I** 294f, 324
Arrian **I** 350
Arsinoë II **I** 23f, 35
Art **I** 96f
Artapanus **I** 264
Artemis of Ephesus **I** 169, 378
Ascension of Moses **I** 257
Asceticism **I** 237; **II** 122f, 153, 156, 230, 327, 333
Asclepius **I** 170, 173–76, 364
Asia (Roman province) **I** 21, 291
Asia Minor **I** 5, 20–22, 45–47, 223; **II** 10, 197f, 241f, 250, 253
Asianism **I** 103f
Associations **I** 56–58, 62, 65–67, 165f, 225, 334f; **II** 337
Assyria **I** 5
Astrology **I** 156–59, 376–80
Astronomy **I** 115, 117, 119, 156f, 377f
Atargatis **I** 192, 196
Atheism **I** 146, 155
Athens **I** 3, 14f, 22, 43, 90, 99, 125f, 181, 320; **II** 109
Attalids **I** 20, 80
Attalus I Soter **I** 20
Attalus II Philadelphus **I** 21
Attalus II Philometor **I** 21
Attic, Atticism **I** 102–4; **II** 296
Attis (see also Magna Mater) **I** 191–94; **II** 231

Augustus **I** 301–7, 334, 340, 367f, 391f

Babrius **I** 121
Babylon **I** 4, 11–14, 117, 156–59, 205, 220f; **II** 250, 293
Bacchanalia **I** 182f, 364
Bactria **I** 10, 26–28
Banking **I** 90f
Baptism **II** 71f, 87, 100, 121f, 159, 179, 205, 211, 229, 264, 269, 294
Bar Kochba **I** 320, 410
Barnabas **II** 91–93, 102, 105–7, 114, 277
Barnabas, Epistle of **II** 5, 276–79
Baruch, First Book of **I** 270
Barch, Second Book of (Apocalypse) **I** 403; **II** 252
Basilides **II** 232
Belial **I** 238f
Berenice I **I** 35
Berenice II **I** 35
Berossus **I** 156, 160
Beth-Din **I** 405–10
Biblicisms **I** 111f
Bilingualism **I** 112f
Biographies **I** 116, 132–35, 137, 276, 375f, **II** 4, 169, 174, 315f
Bion of Borysthenes **I** 154
Bishop, see Episcopacy
Bithynia **I** 21, 46, 297; **II** 294, 334–36
Bolos of Mendes **I** 77
Books, Production of **I** 80–82, 94f, 121f
Botany **I** 115
Byssus **I** 77f
Byzantine text **II** 18

Cabiri **I** 176, 180, 198
Caesar **I** 298–301, 346, 367, 390f
Caesarea Maritima **I** 393; **II** 93, 144
Caesarea Philippi **I** 395; **II** 170
Caesarean text **II** 17f
Calendar **I** 236, 262, 301, 377f, 407
Caligula **I** 308–10, 369f, 397
Callimachus **I** 127
Canon of the NT **II** 5–12, 330f
Canon of the OT **I** 252f
Cappadocia **I** 22, 46f
Carneades **I** 142
Carpocratians **II** 223, 231
Carthage **I** 281, 285f, 289–91
Cassander **I** 14f
Catalogues of Virtues and Vices, see Virtues and Vices
Cato **I** 345
Catullus **I** 339
Celsus **I** 356; **II** 15
Celts (see also Galatians) **I** 16f, 21, 26, 285
Ceramics **I** 78
Cerinthus **II** 204

Authors Discussed in the Text

Bold Roman numerals indicate volume number.

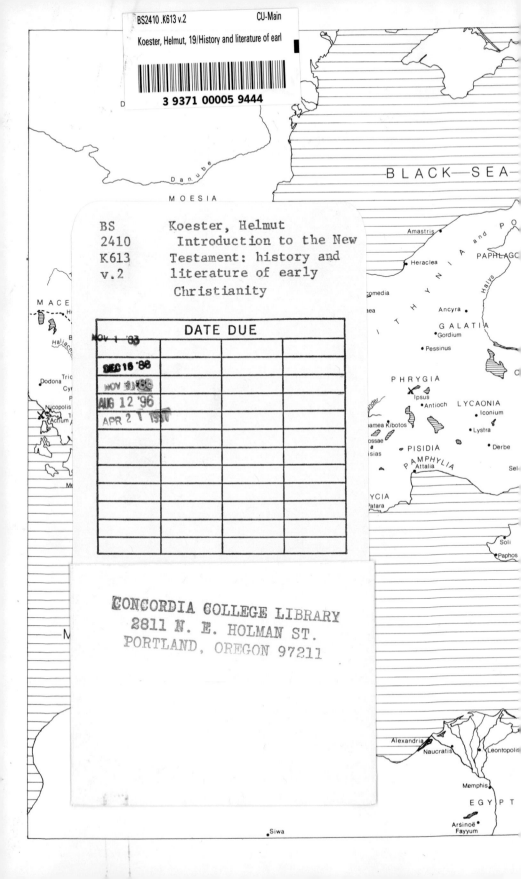

BLACK—SEA

Danube

MOESIA

Amastris

PAPHLAGO

Heraclea

comedia

aea   Ancyra

GALATIA
•Gordium

• Pessinus

PHRYGIA

Ipsus

•Antioch LYCAONIA
          • Iconium

amea Kibotos

ossae

• Lystra

sias   • PISIDIA   • Derbe

PAMPHYLIA
Attalia

YCIA
atara

Soli

Paphos

Alexandria
Naucratis   Leontopolis

Memphis

EGYPT

Arsinoë •
Fayyum

Siwa